# THE GREAT AMERICAN SPORTS PAGE

# ★ THE GREAT ★
# AMERICAN
# SPORTS PAGE

A Century of Classic Columns
from Ring Lardner to Sally Jenkins

JOHN SCHULIAN, EDITOR

Foreword by Charles P. Pierce

LIBRARY OF AMERICA

THE GREAT AMERICAN SPORTS PAGE

Foreword, introduction, headnotes, and volume compilation copyright © 2019 by
Literary Classics of the United States, Inc., New York, N.Y.
All rights reserved.

Published in the United States by Library of America.
www.loa.org

Some of the material in this volume is reprinted with the permission of holders
of copyright and publishing rights. Acknowledgments are on page 377.

Distributed to the trade in the United States by Penguin Random House Inc.
and in Canada by Penguin Random House Canada Ltd.

Library of Congress Control Number: 2018952817

ISBN 978–1–59853–612–6

1   3   5   7   9   10   8   6   4   2

Printed in the United States of America

★ ★ ★

# Contents

★ ★ ★

# Foreword

## by Charles P. Pierce

O N SATURDAY, October 25, 1986, I wrote the same story four times with four different endings, and all between the hours of 11 P.M. and 1 A.M. on an ice-fingered night in the borough of Queens, New York City. The Boston Red Sox and the New York Mets were playing the sixth game of that year's World Series. The Red Sox had a 3–2 lead in games, and they were leading 2–0 when the Mets came to bat in the bottom of the fifth inning. That was the first time I wrote the story.

At the time, I was a sidebar/feature writer for the *Boston Herald*, a tabloid owned by an Australian pirate named Rupert Murdoch, whose enthusiasm in his American properties were sports and political coverage that checked in somewhere to the starboard side of Vlad the Impaler. I was a sportswriter so I was lucky that my soul remained relatively intact. In the fifth inning of that game, I was almost all the way through with my story. I was drowning my prospective reader in lore; Boston had not won a World Series since—all together now—1918, but the whole Curse of the Bambino arsenal of nostalgia had not yet been fully weaponized. (That, as we shall see, would come later that night.) I also was going heavy on the lore because not a helluva lot had happened and I had a deadline looming. And Saturday deadlines for the Sunday newspaper were the most merciless of all.

This was a joke we used to tell at the *Herald* when we all got together down at J. J. Foley's, one of the last great cop-and-newspaper bars. The newspaper was located directly across the Massachusetts Turnpike from Boston's Chinatown neighborhood. Naturally, the print deadlines were fashioned to get the papers to the more distant precincts first. So the joke was that anything submitted after midnight would have to be written in Chinese because only the newspaper circulated in the three blocks around the paper would contain the story. This is a joke that gets funnier in retrospect than it was as October 25, 1986, became October 26, 1986, and the Mets tied the damn game in the bottom of the fifth.

Back into the copy I went, thinning out the lore, changing the emphasis so as to make it easier for me to change the emphasis if the Red Sox blew this game and New York forced a seventh game. The Red Sox scored a run in the seventh. I tinkered a little more. The Mets tied it in their half of the eighth. I reverse-engineered my tinkering back to what it had been before. The two teams went into extra innings. I tinkered more heavily, actually constructing "dummy" ledes that I thought could cover any outcome. This proved to be a very bad call indeed.

In the top of the tenth inning, Boston's Dave Henderson, about whom I'd already written when he'd cracked a pennant-saving home run against the California Angels, parked one into the left field stands. I began to write again about how Henderson was now the unlikeliest hero of all, having saved two postseason series with dramatic home runs. I was still writing this when Boston scratched another run across to lead 5–3. We were now well into those hours in which the conventional *Herald* wisdom had it that I should have been writing in Mandarin. But, then, Bill Buckner—and all the ridiculous events leading up to Bill Buckner—unfolded, and I had to start all over again, writing about a world-historical debacle with fifteen minutes or so left and the Deadline Muse sitting on my shoulder, whispering things like, "Don't forget that Bob Stanley was out there looking like the bystander at a car bombing." To this day, I don't remember what I wrote, but I do remember thinking while enjoying a postgame beer or three that I'd never been happier or more satisfied in my work.

A week or so later, of course, I came down with bronchitis that lasted until Thanksgiving.

In *Much Ado About Nothing*, Shakespeare's Beatrice turns down the heroic Don Pedro by telling him, "No, my lord, unless I might have another for working-days: your Grace is too costly to wear every day." The Deadline Muse is a muse for working days. She is not as costly as the Magazine Muse or the Book Muse or the Novel Muse. She is always overworked, and always underloved, except in retrospect, when all of we suitors come to miss her insistence that we do our best work in the least amount of time and talk of her fondly in her absence.

As time and technology passed, I noticed that the Deadline Muse was being called upon to work harder than before. One of the great attractions of newspapering of any sort was that it was one of the few occupations that required a great amount of hanging around. Hanging around crime scenes and courthouses. Hanging around legislative chambers and press rooms, and ballparks and press boxes. In times like that, the Deadline Muse got time to rest so that she would be strong and true when called upon *in extremis*. Now, though, in this era in which we are not reporters writing stories but, rather, content-producers producing content across many platforms, nobody gets any time off. Hanging around has been replaced by tweeting out into the world every new and tiny thing that floats by as though it were Lindy landing in Paris. The Deadline Muse is worn out, and the occupation of daily sportswriting is exhausting itself in tandem.

I somehow have transitioned to the point where nearly all my work takes place online now and, often, I am asked how I can produce what is said to be a great deal of content—Lord, how I hate that goddamn word—in a short space of time. I tell them, well, once there was a night in Queens, and when I get to that part of the story, in my mind's eye I can see the Deadline Muse again, as young as she used to be, and I hear her calling me to work again.

★ ★ ★

# Introduction

### By John Schulian

THE AMERICAN sports page was more than a section of the newspaper when newspapers monitored the heartbeat of everyday life. It was the inspiration for a twentieth-century ritual now turned sepia. Factory workers wanted scores in the morning and race results in the afternoon. Subway riders and living-room readers ignored the ink that stained their fingers to find out who was in first place. The lot of them could have moved on to the front page's wars, political shenanigans and crime sprees after a minute or two. But whether they were college professors or fresh off the boat, adults or children, men or women, they stayed for the writing that was good enough to spare the sports page from the bottom of a birdcage. Some dared call it art.

When Babe Ruth smote two homers in a World Series game, the first thought to enter Heywood Broun's mind—"The Ruth is mighty and shall prevail"—came clattering out of his typewriter. Just like that, Broun grabbed readers and didn't let go. It was the same when Jimmy Cannon took his devout admirers inside a hero's head: "You're Joe Louis . . . You're Joe DiMaggio . . . You're Willie Mays. . . ." Readers felt what Cannon wrote in the gut. Jim Murray aimed for the funny bone when he served up this classic image of a six-foot-seven slugger: "His strike zone is so big, it should be sub-divided." And the cry went up for more.

It was just what editors and publishers had hoped for back when it finally dawned on them that sports sold newspapers. The penny press had carried stories about horse races and bare-knuckle fights in the 1820s, and the first star scribe, Henry Chadwick, was anointed before the Civil War. Early in the twentieth century, something bigger emerged in Chicago—a loosey-goosey approach to covering sports that embraced bumpkins and oddballs with the same delight it did fireballers and knockout artists. Ring Lardner, who could find the humor in a ballplayer's breakfast, became a national treasure. Grantland Rice championed the "gee whiz" school of sportswriting while his stablemate at the *New York Herald Tribune*, W. O. McGeehan, surveyed the hype and hypocrisy afflicting sports and countered with the "aw nuts" school.

Sportswriters of their generation, no matter which camp they were in, rarely talked to their subjects unless they were in a bar or on a train to the next big game. The *New York Sun*'s Frank Graham set about changing that in the 1930s by recreating conversations he overheard in dugouts, horse barns, and boxing arenas. The result read too much like Frank Merriwell at Yale and not anywhere near enough like the everyday palaver of hard men who, in many cases, had grown up looking at the backside of a mule. But no less than Red Smith called Graham's experiment "the most important single change in my business in my lifetime," and Red didn't say that just because Graham was his best friend. He knew the ear was as important as the eye when it came to depicting ballplayers and prizefighters as flesh and blood.

Still, it took Dick Young—a *New York Daily News* baseball writer born to kick down doors—to lead the press corps' charge into the locker room. He covered the Brooklyn Dodgers in the time of Jackie Robinson, when beanballs, bravery, and monumental change were the order of the day, and he wanted answers, dammit. Answers about strategy and personalities and Robinson's great leap forward. The only way Young was going to get them was by asking questions until he had wrung the truth out of everyone in his crosshairs. Suddenly, a beautiful free-for-all was in session.

I spent sixteen years in newspapers, nearly ten of them as a sports columnist, and when that itch had been scratched, I went to Hollywood to scratch another one. My past became my calling card, a conversation starter whether I was interviewing for a job or, in the instance I remember best, meeting the star of a TV show. The star in this case was Don Johnson, who had rocketed to the top of the ratings and the cover of *Time* magazine with the glitzy, supercharged crime drama *Miami Vice*. He was directing an episode I had written, and he wanted me on location in Miami, mainly, it turned out, to poach the few worthwhile lines I had put in his costar's mouth.

"So," he said over dinner, "they tell me you were a sportswriter."

"I was."

"That's a strange way to make a living, isn't it?"

My mind did cartwheels as I stared across the table at this randy, unshaven heartthrob who played an undercover cop who dressed like a disco pimp, wore white loafers without socks, never blinked during a shoot-out, drove a Ferrari Testarossa while rock music swelled in the background, and had a pet alligator named Elvis.

*I* had a strange job?

Not by my lights, not even when I walked away from it. I had the best job anyone could have on a newspaper. I wrote about any sport that suited my fancy and prowled such sacred precincts as Madison Square Garden, Fenway Park, and Wimbledon. I was just as happy, however, hanging out in a bucket-of-blood boxing gym or trying not to laugh when the Chicago Cubs' sourpuss manager challenged me to a fight. A columnist isn't doing his job if he isn't putting someone's nose out of joint, but I took far greater pride in painting word pictures of Muhammad Ali both in triumph and in despair.

Everywhere I looked in the 1970s and '80s, there were columnists playing the same game I was, each making his or her own distinctive moves beneath a mug shot and a byline set in type bigger than an everyday reporter's. Dave Kindred established himself as the Red Smith of our generation as he moved from Louisville to Washington to Atlanta. Boston's Leigh Montville tickled the language with his sense of the ridiculous. Mike Lupica became the columnist you had to read in New York when he was barely out of swaddling clothes. Diane K. Shah, making history in Los Angeles as the nation's first female big-city sports columnist, didn't believe it was Cary Grant calling to compliment her until she hung up on him and he called back.

We took our cues from the seismic changes that shook sportswriting after World War II. While Dick Young raised hell in the trenches, Stanley Woodward, the *Herald Tribune*'s flinty sports editor, preached anarchy from on high, telling Red Smith and the rest of his staff to "stop godding up those ballplayers." Irreverence and iconoclasm became a way of sports-page life. When the *Philadelphia Daily News*'s boxing writer put up his dukes as a pro and won his first and only fight— by knockout—the paper ran a story that boasted about "the hardest hitting sports staff in creation." In New York, the lovably godawful Mets lurched into existence in 1962 and energized a band of young sportswriters—co-conspirators might be more accurate—known as "chipmunks." They spread fun all the way to the World Series where a pitcher for the un-funny Yankees inspired the ultimate postgame chipmunk question by saying his wife had been feeding their baby during a particularly tense moment. "Breast or bottle?" a *Newsday* columnist asked.

Somehow the chipmunks' cheekiness blended with the heightened professionalism that was coming to the fore across the country by the '80s. Tougher reporting and crisper writing defined powerhouse sports sections in Boston, Los Angeles, Philadelphia, Washington, Dallas, Chicago, Kansas City, Atlanta, Miami, and, of course, New York— mostly big-budget operations that sent writers around the world and filled as many as thirty pages a day. I'm not sure any of them surpassed the juggernaut Woodward assembled at the *Herald Tribune*, nor did any columnist eclipse Ring Lardner, Red Smith, and Jimmy Cannon, but the hard-charging new breed had its virtues. It was irreverent and adversarial, ready to laugh and slow to kowtow, as quick to quote Bob Dylan or James Brown as their predecessors had Shakespeare. Most important, they didn't shy away from tackling race, labor, and economics, subjects that were all but unimaginable on the sports page a generation before.

Long before analysis became a front-page staple, sports columnists and reporters were weaving tapestries of observation and opinion. They chronicled the game-winning homer and the ninety-nine-yard touchdown drive, but they also acted much like, say, drama critics unchained to grill playwrights. You'll find no better examples than Bob Ryan's passionate, uproarious Boston Celtics game stories and Richard Hoffer's elegance on deadline as he immortalizes an Olympic gymnast's heroics. Not surprisingly, Ryan and Hoffer became stars themselves, as did the wordsmiths who began stepping forth in the '80s and '90s to write marathon-length features inspired by *Sports Illustrated*'s legendary bonus pieces. Longform, they're called now. But the name wasn't anywhere near as interesting as the phenomenon of star columnists like the *L.A. Times*'s Bill Plaschke getting out of their thousand-word cages occasionally to write long. Ask Plaschke to give up his column, though, and you would likely see steam come out of his ears.

The column is where the stars of the twentieth-century sports page usually conducted their business, and even with longform now in flower, there are still those scribes who feel the column's magnetic pull. They want the freedom a columnist has to create a world all his own, a place where he can raise hell, tug heartstrings, or seek nobility in a loser's locker room. The old-timers used to churn out seven columns a week, and sometimes covered a beat, too. When one of them was told to take a day off, he thought his editor didn't like him anymore. His 2019 counterpart is on the hook for only three or four, but even so, he can feel the weight of his labors.

He'll wish writing the column wasn't always such a wrestling match with the language. He'll wish he could rap one out in twenty minutes, the way some columnists do. He'll wish he had a better lead or a better idea or maybe any idea at all. He always comes up with something, though, and when he finishes it, he promises himself the next one will be better. This book exists because such promises were kept.

★

I remember myself then, a lad fresh from the provinces and on my own as a grad student in Chicago. I told anyone who would listen that I intended to become a sportswriter. I thought I knew what sportswriting was because I'd seen my name in my hometown papers for playing baseball and read Jim Murray's syndicated column whenever I found it back with the truss ads and public parks golf scores. Then I bought a copy of the pre–Rupert Murdoch *New York Post*, and as I read about the 1968 NBA All-Star Game, I realized how vast my ignorance was.

Here was sportswriting the way I instinctively knew it should be— bright, lively, culturally attuned, unafraid of prickly issues. I zeroed in on Larry Merchant's column probing the psyche of Gus (Honeycomb) Johnson, a ferocious rebounder who sometimes seemed more interested in the gold in his two front teeth. Little did I know of the sports-page revolution Merchant had led in Philly. For the moment, it was enough that he had turned on the light for me.

College sportswriting classes had yet to become fashionable, so I plowed through E. P. Dutton's yearly *Best Sports Stories* anthologies. They weren't as sophisticated as the longform-heavy *Best American Sportswriting* annual that has both replaced and surpassed them, and yet I could get a megadose of inspiration from stories and columns by legends like W. C. Heinz and emerging stars like Robert Lipsyte. Between the lines was a message that great sportswriting wasn't confined to major markets, as Emmett Watson proved with a column out of Seattle about a boxer at the end of the road.

I pressed on, combing used book stores for the best of Smith and Cannon. Got lucky and stumbled across Joe Palmer's sublime *This Was Racing*. Caught a break when Merchant and Murray came out with collections of their own. But no one ever saw fit to wrap hard covers around Sandy Grady's pluperfect deconstructions of Philadelphia sports or Wells Twombly's lyrical takedowns of fools and phonies by the San Francisco Bay. You'll find them in these pages, however, as an acknowledgment that they gave better than they got.

Not that I have righted all wrongs or shined a light on every deserving scribe. I'd need a thousand pages to do that. What I offer you here is a cross section of stellar twentieth-century newspaper sportswriting. My apologies if I have failed to include a favorite of yours. It wasn't out of malice unless you are a Paul Gallico fan. If Gallico is remembered at all, it is likely as the author of *The Snow Goose* and *The Poseidon Adventure*, but in the twenties he was the *New York Daily News*'s precocious sports editor, America's highest-paid sports columnist, and a daredevil whose exploits would inspire George Plimpton. He was also a racist, misogynist, homophobe, and anti-Semite. The proof lies in his book *Farewell to Sport*, which is regarded as a classic by people who ought to read it sometime.

Too bad Sally Jenkins, Jane Leavy, and Diane Shah weren't around to knock him on his bigoted dime. But it wasn't until the last quarter of the century that women began making America's leading sports pages better with their intellect, empathy, courage, wit, and enviable prose styles. Theirs was not an easy row to hoe as they confronted sports-world troglodytes whose wandering hands and lewd proposals made you weep for the women in their private lives. But Shah will tell you she knew she had been accepted when she and two of her press box sisters crossed paths with Red Smith after a ball game and he said, "Hi, fellas."

Problems came in a different package for African American writers once they weren't confined to the proud black newspapers that covered what the white press ignored. As black athletes began to dominate sports, most visibly basketball, white sports editors responded by hiring black writers to cover them. There was no pigeonholing the best of them, though, as they gave the sports page a new dimension from one coast (Michael Wilbon of *The Washington Post*) to the other (Ralph Wiley of the *Oakland Tribune*). As I put this book together, it seemed a sign of progress that I could find Wiley's columns in a collection of his work. Wilbon, meanwhile, never responded to multiple requests for pieces he was proud of. I suppose that's progress of a different sort. Besides, I found two gems by him anyway.

Only Frank Graham was more elusive, but that wasn't any of his doing. He died in 1965. Fortunately, I tracked down his son, by phone, in the fishing village in Maine where he lives. Frank Jr. turned out to have boxes full of his father's work, pasted on shirt cardboards from the laundry. He typed up some of his favorites and mailed them to me. It was a lovely gesture that was made all the lovelier by the fact that he was ninety-three.

The old-timers knew how to dress. You look at photos of them in a press box—World Series time, the fall air crisp—and they're wearing suits and ties, fedoras and tweed overcoats. Not just the big hitters like Damon Runyon and Red Smith, but everybody. There's one sartorial touch they seem to have drawn the line at, though: briefcases. So when a numbers-besotted scribe showed up lugging one, the story goes that Jimmy Cannon shamed him with a single question: "What's in the briefcase, Lenny, decimal points?"

Newspaper sportswriting wasn't about decimal points in those days, or my day, either. At its best, it was about how words were strung together to capture a moment, create a mood, or define a personality. In these pages, you'll find pieces of writing that hopscotch everyday journalism and enter the realm of artistry. W. C. Heinz's 1949 classic, "Death of a Racehorse," weighs in at less than a thousand words, hammered out against an unforgiving deadline, and yet it can stand beside some of our very best short fiction. Just a homely newspaper column built of fact and keen observation, but it has endured all these years and lit a fire in writers who see it as the gold standard.

Would that today's newspapers provided more chances to aim so high. It is, after all, an era rich in wonderful, even brilliant sportswriting. But most of it is floating in cyberspace while too many sports sections resemble skeletons, their staffs downsized, their budgets and page counts diminished. And to think that we got all puffed up back when TV's power simply made us get better. We went places the cameras wouldn't go, chased angles instead of talking heads, and, if we worked on afternoon papers—remember them?—wrote until the sun was coming up.

But as the twenty-first century loomed, there was no beating sports talk radio, not with all those fans with all their opinions out there dialing frantically: "Yo, Vinnie from Manayunk, you're on the air." In less time than it took to bellyache about a bad trade, talk radio was setting the agenda for local sports coverage. ESPN ruled the world round the clock. And the irony was that some of the biggest stars on cable TV and radio were newspaper sports columnists who spent hours gabbing on the air when they could have been doing what made them marketable in the first place.

Then came the train wreck that scrambled daily sportswriting, probably forever. Sports went corporate, athletes made too much money not to toe the party line, and PR honks swarmed around interviews like plant lice. The Internet's sometimes nonsensical demand for immediacy sapped weary writers' energy for art. Metrics buried everything in a blizzard of launch angles, acronyms—WAR, anyone?—and those damned decimal points.

All I can do as I survey this mess is wish that the pure hearts trying to write their way out of it had known Earl Weaver. He managed the Baltimore Orioles when they defined baseball excellence, a wily, profane banty rooster with far too many rough edges to ever get hired today. He picked fights with umpires and feuded with his star pitcher, spun pregame yarns about bush-league life and smoked furtively in the dugout until the last man was out. He pioneered the use of computer printouts, too, but that's beside the point. I'm here to tell you about the day he helped carry my luggage through O'Hare International. When we got where I was going, I bought him a copy of my paper, and Weaver, being the kind of subject every sportswriter needs as much as nouns and verbs, said, "Jesus Christ, a tip."

# THE GREAT AMERICAN SPORTS PAGE

# W. O. McGEEHAN

W. O. Mcgeehan (1879–1933) was the *New York Herald Tribune*'s in-house antidote to hero-worshipping Grantland Rice. Mcgeehan, a professional skeptic with no time for hustlers or dullards, was managing editor of the *San Francisco Bulletin* before he headed east and established his independence as a sports columnist. "If it's a bribe, it's not enough," he said. "If it's a gift, it's too much." He was, not surprisingly, a member in good standing of the Aw-Nuts school of sportswriting. The McGeehan columns offered here stamp him as a progressive thinker regarding female athletes and a cop on the beat when casting a gimlet eye on boxing. He pilloried the sport as "the manly art of modified murder" and mocked Primo Camera, a mob-backed heavyweight contender, as "the tall tower of Gorgonzola." If McGeehan had walked into a sports department fifty years later, he would have been a perfect fit.

★   ★   ★

# Gertrude Ederle vs. the Channel

THE SETTING for the greatest sports story of the year, to my mind, will be the twenty-two miles of sullen gray Channel water between Cape Gris-Nez and Dover early in August, when Gertrude Ederle makes her second attempt to conquer the elements that beat her last year. Only five men out of the hundreds who have tried have made it and not a single woman.

This is more than a great melodramatic sporting event. The Ederle family is installed at the Hotel of the Lighthouse talking it over and Pa

Ederle is planning his celebration in the event of his daughter's victory. And Gertrude said naïvely, "And I'll bet all the women in the world will celebrate that night." That is the keynote of the interest. Swimming the Channel is a supreme test of courage and endurance, requiring a physique which makes victory possible. And a victory for Gertrude Ederle will be one of the greatest feminist stories, as well as one which will appeal to the dullest imagination.

In Paris the gamblers are willing to give heavy odds on the Channel against the young champion of her sex, a girl who is to make the attempt to demonstrate that the members of her sex can possess virtues held previously exclusively by the masculine. She is trying for the second time a feat that only the hardiest and most exceptionally equipped male swimmers have succeeded in accomplishing.

Standing beside Miss Ederle as she sat on one of the rocks near the lighthouse and looked across the gray, sullen water, I'd be inclined to back this girl against the Channel. If there is one woman who can make the swim, it is this girl, with the shoulders and back of Jack Dempsey and the frankest and bravest pair of eyes that ever looked into a face. It is improbable, but not impossible.

At first Miss Ederle gives the impression of being dull, because she is slightly deaf through an injury to her eardrums from swimming and because, like all swimmers, she is a mouth breather. But she is far from dull. She has a sense of humor. She told me of her last attempt, when she swam for an hour on instinct alone, blinded, deaf, and only half conscious. She remembered only the humor of the trip.

She told of the correspondents boarding the tug at Cape Gris-Nez airily waving at her and saying, "See you in Dover." Then she told in words and pantomime how they crawled off on the English side, wan and seasick, and how one of them said, "This is the last time I make any Channel swims." She threw back her bobbed head and laughed with the heartiness of a big boy.

"This time," she said, "I am preparing myself to stay eighteen hours in the water. The last time I was trying for a record. When I start again it will be with the idea of reaching the other side, and I will not quit until I cannot move."

As she spoke she peered through the chill mists that hid the outlines of the English coast. Below, the Channel was growling as it lashed against the rocks with a constant menace. Behind her was standing the north coast of France.

"All I am going to get for this is a roadster. Pa promised me one if I make the swim this time. So I'll be seeing nothing but that roadster on the boat while I am making the swim." A little while later she was cuddling a little baby rabbit, which she had picked up in the fields, against her brown cheek. A strange mixture is this girl, with the simplicity of Shaw's Joan of Arc and the physique and many attributes of a male giant. To picture what eighteen hours in the Channel might seem you must stand with her on the rocks at Cape Gris-Nez.

Consider the ancestry of this young Amazon. Her grandmother was the mother of twenty-one children and she is still alive and active in Stuttgart, on the edge of the Black Forest in Germany. When this swim is over Gertrude is going to visit her. The swimmer herself is one of a family of twelve—one of the old-fashioned German-American families.

Her training quarters are rougher than those of any prize fighter I have ever visited. In fact, the manager of one of these delicate male athletes would seize his fighter and flee at first sight of the Hotel of the Lighthouse, with beds that sag in the middle and running water that never runs. The diet she eats would shock a trainer. It is the diet of a stenographer mixed with pickles. Yet I have heard third-rate prize fighters complaining that they didn't get their proper nourishment even when they had their own chefs.

The loneliness would make even an unimaginative prize fighter mad in a few weeks. But this girl keeps her even temper and her sunny good humor, living day by day with a battlefield by her side. This time she is under the charge of the gray-haired William Burgess, who swam the Channel years ago, and a man who has spent his life studying its changes and its cruel moods. The present plan is to have Gertrude Ederle start from the point on the French coast where he finished and have the light of Cape Gris-Nez guide her through the long, weary miles of darkness and silence, broken only by the growl of the waters.

She was at the door of the lighthouse when I left her with her toy phonograph playing a jazz tune. She held out one of the strong brown hands that will beat against the waters of the Channel and said with that boyish smile, "Good-by, good luck."

I felt that I would sooner be in that tug the day she starts than at the ringside of the greatest fight or at the arena of the greatest game in the world, for this, in my opinion, is to be the greatest sports story in the world.

*1926*

★  ★  ★

# News of a Champion

AD WOLGAST, once lightweight champion of the world, is in the news again briefly. Friends who have been caring for him in California have made application to have him committed to an asylum as hopelessly insane.

For more than ten years Wolgast has been living in a phantom world populated by old prize-ring ghosts. His mind failed him shortly after he lost his championship, and he labored under the hallucination that he was to meet Joe Gans (long since dead) for the lightweight championship. Jack Doyle, a Los Angeles promoter, with more heart than most of the men who make their money out of the manly art of modified murder, took pity on him and assumed full charge of him.

Through Doyle's generosity Ad Wolgast was provided with a little gymnasium, where he did his training. He seldom used to miss a morning on the road. It was his hallucination that he was to meet Joe Gans, dead even before Wolgast's mind went into the fog, in a championship bout. For years he settled down into this routine with only the idea that he must be in condition for the championship bout.

Sometimes they would take him to boxing matches. He always used to say, "I could whip either of them." But he never insisted on meeting any of the fighters he saw. He was concentrating on the phantom bout with Gans. Physically Wolgast seemed to be all that he ever had been, but his mind was gone forever.

I saw Wolgast win the lightweight championship from Battling Nelson in a ring pitched in the adobe mud near Port Richmond, California. For concentrated viciousness, prolonged past forty rounds, that was the most savage bout I have ever seen. Both men were badly enough battered, for in giving Nelson a beating, Wolgast was forced to take almost as much as he gave. It was inevitable that the effects would tell.

Somewhere around the thirtieth round, I think it was, Wolgast was dropped by a body blow and it looked like the end. But he was up in an instant, snarling and lashing at Nelson. After that it was Nelson, the Durable Dane, who showed signs of weakening and whose face began to look like a raw slab of steak. The features were obliterated and only the slit of one eye remained open.

In the forty-second round Nelson was pressing feebly forward while Wolgast's gloves were hurling crimson splashes around the ring every time they struck the battered face. The Dane would not yield an inch, but it had become so cruel that the most hardened ringsiders were calling upon the referee to stop it.

Finally Eddie Smith stepped between the men and pushed Nelson to his corner. The Dane snarled at him, then tried to protest through the twisted and battered mouth. The only sound that came was one such as might have been made by an exhausted and terribly wounded wild animal. Nelson's seconds caught him and pushed him onto the stool in the corner. The referee raised Wolgast's hand. He had become lightweight champion of the world.

Not so long after I saw him lose this title to Willie Ritchie of California, then a young graduate from the amateur ranks. It started out as though Wolgast would rush Ritchie off his feet. The "Cadillac Bearcat" was beating the Californian from the start, when Ritchie landed a wild swing that caught Wolgast flush on the jaw. Wolgast dropped to his knees, all but out. As he was about to collapse he drove two foul punches upward at the Californian. He had the rattlesnake's instinct to strike, even when mortally hurt.

It was Wolgast's fate to have won the championship in one of the hardest fights ever staged, only to have lost it through almost a chance blow—if there is such a thing as a chance blow.

Said one of Wolgast's former managers, "He was one of the greatest fighters I ever knew, and it was a pleasure to manage him. He never cared whom he fought or how often. He would fight anybody I signed up with him.

"Once I tried him out for fun. I knew that he was in his hotel room so I rang him up and told him that I had signed him as a substitute boxer for some bouts that night. The schedule called for him to appear in three hours. 'All right,' he said. 'Wake me up in a few hours, and I'll get ready to go into the ring.'

"'But you haven't asked who it is that you are going to fight,' I said. 'No,' said Wolgast, 'and I don't care. Just wake me up so that I won't be late getting to the ring.' He was that way all the time. He would say, 'Get me anybody for any time, and I'll fight him any time you say.'

"You do not meet that kind of fighter these days, the fellow you can have hop into a ring on a few hours' notice. The boys are very careful, particularly the topnotchers, as to the kind of matches you make for them. They never want to take a chance with any of the rough ones. Can you picture any of the later lightweights being careless about whom they are signed up with?"

From the point of view of the manager there is no doubt that Wolgast was the ideal prize fighter. He always was willing to step into the ring at the command of the mastermind, to take a beating, and to listen to the voice of the manager, shouting, "Go on in. He can't hurt US!"

Nearly all of Wolgast's former managers have their health and are in no danger of the almshouse or the insane asylum. Oh yes. There is no doubt that Ad Wolgast was the ideal prize fighter from the manager's point of view. But poor little Wolgast will be taken to a state insane asylum shortly. The blows that the managers did not feel seem to have had effect upon Wolgast. Perhaps the fighter was just a trifle more sensitive than the manager.

*1927*

## DAMON RUNYON

Damon Runyon (1880–1946) covered his first hanging at age eleven and grew up to create the mythological Broadway world populated by such unforgettable characters as Nathan Detroit, Madame La Gimp, and Harry the Horse. Runyon also found time to write rollicking dispatches about old ballplayers on bandy legs and tapped-out gamblers who substantiated his theory that all life was six-to-five against. He came from Colorado in 1910 to report on baseball for William Randolph Hearst's New York papers, but the press box could hold him for only so long. He went on to cover murder trials by applying the techniques of baseball writing and to capture the vernacular of the streets in the short stories that came to life onstage as *Guys and Dolls*. Ever since then, writers have tried to duplicate the rhythms in the sentences Runyon left behind. They never come better than close.

★   ★   ★

# Stengel's Homer Wins It for Giants, 5–4

THIS IS the way old "Casey" Stengel ran yesterday afternoon, running his home run home.

This is the way old "Casey" Stengel ran running his home run home to a Giant victory by a score of 5 to 4 in the first game of the World Series of 1923.

This is the way old "Casey" Stengel ran, running his home run home, when two were out in the ninth inning and the score was tied and the ball was still bounding inside the Yankee yard.

This is the way—

His mouth wide open.

His warped old legs bending beneath him at every stride.

His arms flying back and forth like those of a man swimming with a crawl stroke.

His flanks heaving, his breath whistling, his head far back.

Yankee infielders, passed by old "Casey" Stengel as he was running his home run home, say "Casey" was muttering to himself, adjuring himself to greater speed as a jockey mutters to his horse in a race that he was saying, "Go on, Casey! Go on."

People generally laugh when they see old "Casey" Stengel run, but they were not laughing while he was running his home run home yesterday afternoon. People—60,000 of 'em, men and women—were standing in the Yankee stands and bleachers up there in the Bronx roaring sympathetically, whether they were for or against the Giants.

"Come on, Casey!"

The warped old legs twisted and bent by many a year of baseball campaigning, just barely held out under "Casey" Stengel until he reached the plate, running his home run home.

Then they collapsed.

They gave out just as old "Casey" slid over the plate in his awkward fashion with Wally Schang futilely reaching for him with the ball. "Billy" Evans, the American League umpire, poised over him in a set pose, arms spread to indicate that old "Casey" was safe.

Half a dozen Giants rushed forward to help "Casey" to his feet, to hammer him on the back, to bawl congratulations in his ears as he limped unsteadily, still panting furiously, to the bench where John J. McGraw, chief of the Giants, relaxed his stern features in a smile for the man who had won the game.

"Casey" Stengel's warped old legs, one of them broken not so long ago, wouldn't carry him out for the last half of the inning, when the Yankees made a dying effort to undo the damage done by "Casey." His place in centerfield was taken by young "Bill" Cunningham, whose legs are still unwarped, and "Casey" sat on the bench with John J. McGraw.

No one expected much of "Casey" Stengel when he appeared at the plate in the Giants' side of the ninth inning, the score a tie at 4 to 4.

Ross Youngs and "Irish" Meusel, dependable hitters, had been quickly disposed of by the superb pitching of "Bullet Joe" Bush.

No one expected Stengel to accomplish anything where they had failed. Bush, pitching as only Bush can pitch in an emergency, soon had two strikes and three balls on "Casey."

He was at the plate so long that many of the fans were fidgeting nervously, wondering why he didn't hurry up and get put out, so the game could go on. "Casey" Stengel is not an imposing figure at bat, not an imposing figure under any circumstances. Those warped old legs have something to do with it. A man with warped legs cannot look very imposing.

People like to laugh at "Casey"—"Casey" likes to make people laugh.

A wayfarer of the big leagues—Brooklyn, Pittsburgh, Philadelphia, and finally New York—he has always been regarded by the fans as a great comedian, a funny fellow, a sort of clown.

The baseball land teems with tales of the strange didoes cut by "Casey" Stengel, whose parents started him out as Charles, with his sayings.

Who knows but that "Bullet Joe" may have been thinking of "Casey" Stengel more as a comedian than as a dangerous hitter when he delivered that final pitch yesterday afternoon? Pitchers sometimes let their wits go wool-gathering.

"Bap"—Stengel's bat connected surely, solidly. The ball sailed out over left field, moving high, moving far.

"Long Bob" Meusel ("Irish" Bob's Yankee brother) and "Whitey"

Witt, the Yankee outfielders, raced toward each other as they marked the probable point of the ball would alight, and in the meantime, "Casey" Stengel was well advanced on his journey, running his home run home.

As the ball landed between Meusel and Witt, it bounded as if possessed toward the left center field fence. Everybody could see it would be a home run inside the yard, if "Casey" Stengel's warped old legs could carry him around the bases.

Witt got the ball about the time Stengel hit third, and about that time Stengel was laboring, "all out." Witt threw the ball in to Bob Meusel, who had dropped back and let Witt go on. Meusel wheeled and fired for the plate, putting all the strength behind the throw. Few men have ever lived who can throw a baseball as well as Bob Meusel.

Stengel was almost home when Meusel's throw was launched, and sensing the throw "Casey" called on all that was left in those warped old legs, called no doubt on all the baseball gods to help him—and they helped.

It is something to win a World Series with a home run, and home run inside the yard.

John J. McGraw perhaps feels that his judgment in taking Stengel on at a time when "Casey" was a general big-league out-cast has been vindicated.

If you are curious to know the origin of the nickname "Casey," it might be explained that Stengel's home-town is Kansas City.

The nickname comes from "K.C." One of these many little coincidences that are always popping out in baseball is the fact that "Casey" and "Bullet Joe" Bush are great pals. They made the baseball tour last Winter as roommates.

Stengel is around 33, if you are seeking more information about the first hero of the World Series of 1923. They call that "old" in baseball. He has been with the Giants since 1921, from the Philadelphia club. He is all right, "Casey" Stengel is, and you can prove it by John J. McGraw.

*1923*

★   ★   ★

# All Horse Players Die Broke

HORSE PLAYERS, like rumpots, swear off occasionally. Usually it is when they are broke and disgusted. That was the case with "The Singing Kid" in Chicago at the close of a racing season some years ago.

He swore by the bones of Sysonby that if he could get a job doing anything, even cleaning the streets, at enough salary to give him board and room he would never look at a form sheet again as long as he lived.

Pat Nash took "The Singing Kid" seriously and put him in charge of his breeding farm in the blue grass region of Kentucky at $150 a month and all found. "The Kid" lived in the manor house with so many servants to wait on him that he did not have to lift a hand.

His duties were light. The neighbors were friendly. A man could scarcely dream of a nicer existence. But when Pat visited the farm as it came on the following spring, he found "The Singing Kid," usually the best of company and the lightest of heart, in morose mood. He did not have much to say for several days, then one evening as they sat before the fire in the comfortable old living room, he said:

"Pat, I want you to know I am very grateful to you for all you have done for me in giving me this place and getting me away from horse racing. I will never forget you. Never as long as I live. But there is something I must discuss with you."

"I know," said Pat gently. "But the racing season is coming on and you must be on your way. Well, good-bye, Singer. Go and pack."

"Good-bye and God bless you, Pat," said "The Singing Kid." "I'm already packed."

I had a wire last week from Dave Butler, movie director and horse racing enthusiast, telling me of the death in Hollywood of "The Singer" as he came to be known in his later years since the appellation "The

Kid" was obviously inappropriate to a pudgy, bald chap with a dignified pince-nez riding his nose.

This was the original "Singing Kid" I am talking about. He had the monicker over forty years. I have known of a score of others who borrowed it or had it applied to them but Arthur Loftus undoubtedly held priority to the title, and all others were infringements.

He once had a really good tenor voice that he exercised professionally in minor vaudeville and back rooms until the horses became a permanent affliction with him. That was a long time ago because he was around Emeryville in the old days, a mere punk, it is true, but a horse player even then. I would put his age at death at past 60. But you never can tell about horse players. They are timeless.

I reckon it must be the outdoor life and the activity. "The Singing Kid" up to the last time I saw him, which was several years ago, was as lively as a grasshopper. His voice did not hold out as well as his legs. He used to come over to my house on Hibiscus Island, down in Dade County, Florida, during the racing season and sing for me, mainly operatic stuff and even I noticed a crack in the upper register of his tones wider than that in the liberty bell.

No one, not even "The Dancer," could root a horse home like "The Singing Kid." He was master of the art of snapping his fingers, which I deem quite necessary in rooting 'em in and which is something I was never able to do. He was a neat fellow and had his own code of ethics. I am sure he never purposely harmed anyone.

Howard Lindsay and I tried to put "The Singing Kid" on the stage playing himself in "A Slight Case of Murder" but after accepting the role, he ran out on us. Ben Lindheimer, the Chicago racing magnate, gave him a job describing the races over the loud speaker to the assembled fans and oddly enough "The Kid" got a horrible attack of mike fright and was a total bust.

He was always a player. He did some handicapping but seemed to rely more on tips from friendly trainers and jockeys and owners. He was a high player in that he would bet all he had which I contend makes a man a higher player than one to whom the losses mean nothing. "The Singing Kid" had considerable money at different times in his life but I am sure that his passing was in strict accordance with the immutable law of racing that all horse players must die broke.

*1944*

## GRANTLAND RICE

Even if Grantland Rice's name means nothing to you, it's entirely possible you have heard someone utter something about the four horsemen of a football apocalypse "outlined against a blue-gray October sky." They are arguably the most famous and certainly the most quoted words in sportswriting history. Rice (1880–1954) wrote them as he piled on adjectives and imagery to describe Notre Dame's backfield running amok against poor Army in 1924. The unofficial leader of the press box's Gee-Whiz contingent, he seemed to see every event he covered as the equivalent of the Trojan War. Some contemporaries mocked him and subsequent generations of sportswriters were even harsher. But Rice, the star of the *New York Herald Tribune*'s sports page and a nationally syndicated columnist during the Roaring Twenties and the Depression, never stopped striving to paint word pictures for audiences in the age before TV. He was best when he took some of the purple out of his prose the way he did in the following story about a once-dominant pitcher recapturing greatness in the '24 World Series. Rice remained true to his vision of sports until the end. When he died, he did it the only place he could—at his typewriter.

★   ★   ★

# Senators Win Title, 4–3

DESTINY, WAITING for the final curtain, stepped from the wings today and handed the king his crown.

In the most dramatic moment of baseball's sixty years of history the wall-eyed goddess known as Fate, after waiting eighteen years, led

Walter Johnson to the pot of shining gold that waits at the rainbow's end.

For it was Johnson, the old Johnson, brought back from other years with his blazing fast ball singing across the plate for the last four rounds, that stopped the Giant attack, from the ninth inning through the twelfth, and gave Washington's fighting ball club its world series victory by the score of 4 to 3, in the seventh game of a memorable struggle.

Washington won just at the edge of darkness, and it was Johnson's great right arm that turned the trick. As Earl McNeely singled and Muddy Ruel galloped over the plate with the winning run in the last of the twelfth, 38,000 people rushed on to the field with a roar of triumph never known before, and for more than thirty minutes, packed in one vast, serried mass around the bench, they paid Johnson and his mates a tribute that no one present will ever forget. It was something beyond all belief, beyond all imagining. Its crashing echoes arc still singing out across the stands, across the city, on into the gathering twilight of early autumn shadows. There was never a ball game like this before, never a game with as many thrills and heart throbs strung together in the making of drama that came near tearing away the soul to leave it limp and sagging, drawn and twisted out of shape.

Washington, facing the last of the eighth inning, was a beaten team, with the dream about dosed out. And then like a heavy blast from hidden explosives a rally started that tied the score, the two most important tallies of baseball lore sweeping over the plate as Bucky Harris's infield blow skirted the ground and suddenly leaped upward over Lindstrom's glove.

It was this single from the great young leader that gave Johnson his third and final chance. For, as the Giants came to bat in the ninth, with the score knotted at 3 and 3, there came once more the old familiar figure slouching across the infield sod to his ancient home in the box. Here once more was the mighty moment, and as 38,000 stood and cheered, roared and raved, Johnson began to set the old-time fast one singing on its way. With only one out in the ninth inning, Frank Frisch struck a triple to deep center, hut in the face of this emergency "Old Barney" turned back to something lost from his vanished youth, and as Kelly tried in vain to bring Frisch home, the tall Giant suddenly found himself facing the Johnson of a decade ago—blinding, baffling speed that struck him out and closed down on the rally with the snap of death.

Johnson was on his way, and neither Destiny nor the Giants could head him off. He had suffered two annihilations, but his mighty moment had come and he was calling back stuff from a dozen years ago. To show that he was headed for another triumph and that young blood was coursing through his veins again, he came to the eleventh and struck out Frisch and Kelly. It was the first time in four years of world series play that any pitcher had struck out the keen-eyed Frisch. But the Fordham Flash today was facing the Johnson that used to be, the Johnson that nailed them all, the high and low alike, with a fast ball that few could see and fewer still could hit.

All this while the drama of the day was gathering intensity from round to round. Washington missed a great chance in the eleventh after Goslin had doubled, but the end was now near at hand. The human heart couldn't hold out many moments longer. The strain was too great for any team or any crowd to stand. Thirty-eight thousand pulses were jumping in a dozen different directions at the same moment as nervous systems were going to certain destruction.

For four innings now Johnson had faced Nehf, Bentley and McQuillan and two of these had been his conquerors. He was on the verge of getting his complete revenge in one sudden swirl of action. Still cool, serene and steady with the old right arm coming through with its easy and endless rhythm, Johnson again rolled back the Giant charge in the twelfth. In these four innings he had fanned five men, and most of them were struck down when a hit meant sudden death.

The long, gray afternoon shadows had now crept almost across the field. There was grave doubt that even another inning could have been played when fate in the shape of a catcher's mask intervened. With one man out and Bentley pitching, Ruel lifted a high foul back of the plate.

Hank Gowdy, one of the most reliable of all who play, started for the ball, but in dancing beneath it his feet became entangled in the mask and before he could regain his balance the ball dropped safely to earth through his hands.

This was the spot which destiny picked as the place to hand "Old Barney" the long delayed crown, for Ruel on the next swing doubled to left. Johnson was safe on Jackson's error at short, and with only one out McNeely decided to follow the Harris attack. He slashed one along the ground to third, and as Lindstrom came in for the ball, for the second time in the game the ball suddenly bounded high over his head as Ruel crossed with the run that brought world series glory to Washington's game and crippled club.

The hit that tied it up and the hit that won were almost identical, perfect duplicates, as each reared itself from the lowly sod as if lifted by a watchful and guiding fate that had decided in advance that Washington must win. In the wake of this hit the ravings and the roarings again came near dislodging the rafters of the big stands. For this was the hit that meant Johnson's triumph, the hit that meant Washington's victory.

No club from the sixty years of play ever came from behind as often to break down the ramparts and get to the top. But Washington had the habit, and even when crippled and almost beaten Harris and his mates refused to waver for a moment as they formed again with what remnants were left to lead another counter charge. It was a home run by Harris that gave Washington its first score, and it was the manager's single that gave Johnson his closing chance to follow the old dream to the end of the route.

While Barnes held the winners to one hit for six innings, he weakened at last, and McGraw threw in Nehf, McQuillan and Bentley in a vain effort to save a waning cause. Washington, needing two games to win on Wednesday night, had won them both by one of the gamest exhibitions in the long span of all competitive sport.

Another perfect day with another spread of blue sky and yellow sun, the seventh in succession, helped to bring about the second

$1,000,000 world series, the first being last year. This made the fourth $1,000,000 program in American sport: Dempsey–Carpentier, Dempsey–Firpo and two world series, with the former fight on top by nearly a million iron men.

The gathering around the Presidential box just before the first salvo was fired indicated the day's first excitement. When the cameramen reached the scene in the scurrying groups they discovered the President and Mrs. Coolidge, Secretary Slemp, Judge Landis, John J. McGraw, Bucky Harris and Clark Griffith all set for the last official pose of the long war's final day. With the ball park packed to the ultimate elbow, the crowd outside was even larger, as endless lines extended back around corners and alongside streets, almost blocking traffic. Inside it was a quieter and more tense gathering than the day before, with a part of the pre-game chatter stilled.

It was not until Warren Harvey Ogden, "The Sheik of Swarthmore," struck out Fred Lindstrom to start the game that rolling waves of sound indicated the amount of suppressed excitement.

After Ogden had walked Frisch he gave way to Mogridge with a string of lefty-handed hitters up, including Terry. The idea was to have Terry announced with a right-hander pitching so that if once removed with a left-hander in he was out of the series.

Great plays began to sparkle early like diamonds shining in the sun. In the second inning Hack Wilson slapped one along the ground at a whistling clip almost over second base. Here was a budding hit, if we ever saw one. But Bluege, who is remarkably fast, cut over and by an almost impossible effort knocked the ball down with his glove, scooped it up with the right and nailed his man at first from short center by a cannonball throw.

In the third inning Joe Judge started one toward right center with a rising inflection. It was on its way to gold and glory when Frank Frisch broke the high jump record and cut off a budding triple. After three innings and a half of brilliant pitching the first big crash came in the fourth. Here, with one out, came Bucky Harris reaching for another laurel sprig. His line drive over Hack Wilson carried into the stands, although Hack almost broke his massive spine in trying to pull down the drive. His impact with the low, green barricade sounded like a barrel of crockery being pushed down the cellar stairs.

Just a moment later the same Hack, having recovered his breath, came racing in for a low, rakish hit by Rice. He dived for the ball and dug it up six inches from the turf, skating along for many feet upon his broad and powerful system, stomach down. Here was another hit totally ruined by fancy fielding.

The sixth was replete with loud noises and much strategy. It was here that the stout Washington defense cracked wide open. Mogridge started the trouble by passing Pep Young. Kelly laced a long single to center, sending Young scurrying around to third. Here McGraw sent in Meusel to hit for Terry and Harris countered by removing Mogridge, the southpaw, and sending Marberry to the rifle pit. Meusel lifted a long sacrifice fly to Sam Rice, scoring Young. Wilson followed with a lusty hit, sending Kelly to third. Here the run getting should have ended.

Jackson tapped one sharply to Judge at first, and Judge, attempting to hurry the play for the plate, fumbled the ball and lost his bearings completely as Kelly scored, Jackson reached first and Wilson moved to second on a simple chance. Gowdy tapped one along the ground toward Bluege, and this brilliant infielder let the ball trickle between his feet to left field as Wilson came over with the third run. It was a pitiful infield collapse after a day of superb support up to this motheaten spot. The infield cave-in gave the Giants two extra runs and a tidy lead.

The eighth was the most dramatic spot of the entire series. It was full of throbs, thrills and noises. With one out, Nemo Leibold, batting for Taylor, doubled down the left field line. This started the racket with a howl and a roar. Ruel then drew his first hit of the series, an infield blow that Kelly knocked down but couldn't field. With the clamor increasing at every moment, Tate, batting for Marberry, walked, filling the bases, with only one out. There was a brief lull as McNeely flied out. The vocal spasm broke loose with renewed fury when Harris rapped one sharply toward Lindstrom, and the ball, after skirting the ground, suddenly bounded high over Lindstrom's head for the single that scored Leibold and Ruel and tied it up. Harris had driven in all three runs and the gathering paid its noisiest acclaim.

It was Art Nehf who checked Washington's assault and it was Walter Johnson who hurried in to face the Giants in the ninth with his third shot at destiny.

For a moment in the ninth he rocked and reeled on the edge of the precipice. With one out Frisch tripled to deep center. But after Johnson had purposely passed Pep Young he struck out Kelly and then led Meusel to an infield out that left Frisch stranded far from home.

Washington came within a span of winning in the ninth. With one gone Joe Judge laced a single to center. Bluege tapped to Kelly at first and Kelly whipped the ball at high speed to Jackson, the ball bounding away from Jackson's glove as Judge raced to third. A man on third and first and only one out—what a chance. But Miller rammed one sharply to Jackson at short and a crushing double play wiped out Washington's chance with Judge almost home.

Groh, batting for McQuillan, opened the ninth with a clean hit. He limped to first and gave way to Southworth. Lindstrom sacrificed, but Johnson, calling on all he had, struck out Frisch and Kelly in a row, Frisch fanning for the first time in four years of world series play.

It was Johnson's day at last.

*1924*

## RING LARDNER

Ring Lardner (1885–1933) liked to say he just mimicked the men who worked the baseball beat before him. His devoted readership, enraptured by the fractured English that stamped him as an original, would hear none of it. In the years 1913 through 1915, he wrote more than sixteen hundred columns and stories for the *Chicago Tribune*, and no one would have complained if he had written sixteen hundred more. When Lardner moved to New York and the Bell Syndicate, his column appeared in a hundred fifty papers, a figure made all the more startling by the short fiction he wrote in his supposed idle hours and the huge success of his first book, *You Know Me Al*, which is still read a century later. There would be more short stories, more books, and more journalism as well as forays into music, plays, and Ziegfeld Follies skits. And Lardner still had time for golf, bridge, the Algonquin Round Table, a happy marriage that produced four sons who became writers, and so much drinking with his pal F. Scott Fitzgerald that Fitzgerald had to flee to France to get some work done. When Lardner died at forty-eight he had done enough living for someone twice his age.

★ ★ ★

# Mordecai Brown: The Reporter's Friend

S O FAR as the big leagues are concerned, Mordecai Brown, they say, is through. If the gentleman from Indiana needs consolation he may perhaps find a bit in the knowledge, hereby imparted to him, that there is more genuine regret among the baseball writers of our beautiful city over his departure than over the passing of any other athlete whose work has redounded to the honor and glory of Chicago, etc.

Brownie was not only the most popular ball player among the ball players, but also far and away the most general favorite among the scribes.

That he was liked and respected by fellow members of the Cub pitching staff, speaks volumes for his personality. Pitchers, most of them, are human, and being human, not apt to harbor the tenderest feelings toward those indubitably their superiors in skill. Brownie was, in his top form, the best of a great pitching corps. Yet every other member of that corps was sincerely fond of him.

However, we are dealing here with his standing with the newspaper men. He was not a live source of news, owing to his reticence. His modesty prevented his giving us valuable columns about himself for use on rainy days.

But he could tell, by looking at you, when you were broke. While you were still wondering from whom to borrow five, he would come up and, without a word, hand you ten.

As present day salaries go, he was drawing far less than he was worth. But he was drawing far more than were we reporters, and knowing this, it hurt him to see us spend. So he did most of the spending for us, against our protest, of course.

We (editorially, this time) never fully appreciated Brownie, though he had done us innumerable favors, until one day in the season of 1909. It was the last day in Philadelphia and the next stop was in New York. We had a tentative engagement in New York at eight-thirty that evening, an engagement we wanted to keep. In the forenoon, we sought out Charley Williams, the walking time-table.

"Is there a train out of here for New York round six o'clock?" we asked.

"Why?"

"I want to get there early this evening."

"So does everybody else," said Charley.

(Everybody was young then.)

"There's a train on the Reading at six," continued Charley, "and we can get it at the station near the park if the game's over in time. I asked Shettsline if he'd start early, but he wouldn't. So we'll just have to take chances."

The P. L. tried to help by selecting as pitcher, Orval Overall, one of the fastest workers in the pastime. Big Orrie proved fast, and effective, too, but no more effective than Sparks of the enemy. At the end of the eleventh, we had given up hope of an extra evening on Broadway, for it was a quarter after five and everything pointed to a long tie.

But in their twelfth, the desperate Cubs fell on the Philly pitcher and drove home two runs, the first of the game.

"Now, if he can just hold 'em!" we said, and started making up the box score.

But the Phillies weren't quite through. The top of their batting order was up, and whoever was lead-off man singled. Otto Knabe walked and the next gentleman sacrificed. A base hit would tie it again, and two such wretched hitters as Magee and Bransfield were in line.

Out went Orrie and in came Brown; the tying run on second base; the crowd barking at him; one out, and Philadelphia's best batsmen to face.

Six balls Brownie pitched, six curve balls, the curvin'est balls we ever saw. And three times apiece Magee and Bransfield swung, and missed three times apiece.

While the Cubs hurriedly changed their clothes, we as hurriedly wrote our story; a story about one per cent as good as the game warranted.

On the train we shook the three-fingered hand.

"Much obliged, Brownie. I've got a date in New York this evening."

"So Charley said," replied Mr. Brown. "Come on in the next car and I'll buy you dinner."

*1916*

★   ★   ★

# Kid's Strategy Goes Amuck
# as Jake Doesn't Die

C INCINNATI, OHIO—Gents: Up to the eighth inning this pm, we was all setting there wondering what to write about and I happened to be looking at Jake Daubert's picture on the souvenir program and all of a sudden Jake fell over and I thought he was dead so I said to the boys: "Here is your story:

"Jacob E. Daubert was born in Shamokin, Pa., on the 17 of April, 1886, and lives in Schuykill, Pa., and began playing with the Kane, Pa., club in 1907. With Cleveland in 1908 and Toledo for two years. Joined the Brooklyn club in 1910 and remained there until this season. Then joined the Cincinnati Reds and fell dead in the 8th inning of the 1st game of the world serious."

So everybody got up and cheered me and said that was a very funny story but all of a sudden again Jake stood up and looked at the different pts. of the compass and walked to 1st. base and wasn't dead at all and everybody turned around and hissed me for not giving them a good story.

Well gents, I am not to blame because when a man has got a fast ball like Grover Lowdermilk and hits a man like Jake in the temple, I generally always figure they are dead and the fact that Jake got up and walked to 1st base is certainly not my fault and I hope nobody will hold it vs. me.

That was only one case where Mr. Gleason's strategy went amuck. His idear there was to kill the regular 1st. baseman and then all Mr. Moran would have left to do would be to either stick Dutch Reuther on 1st. base where he couldn't pitch or else stick Sherwood Magee over there where he couldn't coach at third base. But Jake gummed all up by not dying.

Well another part of Mr. Gleason's strategy was dressing the White Sox in their home uniforms so as they would think they was playing on the home grounds in front of a friendly crowd but the trouble with that was that the Reds was all dressed in their home uniforms so as you couldn't tell which club was at home and which wasn't and it made both of them nervous.

Then to cap off the climax Mr. Gleason goes and starts a pitcher that everybody thought he was going to start which took away the element of surprise and made a joker out of the ball game. If he had of only started Erskine Mayer or Bill James or any of the other boys that I recommended why the Reds breath would have been took away and even if they had of hit they couldn't of ran out their hits.

The trouble with the White Sox today was that they was in there trying to back up a nervous young pitcher that never faced a big crowd in a crux before and when he got scared and blowed why it was natural for the rest of them to also blow up. But just give these young Chicago boys a chance to get use to playing before a big crowd with money depending on it and you will be surprised at how they get on their ft. and come back at them.

Nobody should ought to find fault with Mr. Gleason, however, for what happened today. As soon as it was decided that they would have 9 games in this serious why the Kid set down and figured that the rules called for 9 men on a side and if 1 Red was killed per day and the serious run the full 9 games why they would only be 1 man left to play the final game and 1 man cant very well win a ball game even vs. the White Sox the way they looked. But Daubert didn't die as expected and they will know better next time then to hit a left handed 1st baseman in the egg.

As for the game itself they has probably never been a thriller game in a big serious. The big thrill come in the 4th innings when everybody was wondering if the Sox would ever get the 3rd man out. They finely did and several occupants of the press box was overcome. The White Sox only chance at that pt. was to keep the Reds in there hitting till darkness fell and make it a illegal game but Heinie Groh finely hit a ball that Felsch could not help from catching and gummed up another piece of stratagem.

Before the game a band led by John Philip Sousa played a catchy air called the Stars and Stripes Forever and it looks to me like everybody would be whistling it before the serious runs a dozen more games.

It now looks like the present serious would be 1 big surprise after another and tomorrow's shock will occur when the batterys is announced which will be Rube Bressler for the Reds and Lefty Sullivan for the Sox. This will be the biggest upset of the entire fiasco.

I seen both managers right after today's holy cost and Moran said hello old pal, and Gleason said hello you big bum so I am picking the Reds from now on.

*1919*

★   ★   ★

# The Perils of Being a Football Writer

WELL FRIENDS here it is the middle of the football season and maybe your favorite team looks like it will win the championship, and I don't want to be no kill joy but I can't resist from telling you what a treat you missed this fall namely I was going to write up some of the big games down east but at the last minute the boss said no. He didn't state no reasons but I wouldn't be surprised if I knew what they was and guess he is right for once. I don't know nothing about the game but that don't seem to stop a few of the other boys that is writeing it up and I doubt if my mgr. took that part of it into consideration but I guess he felt like my write ups would be kind of silly and I might get smart and introduce a spirit of levity into my write ups which would be out of keeping with a game which is almost sacred you might say and the coaches and aluminum of all the different colleges would be off of me for life. Then in the 2d place maybe he asked the different newspapers if they wanted the stuff and they all said no. If that is the case it may of had something to do with his decision as he is funny that way.

Well anyway I ain't going to write up on football games but wile we are on the subject I would like to say a few wds. in regards to this great autumn complaint and firstly I beg to assure my readers that when informed that my services as football reporter was neither required or desired I managed to not break down in public because I once had that job for several seasons and I wouldn't number it amongst the melons of journalism.

From the middle of Sept. till xmas a football reporter can't go in his office without they s a bunch of letters from students or old grads or the coaches themselfs and the letters always starts out by calling you some name and then the writer goes on to say why and the he—ll don't you give more space to the old Yellow and Pink. All we ask is a square deal, but we ain't getting it. By a square deal they mean 8 columns about the old Yellow and Pink and nothing about nobody else and the 8 columns has got to be 8 columns of glory hallelujah. Maybe it's necessary to mention that the Yellow and Pink was beat 98 to 0 last Saturday by the Old Mauve, but you are supposed to excuse this on the grounds that Buster Gifford the Yellow quarterback, was out of the game with a hangnail, but even at that the old Yellow would of rallied and tied the score in the 4th period only just as they were getting started, Jesse James, the head lineman, called an offside and the 5 yd penalty took the heart out of our boys. Coach Dunglebury says the penalty was a outrage as none of his men was ever offside in their life. He had learned them different.

Well friends when a man is a football reporter he gets acquainted with the different coaches and asst. coaches and theys a few of them that is as good fellows as you want to meet a specially some of the asst coaches and some of my best friends is asst coaches and a few head coaches too. And if any of the last named is reading this article I want them to understand that they are not the ones I am talking mean about. It's the ones that ain't reading this article that I refer to when

I say that they's no class of people that compares with head coaches when it comes to fair mindness unlest it's the boys that wrote the official communiques during the war.

Dureing my turn of service as a football expert they was numerous occasions when different head coaches spent the sabbath writeing a letter to my sporting editor asking him to give me the air as a special favor to them. And they were also 2 occasions when coaches wrote to him and said that my write up of their game the day before was the best football report they had ever read and lest my readers should think I am bragging I will hasten to exclaim that in each of these 2 cases the teams who these gents coached had win a close game and my articles was nothing but hymns of praise for how well the teams were coached.

One of a football reporter's little chores is generally to look up both coaches after the game and see what they have got to say for themself. The coach of the winning team pretty near kisses you but you don't no sooner than lay eyes on the other guy when you realize for the first time that the result of the game was your fault. I won't repeat none of the alibis that these birds have thought up as you would think I was copying out of Joe Miller's joke book but instead of that I will tell you about the time I got the surprise of my young life and that was up to Ann Arbor, Mich. Cornell and Michigan had just had a alleged contest and the score was something like 35 to 10 in favor of Cornell. So afterwards I went in the Michigan dressing room to see Mr Yost and there he was smileing from ear to ear and I says

"Well what about it?"

"Well," he says, "I guess we was lucky to score."

The trainer worked on me for a hr.

I don't know how they are running it out west now days but here in the east the coaches has a meeting in the off season and picks out the officials for their next season's games and here is another place where fair play and sport for sport's sakes comes leaping to the surface like a ton of lead. I don't need to go into no details but it would be kind of fun to see the same system tried out in big league baseball, namely let the managers pick out their own umpires. As soon as a ball club lost a game, why the manager would say, "He can't never umpire no more games for me" and when 8 games was lost the manager would be out of umpires and congress would half to pass conscription.

And it would also be fun if the football coaches was allowed to tell the newspapers who they could send to report their games. A lot of the boys that is now writeing up the games would have their Saturdays free for golf.

*1921*

## HEYWOOD BROUN

Heywood Broun (1888–1939) touched every base he could get to in his short life—sports reporter, war correspondent, political columnist, theater critic, book reviewer, magazine writer, novelist—and he managed to help found a union for newspaper wage slaves, too. He captured Babe Ruth's freewheeling majesty as a baseball writer for the *New York World*, and he used the Babe as inspiration for a character in his novel *The Sun Field*. Broun was equally memorable when writing about boxing and football, and he wasn't above making sport of the Ivy League. He had attended Harvard but hadn't hung around long enough to pick up a degree or learn how to make himself presentable. Black Jack Pershing, the legendary World War I general, surveyed the writer's slovenly attire at their first meeting and asked, "Have you fallen down, Mr. Broun?" Let's just say Broun wasn't a slave to fashion.

★ ★ ★

# This Side of Paradise?

PRINCETON, HITHERTO believed to be this side of paradise, sent a line smash through the pearly gates of this afternoon and defeated Yale by 20–0. The score would have been larger but for the brilliant work of Into. He was a tough proposition. It might even be said that he was a tough preposition. He was stalwart on defense, good on attack, but a bad man to end a sentence with.

This, however, is supposed to be a skipping story of the game and ought to start at the beginning. We trust that the reader will take it for granted that the Palmer Stadium was full, the hotels crowded, the town gay with bunting and pretty girls. This year they are wearing woolen stockings.

Just before the whistle blew, Captain Tim Callahan of Yale and Mike Callahan of Princeton walked out into the middle of the gridiron. The referee said: "I guess I don't have to introduce you boys," and he was quite right, because the Callahans are brothers.

Mrs. Callahan believes in scattering her sons. She follows the old adage of "Don't put all your eggs in one basket." There is still another Callahan who is preparing for Ursinus. Mrs. Callahan believes that by trying all the colleges at least one of her sons is going to get an education.

Tim asked, "What's the news from home?" And Mike said, "Well, I had a letter last week," but before he could read it the referee interrupted by tossing a coin, and, as Tim is the elder, Mike let him win and choose his own goal. It was the only thing Yale won during the afternoon.

The two captains then returned to the side lines and gathered their respective teams around them for a few last words. Tim said, "Fight hard boys!" and Mike said, "Smash 'em boys!" These are brave words, but it's in the breed.

Then the game began, and we noticed as it went along that, though the passes tossed by the Murphys, the Gilroys, and the Garritys did not always go to the designated receiver, there was generally some Irishman there to catch them.

Franklin Pierce Adams, who sat in the next seat, promised to give us first chance on anything he might say during the game, but after two periods the best he could do was to remark that there were three great plunging backs on the gridiron. "And the greatest of these is Garrity." Then he left to go to another place in the stand where he had some friend who hadn't heard it.

Princeton began as if to sweep Yale right off the field. Yale had punted and, following the kickoff, Lourie went around right end for thirty-five yards. Whenever a Yale man approached, Lourie stuck out his thumb, like little Jack Horner, and proceeded about his business. It was most enjoyable.

Damon Runyon immediately declared that he was going to send his son to Princeton and Frank O'Malley said he was also going there. That will be mighty convenient in the big game of 1936, because whenever Harvard needs five or six yards for a first down the quarterback will give the ball to H. Broun III and say, "Smash Runyon!" And if a scoring play is needed he can be sent around O'Malley.

However, although Princeton gained a lot of ground nothing came of it in the first period and Runyon began to weaken a little on his decision and said he heard Penn State well spoken of.

Just after the second period began Murray sent a beautiful drop kick over from the thirty-five-yard line at a hard angle. Your correspondent thinks it safe to assume that the readers of the *Tribune* will realize that much cheering from the Princeton stands followed and all that will be omitted.

With the half almost ended, Princeton had the ball on Yale's forty-yard line and big Keck dropped back for what seemed to be a try for a placement goal. Many in the stands and some on the field were suspicious, but Princeton carried out the deception admirably. The ball was passed to Lourie, who lay prone, and he made a motion as if to place it on the ground. Then he jumped up and began to run.

Keck was ahead of him, and it was hard to see Lourie from in front. He ran toward the Yale goal. One man in Blue was chasing him and seemed to stretch out his hand and say "Tag." He failed to think of this, and in the race for the goal Lourie was first, with the Yale man a good second.

Musing between the halves as Yale and Princeton sang about God and Country, and Yale and Old Nassau and Princeton's honor, and the rest of the sentiments which go to make up an afternoon, we began to reflect that numbering the players didn't help as much as we thought it would. After all it would be almost as satisfactory to know that a touchdown had been scored on a pass from one Princeton man to another as that it had come from 16 to 28 to somebody who looked a little like

39, but might be 7. Of course, it might help a little if they would use nonpareil instead of agate.

Princeton's touchdown in the third quarter was easy, for Murphy muffed a twisting punt from Scheerer and Mike Callahan carried the ball over the line. We noticed when Murphy went out of the game a little later that he buried his head in his hands and seemed terribly broken up about his error.

It is a great pity that all the circumstances of a big game compel young college players to take everything so seriously. Looking at the universe from a cosmic point of view, it doesn't make much difference that Murphy dropped the punt, but he could not see it that way.

Princeton scored again when Keck kicked a placement goal from Yale's thirty-six-yard line after a fair catch. Keck has great dramatic ability as well as skill in kicking goals. In the third period they carried him off the gridiron, and a few minutes later he turned up in the line-up and hit the crossbar from the fifty-yard line. But for his injury, he would undoubtedly have booted the ball over the wall of the stadium. At this point there was not a little sparring back and forth, and Yale sent in Eddie Eagan, the Olympic light heavyweight champion.

By and by the whistle blew, and again we think it is safe to assume that the reader knows that all the Princeton men from years and years back came to the field to snake-dance and throw their hats over the goal posts.

Mike went over to Tim and took out the letter to begin where he had been interrupted by the referee.

"Aunt Sally's a little better," he said.

"Damn Aunt Sally!" said Tim.

*1920*

★　★　★

# The Orthodox Champion

THE ENTIRE orthodox world owes a debt to Benny Leonard. In all the other arts, philosophies, religions and what nots conservatism seems to be crumbling before the attacks of the radicals. A stylist may generally be identified to-day by his bloody nose. Even in Leonard's profession of pugilism the correct method has often been discredited of late.

It may be remembered that George Bernard Shaw announced before "the battle of the century" that Carpentier ought to be a fifty to one favorite in the betting. It was the technique of the Frenchman which blinded Shaw to the truth. Every man in the world must be in some respect a standpatter. The scope of heresy in Shaw stops short of the prize ring. His radicalism is not sufficiently far reaching to crawl through the ropes. When Carpentier knocked out Beckett with one perfectly delivered punch he also jarred Shaw. He knocked him loose from some of his cynical contempt for the conventions. Mr. Shaw might continue to be in revolt against the well-made play, but he surrendered his heart wholly to the properly executed punch.

But Carpentier, the stylist, fell before Dempsey, the mauler, in spite of the support of the intellectuals. It seemed once again that all the rules were wrong. Benny Leonard remains the white hope of the orthodox. In lightweight circles, at any rate, old-fashioned proprieties are still effective. No performer in any art has ever been more correct than Leonard. He follows closely all the best traditions of the past. His left hand jab could stand without revision in any textbook. The manner in which he feints, ducks, sidesteps and hooks is unimpeachable. The crouch contributed by some of the modernists is not in the repertoire of Leonard. He stands up straight like a gentleman and a champion and is always ready to hit with either hand.

His fight with Rocky Kansas at Madison Square Garden was adver-
tised as being for the lightweight championship of the world. As a matter of fact much more than that was at stake. Spiritually, Saint-Saëns,
Brander Matthews, Henry Arthur Jones, Kenyon Cox, and Henry
Cabot Lodge were in Benny Leonard's corner. His defeat would, by
implication, have given support to dissonance, dadaism, creative evolution and bolshevism. Rocky Kansas does nothing according to rule.
His fighting style is as formless as the prose of Gertrude Stein. One
finds a delightfully impromptu quality in Rocky's boxing. Most of the
blows which he tries are experimental. There is no particular target.
Like the young poet who shot an arrow into the air, Rocky Kansas
tosses off a right hand swing every once and so often and hopes that it
will land on somebody's jaw.

But with the opening gong Rocky Kansas tore into Leonard. He was
gauche and inaccurate but terribly persistent. The champion jabbed
him repeatedly with a straight left which has always been considered
the proper thing to do under the circumstances. Somehow or other it
did not work. Leonard might as well have been trying to stand off a rhi-
noceros with a feather duster. Kansas kept crowding him. In the first
clinch Benny's hair was rumpled and a moment later his nose began
to bleed. The incident was a shock to us. It gave us pause and inspired
a sneaking suspicion that perhaps there was something the matter
with Tennyson after all. Here were two young men in the ring and
one was quite correct in everything which he did and the other was all
wrong. And the wrong one was winning. All the enthusiastic Rocky
Kansas partisans in the gallery began to split infinitives to show their
contempt for Benny Leonard and all other stylists. Macaulay turned
over twice in his grave when Kansas began to lead with his right hand.

But traditions are not to be despised. Form may be just as tough
in fiber as rebellion. Not all the steadfastness of the world belongs
to heretics. Even though his hair was mussed and his nose bleeding,
Lenny continued faithful to the established order. At last his chance
came. The young child of nature who was challenging for the championship dropped his guard and Leonard hooked a powerful and entirely

orthodox blow to the conventional point of the jaw. Down went Rocky Kansas. His past life flashed before him during the nine seconds in which he remained on the floor and he wished that he had been more faithful as a child in heeding the advice of his boxing teacher. After all, the old masters did know something. There is still a kick in style, and tradition carries a nasty wallop.

*1922*

## FRANK GRAHAM

In the early 1930s, when he was *The New York Sun*'s newly minted sports columnist, Frank Graham (1893–1965) started going into dugouts and dressing rooms for the sole purpose of listening to what was being said in them. He took no notes but remembered as much as he could so he could sit down at his typewriter and re-create it. The result thrilled readers hungry for insight into their heroes. Read from a twenty-first-century perspective, however, the conversations Graham recounted seem stiff and lifeless, like something from a boy's novel. Still, Red Smith wasn't wrong when he called Graham's bold step forward "the most important single change in my business in my lifetime." It was just that other writers would improve on what Graham was the first to do. Graham, meanwhile, left his mark with the kind of visceral, evocative columns collected here. His eyes, it seems, worked far better than his ears.

★ ★ ★

# A Show They Will Never Forget

THE RING may have seen a better fighter than Joe Louis, but it never saw a greater one during a span of two minutes than he was at the Yankee Stadium last night when he hammered Max Schmeling into a state of helplessness. The fight no sooner had begun than it was over. But in two minutes and four seconds Louis gave the crowd a show it never will forget. A show that left it breathless and startled and perhaps a little frightened.

Louis had jabbed Schmeling and rocked him with short lefts and rights, and Schmeling had hit him twice with a right hand, once in close and again at long range. But the German's defenses hadn't disturbed Louis and now they were sparring close to the ropes, and suddenly Louis nailed Schmeling with a left hook to the jaw.

Schmeling's knees buckled, and there was pain and panic in his eyes. Frantically he clutched the top rope to keep from falling, and now Louis was beating him frightfully about the head and body, and his punches froze Max to the ropes. Louis hit him a terrible punch in the stomach and he groaned "Oh! Oh!" Now, as he twisted about in an effort to escape, the rope was across his throat, and he hung there, and then Louis beat him off the rope to the canvas.

He was up at a count of three, and Louis was upon him again. Now he was paying the German off for his assurance, for his thinly veiled contempt for a man he once had outwitted and cruelly beaten. And there was no mercy in those smoldering eyes, deep set in a sullen face. He knocked Schmeling down again and when Max hit the floor a third time, Max Machon hurled a towel into the ring, for Schmeling was completely gone.

Arthur Donovan, the referee, picked the towel up and hurled it back across the ropes. And now Donovan stepped between the men and waved Louis to his corner and helped to pick Schmeling up as the German's white-faced seconds crowded up through the ropes.

It was over as quickly as that, and Louis was the undisputed heavyweight champion of the world. When he entered the ring last night he was champion of the world—save for Schmeling, the man who had knocked him out and whose shadow lay across his claim to greatness.

But now Schmeling had gone the way of all others who had opposed him, except Bob Pastor and Tommy Farr. The way of Carnera and poor, pitiful Levinsky and Max Baer and Sharkey and Jim Braddock and the rest. He had smashed Schmeling and, along with him, a lot of fine-spun theories about his fear of the German, his inability to keep away from Schmeling's right hand and the unlikelihood that even in an emergency he could change the style of fighting into which he had settled.

For last night he wasn't a shuffling counter fighter, but forced a relentless pace and blasted Schmeling's strategy to pieces with his fists. Whatever doubts he may have had in the long months since Schmeling stretched him, horribly beaten, in that same ring, had disappeared. There was no hesitancy about him, no caution, no fear of the German. He didn't waste a second, but walked into Schmeling and beat him down, and they raised his hand in victory, and he stood there concealing his elation with a mask of saffron flesh.

Short as the fight was, Louis's victory was so devoid of fluke or accident that no room was left for excuse of alibi on Schmeling's part. Nor did Max offer one. He simply said that an early blow over his left kidney had deadened his body and sapped the power from his legs and after that he had no chance, because he could not move about to escape the champion's raking fists.

Short as it was, the fight smoothed the years ahead for Louis and left him standing alone. If Baer, who was in a ringside seat last night, can be induced to climb in there with Louis again there will be a fight in September, and the mob will go for it, for the mob likes Baer—or hates him—and Louis would draw with anybody.

But now that Schmeling has been battered out of the heavyweight scene there is no one who can beat Louis, including Farr, who once held him off for fifteen rounds, and Pastor, who scurried before him for ten. Again the ring is dominated so completely by a man that he dwarfs his rivals.

This latest triumph of Louis's was by all odds his greatest. Jim Corbett once said that in the life of every champion there came a night when he had everything. Such a night was last night in the life of Joe Louis. He may never hold that peak again, but he held it last night for two minutes and four seconds, which was all that was necessary.

Out of the whirl and blur of Louis's punches come two mind pictures. One is of a sleek and smiling German bowing to the crowd when he was introduced. The other of a battered, brain-fogged tortured victim being helped through the ropes by his handlers a few minutes after. His dreams of returning to Berlin in triumph, champion of the world again, were shattered and fell about him.

*1938*

★   ★   ★

# Ex-Champion

I T CAME over the Associated Press teletype: "Cleveland—Jimmy Doyle, 148, Los Angeles, stopped Lew Jenkins, 141, Sweetwater, Tex. (4)."

It got into the paper. Down at the bottom of a column, set in agate type, which is the smallest type they have in the composing room. It was thrown in, as it should have been, with a lot of other fight results.

Yet behind that brief line was a story. A story of a strong, tough kid on his way up battering an old guy around the ring, and beating him so badly that the referee had to step in and stop it because it wasn't a contest any longer and the old guy might have been seriously hurt . . . an old guy who, not so very long ago, was the lightweight champion of the world.

Remembering Jenkins the way he was when he first hit the big time is easy because it was only six years ago, when he came out of the small clubs in the outlying sections of Brooklyn. He had won four or five fights in a row on the fringes of the town and now, for the first time, he was crawling through the ropes in Madison Square Garden.

Behind him . . . behind those few fights in Brooklyn . . . lay rough and crowded years. He had worked as a cotton picker and had served a hitch in the Regular Army. He had banged around the Southwest in an old rattletrap car and slept in tourist cabins and flop joints and fought in Dallas and Houston and Los Angeles and San Antonio and many of the small towns in between, picking up a few bucks and moving on . . .

and stopping somewhere to fight again. He had had a couple of dozen fights that are in the book and lots of others that aren't. He had moved up through the Middle West and fought in and out of Chicago. He had won fights and he had lost them, but for a long time nobody had paid any attention to him. Then he had put together a series of knockouts and now he was in the Garden.

He was in with a fellow named Billy Marquart, out of Winnipeg, who was being schooled by Jack Hurley, the manager who had hit the pot of gold with Billy Petrolle. Hurley thought Marquart was ready and threw him in with Jenkins, and for two rounds Marquart gave Jenkins a beating and in the third round he had Jenkins on the ropes and was setting him up for a knockout when Jenkins nailed him with a right hand on the chin and staggered him. Then Jenkins drove him across the ring and knocked him through the ropes and tried to follow him through, punching at him as he was tangled in the strands. The referee dragged Jenkins back, and somehow Marquart got to his feet and Jenkins leaped in at him again and this time he knocked him out.

Now everybody raved about Jenkins, calling him a vest-pocket Dempsey and a killer and the greatest puncher the lightweights had seen in a very long time. He could punch. There was no doubt about that. He was a scrawny guy with a long, thin neck and a chin to match and he couldn't box very well but he could knock down anybody he could hit and he was hot now and it looked as if he could hit anybody.

He took a trip back to Dallas and knocked out a third-rater named Chino Alvarez in one round and then he came back to New York and they matched him with Tippy Larkin, who was just coming to the front and had built up a great following in New Jersey, and in the first round he hit Larkin on the chin and stiffened him.

His real manager was Fred Browning, who owned some race horses and had a piece of a short-lived race track in Texas and also owned some night spots in Dallas and Fort Worth. Browning had had a paper on him for a long time, which is the way they describe a contract on Jacobs Beach, but had paid scant attention to him, if any, until he started knocking everybody out. Now Browning was back in the picture and he leased Jenkins to Hymie Caplin on a percentage basis and Caplin maneuvered a match for Jenkins with Lou Ambers, the lightweight champion.

It is easy, too, to remember Jenkins that night—the greatest night he ever had known or would know again, for after that night he pinwheeled toward obscurity, winning a few fights as he went along, but heading inevitably back toward the pugilistic heap from which, so lately, he had come up swinging.

You take the average fighter who gets a crack at a title and two hours or so before he is going into the ring you will find him lying down, or maybe sitting around in some quiet spot trying to keep his nerves under control until he gets into the ring when, as soon as the bell rings, he will have a firm grip on his nerves again because he will be in action. But two hours before he went into the ring with Ambers, Jenkins was touring the restaurants in the midtown area, going in with Hymie and shaking hands with the customers.

He had on an old, rumpled suit and a flannel shirt with no tie and his hair was sticking up. He went around, shaking hands, stopping now and then at a table to talk with those sitting there and sometimes there was a smile on his seamed and scarred and leathery face. You would have thought he was going to fight some stumble bum in an out-of-the-way club, for all the tension he showed, and when he smiled it was because someone had asked him how he thought he would do against Ambers.

Two hours later he knocked Ambers out in the third round, and now, with the cotton fields and the Army and the flop joints of the Southwest behind him he was the lightweight champion of the world.

He held the peak for a little while and then, as though destiny had marked the way so plainly for him, he slipped, skidded and whirled down. He reached a point where no matchmaker would use him . . . and then we were in the war and he joined the Coast Guard.

He showed up once in a while in his bell-bottomed trousers before the war took him to the far places. He was in better shape than he had been the last few times he had been seen in a ring and some of his friends thought that the regular life he was leading, eating well, hitting the sack early and getting plenty of hard work to tire him out through the day and using up the energy he once spent to buy his idea of fun would fit him for a return to the ring.

Maybe it did. He was in there with a good fighter in Cleveland the other night. Maybe he can go on fighting, picking up a few dollars here and there. What else can he do to make a living?

*1945*

## WESTBROOK PEGLER

Westbrook Pegler (1894–1969) was always the last writer out of the press box. He was a wordsmith, and the pains he took with his prose ate up the clock. It would be an understatement to say he wrote magnificently for the *Chicago Tribune* and the Scripps Howard syndicate, particularly about Hitler and the Nazi presence at the 1936 Winter Olympics, but his innate crankiness opened the door to political commentary. Though he won a Pulitzer Prize in 1941 for exposing the connection between organized crime and Hollywood labor unions, Pegler spent more time bashing Franklin and Eleanor Roosevelt, the New Deal, and the civil rights movement. He picked fights with his publisher, lost a pricey libel suit, and ultimately became so extreme that he got drummed out of the John Birch Society. Looking back at his career, the rueful Pegler admitted his problems began when he left sportswriting and, in his memorable phrase, "went cosmic."

★ ★ ★

# The Called Shot Heard Round the World

THERE, IN the third ball game of the World Series, at the Cubs' ball yard on the north side yesterday, the people who had the luck to be present saw the supreme performance of the greatest artist the profession of sport has ever produced. Babe Ruth hit two home runs.

Now, Lou Gehrig also hit two home runs, and Jimmy Foxx of the Athletics or any other master mechanic of the business might have hit three or four home runs and you would have gone away with the same impression that a factory tourist receives from an hour of watching a big machine lick labels and stick them on bottles of mouthwash or pop. The machine might awe you, but would you love it?

The people who saw Babe Ruth play that ball game and hit those two home runs against the Cubs came away from the baseball plant with a spiritual memento of the most gorgeous display of humor, athletic art and championship class any performer in any of the games has ever presented.

The Babe is 38 years old, and if you don't know that he is unable to hike as far for fly balls or stoop as nimbly as he used to for rollers coming to him through the grass, that must be just your own fault, because he would not deceive you. As an outfielder he is pretty close to his past tense, which may mean that one more year from now he will be only a pinch-hitter. He has been breaking this news all year to himself and the customers.

Why, when Bill Jurges, the human clay pigeon, hit a short fly to him there in left field and he mauled it about, trying for a shoestring catch, he came up off the turf admitting all as Jurges pulled up at second.

The old Babe stood up, straightened his cap and gesticulated vigorously toward Earl Combs in center. "Hey!" the old Babe waved, "my dogs ain't what they used to be. Don't hit them out to me. Hit to the young guy out there."

The customers behind him in the bleachers were booing him when the ball game began, but they would have voted him president when it was over, and he might not be a half-bad compromise, at that.

Somebody in the crowd tossed out a lemon which hit him on the leg. Now there are sensitive ball players who might have been petulant at that and some stiff-necked ones who could only ignore it, boiling inwardly. But the Babe topped the jest. With graphic gestures, old Mr. Ruth called on them for fair play. If they must hit him with missiles, would they please not hit him on the legs? The legs weren't too good anyway. Would they just as lief hit him on the head? The head was solid and could stand it.

I am telling you that before the ball game began the Babe knew he was going to hit one or more home runs. He had smacked half a dozen balls into the right-field bleachers during his hitting practice and he knew he had the feel of the trick for the day. When his hitting practice was over he waddled over toward the Cubs' dugout, his large abdomen jiggling in spite of his rubber corsets, and yelled at the Cubs sulking down there in the den, "Hey, muggs! You muggs are not going to see the Yankee Stadium any more this year. This World Series is going to be over Sunday afternoon. Four straight."

He turned, rippling with the fun of it and, addressing the Chicago customers behind third base, yelled, "Did you hear what I told them over there? I told them they ain't going back to New York. We lick 'em here, today and tomorrow."

The Babe had been humiliating the Cubs publicly throughout the series. They were a lot of Lord Jims to him. They had had a chance to be big fellows when they did the voting on the division of the World Series pool. But for a few dollars' gain they had completely ignored Rogers Hornsby, their manager for most of the year, who is through with baseball now apparently without much to show for his long career, and had held Mark Koenig, their part-time shortstop, to a half share. The Yankees, on the contrary, had been generous, even to ex-Yankees who were traded away months ago, to their deformed bat boy who was run over and hurt by a car early in the season, and to his substitute.

There never was such contempt shown by one antagonist for another as the Babe displayed for the Cubs, and ridicule was his medium.

In the first inning, with Earle Combs and Joe Sewell on base, he sailed his first home run into the bleachers. He hit Charlie Root's earnest pitching with the same easy, playful swing that he had been using a few minutes before against the soft, casual service of a guinea-pig pitcher. The ball would have fallen into the street beyond the bleachers under ordinary conditions, but dropped among the patrons in the temporary seats.

The old Babe came around third base and past the Cubs' dugout yelling comments which were unintelligible to the patrons but plainly discourteous and, pursing his lips, blew them a salute known as the Bronx cheer.

He missed a second home run in the third inning when the ball came down a few feet short of the wire screen, but the masterpiece was only deferred. He hit it in the fifth, a ball that sailed incredibly to the extreme depth of center field and dropped like a perfect mashie shot behind the barrier, long enough to clear it, but with no waste of distance.

Guy Bush, the Cubs' pitcher, was up on the top step of the dugout, jawing back at him as he took his turn at bat this time. Bush pushed back his big ears, funneled his hands to his mouth, and yelled raspingly at the great man to upset him. The Babe laughed derisively and gestured at him. "Wait, mugg, I'm going to hit one out of the yard." Root threw a strike past him and he held up a finger to Bush, whose ears flapped excitedly as he renewed his insults. Another strike passed him and Bush crawled almost out of the hole to extend his remarks.

The Babe held up two fingers this time. Root wasted two balls and the Babe put up two fingers on his other hand. Then, with a warning gesture of his hand to Bush, he sent him the signal for the customers to see.

"Now," it said, "this is the one. Look!" And that one went riding in the longest home run ever hit in the park.

He licked the Chicago ball club, but he left the people laughing when he said good-bye, and it was a privilege to be present because it is not likely that the scene will ever be repeated in all its elements. Many a hitter may make two home runs, or possibly three in World Series play in years to come, but not the way Babe Ruth made these two. Nor will you ever see an artist call his shot before hitting one of the longest drives ever made on the grounds, in a World Series game, laughing and mocking the enemy with two strikes gone.

*1932*

★  ★  ★

# The Olympic Army

G ARMISCH-PARTENKIRCHEN—Everything is said to happen for the best, and whatever anyone may think of the sporting propriety of our taking part in the political, military and sporting activities here in Garmisch, the experience should show a net profit to the United States.

Such shoving around as the populace received at the hands of the young strong-armed squad of Hitler bodyguards appropriately, though ingenuously, named the Black Guards, was never seen in the United States, even in the heyday of Jimmy Walker or Huey P. Long.

American athletes and the journalists of all nations sent to cover the program of sports known as the Winter Olympics, saw a perfect demonstration of military dictatorship, and there were those among the throng who agreed that if this is what Huey was promoting in Louisiana they will be glad to have none of the same.

The dictator held ten thousand people in the grandstand of the rink where the figure skating took place until he was ready to take his leave, and before the event they paved his way with such idolatrous care that it made no difference whether anyone else reached the scene or not.

Thousands of people were herded this way and that in the snow who had bought tickets or were trying to buy tickets to see the sport, and thousands were shunted off and away from the inclosure by long cordons of officious, beefy young Nazis in various uniforms, whose only duty was to flatter and accommodate the house painter who became the head man of the third Reich. It was a magnificent display of strong-arm authority wholly corroborating the old tradition that the German people's favorite sport is to be shoved around by men in uniform.

The road approaching the stadium was held clear by a double cordon of troops in brown uniforms who are supposed not to be soldiers but a civilian labor corps, although they dress like soldiers, with a swastika worn on the left arm, and perform military drill with shovels instead of guns.

At the head of the line near the stadium the Black Guards took their stand. They are a special corps, like the King's Life Guard in England, except that they are all young, athletic, tall and of overbearing demeanor. They wear fine black uniforms which flatter the youthful figure of a man, and wear on the left sleeve in silver embroidery the name "Adolf Hitler." They were wearing black tin hats, and the very atmosphere was vibrant with oppression and a sense of the importance of the Leader.

Your correspondent has seen in his time such men as Edison, Ford, Shaw, Einstein, Mussolini, Clemenceau and Eugene Debs, and therefore might have been a trifle slow to take spark. It seemed a secondary experience, not to say an anticlimax, to witness Adolf Hitler, but to the German government, which had invited the athletes of the world to Garmisch in the name of sport and human brotherhood, it was a tremendous affair.

The Olympics were of secondary importance, if any. This was the dictator's day, and it is a good thing for the Americans present that this was so, because they have nothing important to learn from the athletes, but much to learn about absolute authority in government.

You must picture this town. Ten thousand swastikas stir faintly in the light winter wind along the streets of Garmisch-Partenkirchen. The flag is the color of blood, with a white circle containing an ancient device in black. The swastika flies from every house and store, and some homes are adorned with long ribbons of little pennants strung together from window to window, fifty or a hundred swastikas in a row.

Soldiers are everywhere in Garmisch-Partenkirchen, where the athletes of many nations are competing on ice and snow in the brotherhood of sports. There are soldiers in the old German field gray, soldiers of the labor corps in brown, and special soldiers of the Black Guard in black and silver. All the soldiers wear the swastika, and it is seen again on the red post-office trucks and the army transports, which go tearing through the streets off into the mysterious mountains splashing melted slush onto the narrow footway.

This motor transport gives a strange suggestion of war in the little mountain resort where sportsmen are drawn together in a great demonstration of friendship. When the United States held the winter Olympics at Lake Placid, the only armed force in sight was a small detachment of New York State Police with service pistols and cartridge belts, and they were there only to regulate motor traffic.

I do not know why there are so many troops and so much army transport in Garmisch, and I hesitate to inquire unless that be construed as an effort to obtain military information. I was not interested in military affairs but only in sport, and the great international Olympic ideal of amity through chivalrous competition.

I know the ideal by heart, having heard it many times in speeches and read it in statements by Mr Avery Brundage, the president of the American Athletic Union, who brought the American team over to this armed camp, and by other idealists in the Olympic organization who joined Mr Brundage in the enjoyment of official courtesies and flattery delivered in the elegant style of the Old World.

We ought to treat Mr Brundage's vanity better at home. Perhaps an official dinner at the White House would equalize some of the honor which the Germans have shown him in their campaign to overpower disgust in America and procure the participation of American athletes.

The big army trucks which roar up the hills are painted in camouflage and loaded with soldiers. The little officers' cars built on the design of the old-fashioned low-neck hack are camouflaged too, and the scene is strongly reminiscent of the zone behind the front when divisions were being rushed to the sector of the next offensive.

Up to this time no artillery has been seen. I take it that the brotherhood games of the Winter Olympics run under the auspices of Nazi sportsmanship are only infantry action up to this writing. They may be saving their heavy stuff, their tanks and bombers for the summer program.

Well, I am glad I was here for this particular day, and I insist that as matters turned out it was a good thing to send an American team. If they didn't learn their lesson this time they are beyond teaching. At home we have never found it necessary to mobilize an army for a sport event, and even Huey himself, when he went on tour with his football team, carried only a few selected gunmen whose function was strictly retributive in the end.

*1936*

## JOE PALMER

Joe Palmer (1904–1952) was a comet who streaked across the sky for six short years at the *New York Herald Tribune* and then did his readers the great disservice of dying at forty-eight. He wrote about horse racing with such joy, wit, and integrity that his prose was devoured even by those who didn't know a fetlock from a furlong. To Palmer the great Man o' War "was as near to a living flame as horses ever get," but he brought the winner's circle into perspective by writing "All men are equal on the turf or under it." And to think this University of Kentucky graduate and University of Michigan Ph.D. candidate almost took a wrong turn into academe. Employment at a horse breeders' magazine rescued him, and Red Smith, recognizing a rare talent, steered him to the *Herald Tribune*. The best of Palmer's work was collected in a book called *This Was Racing*. It is, alas, out of print.

★　★　★

# Stymie—Common Folks

ON THE cold blustery afternoon of Jan. 28, 1921, several hundred persons huddled in the wind-swept stands of the old Kentucky Association track at Lexington to see one horse gallop past them. Down he came, a great red chestnut with a copper mane and a high head, flying the black and yellow silks of Samuel D. Riddle. This was Man o' War, leaving the race tracks forever.

Fourteen years passed before Lexington considered another horse worth a turnout. Then, on March 11, 1935, some 500 citizens assembled, on a foul, wet afternoon, to see Equipoise take his last public gallop. This was at the private track of the C. V. Whitney farm, because it was in that unbelievable two-year period when Lexington had no public race track.

The next performance, and as far as I know the last one, came on Aug. 8, 1943, when Calumet Farm Celebrated "Whirlaway Day." By this time the Chamber of Commerce had got into the act, and there was a remarkable spate of Congressmen, Southern oratory, news cameras and radio announcers. This is not a complete list.

It is unlikely (though you can never tell about a chamber of commerce) that there will be any such doings over Stymie, when he arrives to enter the stud at Dr. Charles Hagyard's Green Ridge Farm. It isn't that the other three were Kentuckians coming home, and that Stymie's an outlander from Texas. It was thoroughly appropriate that Stymie should have his final public appearance at Jamaica, because he's a Jamaica kind of horse. Though I have no doubt he will do well in the stud, his kinship is with the race track, not the breeding farm.

Man o' War, Equipoise and Whirlaway all were equine royalty from the day they were foaled. Stymie was common folks. It is true that he carries the blood of both Equipoise and Man o' War, but all pedigrees are purple if you go back a little. He was the son of a horse that had won two common races, out of a mare that couldn't win any. Nobody ever thought the first three were anything but good. Stymie began as a $1500 plater that couldn't get out of his own way.

Stymie wasn't, of course, as good as any of the three. But he was immeasurably tougher. Could he have got to the races one more time, he would have started as many times as all three of the others together. If you want to clutter your mind with a perfectly useless bit of information, Man o' War made his reputation by blazing nineteen miles and five furlongs; Equipoise, stopping now and then to grow a new hoof, ran just a trifle over fifty miles in competition. Whirlaway lasted a little longer, and lacked half a furlong of running sixty-six miles. But Stymie's journey to leadership among the world's money winners took him 142 miles, plus half a furlong and sixty yards. That's more than the other three together.

Man o' War and Equipoise and Whirlaway each won the first time out, at short odds, as they were expected to do. Stymie was 31 to 1 in a $2500 claiming race and he ran as he was expected to do, too, finishing seventh. He was out fourteen times before he could win, and that was a $3300 claimer.

You are not to imagine that Stymie was accidentally and mistakenly dropped into a claiming race before any one appreciated his quality. He ran twelve times in claiming races and got beat in eleven of them. He was, until the fall of his two-year-old season, right where he belonged. Then, from this beginning, he went on to win $918,485.

This is, you will see, basically the story of the ugly duckling, of Cinderella among the ashes, of Dick Whittington and his cat, and of all the world's stories none has ever been preferred to that which leads to the public and very glorious triumph of the oppressed and the downtrodden. Jamaica's horseplayers are to some extent oppressed and downtrodden, and perhaps in Stymie they find a vicarious success.

The horse envisioned by a breeder, in Kentucky or elsewhere, is the son of a Derby winner out of an Oaks mare, which can sweep the futurities at two and the classics at three, and then come back to the stud to send other great racers to the wars. These are, roughly, the specifications which fit such horses as Citation and Count Fleet and War Admiral, and the like.

But the race trackers, I think, save most of their affection for the Exterminators and the Stymies and the Seabiscuits, who do it the hard way in the handicaps, pounding out mile after bitter mile, giving weight and taking their tracks wet or dry, running for any jockey, and trying with what they've got, even when they haven't got enough. That's why Stymie fitted a farewell at Jamaica better than a welcome in Kentucky.

He's a curious horse, this obscurely bred Texas product. This tourist leaned on Jack Skinner's back fence at Middleburg one December for maybe a half hour, just studying Stymie, which did not return the compliment, but went on picking at the scanty winter grass. Except for the crooked blaze which gives him a devil-may-care expression, he's the most average horse you ever saw. Not tall, not short, not long, not close-coupled. Good bone, good muscle, good chest—nothing outstanding, nothing poor. As a result, of course, he is almost perfectly balanced, and maybe this is what makes him tick.

However, there is another matter. When Stymie comes to the peak of condition, he exudes vitality so you expect to hear it crackle. He comes to a hard, lean fitness that you seldom see in domestic animals, unless in a hunting dog that has been working steadily, or perhaps a hunter that has been having his ten miles a day over the fields. This is when, as Hirsch Jacobs says, he gets "rough." It isn't temper or meanness. He just gets so full of himself that he wants things to happen.

The faster he goes the higher he carries his head, which is all wrong according to the book, but is a characteristic of the tribe of Man o' War, to which he is inbred. This tourist, who doesn't scare easily in print, will long remember the way Stymie came around the turn in the Pimlico Cup Handicap with his copper mane flying in the wind, making pretty good horses look as if they had just remembered a pressing engagement with the quarter pole.

He is not a great horse, in the sense that Man o' War and Equipoise were great. He isn't versatile. There are dozens of horses around that can beat him at a mile, and even at a mile and a quarter he would have trouble with Armed or Lucky Draw, just as he had trouble with Devil Diver. He can't make his own pace and he can't win slow races. He needs something up ahead to draw the speed from the field, to soften it up for his long, sweeping rush at the end.

But give him a field with speed in it, at a mile and a half or more, and horses had better get out of his way, even Whirlaway.

Anyway, another fine and ardent and satisfactory story of the turf was brought to a close at Jamaica. And it was happy to note that, for all the long campaign, it was no battered and limping warrior which left us. Stymie never looked better with his bronze coat in great bloom, and the high head carried as proudly as ever.

As he stood for the last time before the stands, people around the winner's enclosure were shouting to his groom, "Bring him in here, for just one more time."

The groom didn't obey, and probably he was right. Stymie never got in a winner's circle without working for it. It was no time to begin.

*1949*

★   ★   ★

# Samuel Doyle Riddle

O N June 30, 1861, Matt Winn was born in Louisville, Ky. On the following day Samuel Doyle Riddle was born in Glen Riddle, Pa. Being an extremely stubborn man, Mr. Riddle outlived his contemporary by something more than a year. His death a few days ago removed one of the few remaining links which bound racing of today to the racing of the previous century, and in fact if there is any older man now living who played an important part in the long pageant of racing his name escapes me at the moment.

This tourist knew Mr. Riddle for some fifteen years, and had various arguments ranging from mild to bitter with him, as anyone who knew him that long was sure to have. But he has always been honored in this corner for one somewhat peculiar reason: he never forgot that Man o' War was a horse.

If this seems an obvious thing to remember, then you were not well acquainted with Man o' War. He was as near to a living flame as horses ever get, and horses get closer to this than anything else. It was not merely that he smashed his opposition, sometimes by a hundred lengths, or that he set world records, or that he cared not a tinker's curse for weight or distance or track or horses.

It was that even when he was standing motionless in his stall, with his ears pricked forward and his eyes focused on something slightly above the horizon which mere people never see, energy still poured from him. He could get in no position which suggested actual repose, and his very stillness was that of the coiled spring, of the crouched tiger.

All horses, and particularly all stallions, like to run, exultant in their strength and power. Most of them run within themselves, as children run at play. But Man o' War, loose in his paddock at Faraway, dug in as if the prince of all the fallen angels were at his throat-latch, and great chunks of sod sailed up behind the lash of his power. Watching, you felt that there had never been, nor could ever be again, a horse like this.

Well, this fiery thing of blood and bone (a bow to Mr. Masefield here) was Mr. Riddle's own. It could very easily have gone to his head. I tell you this as one who has seen people make fools of themselves over far lesser horses. Mr. Riddle was much prouder of Man o' War than you are of your children, and probably with more reason, and possession of him was a stately music. But he didn't spend his time feeding sugar to the horse, or drooling over him. He remembered that even if Man o' War was the most magnificent horse ever, he was still a horse, and that his interests lay in hard oats and clean hay and good grooming and a comfortable stall, and that is what he got.

Any number of people had bright ideas about Man o' War nearly always to their personal enrichment. The movies wanted him. There was a very remunerative scheme to tour him around the country for exhibition. At all such propositions Mr. Riddle snorted. The verb here has been very carefully chosen, and when Mr. Riddle snorted at a proposition, then that proposition lay dead and partly decomposed.

With the hundreds of thousands of people who wanted to see Man o' War he was always very fair. Faraway lay open, from nine in the morning until four in the afternoon, and anyone who wished could drive up and park and go into the stable and see Man o' War. It must have been expensive, because it involved keeping one groom always on duty to show the horse, and another to step on the cigarettes which visitors threw down in the stable, but there was never any variance to the pattern.

Mr. Riddle was not always a model of old southern Pennsylvania courtesy. The day that Whirlaway beat War Relic by the length of one flaring nostril in the Saranac Handicap was an instance. Mr. Riddle had looked at the motion pictures (Saratoga had a different camera then) and was convinced War Relic had won. He said so in clear ringing tones, and the entrance to the Saratoga clubhouse, which I should estimate at about ten feet wide, fit him just about the way the Panama Canal fits the U.S.S. Missouri. He had a cane in one hand and a racing paper in the other, and there were only a few inches of clearance on each side.

But he could be a very good companion and a gracious host, and a fine teller of tales, particularly of the days when racing had not bartered color and intrigue and verve for mere dull honesty. I suppose his death releases one of these which, since it happened when Mr. Riddle was a young man, must antedate 1900.

It was at a hunt race meeting, which included a jumping race with eight starters, all ridden by amateur riders. Naturally they fixed it, and because they did not trust one another inordinately, each rider was required to put up a $300 bond that he would let the elected horse win.

Some of this seeped out to the bookmakers in residence, so the prices went crazy and one rider, who was on a horse which should have been a legitimate second choice at perhaps 3 to 1, noted that he was being held instead at 10 to 1. So, through a confederate, he bet $400 on himself and stole off to a long lead.

Nobody bothered about him, because it was assumed that in due course his horse would "bolt" or that he would roll off at the next low fence. By the time anyone realized that the double steal sign was on, it was too late for anyone to go out and throw him down, though it was tried. So he forfeited his $300 bond and won $4000.

"There was a little hotel near the course where the riders and some of the trainers stayed," Mr. Riddle remembered. "I was over there after the race. The winner was barricaded in his room, and the others were outside the door, howling in the hall." He did not say whether, when he departed, six or seven riders were left howling in the hall, and it did not seem good manners to ask.

"I always remember that fellow," he chuckled. "He was one man whose word was as good—just exactly as good—as his bond."

*1951*

## SHIRLEY POVICH

One can't help wondering if there will ever be another sports columnist like Shirley Povich (1905–1998) both for what he wrote and for the grace and decency that defined him. In eight decades at *The Washington Post*, he never lost his sense of wonder or caved in to the cynicism the press box breeds. When he wrote about Lou Gehrig's tearful farewell to baseball, Povich relied on his vast store of compassion without lapsing into sloppy sentiment. Don Larsen's perfect game in the 1956 World Series sat at the other end of the emotional spectrum, inspiring Povich to craft a small masterpiece that hums with excitement and exquisite detail. He stayed with his daily column until 1974 and wrote occasional essays after that. He turned in his last one the day before he died. He was ninety-two.

★　★　★

# Iron Horse "Breaks" as Athletic Greats Meet in His Honor

NEW YORK, July 4—I saw strong men weep this afternoon, expressionless umpires swallow hard, and emotion pump the hearts and glaze the eyes of 61,000 baseball fans in Yankee Stadium. Yes, and hard-boiled news photographers clicked their shutters with fingers that trembled a bit.

It was Lou Gehrig Day at the stadium, and the first 100 years of baseball saw nothing quite like it. It was Lou Gehrig, tributes, honors, gifts heaped upon him, getting an overabundance of the thing he wanted least—sympathy. But it wasn't maudlin. His friends were just letting their hair down in their earnestness to pay him honor. And they stopped just short of a good, mass cry.

They had Lou out there at home plate between games of the double-header, with the 60,000 massed in the triple tiers that rimmed the field, microphones and cameras trained on him, and he couldn't take it that way. Tears streamed down his face, circuiting the most famous pair of dimples in baseball, and he looked chiefly at the ground.

Seventy-year-old Ed Barrow, president of the Yankees, who had said to newspapermen, "Boys, I have bad news for you," when Gehrig's ailment was diagnosed as infantile paralysis two weeks ago, stepped out of the background halfway through the presentation ceremonies, draped his arm across Gehrig's shoulder. But he was doing more than that. He was holding Gehrig up, for big Lou needed support.

As he leaned on Barrow, Gehrig said: "Thanks, Ed." He bit his lip hard, was grateful for the supporting arm, as the Yankees of 1927 stepped to the microphone after being introduced. Babe Ruth, Bob Meusel, Waite Hoyt, Herb Pennock, Benny Bengough, Bob Shawkey, Mark Koenig, Tony Lazzeri, all of the class of '27 were there. And Gehrig had been one of them, too. He had been the only one among them to bestride both eras.

Still leaning on Barrow, Gehrig acknowledged gifts from his Yankee mates, from the Yankee Stadium ground crew, and the hot dog butchers, from fans as far as Denver, and from his New York rivals, the Giants. There was a smile through his tears, but he wasn't up to words. He could only shake the hands of the small army of officials who made the presentations.

He stood there twisting his doffed baseball cap into a braid in his fingers as Manager Joe McCarthy followed Mayor La Guardia and Postmaster General Farley in tribute to "the finest example of ball player, sportsman and citizen that baseball has ever known," but Joe McCarthy couldn't take it that way, either. The man who has driven the highest-salaried prima donnas of baseball into action, who has baited a thousand umpires, broke down.

McCarthy openly sobbed as he stood in front of the microphone and said, "Lou, what else can I say except that it was a sad day in the life of everybody who knew you when you came to my hotel room that day in Detroit and told me you were quitting as a ball player because you felt yourself a hindrance to the team. My God, man, you were never that."

And as if to emphasize the esteem in which he held Gehrig though his usefulness to the Yankees as a player was ended, McCarthy, too, stepped out of the fringe full into the circle where Gehrig and Barrow stood and half embraced the big fellow.

Now it was Gehrig's turn to talk into the microphone, to acknowledge his gifts. The 60,000 at intervals had set up the shout, "We want Lou!" even as they used to shout, "We want Ruth"—yells that they reserved for the only two men at Yankee Stadium for which the crowd ever organized a cheering section.

But Master of Ceremonies Sid Mercer was anticipating Gehrig. He saw the big fellow choked up. Infinitesimally Gehrig shook his head, and Mercer announced: "I shall not ask Lou Gehrig to make a speech. I do not believe that I should."

They started to haul away the microphones. Gehrig half turned toward the dugout, with the ceremonies apparently at an end. And then he wheeled suddenly, strode back to the loud-speaking apparatus, held up his hand for attention, gulped, managed a smile and then spoke.

"For weeks," said Gehrig, "I have been reading in the newspapers that I am a fellow who got a tough break. I don't believe it. I have been a lucky guy. For 16 years, into every ball park in which I have ever walked, I received nothing but kindness and encouragement. Mine has been a full life."

He went on, fidgeting with his cap, pawing the ground with his spikes as he spoke, choking back emotions that threatened to silence

him, summoning courage from somewhere. He thanked everybody.
He didn't forget the ball park help; he told of his gratitude to newspapermen who had publicized him. He didn't forget the late Miller
Huggins, or his six years with him; or Manager Joe McCarthy, or the
late Col. Ruppert, or Babe Ruth, or "my roommate, Bill Dickey."

And he thanked the Giants—"The fellows from across the river,
who we would give our right arm to beat"—he was more at ease in
front of the mike now, and he had a word for Mrs. Gehrig and for the
immigrant father and mother who had made his education, his career,
possible. And he denied again that he had been the victim of a bad
break in life. He said, "I've lots to live for, honest."

And thousands cheered.

*1939*

★    ★    ★

# Larsen Pitches 1st Perfect Game in Series History

N EW YORK, Oct 8, 1956—The million-to-one shot came in. Hell
froze over. A month of Sundays hit the calendar. Don Larsen today
pitched a no-hit, no-run, no-man-reach-first game in a World Series.

On the mound at Yankee Stadium, the same guy who was knocked
out in two innings by the Dodgers on Friday came up today with one
for the record books, posting it there in solo grandeur as the only Perfect Game in World Series history.

With it, the Yankee righthander shattered the Dodgers, 2–0, and
beat Sal Maglie, while taking 64,519 suspense-limp fans into his act.

First there was mild speculation, then there was hope, then
breaths were held in slackened jaws in the late innings as the big mob

wondered if the big Yankee righthander could bring off for them the most fabulous of all World Series games.

He did it, and the Yanks took the Series lead three games to two, to leave the Dodgers as thunderstruck as Larsen himself appeared to be at the finish of his feat.

Larsen whizzed a third strike past pinch-hitter Dale Mitchell in the ninth. That was all. It was over. Automatically, the massive 226-pounder from San Diego started walking from the mound toward the dugout, as pitchers are supposed to do at the finish.

But this time there was a woodenness in his steps and his stride was that of a man in a daze. The spell was broken for Larsen when Yogi Berra stormed on to the infield to embrace him.

It was not Larsen jumping for joy. It was the more demonstrative Berra. His battery-mate leaped full tilt at the big guy. In self defense, Larsen caught Berra in mid-air as one would catch a frolicking child, and that's how they made their way toward the Yankee bench, Larsen carrying Berra.

There wasn't a Brooklyn partisan left among the 64,519, it seemed, at the finish. Loyalties to the Dodgers evaporated in sheer enthrall-ment at the show big Larsen was giving them, for this was a day when the fans could boast that they were there.

So at the finish, Larsen had brought it off, and erected for himself a special throne in baseball's Hall of Fame, with the first Perfect Game pitched in major league baseball since Charlie Robertson of the White Sox against Detroit 34 years ago.

But this was one more special. This one was in a World Series. Three times, pitchers had almost come through with no-hitters, and there were three one-hitters in the World Series books, but never a no-man-reach-base classic.

The tragic victim of it all, sitting on the Dodger bench, was sad Sal Maglie, himself a five-hit pitcher today in his bid for a second Series victory over the Yankees. He was out of the game, technically, but he was staying to see it out and it must have been in disbelief that he saw himself beaten by another guy's World Series no-hitter.

Mickey Mantle hit a home run today in the fourth inning and that was all the impetus the Yankees needed, but no game-winning home run ever wound up with such emphatic second-billing as Mantle's this afternoon.

It was an exciting wallop but in the fourth inning only, because after that Larsen was the story today, and the dumb-founded Dodgers could wonder how this same guy who couldn't last out two innings in the second game could master them so thoroughly today.

He did it with a tremendous assortment of pitches that seemed to have five forward speeds, including a slow one that ought to have been equipped with back-up lights.

Larsen had them in hand all day. He used only 97 pitches, not an abnormally low number because 11 pitches an inning is about normal for a good day's work. But he was the boss from the outset. Only against Pee Wee Reese in the first inning did he lapse to a three-ball count, and then he struck Reese out. No other Dodger was ever favored with more than two called balls by Umpire Babe Pinelli.

Behind him, his Yankee teammates made three spectacular fielding plays to put Larsen in the Hall of Fame. There was one in the second inning that calls for special description. In the fifth, Mickey Mantle ranged far back into left center to haul in Gil Hodges' long drive with a back-hand shoetop grab that was a beaut. In the eighth, the same Hodges made another bid to break it up, but Third Baseman Andy Carey speared his line drive.

Little did Larsen, the Yankees, the Dodgers or anybody among the 64,519 in the stands suspect that when Jackie Robinson was robbed of a line drive hit in the second inning, the stage was being set for a Perfect Game.

Robinson murdered the ball so hard that Third Baseman Andy Carey barely had time to fling his glove upward in a desperate attempt to get the ball. He could only deflect it. But, luckily, Shortstop Gil

McDougal was backing up and able to grab the ball on one bounce. By a half step, McDougal got Robinson at first base, and Larsen tonight can be grateful that it was not the younger, fleeter Robinson of a few years back but a heavy-legged, 40-year-old Jackie.

As the game wore on, Larsen lost the edge that gave him five strikeouts in the first four innings and added only two in the last five. He had opened up by slipping called third strikes past both Gilliam and Reese in the first inning.

Came the sixth, and he got Furillo and Campanella on pops, fanned Maglie. Gilliam, Reese and Snider were easy in the seventh. Robinson tapped out, Hodges lined out and Amoros flied out in the eighth. And now it was the ninth, and the big Scandinavian-American was going for the works with a calm that was exclusive with him.

Furillo gave him a bit of a battle, fouled off four pitches, then flied mildly to Bauer. He got two quick strikes on Campanella, got him on a slow roller to Martin.

Now it was the left-handed Dale Mitchell, pinch-hitting for Maglie. Ball one came in high. Larsen got a called strike.

On the next pitch, Mitchell swung for strike two.

Then the last pitch of the game: Mitchell started to swing, but didn't go through with it.

But it made no difference because Umpire Pinelli was calling it Strike Number Three, and baseball history was being made.

Maglie himself was a magnificent figure out there all day, pitching hitless ball and leaving the Yankees a perplexed gang, until suddenly with two out in the fourth, Mickey Mantle, with two strikes called against him, lashed the next pitch on a line into the right field seats to give the Yanks a 1–0 lead.

There was doubt about that Mantle homer because the ball was curving and would it stay fair? It did. In their own half of the inning, the Dodgers had no such luck. Duke Snider's drive into the same seats had curved foul by a few feet. The disgusted Snider eventually took a third strike.

The Dodgers were a luckless gang and Larsen a fortunate fellow in the fifth. Like Mantle, Sandy Amoros lined one into the seats in right, and that one was a near-thing for the Yankees. By what seemed only inches, it curved foul, the umpires ruled.

Going into the sixth, Maglie was pitching a one-hitter—Mantle's homer—and being out-pitched. The old guy lost some of his stuff in the sixth, though, and the Yankees came up with their other run.

Carey led off with a single to center, and Larsen sacrificed him to second on a daring third-strike bunt. Hank Bauer got the run in with a single to left. There might have been a close play at the plate had Amoros come up with the ball cleanly, but he didn't and Carey scored unmolested.

Now there were Yanks still on first and third with only one out, but they could get no more. Hodges made a scintillating pickup of Mantle's smash, stepped on first and threw to home for a double play on Bauer who was trying to score. Bauer was trapped in a run-down and caught despite a low throw by Campanella that caused Robinson to fall into the dirt.

But the Yankees weren't needing any more runs for Larsen today. They didn't even need their second one, because they were getting a pitching job for the books this memorable day in baseball.

*1956*

# RED SMITH

Walter Wellesley Smith (1905–1982) claimed he was named after three women's colleges. In print, however, he was Red, the nickname he went by even after his hair turned white. He arrived in New York at the relatively advanced age of forty and his column, a marvel of elegance, droll humor, and genuine affection for the characters he encountered, quickly became the anchor of the *Herald Tribune*'s gold-standard sports department and a nationally syndicated hit. Hard times struck in the 1960s when his friend and editor, Stanley Woodward, died and the *Herald Trib* went out of business. Smith found a safe haven at *The New York Times* in 1971. Five years later, he won a long-overdue Pulitzer Prize. In a just world, he would have been the first sportswriter to receive one. When he was the second, he set aside his usual courtly charm and tore the wood from his plaque so he could use it for kindling.

★   ★   ★

# A Horse You Had to Like

I F THIS bureau had a prayer for use around horse parks, it would go something like this: Lead us not among bleeding-hearts to whom horses are cute or sweet or adorable, and deliver us from horse-lovers. Amen.

In this case, issue is not taken on the rhetorical grounds adopted by James Thurber when he observed that to him the expression, "dog lover," meant one dog that was in love with another dog. Rather, the idea here is merely to get on record with an opinion that horses are animals which a guy can like and admire and have fun betting on or just watching. This is no knock at love, which is for blondes.

With that established, let's talk about the death of Seabiscuit the other night. It isn't mawkish to say, there was a racehorse, a horse that gave race fans as much pleasure as any that ever lived, and one that will be remembered as long and as warmly. If someone asked you to list horses that had, apart from speed or endurance, some quality that fired the imagination and captured the regard of more people than ever saw them run, you'd have to mention Man o' War and Equipoise and Exterminator and Whirlaway and Seabiscuit. And the honest son of Hard Tack wouldn't be last.

It wasn't primarily his rags-to-riches history that won Seabiscuit his following, although reaching success from humble beginnings never dims a public figure's popularity. It wasn't the fact that he won more money than any other horse up to his time, although that hurt neither his reputation nor his owner. He wasn't a particularly handsome horse, nor especially big or graceful, and he never was altogether sound. Up to now, his get have not made him famous as a sire. The quality he had was expressed one day by a man in the press box who said, "Look at his record. He's the Canzoneri of horses."

Look at his record and you see what the man meant. Just as Tony Canzoneri barnstormed through the fight clubs of the land taking on everyone they tossed at his head, so Seabiscuit made the rounds of most of the mile tracks between the oceans, and left track records at more than a few. Hialeah Park (his record reads), Bowie, Havre de Grace, Jamaica, Rockingham, Narragansett, Suffolk, Saratoga, Aqueduct, Agawam, Empire City, Pimlico, Belmont, Detroit, River Downs, Bay Meadows, Santa Anita, Tanforan, Laurel, Agua Caliente, Arlington, Del Mar, Hollywood.

He didn't always win, of course. Indeed, he was whipped seventeen times hand-running in allowance purses and maiden races and claimers before he won one, and that one was worth $750. Those were the days when he went unclaimed for $2,500.

It has often been written how his first owner, Ogden Phipps, tossed him away for $8,500 in a private sale to Charles S. Howard. Actually, Phipps did all right with him. Seabiscuit ran forty-seven times and won nine races for his breeder; his winnings and sale price brought Phipps $26,965. No one could have guessed he would earn $419,265 racing for Howard.

In these days when a Shetland pony won't break out of a walk for less than $50,000, earnings are an unsatisfactory measure of a horse's class. Seabiscuit's record of $437,730 has been surpassed by several horses. But he had to work for most of his. He often came out of a race with $25 or $50 in third or fourth money, and he had to make three runs at the Santa Anita Handicap, losing twice by a nose, before he grabbed his biggest prize of $86,650.

With the news story of his death was a photograph of Seabiscuit with Red Pollard, his regular jockey. It brought to mind several names that were associated with the horse. There was his owner, who was known as "Lucky Charley" Howard when his stable, led by Seabiscuit, was polishing off stakes like mad, making him first among money-winning owners. They haven't started running benefits for Howard yet—he was nineteenth among owners, with purses of $182,885 last year—but you don't see those red and white silks out front as often as you did, and they don't call him "Lucky Charley" any more.

There was Pollard, who certainly wasn't ever called lucky. The little redhead rode to fame on Seabiscuit, but he missed the ones he wanted most. He'd been second, beaten a nose by Rosemont, in the Santa Anita Handicap of 1937 and he was getting ready for a second shot the following year when he got busted up in a spill. Had to sit back and look on while his horse lost the same race by the same margin, this time to Stagehand.

He was just about recovered from that injury when he came East to ride Seabiscuit in New England. A gypsy horseman, a friend, asked him to work a two-year-old for him. The colt bolted and smashed Pollard's left leg. He was still laid up when Seabiscuit ran the most memorable race of all, the match with War Admiral.

Seabiscuit broke down in his next start and Pollard went to the farm with him, put in a year helping to bring him around. They came back together in 1940, and together they finally won the $100,000 handicap. One hasn't heard much of Red since, although he was still riding a fair share of winners last year.

There's Tom Smith, who trained Seabiscuit. He's changed jobs, and things haven't been entirely smooth for him. Just got back this year after his suspension in that ephedrine case.

And then there was Georgie Woolf, who rode Seabiscuit in the match with War Admiral, the best horserace these eyes have seen. That was the race where Sam Riddle, War Admiral's owner, dictated virtually all the conditions, including a walk-up start because his horse didn't like gates.

Ed Christmas was talking about Woolf recently, recalling how he used an old trick of quarter-horse racing to steal the start from Charley Kurtsinger, who didn't have his experience of racing on the Western plains. As they walked up to the line, Georgie kept Seabiscuit's head turned in toward War Admiral, determined that if he didn't get away alone he'd leave no room for War Admiral to dart past him. If ever a rider swiped a race, Woolf swiped that one at the start, leaping away ahead of a horse that was habitually first out of the gate.

Georgie Woolf? He's dead, too.

1947

★ ★ ★

# Next to Godliness

THE GAME has been over for half an hour now, and still a knot of worshippers stands clustered, as around a shrine, out in right field adoring the spot on the wall which Cookie Lavagetto's line drive smote. It was enough to get a new contract for Happy Chandler. Things were never like this when Judge Landis was in.

Happy has just left his box. For twenty minutes crowds clamored around him, pushing, elbowing, shouting hoarsely for the autograph they snooted after the first three World Series games. Unable to get to Lavagetto, they were unwilling to depart altogether empty-handed. Being second choice to Cookie, Happy now occupies the loftiest position he has yet enjoyed in baseball. In Brooklyn, next to Lavagetto is next to godliness.

At the risk of shattering this gazette's reputation for probity, readers are asked to believe these things happened in Ebbets Field:

After 136 pitches, Floyd Bevens, of the Yankees, had the only no-hit ball game ever played in a World Series. But he threw 187 and lost, 3 to 2.

With two out in the ninth inning, a preposterously untidy box score showed one run for the Dodgers, no hits, ten bases on balls, seven men left on base, and two more aboard waiting to be left. There still are two out in the ninth.

Hugh Casey, who lost two World Series games on successive days in 1941, now is the only pitcher in the world who has won two on successive days. One pitch beat him in 1941, a third strike on Tommy Henrich, which Mickey Owen didn't catch. This time he threw only one pitch, a strike to Tommy Henrich, and this time he caught the ball himself for a double play.

Harry Taylor, who has had a sore arm half the summer, threw eleven pitches in the first inning, allowed two hits and a run, and fled with the bases filled and none out. Hal Gregg, who has had nothing at all this summer—not even so much as a sore arm—came in to throw five pitches and retired the side. Thereafter Gregg was a four-hit pitcher until nudged aside for a pinch hitter in the seventh.

In the first inning George Stirnweiss rushed behind second base and stole a hit from Pee Wee Reese. In the third Johnny Lindell caught Jackie Robinson's foul fly like Doc Blanchard hitting the Notre Dame line and came to his feet unbruised. In the fourth Joe DiMaggio caught Gene Hermanski's monstrous drive like a well-fed banquet guest picking his teeth and broke down as he did so. Seems he merely twisted an ankle, though, and wasn't damaged.

Immediately after that play—and this must be the least credible of
the day's wonders—the Dodger Simp-Phony band serenaded Happy
Chandler. The man who threw out the first manager for Brooklyn this
year did not applaud.

In the seventh inning two Simp-Phony bandsmen dressed in mot-
ley did a tap dance on the roof of the Yankees' dugout. This amused the
commissioner, who has never openly opposed clowning.

In the eighth Hermanski smashed a drive to the scoreboard. Henrich backed against the board and leaped either four or fourteen feet
into the air. He stayed aloft so long he looked like an empty uniform
hanging in its locker. When he came down he had the ball.

In the ninth Lindell pressed his stern against the left-field fence
and caught a smash by Bruce Edwards. Jake Pitler, coaching for the
Dodgers at first base, flung his hands aloft and his cap to the ground.

And finally Bucky Harris, who has managed major-league teams in
Washington, Detroit, Boston, Philadelphia, and New York, violated all
ten commandments of the dugout by ordering Bevens to walk Peter
Reiser and put the winning run on base.

Lavagetto, who is slightly less experienced than Harris, then dem-
onstrated why this maneuver is forbidden in the managers' guild.

Cookie hit the fence. A character named Al Gionfriddo ran home.
Running, he turned and beckoned frantically to a character named
Eddie Miksis. Eddie Miksis ran home.

Dodgers pummeled Lavagetto. Gionfriddo and Miksis pummeled
each other. Cops pummeled Lavagetto. Ushers pummeled Lavagetto.
Ushers pummeled one another. Three soda butchers in white ran onto
the field and threw forward passes with their white caps. In the tangle
Bevens could not be seen.

The unhappiest man in Brooklyn is sitting up here now in the far
end of the press box. The "v" on his typewriter is broken. He can't write
either Lavagetto or Bevens.

1947

★   ★   ★

# Miracle of Coogan's Bluff

N OW IT is done. Now the story ends. And there is no way to tell it. The art of fiction is dead. Reality has strangled invention. Only the utterly impossible, the inexpressibly fantastic, can ever be plausible again.

Down on the green and white and earth-brown geometry of the playing field, a drunk tries to break through the ranks of ushers marshaled along the foul lines to keep profane feet off the diamond. The ushers thrust him back and he lunges at them, struggling in the clutch of two or three men. He breaks free, and four or five tackle him. He shakes them off, bursts through the line, runs head-on into a special park cop, who brings him down with a flying tackle.

Here comes a whole platoon of ushers. They lift the man and haul him, twisting and kicking, back across the first-base line. Again he shakes loose and crashes the line. He is through. He is away, weaving out toward center field, where cheering thousands are jammed beneath the windows of the Giants' clubhouse.

At heart, our man is a Giant, too. He never gave up.

From center field comes burst upon burst of cheering. Pennants are waving, uplifted fists are brandished, hats are flying. Again and again the dark clubhouse windows blaze with the light of photographers' flash bulbs. Here comes that same drunk out of the mob, back across the green turf to the infield. Coattails flying, he runs the bases, slides into third. Nobody bothers him now.

And the story remains to be told, the story of how the Giants won the 1951 pennant in the National League. The tale of their barreling run through August and September and into October. . . . Of the final day of the season, when they won the championship and started home with it from Boston, to hear on the train how the dead, defeated

Dodgers had risen from the ashes in the Philadelphia twilight. . . . Of the three-game play-off in which they won, and lost, and were losing again with one out in the ninth inning yesterday when— Oh, why bother?

Maybe this is the way to tell it: Bobby Thomson, a young Scot from Staten Island, delivered a timely hit yesterday in the ninth inning of an enjoyable game of baseball before 34,320 witnesses in the Polo Grounds. . . . Or perhaps this is better:

"Well!" said Whitey Lockman, standing on second base in the second inning of yesterday's play-off game between the Giants and Dodgers.

"Ah, there," said Bobby Thomson, pulling into the same station after hitting a ball to left field. "How've you been?"

"Fancy," Lockman said, "meeting you here!"

"Ooops!" Thomson said. "Sorry."

And the Giants' first chance for a big inning against Don Newcombe disappeared as they tagged Thomson out. Up in the press section, the voice of Willie Goodrich came over the amplifiers announcing a macabre statistic: "Thomson has now hit safely in fifteen consecutive games." Just then the floodlights were turned on, enabling the Giants to see and count their runners on each base.

It wasn't funny, though, because it seemed for so long that the Giants weren't going to get another chance like the one Thomson squandered by trying to take second base with a playmate already there. They couldn't hit Newcombe, and the Dodgers couldn't do anything wrong. Sal Maglie's most splendrous pitching would avail nothing unless New York could match the run Brooklyn had scored in the first inning.

The story was winding up, and it wasn't the happy ending that such a tale demands. Poetic justice was a phrase without meaning.

Now it was the seventh inning and Thomson was up, with runners on first and third base, none out. Pitching a shutout in Philadelphia last Saturday night, pitching again in Philadelphia on Sunday, holding the Giants scoreless this far, Newcombe had now gone twenty-one innings without allowing a run.

He threw four strikes to Thomson. Two were fouled off out of play. Then he threw a fifth. Thomson's fly scored Monte Irvin. The score was tied. It was a new ball game.

Wait a moment, though. Here's Pee Wee Reese hitting safely in the eighth. Here's Duke Snider singling Reese to third. Here's Maglie wild-pitching a run home. Here's Andy Pafko slashing a hit through Thomson for another score. Here's Billy Cox batting still another home. Where does his hit go? Where else? Through Thomson at third.

So it was the Dodgers' ball game, 4 to 1, and the Dodgers' pennant. So all right. Better get started and beat the crowd home. That stuff in the ninth inning? That didn't mean anything.

A single by Al Dark. A single by Don Mueller. Irvin's pop-up, Lockman's one-run double. Now the corniest possible sort of Hollywood schmaltz—stretcher-bearers plodding away with an injured Mueller between them, symbolic of the Giants themselves.

There went Newcombe and here came Ralph Branca. Who's at bat? Thomson again? He beat Branca with a home run the other day. Would Charley Dressen order him walked, putting the winning run on base, to pitch to the dead-end kids at the bottom of the batting order? No, Branca's first pitch was a called strike.

The second pitch—well, when Thomson reached first base he turned and looked toward the left-field stands. Then he started jumping straight up in the air, again and again. Then he trotted around the bases, taking his time.

Ralph Branca turned and started for the clubhouse. The number on his uniform looked huge. Thirteen.

*1951*

## JIMMY CANNON

They loved him or hated him. There was never any middle ground when it came to Jimmy Cannon (1909–1973) among the straphangers, dock-workers, bet-the-rent gamblers, and future sportswriters who read him three hundred times a year. A child of Greenwich Village, he grew up to become Damon Runyon's protégé, Joe DiMaggio's confidante, and the best reason to buy the *New York Post* from 1946 until he jumped to the *Journal-American* in '59 and became the country's best-paid sports columnist. The big money—some said a thousand dollars a week, others twice that—didn't change him, though. He was still Jimmy Cannon with his bluesy cadences, stubborn humanity, and "Nobody asked me, but" exercises in saloon wit. After a stroke left him lying on his apartment floor for days before he was found, he said what only he could: "I kept thinking I was Billy Conn trying to get up against Joe Louis in 1941."

★  ★  ★

# DiMaggio

THE MORNING sun was hot as we came out of the inlet and a big yellow turtle went by as the cruiser started up the Florida coast. The sails were running off Hobe Sound and on the way up from Palm Beach the mate baited the stern lines and the outriggers with mullet. We picked up the other boats and most of them were having a good day. The majority were flying white pennants and you run one up every time you get a sail. Some had red flags in the rigging which meant they had landed a sail but had thrown it back into the sea. It had been dark and rainy in Florida and this was the first day the boats had been out in a long time. The beaches were deserted and the nightclubs were getting a big play. The people who came to get the sun stayed up very late in the joints, where they burned big logs in the fireplaces. We wore our overcoats at night and the radio described the snowstorms in New York and then we'd say it was all right being in Florida even if we had to sleep in our bathrobes.

But now the bait was skipping on the surface and DiMag was sitting with the pole leaning against his right leg. DiMag knows a lot about it and he enjoys it very much. He was very excited but he fishes the way he does everything else. It was impossible to look at him and know how big a kick he was getting out of it. The mate was only 17 and he was stripped to the waist and very brown and very impressed that he was fishing Joe.

He showed us a skin-scraped bruise on his right forearm.

"Sail did it last week," he explained, proudly.

"How?" DiMag asked.

"He hit me with his bill," the kid explained.

The kid pointed to the zigzagging thread of a scar across his brown belly.

"Last season one of them ripped me open with his bill," the boy said with great dignity.

The sky darkened temporarily and it was rough for a while. One of the party went down into the small cabin and was sick. Some of the Yanks used to kid Joe and say he got sick on a ferry boat. They told it because his father was a fisherman and Joe was raised on the waterfront of San Francisco. But he sat there all day, eating black olives out of a jar, a big angular quiet man in a T-shirt, watching the mullet dragging on his line. The pole jerked and DiMaggio rose and the mate shouted: "Sail . . . sail . . . sail!"

The sail gets its fish by hitting it with its bill and stunning it. Then it comes back and swallows it. The sail hit the bait and came again and DiMaggio pulled the hook into him. I do not find any pleasure in fishing. But I understand the excitement of it when a fish has the strength and the gameness of a sail. This sail was going and the line spun on the reel and made a little song.

"Don't lose him, Joe," the mate yelled.

"Don't worry," Joe said.

The sail was traveling and Joe said: "Watch out. It's going to break water." The sail fish came up out of the sun-burnished sea in a flapping leap. It went up straight gleaming and quivering and then it was gone. It had a lot of fight. I wanted Joe to get a fish but when I thought of the hook in its mouth and how game it was I wanted it to shake free.

After thirty minutes Joe brought the fish in close. The kid put on gloves and leaned over the side, a sawed-off baseball bat in his right hand. He grabbed the bill and pulled it up over the rail. The kid was excited and missed with the bat but finally hit it. It was a big one, 7 foot 10 inches.

On the way in the terns and gulls came over and dropped down as the mate took in the lines. They hovered over the bait, going after it in drifting passes. The people on the boat clapped their hands and the birds flew off. But one of them arose with the bait in his mouth. It went up straight, the line loose and curved beneath it.

"I got him hooked," Joe said.

The gull glided in desperate circles over the boat, the mullet in its beak. The other birds fought it for the fish and it slid away from them and fought the hook at the same time. It was like flying a kite in a great wind. DiMag gave him plenty of room to fly and gently tried to shake the hook loose. It came down to the surface. The line tightened. The gull was dragged through the wake. Joe tried to pull it out of the sea but it was tired and flopped down again.

"I hope I don't drown him," Joe said. "It will take all the fun out of the whole day."

The bird rose again, slowly and with great effort. It wavered over the boat, the others flying around it, trying to get the fish in its mouth. But unexpectedly the fish fell out and the line with it. The mullet dropped into the sea and a pelican got it.

The gull fell but started up again. It was deformed by fatigue and the fight was one-sided and slow. It seemed as though a mysterious pressure was forcing it down into the sea. It was very weak and flew that way, rising and falling. We watched it go that way, trying to reach the land, until it flew out of sight.

*1948*

★　★　★

# You're Billy Graham

YOU'RE BILLY GRAHAM who was a champion but it isn't in the book. Inside, where a man keeps the trophies of his life, you know you were a champion. But you never held a title and you never took down the champion's end of a touch.

You're through with the fight racket. The guys who run it should grieve. You were an ornament of the filthiest game men work at in this country. The ugly business has to have more like you if it intends to survive. You fought 126 fights for money and not one of them was disfigured by larceny. No champion ever had more pride or dignity. But you depart, not as a champion, but as a respected main event pug.

You weren't a great fighter. But you walked down a street or entered a gymnasium as though you were a champion. Champions don't always hold titles. But you can't hock an attitude. Honor doesn't draw interest in any bank.

It might console you because you know this. It isn't enough though. Guys fight for money. You're no exception. You're not wealthy but you are not busted, either. But you should have made more. The championship meant a lot to you. It guaranteed you a life without economic fear. Now, after picking up, you haven't much time for leisure. You haven't a fortune to invest. You put more into the fight racket than you took out.

You beat Kid Gavilan in February of '50. You lost to him in December of that year. But the big one happened in August of '51. You won that one. You took it but they gave the decision to Gavilan. You needed that one. That was the one that would have put you in the boxing guides as the welterweight champion.

You never could punch. But no one ever knocked you down. Not a second was ever counted over you. You were a formal boxer who knew all the subtle moves. You schemed to set them up, hit and move. You weren't flashy or exceptionally fast. You had a conservative style. It was formed by your knowledge of your business.

You had another shot at Gavilan in Cuba in '52. You weren't feeling well. He beat you that night. But you carry a memory from that fight. You always had to step and block and punch sneakily to get a decision. You didn't take guys out with a rap. You made your fight, a sedate and careful boxer, the only way your talent allowed.

In Havana you hit Gavilan with a right hand. You felt him going. You saw him sag. This was a tough guy who took a punch as well as you did. But the last time with Gavilan you stunned him. This pleased you.

You, who were bitterly humorous about your inability to hurt people, nailed Gavilan that night. It didn't work. You weren't a puncher and he slipped away. It astonished you and flattered you. Maybe, you thought, if you had to do it again, you might study balance. Perhaps, you could punch. But it was too late then. Your style was shaped. You were a steady boxer. You didn't thrill them. But anyone who understood the fight racket admired you.

You beat Ray Robinson in the amateurs. You took a lot of good fighters but never again beat a truly great one. It was your honesty that impressed people most. You were game by the standards of your fierce trade. You fought as well as you could every night you were paid to perform. But you never held a title. And you would like to be in the book.

You lived the way you fought. Of course, you took the old lady to dinner at Shor's once in a while. You dropped by the Copa when an act appealed to you. But you didn't use yourself up on the night shift. You were a neighborhood guy. Your old man owned a saloon on the East Side. Hardly a night passed by without a guy singing "When Irish Eyes Are Smiling." It was that kind of a joint.

You liked a glass of beer and side street barrooms where men remembered the old country in songs when they were drinking. You trained well. You had to. You didn't have the big gifts. Condition was one of your assets. After losing to Chico Vejar, you decided the fight racket belonged to the kids. You were right.

The likes of Vejar shouldn't beat you. You could always handle club fighters. Kids who piled in on you didn't bother you. But your legs were good then. The jab was accurate. The wind lasted then. Guys such as Vejar used to be marks. But you were seized by the sluggishness of middle age that attacks athletes in their youth.

You were turned out of your style in your last fight. Tavern oracles, taking it on the television, were excited by the way you lost to Vejar. They enjoyed your desperation. You were behind. So you tried to bust him out with a right hand. It is the way a good fighter goes. But here was proof you couldn't go 10 rounds with an awkward kid if he pressed you. Panic turned you into a slugger.

When fatigue caused you to stand and punch with Vejar, then you conceded you no longer were a pug. The fight racket shills do a lot of bragging at stags and beefsteaks and boys' club fetes. They generally list the men who were better than their rotten sport. They should include you every time they mention guys the fight racket couldn't ruin. You're Billy Graham who was a champion but it isn't in the book.

*1955*

★   ★   ★

# Doc Kearns

T TOOK him eighty years, but Doc Kearns, who died yesterday, finally proved he was right. Daytime's for sleeping. Nights are for laughs. The working day is nine to five. Doc never played a hand in that game.

Funerals aren't held at night. You get married in the daytime, and indicted. That's when you visit doctors' offices. Bill collectors seldom bother you after dark. Night was Doc's country.

I imagined it would have amused Doc to go out in his sleep at night in the solitude of his old man's bed. He'd probably say that's what killed him. Doc never trusted guys who set their alarm clocks to go off before noon.

This was the greatest of all hustlers. He schemed for the edge in every proposition. Chances are he had figured some angle to duck death. Whatever it was, Doc had it swinging for him for a long while. The doctors forced him to turn in early. He spent all he had and most of his life buying a piece of the night in every town he was ever in. Doc made very few sensible investments.

Lately, he was on coffee, and a stranger in the nights of his final years. Instead of cafes, Doc played the rib joints and the delicatessens. Curfew-honoring cabarets with minimum charges where the masters of ceremonies announce the wedding anniversaries of suburban couples didn't appeal to him. Why if you get bagged and slug a guy, they call a cop. He went for more in a night in Texas Guinan's than the modern nightclubs grab in a week.

Doc didn't realize he was a relic commemorating the myth of the Twenties. He was left over from another era, a man misplaced by time. He claimed he made $19,000,000 managing Jack Dempsey, but he was a guy who never talked small numbers. Cut that in half and then divide by two again and you wouldn't be giving him the worst of it. But it was still more than anyone else ever took out of the fight racket.

He did the business for Dempsey, Mickey Walker, Jackie Fields, Joey Maxim and Archie Moore when they were champions. Briefly, he handled Abe Attell, Benny Leonard, Stanley Ketchel, Ace Hudkins, Harry Wills, and Sam Langford. Short or holding, hustling a stiff or a great fighter, Kearns always acted as though he was headed for a promoter's office to pick up his cut of a million-dollar gate.

Doc died busted. If the guys who owed him had paid off, he would have been wealthy. On the last day of his life Doc was starting all over again at eighty. He was shilling for a kid heavyweight named Jefferson Davis. Of course, Davis was another Dempsey. They all were, if Doc owned their contract.

He was a rogue, all right, but all he wanted money for was to spread around. At once, Doc was a con man and a mark. He clipped many a sucker but he was the biggest one of all.

They padded his checks in the joints. The moochers bit him with stories he knew were lies. He gave it away in big chunks, and held still for touches that were never repaid.

Doc got rid of money as though no fight ever drew less than a mill. The party was over in the Thirties. Often he was out scuffling for rent money. But circumstances never altered his personality or corrupted his faith in himself. He was a game old man.

Once, after a spell of impoverished obscurity, Doc arrived in New York with Jimmy Adamick, a mediocre heavyweight. He hit the Tavern, then run by Toots Shor, on the first bounce. He immediately bought a round for the house.

The whiskey eventually transported him back to the affluent past. He ordered the maitre d' to bring him everybody's check. No one reaches when the Doc's springing. He signed them, and asked Shor for a loan of two hundred. Doc staked the help, from the busboy to the chef, with the two Cs. He left the place tapped out.

It was never any good between Doc and Dempsey once they split.

Shortly after their break, Joe Benjamin, the old lightweight, gave Doc some advice.

"Jack's hot as you," Benjamin said. "Let him cool out and it'll straighten out."

"Tell him he needs me more than I need him," Kearns said.

Of course, Doc was wrong but he believed that until he went to sleep Saturday night. They spoke but neither ever forgave the other. There was never a combination like them in all the ages of sports.

Off the Loop in Chicago, years afterward, Doc ran a one-bartender saloon. Times were tough. A gambler came in with a large party. He ordered champagne and caviar to build up the check. Doc got his load on. When the bookmaker called for the bill, there wasn't any. Doc had snatched it. A week later, the joint closed. Doc was a player, not a dealer.

On the afternoon before he died, Doc called Oscar Fraley, his biographer.

"When we going to Las Vegas?" asked Kearns who would die that night.

Too bad Doc didn't make it, the joints never fold in Vegas. That kind of action could keep a man alive forever.

*1963*

## WENDELL SMITH

It was Wendell Smith (1914–1972) who recommended that the Brooklyn Dodgers sign Jackie Robinson. When the Dodgers did just that in 1946, Smith, sports editor and columnist of the *Pittsburgh Courier*, became Robinson's friend, chronicler, and guiding light. Robinson endured a brutal welcome to the world of baseball, but Smith was in the crosshairs of hatred, too. Exiled to what was called "the colored section" of ball parks, he wrote his stories on a portable typewriter in his lap because he was banned from the press box. Only gradually would things change for the better. While Robinson was playing his way into the Hall of Fame, Smith became the first African American reporter at the *Chicago Herald-American* and later a sports columnist for the *Chicago Sun-Times* and a sports anchor for a local TV station. Their lives would always be intertwined, a fact that was underscored after Robinson died in 1972. Smith died almost a month later to the day.


★   ★   ★

# It Was a Great Day in Jersey

JERSEY CITY, New Jersey—The sun smiled down brilliantly in picturesque Roosevelt Stadium here Thursday afternoon and an air of excitement prevailed throughout the spacious park, which was jammed to capacity with 25,000 jabbering, chattering opening day fans . . . A seething mass of humanity, representing all segments of the crazy-quilt we call America, poured into the magnificent ball park they named after a man from Hyde Park—Franklin D. Roosevelt—to see

Montreal play Jersey City and the first two Negroes in modern baseball history perform, Jackie Robinson and Johnny Wright . . . There
was the usual fanfare and color, with mayor Frank Hague chucking
out the first ball, the band music, kids from Jersey City schools putting on an exhibition of running, jumping and acrobatics . . . There
was also the hot dogs, peanuts and soda pop . . . And some guys in the
distant bleachers whistled merrily: "Take Me Out to the Ball Game"
. . . Wendell Willkie's "One World" was right here on the banks of the
Passaic River.

The outfield was dressed in a gaudy green, and the infield was as
smooth and clean as a new-born babe . . . And everyone sensed the
significance of the occasion as Robinson and Wright marched with
the Montreal team to deep centerfield for the raising of the Stars
and Stripes and the "Star-Spangled Banner" . . . Mayor Hague strut-
ted proudly with his henchmen flanking him on the right and left
. . . While the two teams, spread across the field, marched side by
side with military precision and the band played on . . . We all stood
up—25,000 of us—when the band struck up the National Anthem . . .
And we sang lustily and freely, for this was a great day . . . Robinson
and Wright stood out there with the rest of the players and dignitaries,
clutching their blue-crowned baseball caps, standing erect and as still
as West Point cadets on dress parade.

No one will ever know what they were thinking right then, but
I have traveled more than 2,000 miles with their courageous pio-
neers during the past nine weeks—from Sanford, Fla., to Daytona
Beach to Jersey City—and I feel that I know them probably better
than any newspaperman in the business . . . I know that their hearts
throbbed heavily and thumped a steady tempo with the big drum
that was pounding out the rhythm as the flag slowly crawled up the
centerfield mast.

And then there was a tremendous roar as the flag reached its crest
and unfurled gloriously in the brilliant April sunlight . . . The 25,000
fans settled back in their seats, ready for the ballgame as the Jersey

City Giants jogged out to their positions . . . Robinson was the second batter and as he strolled to the plate the crowd gave him an enthusiastic reception . . . They were for him . . . They all knew how he had overcome many obstacles in the deep South, how he had been barred from playing in Sanford, Fla., Jacksonville, Savannah and Richmond . . . And yet, through it all, he was standing at the plate as the second baseman of the Montreal team . . . The applause they gave so willingly was a salute of appreciation and admiration . . . Robinson then socked a sizzler to the shortstop and was thrown out by an eyelash at first base.

The second time he appeared at the plate marked the beginning of what can develop into a great career. He got his first hit as a member of the Montreal Royals . . . It was a mighty home run over the leftfield fence . . . With two mates on the base paths, he walloped the first pitch that came his way and there was an explosive "crack" as bat and ball met . . . The ball glistened brilliantly in the afternoon sun as it went hurtling high and far over the leftfield fence . . . And, the white flag on the foul-line pole in left fluttered lazily as the ball whistled by.

Robinson jogged around the bases—his heart singing, a broad smile on his beaming bronze face as his two teammates trotted homeward ahead of him . . . When he rounded third, Manager Clay Hopper, who was coaching there, gave him a heavy pat on the back and shouted: "That's the way to hit that ball!" . . . Between third and home-plate he received another ovation from the stands, and then the entire Montreal team stood up and welcomed him to the bench . . . White hands slapping him on his broad back . . . Deep Southern voices from the bench shouted, "Yo sho' hit 'at one, Robbie, nice goin' kid!" . . . Another said: "Them folks 'at wouldn't let you play down in Jacksonville should be hee'ah now. Whoopee!" . . . And still another: "They can't stop ya now, Jackie, you're really goin' places, and we're going to be right there with ya!" . . . Jackie Robinson laughed softly and smiled . . . Johnny Wright, wearing a big, blue pitcher's jacket, laughed and smiled . . . And, high up in the press box, Joe Bostic of the Amsterdam News and I looked at each other knowingly, and, we, too, laughed and smiled . . . Our hearts beat just a bit faster, and the thrill ran through us like champagne bubbles . . . It was a great day in Jersey . . . It was a great day in baseball!

But he didn't stop there, this whirlwind from California's gold coast . . . He ran the bases like a wild colt from the Western plains. He laid down two perfect bunts and slashed a hit into rightfield . . . He befuddled the pitchers, made them balk when he was roaring up and down the base paths, and demoralized the entire Jersey City team . . . He was a hitting demon and a base-running maniac . . . The crowd gasped in amazement . . . The opposing pitchers shook their heads in helpless agony . . . His understanding teammates cheered him on with unrivaled enthusiasm . . . And Branch Rickey, the man who had the fortitude and courage to sign him, heard the phenomenal news via telephone in the offices of the Brooklyn Dodgers at Ebbetts Field and said admiringly—"He's a wonderful boy, that Jackie Robinson—a wonderful boy!"

When the game ended and Montreal had chalked up a 14 to 1 triumph, Robinson dashed for the club house and the showers . . . But before he could get there he was surrounded by a howling mob of kids, who came streaming out of the bleachers and stands . . . They swept down upon him like a great ocean wave and he was drowned in a sea of adolescent enthusiasm . . . There he was—this Pied Piper of the diamond—perspiration rolling off his bronze brow, idolizing kids swirling all around him, autograph hounds tugging at him . . . And big cops riding prancing steeds trying unsuccessfully to disperse the mob that had cornered the hero of the day . . . One of his own teammates fought his way through the howling mob and finally "saved" Robinson . . . It was Red Durrett, who was a hero in his own right because he had pounded out two prodigious home runs himself, who came to the "rescue." He grabbed Robinson by the arm and pulled him through the crowd. "Come on," Durrett demanded, "you'll be here all night if you don't fight them off. They'll mob you. You can't possibly sign autographs for all those kids."

So, Jackie Robinson, escorted by the red-head outfielder, finally made his way to the dressing room. Bedlam broke loose in there, too . . . Photographers, reporters, kibitzers and hangers-on fenced him in . . . It was a virtual madhouse . . . His teammates, George Shuba, Stan Breard, Herman Franks, Tom Tatum, Marvin Rackley and all the others, were showering congratulations on him . . . They followed him into the showers, back to his locker and all over the dressing room . . . Flash bulbs flashed and reporters fired questions with machine-gun like rapidity . . . And Jackie Robinson smiled through it all.

As he left the park and walked out onto the street, the once-brilliant sun was fading slowly in the distant western skies . . . His petite and dainty little wife greeted him warmly and kindly. "You've had quite a day, little man," she said sweetly.

"Yes," he said softly and pleasantly, "God has been good to us today!"

*1946*

## W. C. HEINZ

When W. C. Heinz (1915–2008) came home from covering World War II with uncommon distinction, his editors at *The New York Sun* greeted him with what they considered a prize assignment: a reporting job in the paper's Washington bureau. Heinz—Bill to his friends—reacted as if he had been offered a whiff of Hitler's dirty socks. He yearned to write sports. His editors, harboring the disdain for fun and games typical of their breed, couldn't understand why, and probably never did. But, while the *Sun* folded in 1950, the intrepid Heinz eventually got where he wanted to go. He flew with the eagles as a magazine writer and author of books of both fiction and nonfiction, and yet the newspaper sports columns he wrote before all that endure. They are rich in tragedy, laughter, and moments that still give a reader the kind of chill bumps Washington rarely provides.

★　★　★

# Down Memory Lane with the Babe

THE OLD Yankees, going back twenty-five years, were dressing in what used to be the visiting clubhouse in the Yankee Stadium, some of them thin, some of them stout, almost all of them showing the years. Whitey Witt was asking for a pair of size 9 shoes. Mike McNally, bending over and going through the piles of uniforms stacked on the floor, was looking for a pair of pants with a 48 waist.

"Here he is now," somebody added, but when he said it he hardly raised his voice.

The Babe was the last to come in. He had on a dark suit and a cap oyster white. He walked slowly with a friend on either side of him. He paused for a moment and then he recognized someone and smiled and stuck out his hand.

They did not crowd him. When someone pointed to a locker he walked to it and it was quiet around him. When a few who knew him well walked up to him they did it quietly, smiling, holding out their hands.

The Babe started to undress. His friends helped him. They hung up his clothes and helped him into the parts of his uniform. When he had them on he sat down again to put on his spiked shoes, and when he did this the photographers who had followed him moved in. They took pictures of him in uniform putting on his shoes, for this would be the last time.

He posed willingly, brushing a forelock off his forehead. When they were finished he stood up slowly. There was a man there with a small boy, and the man pushed the small boy through the old Yankees and the photographers around Ruth.

"There he is," the man said, bending down and whispering to the boy. "That's Babe Ruth."

The small boy seemed confused. He was right next to the Babe and the Babe bent down and took the small boy's hand almost at the same time as he looked away to drop the hand.

"There," the man said, pulling the small boy back. "Now you met Babe Ruth."

The small boy's eyes were wide, but his face seemed to show fear. They led the Babe over to pose him in the middle of the rest of the 1923 Yankees. Then they led him into the old Yankee clubhouse—now the visiting clubhouse—to pose in front of his old locker, on which is painted in white letters, "Babe Ruth, No. 3."

When they led him back the rest of the members of the two teams of old Yankees had left to go to the dugouts. They put the Babe's gabardine topcoat over his shoulders, the sleeves hanging loose, and they led him—some in front of him and some in back in the manner in which they lead a fighter down to a ring—down the stairs and into the dark runway.

They sat the Babe down then on one of the concrete abutments in the semi-darkness. He sat there for about two minutes.

"I think you had better wait inside," someone said. "It's too damp here."

They led him back to the clubhouse. He sat down and they brought him a box of a dozen baseballs and a pen. He autographed the balls that will join what must be thousands of others on mantels or under glass in bureau drawers or in attics in many places in the world.

He sat then, stooped, looking ahead, saying nothing. They halted an attendant from sweeping the floor because dust was rising.

"I hope it lets up," the Babe said, his voice hoarse.

"All right," somebody said. "They're ready now."

They led him out again slowly, the topcoat over his shoulders. There were two cops and one told the other to walk in front. In the third base dugout there was a crowd of Indians and 1923 Yankees and they found a place on the bench and the Babe sat down behind the crowd.

"A glove?" he said.

"A left-handed glove," someone said.

They found a glove on one of the hooks. It was one of the type that has come into baseball since the Babe left—bigger than the old gloves with a mesh of rawhide between the thumb and first finger—and the Babe took it and looked at it and put it on.

"With one of these," he said, "you could catch a basketball."

They laughed and the Babe held the mesh up before his face like a catcher's mask and they laughed again. Mel Allen, at the public address microphone, was introducing the other old Yankees. You could hear the cheering and the Babe saw Mel Harder, the former Cleveland pitcher, now a coach.

"You remember," he said, after he had poked Harder, "when I got five for five off you and they booed me?"

"Yes," Harder said, smiling. "You mean in Cleveland."

The Babe made a series of flat motions with his left hand.

"Like that," the Babe said. "All into left field and they still booed the stuff out of me."

The Babe handed the glove to someone and someone else handed him a bat. He turned it over to see Bob Feller's name on it and he hefted it.

"It's got good balance," he said.

"And now—" Allen's voice said, coming off the field.

They were coming to boo Babe now. In front of him the Indians moved back and when they did the Babe looked up to see a wall of two dozen photographers focused on him. He stood up and the topcoat slid off his shoulders onto the bench.

"—George Herman," Allen's voice said, "Babe Ruth!"

The Babe took a step and started slowly up the steps. He walked out into the flashing of flash bulbs, into the cauldron of sound he must know better than any other man.

*1948*

★   ★   ★

# Death of a Racehorse

THEY WERE going to the post for the sixth race at Jamaica, two year olds, some making their first starts, to go five and a half furlongs for a purse of four thousand dollars. They were moving slowly down the backstretch toward the gate, some of them cantering, others walking, and in the press box they had stopped their working or their kidding to watch, most of them interested in one horse.

"Air Lift," Jim Roach said. "Full brother of Assault."

Assault, who won the triple crown . . . making this one too, by Bold Venture, himself a Derby winner, out of Igual, herself by the great Equipoise. . . . Great names in the breeding line . . . and now the little guy making his first start, perhaps the start of another great career.

They were off well, although Air Lift was fifth. They were moving toward the first turn, and now Air Lift was fourth. They were going into the turn, and now Air Lift was starting to go, third perhaps, when suddenly he slowed, a horse stopping, and below in the stands you could hear a sudden cry, as the rest left him, still trying to run but limping, his jockey—Dave Gorman—half falling, half sliding off.

"He broke a leg!" somebody, holding binoculars to his eyes, shouted in the press box. "He broke a leg!"

Down below they were roaring for the rest, coming down the stretch now, but in the infield men were running toward the turn, running toward the colt and the boy standing beside him, alone. There was a station wagon moving around the track toward them, and then, in a moment, the big green van that they call the horse ambulance.

"Gorman was crying like a baby," one of them, coming out of the jockey room, said. "He said he must have stepped in a hole, but you should have seen him crying."

"It's his left front ankle," Dr. J. G. Catlett, the veterinarian, was saying. "It's a compound fracture; and I'm waiting for confirmation from Mr. Hirsch to destroy him."

He was standing outside one of the stables beyond the backstretch, and he had just put in a call to Kentucky where Max Hirsch, the trainer, and Robert Kleberg, the owner, are attending the yearling sales.

"When will you do it?" one of them said.

"Right as soon as I can," the doctor said. "As soon as I get confirmation. If it was an ordinary horse I'd done it right there."

He walked across the road and around another barn to where they had the horse. The horse was still in the van, about twenty stable hands in dungarees and sweat-stained shirts, bare-headed or wearing old caps, standing around quietly and watching with Dr. M. A. Gilman, the assistant veterinarian.

"We might as well get him out of the van," Catlett said, "before we give him the novocaine. It'll be a little better out in the air."

The boy in the van with the colt led him out then, the colt limping, tossing his head a little, the blood running down and covering his left foreleg. When they saw him, standing there outside the van now, the boy holding him, they started talking softly.

"Full brother of Assault." . . . "It don't make no difference now. He's done." . . . "But damn, what a grand little horse." . . . "Ain't he a horse?"

"It's a funny thing," Catlett said. "All the cripples that go out, they never break a leg. It always happens to a good-legged horse."

A man, gray-haired and rather stout, wearing brown slacks and a blue shirt walked up.

"Then I better not send for the wagon yet?" the man said.

"No," Catlett said. "Of course, you might just as well. Max Hirsch may say no, but I doubt it."

"I don't know," the man said.

"There'd be time in the morning," Catlett said.

"But in this hot weather—" the man said.

They had sponged off the colt, after they had given him the shot to deaden the pain, and now he stood, feeding quietly from some hay they had placed at his feet. In the distance you could hear the roar of the crowd in the grandstand, but beyond it and above it you could hear thunder and see the occasional flash of lightning.

When Catlett came back the next time he was hurrying, nodding his head and waving his hands. Now the thunder was louder, the flashes of lightning brighter, and now rain was starting to fall.

"All right," he said, shouting to Gilman. "Max Hirsch talked to Mr. Kleberg. We've got the confirmation."

They moved the curious back, the rain falling faster now, and they moved the colt over close to a pile of loose bricks. Gilman had the halter and Catlett had the gun, shaped like a bell with the handle at the top. This bell he placed, the crowd silent, on the colt's forehead, just between the eyes. The colt stood still and then Catlett, with the hammer in his other hand, struck the handle of the bell. There was a short, sharp sound and the colt toppled onto his left side, his eyes staring, his legs straight out, the free legs quivering.

"Aw—" someone said.

That was all they said. They worked quickly, the two vets removing the broken bones as evidence for the insurance company, the crowd silently watching. Then the heavens opened, the rain pouring down, the lightning flashing, and they rushed for the cover of the stables, leaving alone on his side near the pile of bricks, the rain running off his hide, dead an hour and a quarter after his first start, Air Lift, son of Bold Venture, full brother of Assault.

*1949*

## DICK YOUNG

Dick Young (1917–1987) was a terror in his final years, jumping to the *New York Post* from its rival tabloid the *Daily News*, running Tom Seaver out of town, feuding with the revered Red Smith, and playing footsie with millionaire team owners while forever posing as the voice of the people. Young made it easy to forget his seismic impact on baseball writing. When the *News* was selling two million copies a day, he was the reason as much as anybody. He talked to the ballplayers. He gave Jackie Robinson a fair shot and put himself in front of everybody he ever ripped. He had a breezy writing style no matter what the sport— "This belongs on page three with the rest of the ax murders"—but it was always baseball that made his sentences crackle. "It may not seem innovative now," said Vic Ziegel, a reader who became a press box rival, "but at the time we felt like people must have in the Twenties when they first heard Louis Armstrong."

★  ★  ★

# Beloved Enemy

HISTORY AND hysteria were made at Ebbets Field yesterday. The most dramatic, pulse-pounding pennant race ever ended in a tie between the Brooks and Cards—requiring an unprecedented best two-of-three playoff to determine the NL champ. And the thrilling finish had that typically bizarre Brooklyn touch. The Dodgers had lost their vital last game to Boston, 4–0. They lost it because they couldn't clip masterful Mort Cooper for more than four separated singles . . . because Billy Herman had struck a vengeful double that led to the only run in the first eight frames . . . and because relievers Kirby Higbe and Hugh Casey had turned that one-run deficit of Vic Lombardi's into a ninth-inning collapse by getting cuffed for three more tallies.

And yet, as each Boston run rushed across in the ninth, the wild cheering of the 30,756 Faithful grew louder until it reached a madness matched only by a Times Square New Year's Eve demonstration. Here was the strangest sight ever seen in this strangest piece of territory on earth. Here was Brooklyn blowing its vital last game beyond recall—a defeat which ostensibly could cost them the pennant—yet the fans were going insane with joy!

The explanation of this unbelievable behavior, of course, is that word of the Cub rally in St. Louis had just spread through the stands. The portable-radio grapevine flashed the word from section to section. "The Cubs have tied the score. . . . The Cubs are ahead. . . . The Cubs have scored again. . . . And again."

Meanwhile, on the field below, the Braves are scoring again. . . . And again. . . . And again. Higbe has taken over the 1–0 game left him by Li'l Lom, whose valiant four-hit try had just fallen short of Cooper's sparkling performance. But Higbe doesn't have it this time. With one down, he walks Fernandez. Then Ryan rams a hit through the left side and Gillenwater loops another to right for a run.

Now it seems hopeless, but Durocher rushes in Casey, just in case. And Hughie doesn't have it either. Cooper crams a single past Reese's diving glove for another run. Pee Wee then climbs a cloud to spear Culler's bullet, but Hopp pounds another hit through the right hole for the third marker of the stanza. Meanwhile, the stands are rocking with cheers. Because, for every Brave running across the plate, a Cub is doing likewise—and more—a thousand miles away.

Soon the game ends and, instead of gloom, there's a spirit of cheerful expectation among the Faithful. The public address system booms: "Inning by inning results of the Cub-Cardinal game will be posted. Those wishing to remain may do so." Many hundreds did, milling around the stands—cheering when the Cubs scored, and groaning slightly when the Cards scored.

Then came the flash: Cards lose! The pennant tie had been salvaged.

And they went home happy—happy and excited, and still hoping for the Dodger victory, just as they had when the game started. At that time they were cheering every Boston out, every Brooklyn hit, even every strike thrown by Lombardi. Money rode on each pitch, and the nervous tension, like the grey haze that hung over the field, could almost be cut with a knife.

But the dark day was more of an aid to a man with Cooper's speed, than to a stuff pitcher like Lombardi. And what's more, Mort, who had blanked the Giants only three days before, had perfect control. He didn't walk a man, was constantly ahead of the batters, and only once let the Brooks get a man to third.

Lom was fine, too, but half of the four hits he yielded were coupled in the third stanza for the only run Boston really needed. And it was Herman, the man Brooklyn had let go because it was felt that he couldn't help them win the pennant, who almost cost them the flag.

Cooper personally had opened the inning with the first Boston hit. Herman then punched the big blow—a slicing liner that banged low off the right field fence just inside the foul pole for two bases, shooting Mort to third. Holmes then sent Furillo sprinting into left-center for his liner, and Cooper romped over easily after the grab.

And that run he had scored was all the big right-hander needed. Only in the eighth did the Brooks demonstrate a scoring threat of even mediocre proportions. With one down, Edwards made first because Culler's peg of his grounder pulled Hopp off the bag. Medwick then swung for Lombardi and cracked the first pitch through the middle for a single that sent Edwards to second. Here Stanky slammed a bouncer wide of first. Hopp hustled over, fell into a sitting position as he grabbed the ball, but made a spectacular peg to second for the hairline force on pinch-runner Rojek—with Edwards pulling up at third. Lavagetto then drove to left. It was long and deep. Litwhiler coasted back under it, waited patiently for the ball to descend, and squeezed it.

There the tense duel ended. Within the next few minutes, it was a shamble. Higbe and Casey were banged from the box—giving up as many hits in their brief term as Li'l Lom had all day.

By then the Faithful didn't care what they were watching. They were really in St. Louis, every one of 'em.

*1946*

★   ★   ★

# Obit on the Dodgers

THIS IS called an obit, which is short for obituary. An obit tells of a person who has died, how he lived, and of those who live after him. This is the obit on the Brooklyn Dodgers.

Preliminary diagnosis indicates that the cause of death was an acute case of greed, followed by severe political complications. Just a year ago, the Brooklyn ball club appeared extremely healthy. It had made almost a half million dollars for the fiscal period, more than any other big league club. Its president, Walter O'Malley, boasted that all debts had been cleared, and that the club was in the most solvent condition of its life, with real estate assets of about $5 million.

O'Malley contends that unhealthy environment, not greed, led to the demise of the Dodgers in Brooklyn. He points out that he became aware of this condition as long ago as 1947, when he began looking around for a new park to replace Ebbets Field, capacity 32,000.

At first, O'Malley believed the old plant could be remodeled, or at least torn down and replaced at the same site. But, after consultation with such a prominent architect as Norman Bel Geddes, and the perusal of numerous blueprints and plans, O'Malley ruled out such a possibility as unfeasible.

So O'Malley looked around for a new lot where he could build this bright, new, salubrious dwelling for his Dodgers; a dream house, complete with plastic dome so that games could be played in spite of foul weather, a plant that could be put to year-round use, for off-season sports and various attractions.

O'Malley suggested to the City of New York that the site of the new Brooklyn Civic Center, right outside the Dodger office windows in Boro Hall, would be ideal for the inclusion of a 50,000 seat stadium—a War Memorial stadium, he proposed.

That was all very patriotic, the City Planning Commission said, but not a stadium; not there. Sorry.

So, O'Malley looked farther, and hit upon the area at Flatbush and Atlantic Avenues—virtually the heart of downtown Brooklyn, where all transit systems intersect, and where the tired Long Island Rail Road limps in at its leisure. O'Malley learned that a vast portion of the neighborhood, which included the congested Ft. Greene market, had been declared a "blighted area" by city planners who had earmarked it for rehabilitation.

Here began one of the most forceful political manipulations in the history of our politically manipulated little town. With O'Malley as the guiding spirit, plans for establishment of a Sports Authority were born. It would be the work of such an Authority to issue bonds and build a stadium with private capital—utilizing the city's condemnation powers to obtain the land.

With O'Malley pushing the issue through his lifelong political contacts, the bill was drafted in Albany, passed overwhelmingly by the City Council, squeezed through the State Legislature by one vote, and ultimately signed into law by Governor Harriman.

At that moment, April 21, 1956, the prospects for a new stadium, and a continuance of Brooklyn baseball were at their highest. Thereafter, everything went downhill. City officials, who had supported the bill originally, in the belief Albany would defeat it, went to work with their subtle sabotage. Appropriations for surveys by the Sports Center

Authority were cut to the bone, and O'Malley shook his head knowingly. He was getting the works.

O'Malley, meanwhile, had been engaging in some strange movements of his own. He had leased Roosevelt Stadium, Jersey City, for
three years with the announced intention of playing seven or eight
games a season there. Later, he sold Ebbets Field for $3,000,000 on
a lease-back deal with Marv Kratter. The lease made it possible for
O'Malley to remain in Brooklyn, in a pinch, for five years. He had no
intention of doing so—it was just insurance against things blowing up
at both political ends.

Why was Ebbets Field sold?

Politicians claimed it was an O'Malley squeeze on them. O'Malley
claimed it was a manifestation of his good intentions; that he was con-
verting the club's assets into cash so that he might buy Sports Authority bonds and help make the new stadium a reality.

Then, O'Malley moved in a manner that indicated he didn't believe
himself. At the start of '57 he visited Los Angeles. Two months later,
he announced the purchase of Wrigley Field. Shortly thereafter, Los
Angeles officials, headed by Mayor Paulson and County Supervisor
Ken Hahn, visited O'Malley at Vero Beach, Fla.

It was there, on March 7, that serious consideration of a move to
Los Angeles crystallized in the O'Malley mind. He made grandiose
stipulations to the L.A. authorities—and was amazed to hear them
say: "We will do it."

From then on, Los Angeles officials bore down hard on the project,
while New York's officials quibbled, mouthed sweet nothings, and
tried to place the blame elsewhere. With each passing week, it became
increasingly apparent the Dodgers were headed west—and, in an election year, the politicians wanted no part of the hot potato.

Bob Moses, park commissioner, made one strong stab for New York.
He offered the Dodgers park department land at Flushing Meadow—
with a string or two. It wasn't a bad offer—but not as good as L.A.'s.

By now, O'Malley's every move was aimed at the coast. He brought
Frisco Mayor George Christopher to dovetail the Giant move to the

coast with his own. He, and Stoneham, received permission from the NL owners to transfer franchises.

That was May 28—and since then, O'Malley has toyed with New York authorities, seeming to derive immense satisfaction from seeing them sweat unnecessarily. He was repaying them.

Right to the end, O'Malley wouldn't give a flat, "Yes, I'm moving"—as Stoneham had done. O'Malley was using New York as his saver—using it to drive a harder bargain with L.A.'s negotiator Harold McClellan, and using it in the event the L.A. city council were to reject the proposition at the last minute.

But L.A., with its mayor whipping the votes into line the way a mayor is expected to, passed the bill—and O'Malley graciously accepted the 300 acres of downtown Los Angeles, whereupon he will graciously build a ball park covering 12 acres.

And the Brooklyn Dodgers dies—the healthiest corpse in sports history. Surviving are millions of fans, and their memories.

The memories of a rich and rollicking history—dating back to Ned Hanlon, the first manager, and skipping delightfully through such characters as Uncle Wilbert Robinson, Casey Stengel, Burleigh Grimes, Leo Durocher, Burt Shotten, Charley Dressen and now Walt Alston. The noisy ones, the demonstrative ones, the shrewd and cagey ones, and the confused ones. They came and they went, but always the incredible happenings remained, the retold screwy stories, the laughs, the snafued games, the laughs, the disappointments, the fights, and the laughs.

And the players: the great ones—Nap Rucker, Zack Wheat, Dazzy Vance, Babe Herman, Dolph Camilli, Whit Wyatt, Dixie Walker; the almost great ones but never quite—like Van Lingle Mungo and Pete Reiser; the modern men who made up the Dodgers' golden era—Duke Snider, Preacher Roe, Hugh Casey—and the man who made history, Jackie Robinson, and the boy who pitched Brooklyn to its world championship in 1955, Johnny Podres.

And the brass: the conflicts of the brothers McKeever, and the trials of Charley Ebbets; the genuine sentimentality of Dearie Mulvey and the pride of her husband, Jim Mulvey; the explosive achievement of Larry MacPhail, the unpopular but undeniable success of Branch Rickey—and now, Walter O'Malley, who leaves Brooklyn a rich man and a despised man.

*1957*

★   ★   ★

# Hutch

I T WAS the last day in Cincinnati. Shortly, the game would start, and several of the newsmen stood around Fred Hutchinson, at the tip of the Cincy dugout, and talked about the importance of it. They realized what they were saying sounded hollow and petty because how important can it be, the winning or losing of a ball game, or a pennant, when the man you talk to is losing his life.

They tried not to notice the heavy gray at the temples, which had appeared almost overnight, the sometimes thickened speech, the dark blue suit that hung so loosely on what remained of this wonderful man.

"I think I'll get out of here," he said, "before I get in the way," and he turned to go upstairs to the glass-fronted booth on the roof, where he would sit and watch his ball game.

Two months earlier, Fred Hutchinson had told Bill DeWitt he could no longer continue as manager of the Reds, and they decided Hutch should take a leave of absence, and that Dick Sisler would be acting manager in the interim.

The interim. It was a game they played, and Hutch played it with them. He played it right out to the end. When someone was stupid enough to ask how he felt, Hutch would brazen it through, and make vague reference to a sciatic nerve that was causing him some trouble, but it wasn't too bad.

He knew how bad it was, but he played the game with all of them. Only a very few people did he let know he knew, and one of these was Dick Sisler. Hutch had rejoined the team after a visit to his doctor in Seattle, and the doctor had told him the truth. The doctor had told him that the treatments were not going to work, and it tore the heart out of the doctor to tell him that, because the doctor was his brother.

When Hutch rejoined the team in Los Angeles, he called Dick Sisler to his room. Hutch lighted up a cigaret and took a deep drag, and Sisler knew something was up because he hadn't seen a cigarette in Hutch's hand for months before.

"You know what I have?" Hutch said.

Sisler nodded, and played the game. He mentioned a mutual friend whom both knew had had cancer for years, and was living with it. "It can be the same with you," Dick said.

Hutch wasn't playing. "It's not the same thing," he said. "What I have is terminal."

Hutch stayed with the team, and quickly the telltale signs mounted. The Reds' uniforms bear the name of the player across the back of the shirt, lettered in a semicircle from shoulder to shoulder. It took a man with an expansive back to wear the letters HUTCHINSON across his back. Then, one day you noticed that the name couldn't be read because there were folds in the uniform he wore. By All-Star Game, where they made him a coach, he walked in a pained limp, but he walked to that coaching box each inning, and back again, and he paced in that coaching box, a limping pace, with his fists clenched, and the people at Shea Stadium cheered his name, because they too played the game.

You wondered why this wonderful man was wasting his last months working with the ball club instead of taking his family back to Anna Maria Island in the Gulf of Mexico, and spending the precious small time with them, and then you heard of a story that gave the answer.

Hutch's coach and very close friend, Reggie Otero, was fingering through a sports section earlier in the season, and he came across a wirephoto of Birdie Tebbetts. It showed the Cleveland manager on a Florida beach, recovering from a heart attack.

"Look-a-here," said Otero with his decided Cuban accent, and he shoved the paper under Hutch's nose. "You see the way Birdie is taking it easy on the beach? Why you don't do the same theeng?"

Hutchinson looked at the picture and tossed the paper onto the floor. "That's what he likes to do, fine," said Hutch. "I'm doing what I like to do."

Hutch couldn't stand sympathy, and he could tolerate alibis even less. He despised ballplayers who made excuses, and he lost hard. Yet there was this sentimental streak within him, a yard wide, which he fought to subdue. But then he'd have a couple of drinks, and the yard wide would come gushing out of him, usually in the form of a song, which he sang with a sweet, soft voice that seemed to come from a ventriloquist, and not from the big, gruff man.

At the annual spring training party, which Hutch tossed for his players and friends, somebody unthinkingly asked Hutch to sing. He didn't have to be asked twice. He walked over to his daughter, Patricia, who is 16, and he sang their favorite song. He sang "I Understand," and the tears rolled unchecked down the face of Patricia Hutchinson.

The season flew by for Fred Hutchinson. It might have lasted for a few days more if Cincy had been able to win that last day, and force a play-off, but Cincy lost, and in the quiet clubhouse afterward, Dick Sisler said he was proud of the Reds, but was sorry they hadn't been able to win it "for that guy over there," and he pointed across the room where players were coming up to Hutch, one and two at a time, and shaking his thin hand, and saying, "See you in the spring."

Hutch looked them in the eye, and could pretend no longer.

"See you around," he said.

*1964*

## EMMETT WATSON

Emmett Watson (1918–2001) found his voice as a sportswriter just as American soldiers came marching back from World War II. Worried that his editor at *The Seattle Star* might not be on the same wavelength, he left a note saying his column on a battle-scarred football hero was a literary experiment, nothing more. The column ended up on the front page and Watson was a made man. He would go on to write for the city's other dailies, *The Times* and the *Post-Intelligencer*, and become a three-dot general-interest columnist with a literary flair and an abiding sense of civic responsibility. And yet all Watson ever wanted to be was a professional baseball player. He lasted two days as a teenaged catcher in the Pacific Coast League, proving yet again that typewriter keys are easier to hit than a curveball.

★　★　★

# Goal-Line Stand in France Brings Freddy Back

YOU COME back older, heavier, smarter, and with a decent respect for being alive—you return with scars on your back, and a jagged one across your chest, to a game they said you'd never play again.

It's a nice day. You come out of the tunnel in front of 40,000 people, and the sunlight hits the gold "33" on your jersey, a nicer number than a G.I. dog tag.

The program says you're Fred Provo, a left halfback.

The student section, bigger than it's ever been before, is yelling like every other section of its kind, and most of the rooters don't remember when Freddy Provo was a third-string halfback in 1942.

The Husky left half, who runs like there was a law against being tackled, is back to play a safer game. He had a large piece of the second World War laid right in his lap as a 21-year-old sophomore.

No, thank you, please, not any more. Let's toss a coin, or argue the next one out—wars are dangerous.

The kid from Vancouver, Wash., was helping the 82nd Airborne Division push up the lower belly of the Belgian Bulge. A long way from the Beta Theta Pi House, where the meals are good and the biggest hazard is a touch by one of the brothers.

Freddy Provo got hit, a piece of a German mortar clipped him across the chest, high up on the right side. Not so bad; walk a thousand yards to the aid station and they'll fix you up. But one doesn't walk in the middle of a war; he crawls and zigs and zags.

After 500 yards there is a weakness which comes from loss of blood. "To hell with this," said Freddy Provo. "We'll walk a while."

For 500 yards more you walk on borrowed time and thank your stars the German boys with rifles are afflicted with a temporary astigmatism.

The aid station is friendly. They've got you on a table and everything is set for the Army medics to go in and get that piece of mortar.

But suddenly there isn't any aid station. There is a loud noise from a German 88-millimeter job, arriving uninvited. Some of the others are on the floor and when the debris clears, you are worse off than ever.

Three pieces of the German shell have been added to the one you had before. Tech. Sergt. Provo has become a nonvoting stockholder in Krupp Munitions, Ltd.

The Husky stadium looks good these days, some two years later, and even U.C.L.A. and U.S.C. are friendly in their off moments. It's nice to be back, but the stand at the goal line in a hospital in France—well, it's nice to be back.

There was a friendly Army doctor, who took a great deal of pride in his work. He went into Tech. Sergt. Provo's chest and shoulder, removing the bits of metal. Very close.

"Everything's going to be all right," the doctor said. "No matter what they tell you later, you'll play football again. None of the nerves are damaged. The muscles will heal. Just hang in there . . . take it easy."

The other doctors shook their heads. Not so good. Football? Not a chance.

For six months you lay in the hospital, often thinking of home. Of frosh football at Washington in 1941; of varsity ball in '42, enough to make a letter.

And the high school league at Vancouver, under Dutch Shields. The Southwest Conference prep battles, when you were a star, on the first team. Those were the days you'd run wild against Aberdeen, wrecking Phil Sorboe's defense.

"That Provo," he'd say, "he beat me again."

A nice guy, Sorboe. Coaching now at Washington State. Maybe you'll get a crack at the Cougars when you get back to Washington. If you ever play again.

But Tech. Sergt. Provo kept on remembering what the other doctor had said: "You'll play again, no matter what they tell you."

In the hospital a big fullback from Cornell, himself a casualty, helped Tech. Sergt. Provo exercise the arm he used to throw bases with. A lot of work, every day.

"Keep trying, kid," the fullback said. "You won't be a third stringer when you go back to Washington. You're putting on weight."

You walk down East 47th Street from the Beta House, older than the others, heavier than when you left, and, like the Cornell fullback said, no longer on the third team.

It was quite a war, but next time let's have the diplomats fight it out with adjectives at thirty paces.

Football? We've won two and lost three. But there was that

satisfying battle against Washington State at Pullman, three weeks ago. Just like old times.

"That Provo," Sorboe said, after the game. "He beat me again."

*1946*

★    ★    ★

# End of the Line for Leo

I T WAS late afternoon and there were a few people hanging around the gym watching Harry Mathews skip rope. Jack Hurley motioned toward the back room, which was bare of furniture and looked out on First Avenue. Leo Lokovsek propped himself on the window ledge and looked down at the people hurrying about their business.

The side of his face away from the window was shadowed, and you could hardly see the jagged scars around his cheek, ear and temple. It had been three weeks now since the automobile crash outside Everett; three weeks since they had called the priest to the hospital where Leo lay unconscious for twelve hours.

"I got you down here," Hurley said, "to tell you that Leo is through. He isn't going to fight no more."

Lokovsek had come into the gym, feeling well, ready to work out. The Deacon called him into the office, where he told him: "You're all through." Lokovsek argued and pleaded. The X rays had shown no fracture; the doctor had assured him his head was sound.

Hurley tried to explain how it was with Ernie Schaaf, when Primo Carnera killed him with a light left jab. He told him about Lem Franklin, who had a previous head injury that nobody knew about, and how Franklin collapsed and died in the ring without being hit a solid punch.

"Not if all the doctors in the Mayo Clinic told me this boy could fight," Hurley said. "Not even then. He's finished."

"Would you fight for somebody else, Leo?"

Hurley answered the question. "I can't control his life," the Deacon said. "What he does is his own business now. But I think I've convinced him he shouldn't."

Lokovsek nodded.

It was easy then to remember the months of patient training in the gym, the long lean strong body, with the sharp reflexes, the smooth blend of balance and leverage. Experts conceded Lokovsek was a real possibility. It was easy to remember the night in Hoquiam, his first fight, his first knockout, how he drew the deep breath of satisfaction and there was nothing ahead but fight and build-up and fight again— with perhaps a fortune waiting.

Nothing had changed except, possibly, a minute broken blood vessel in his head; something Hurley was afraid of.

"You're young," Hurley said. "You've got a wife and baby to look out for. You got your whole life ahead of you, and if you've got the guts to fight, you should have the guts to start over."

Hurley walked to the door, paused and turned. The steel-rimmed glasses and the tight mouth gave his face a prissy expression.

"They'll come at you," he was saying, in a soft voice. "They'll come at you with money. Parasites. They'll give you money to fight again, because they know you're good and they know they can get it back out of you. Don't go.

"Just remember, I could let you fight. I chase a buck as hard as any man. I could use you for a year in easy fights and then I could back off. I like money real well, but I won't make my money that way."

Hurley went through the door and on out into the gym. Lokovsek was staring hard at his fists, clenched in his lap, and it was easy to think how things might have been.

The build-up already was well on its way. Even now, in the East, they are waiting the word on Hurley's heavyweight. Lokovsek was a natural for the build-up, with his easy, friendly ways, handsome, photogenic face, and a deep, warm sense of humor.

"When he first told me," the fighter said, "I got all sorts of crazy notions. I went away from him mad and disappointed, and I thought about getting somebody else to manage me. I was going to show him.

"Then I remembered something that happened in that fight in Vancouver. The guy was mussing me up a little. I got a flash of Jack in my corner and I remember thinking: 'Nobody can beat me. I'm Hurley's fighter.' Then I knew that Jack was right, and I would have to quit."

Outside the lights were coming on and traffic thickened in the streets. The faint sound of a bag being punched came through the walls, and Leo again looked down at his hands.

"I was going to do so much," he said. "I was going to be champion of the world. All through my life I'll wonder if I could have made it. Now I'll never know."

*1953*

## BLACKIE SHERROD

To understand how Blackie Sherrod (1919–2016) became a Texas legend, you might consider the day he hired a baseball writer simply because the young whippersnapper did a hook slide in front of his desk. Or maybe you could turn to the column in which he wrote that Roger Staubach rescuing the Dallas Cowboys from a wretched performance "was like putting a cherry on a glass of buttermilk." Sherrod passed his sense of perspective on to future stars Dan Jenkins, Edwin (Bud) Shrake, and Gary Cartwright when he was sports editor of *The Fort Worth Press* from 1946 to 1958. Then he turned Dallas into his personal fiefdom, writing a column for the *Times Herald* and, later, the *Morning News* that read, someone said, as though he had invited the English language up on the front porch for some four-alarm chili and a Dr Pepper. He never spoiled the mood by revealing his given name: William Forrest Sherrod.

★   ★   ★

# Old Buster in Ivyland

N EW YORK—As long as he's in the vicinity, don't you know, a chap should certainly take in The Game.

And iffen you don't know what The Game is, then you ain't got a large amount of couth and don't stand there wiping your nose on your sleeve and mumbling apologies.

The Game is the annual football contest between the Harvards and the Yales and it is never referred to by any other title. In New England, the citizens and the news media simply speak of The Game. On the front of the program, the printing says nothing about the Harvards and the Yales. It says, The Game, in letters four inches high.

(It ain't Harvard, anyways. It's Hahvud. Watch that stuff.)

And so it happened that our aging hero was in Boston last weekend to witness an execution, and someone pressed a ticket to The Game into his sweaty palm.

"You owe it to yourself, old fellow," said the benefactor.

Old fellow finished quaffing his nut brown and banged the oaken table with the pewter tankard.

"By jove," says we, squaring tiny shoulders, "consider it done."

New England had been blessed with a wondrous Indian summer. But come Saturday of The Game, and the very weather turned austere and haughty. Freeze the marrow of your Southern bones.

"We could stay in the hotel and watch it on television," says we bravely, feigning pneumonia.

"Nonsense," growled our guide. "It's the day of The Game."

And so, with a merry chattering of teeth, we set forth and never shall we rue the day. We will give you Ringling Brothers, Barnum and Bailey and 18 points and take The Game every ruddy time.

Hahvud is a vast collection of old red brick buildings with gables and white window trim and ivy turned rusty by the season. And over its many acres pour these denizens of a corduroy world—brown pageantry of parkas and suede boots, of teeth braces and horn rim glasses, of fuzzy little hats with shaving brushes on the bands and, yet, of heavy raccoon coats calculated to give Big Daddy Lipscomb a severe hernia.

Station wagons crowd upon the premises. The tailgates are let down and all sorts of goodies, solid and liquid, are set forth. A cheerful old gal in fur boots and a diamond roughly the size of a turkey egg sets up a portable charcoal grill and wafts a hamburger scent all over the place while her hubby pours ready-mixed martinis for the guests.

Big canvas tents dot the landscape with signs like Harvard Class of '37, and inside are tables of delicate sandwiches and coffee and fellowship. There are Rugby games on fields adjacent to the stadium, which is a 57-year-old horror of stone copied after the Acropolis of Athens—with wooden plank seating and huge pillars and dark passageways.

And there is a great abundance of spirits, the better to fight off the rigors of weather and the fact that absolutely no seat cushions are sold in the stadium.

This one dignified old gent in Tyrolian hat, Tattersall vest and stout brogues stood discreetly behind a rock wall and produced a brown bottle from somewhere in his Brooks Brothers garments. He pulled heroically at the stuff, while his freshly powdered wattles quivered in protest, and went into a spell of coughing and eye-watering.

You just knew that this fine gent would never repeat this torture on any other day of the year. He usually sat in a lush leather chair at the club and had Jarvis or Cleve or Hamilton fetch him an ale for his appetite.

But, by gad, sir, this was The Game and these things have to be done.

The Hahvud band warmed up on a nearby pasture and these lads were a bit unbelievable. They were clad in dusty black loafers, wrinkled white ducks, red flannel blazers and red ties that were wonderfully askew.

One wore a beret. Another, an eye patch. Most had unfortunate complexions and thick glasses and difficulty determining which was the right foot and which was the left foot for the purpose of marching.

This, we thought with a certain amount of disdain, was certainly going to be something. If they can play Come to Jesus in whole notes, then we are President Grover Cleveland.

But, as we watched, this scraggly bunch meandered out on the field for a pre-game concert and played the most crisp, most beautifully disciplined music you can ever imagine.

It wasn't a handsome crowd. Most of the gals looked as if they had their hair beat off with a wet rope and they wore the thick black stockings and stood pigeon-toed. And the menfolk were mostly short with florid cheekbones and tight collars.

But it was wonderfully mannered. There was no harsh shoving and gouging and pushing. Neither was there any belligerency nor any gritted-teeth alumni intent on hanging the coach in effigy. What there was, was subdued gaiety and an abundance of good naturedness.

The game was much. A really fine Yale running back named Ken Wolfe dashed 40-odd yards on the first play and the Hahvuds were never in contention. There was cheering and there was booing, but mostly there was enjoyment of the day and the festivities and of the hamburgers on the tailgate grill.

And so, it seemed to this scarred fugitive from the grim, grim world of Southwest football, that The Game isn't The Game at all, in our provincial terms.

Rather it's a holiday to be anticipated and relished, a place to take your best gal with a calm realization that there has to be a loser just as there has to be a winner, and the sky ain't gonna fall down, regardless of the result.

The Hahvuds lost, to be sure, and the pure blue amateur sky stayed up there and everybody had a ball and who's to say these citizens ain't got the right idea?

*1960*

★  ★  ★

# Changing Tastes

I T WAS with considerable curiosity and not a little squeamishness that us traditional codgers read about Grant Teaff and His Amazing Worm Act. You know, about how the Baylor football coach inspired his charges into upsetting the Texas Longhorns by dropping a real live earthworm in his mouth during his pre-game sermon. Correction: real dead earthworm. Big ole rascal, Teaff said with a certain pride.

The coach's act was a demonstration, don't you see, of some Aggie joke about how a successful fisherman kept his bait warm in the winter. If you haven't heard it, stop me for goodness sakes. None of us wish to go through *that* again.

Teaff, if you didn't know, has gained a reputation around the country for his inspirational messages, both to religious bodies as a stimulant to their faith fervor, and to business groups as a motivating force toward success. Some of his motivation talks are recorded as albums and sold. So you're not dealing just with a carnival geek, eating live pullets for a pint of wine, but a professional motivator.

Besides, it was just an act.

"I didn't swallow it," said Teaff. "Honest, I didn't."

There are those naturalists who will probably hold that a nice clean earthworm is a lot better for the system than a wad of chewing tobacco in your trough or a pinch between cheek and gum or, for that matter, a ladle of four-alarm chili. I can remember the immortal words of the late Benny Bickers, a midnite philosopher hereabouts, who once said, "Dammit, it's *my* mouth. I can haul coal in it if I want to!"

There are those who claim Teaff's Amazing Worm Act was designed not only to whip his Bears into a glorious froth, but to attract heavy newspaper ink that would aid his recruiting program, just now swinging into earnest action. After all, the coach of a 2–8 team normally doesn't make the headlines all that much unless he wrestles an alligator at halftime or rents a hotel room and smokes in bed.

("If that's what it takes to coach," said A&M's Tom Wilson, "then I'm in the wrong business.")

Frankly, some of us fail to recognize how The Amazing Worm Act can help Baylor recruiting. Oh, Grant might attract an early bird or two, but he could also find the modern jock will opt for Barry Switzer doing The Hustle on the parlor carpet or Lou Holtz springing a nice clean card trick at the dining room table. The Amazing Worm Act demands a specialized audience, preferably one that hasn't just eaten. You must hand it to Teaff for taking a calculated risk. He could have hiccupped.

Still, The Amazing Worm Act is a noteworthy milestone, I suppose, because it marks a definite stage of progress in motivation talks. There was a time when a little frog-voiced coach could pull out his handkerchief and ask the boys to win one for the Gipper, and let it go at that.

Gosh, once Abe Lemons' Oklahoma City basketball team got 20 points behind at halftime and Abe, of all people, was stricken mute for a motivating talk in the locker room.

"I had a speech for 10 points behind, or 11 or 15," said Abe, "but I never figured on 20." So Abe silently motioned his cowering lads back to the court and held a scrimmage until the other team showed up to start the second half.

Tom Landry, once trying to goad his laggard Cowboys into furious shame, made a show of removing his championship ring at halftime. It made the squad mad alrighty, but not at the other side. At *him*.

Darrell Royal was never one for halftime oratory but at one Cotton Bowl intermission, he suggested to the Texas squad: "There's a helluva fight going on out there on the field. Why don't you fellows join it?"

Once the Fighting Irish were stirred to fanatical delivery when after a long wait, Knute Rockne stuck his bald head in the door and removed his hat. "Pardon me, ladies, I thought this was the Notre Dame dressing room," he said and left.

But now motivation is big league. It was only a few years ago that Al Conover, trying to spur his Rice Owls to wilder efforts against Arkansas, grabbed a chair and threw it through a locker-room window. Then you may have read last year about the high school coach somewhere who brought a live chicken to the practice field and ordered his players to kick it to death to demonstrate their determination.

And just last season, a Florida high school coach bit the head off a live frog to illustrate what *could* be done if a person set his mind to it.

Doubtless all these audiences were stimulated to superior performance. Certainly it seemed to work at Baylor. According to witnesses, when Teaff finished his act, the Bears almost tore the walls down in their rush to get on the field and whomp the Longhorns. Personally I don't much blame them. If a man is standing there biting on a live frog or dropping worms in his mouth, I wouldn't be too eager to stay in the same room with him, either.

*1978*

★   ★   ★

# Zero Is Hero

I T WILL never be recorded, of course, that Larry Cole is a rank traitor. Nowhere will history list him alongside Brutus and Benedict and Shoeless Joe Jackson. Nevertheless it is known to a few discerning observers that the Cowboy mossback has betrayed a dignified, dedicated group.

Were this Abraham Lincoln's time, it would be the firing squad for Bubba. In Rome, it would be 15 rounds against the lions, winner take all. In Cuba, he would be hanging by two of his 10 thumbs.

The reason Larry Cole will escape the everlasting stigma is that the outfit he betrayed is really not an organization at all. It is an unbrotherhood, a non-lodge. To be organized would destroy it.

This, of course, is the exclusive Zero Club which was fermented a dozen years ago in Cowboy training camp. Charter members were three large flaxen linemen named Larry, Pat and Blaine. Their last name was Who. They were swathed in anonymity and gloried in it. (Actually, there is very little else you *can* do in it.)

The Zero Club was just that. The members met occasionally in the dorm room of Cole or Pat Toomay or Blaine Nye, assumed a prone position and did nothing. To do *something* would have violated their by-laws, if they ever had any. Their motto was *Apathy über alles*, which you immediately recognize as the famous old German cry "Apathy above everything."

Occasionally Toomay or Nye would speak forth on the healthgiving qualities of inertia but Cole rarely said anything. Mostly he would lie on his back and roll his eyes and, over his 13 seasons, became quite proficient at this.

These meetings were faithfully chronicled by our man Frank Luksa, who himself is not adverse to sprawling horizontally and studying a fleecy cloud or two. Says it affords him deep insight about the mystery of professional football and also is pretty good for the sinus. So *he* says. Frankly I have never found it so, especially about the sinus.

The Zero Clubbers were never asked for autographs nor photographed nor interviewed.

They were convinced they were destined to spend their football careers unrecognized by the public and maybe even by coaches and teammates and this was quite all right by them. In anonymity, there is peace. Not much money, but peace.

In a way, I presume, all three have betrayed their fraternity. Toomay deserted oblivion when he wrote a book and put his own name on it, an act that frequently calls attention to oneself. He lives in our midst, has a raven on his windowsill and is writing like mad on other tomes.

Nye quit the Cowboys in his prime, making modest headlines that destroyed his anonymity. This surprised him greatly. He thought no one would notice his *absence*, because they never noticed his *presence*. Blaine had all sorts of graduate degrees, in physics and things, and he is off in California probably making nuclear bombs, hopefully for our side.

But Cole's fall is the topper of all. He pulled it Sunday, flaunted it even, there in the Cowboys' lethargic 14–10 edging of the downtrodden Washingtons.

Bubba is going into the *record* book, for heaven sakes. He will never be anonymous again. His name will live forever. I mean, this is like having a disease named for you.

L-a-r-r-y C-o-l-e, scrubbed of its incognito, will be inscribed in Cowboy history right there alongside Bob Lilly, the founder of defensive football as we know it today.

Most touchdowns by a defensive lineman: Four!

The fourth came in the fourth quarter at Texas Stadium, and it was decorated with distinction. When Randy White jerked Redskin passer Mike Kruczek groundward and the ball plopped pitifully into the air, suspended and helpless like a clay pigeon, there was our man Bubba careening along in White's impressive wake.

He captured it with a rare technique. First he butted it with his face guard just to show the dang thing who was boss. Then he bounced it off his taped hands.

"I finally trapped it with all my thumbs," he said, forming a bushel basket with his hams. And then he seized the thing in his right paw like a loaf of Mrs. Baird's finest rye bread and set a course of approximately 345 degrees.

He was forced to demonstrate 187 times for all us serious historians who assaulted him in clustered shifts after the game. He thought it rather amusing that so much ado was made of his deed. His words were polite enough but there was laughter just under the surface. After all, he said in an aside, it's not as if it were the *first* time it's happened.

Cole ran his prize 43 strides into the end zone, much in the manner of a logging train.

"The first thing I thought when I saw those old bow legs start moving," said Randy White, "was HE'S GONNA MAKE A TOUCHDOWN!"

"When I got to the 15," said Cole, "I thought, 'Could it be? Could it be?'"

Next, his biggest concern was dodging congratulating teammates so he could make his almighty left-hand spike. "I thought about doing one of those Billy Johnson waddles in the end zone," he said, "but I probably would have thrown my back out."

Larry's fourth touchdown is even more memorable because it sent Dallas ahead 14–3, a cushion that survived a late Redskin score.

And even more—because all four of his touchdowns have come against Washington. The first three came in his first four games against the Redskins, a century or so ago.

"I'd like to hear the Vegas odds on *that*," he said blissfully. But then Larry realized he was in the spotlight.

"Hey, I'm out there with all those studs—Randy and Harvey Martin and Ed Jones. I'm just an old dog picking up their scraps. That was Randy's play today."

His act brought a gruff appraisal from a betrayed Zero Clubber.

"Any time Bubba Cole scores the winning touchdown for the Cowboys," said Toomay, "things aren't going right."

He was correct. It was not a day for the Cowboy scrapbook. It was sort of a nothing game. Somebody suggested, indeed it was a game for the Zero Club. It could be its highlight film.

"This is all entertainment business," said Cole. "I shot J.R., right?"

But it was no special surprise, even though it has been 11 long scoreless seasons since Cole pulled his last touchdown shenanigan.

"I had an eerie feeling all day long that I was going to score a touchdown. It's crazy to say that, but I did have this really eerie hunch. I guess because it was the Redskins."

Have you ever had that eerie feeling before?

"Yes."

And . . . ?

"It didn't happen," said the traitor.

*1980*

## JIM MURRAY

Jim Murray (1919–1998) turned the *Los Angeles Times*'s sports page into a comedy club with neither a ten-dollar cover nor a two-drink minimum. In the last four decades of the twentieth century, he wrote four, five, even six columns a week, churning out one-liners faster than a stand-up comic with his pants on fire. Every once in a while, Murray would invite readers into his personal life and deliver a column that was as heartfelt as it was unforgettable, but it was the laughs that kept readers coming back. His reward was a Pulitzer Prize, the business of the two hundred papers that ran his syndicated column, and the heart of L.A., a city supposedly without one. Even at the end, when his cultural references were as dated as a Stutz Bearcat, Murray remained a local institution, his great lines seemingly part of every conversation. He had a million of them.

★   ★   ★

# As White as the Ku Klux Klan

GREENSBORO—OK, rest easy, Jefferson Davis! Put down the gun, John Wilkes Booth. Let's hear a chorus of Dee-eye-ex-eye-eee! Run up the Stars and Bars. You won't have to blindfold that Confederate general's statue after all. Downtown Tobacco Road is still safe from the 20th century.

The Masters golf tournament is as white as the Ku Klux Klan. Everybody in it can ride in the front of the bus.

There's nothing the Supreme Court can do about it. Integration fell about 18 strokes or 20 Masters points short. Integration missed the cut.

The one break Charlie Sifford couldn't read and compensate for was the one which made him, like, an eighth-generation American, if only a third-generation free man. "Only in America," as the fellow says. Twenty golf champions had a clear shot at redressing a longtime wrong but they drove it in the deep rough. They double-bogeyed a chance to do something for golf, for themselves, for their country.

Charlie Sifford should have been Chinese, I guess, instead of Carolinian. An accident of birth keeps his clubs in the trunk of the car this week.

The circumstances are well known, but I will recount them briefly here, to the accompaniment of the *Battle Hymn of the Republic* and a recitation of the Gettysburg Address.

Charlie Sifford is a golfer, an American, a gentleman. He is not, however, a Caucasian. Until 1961, this seriously interfered with his life, liberty, and pursuit of happiness, to say nothing of his occupation—because golf was a "Members Only" club till then. They didn't publish the 14th Amendment in *Golf Digest*. It wasn't covered under the "free drop" rule.

Charlie was almost 40 years old before he got to play with the big boys. You can make book Arnold Palmer couldn't have overcome a handicap like that. You would have thought the other guys would give him two-a-side at first, just to be fair.

Charlie didn't need them. Even though some tournaments still had the bedsheet on—retreating behind the "invitational only" subterfuge, Charlie had become dangerous competition. He won two important tournaments, the Hartford and Los Angeles. If you think that's easy, you don't know golf. If you think that's even possible (with Charlie's late start), you're an optimist.

Now, the Masters is an unusual tournament. It was Bobby Jones' dream—and a man is entitled to do in his dreams what he wishes. What Bobby wished was to make it a sort of glorious annual reunion for certified legends of the game—never mind that some of them became fossilized.

The country took to the tournament. So did the world. Golf journalists from two continents wrote tone poems about the course. It became a "bonus" event. Winning it was like getting a seat on the Stock Exchange.

Bobby had to change it—or it would've become known as the "Fossils" instead of the "Masters." He kept six positions for non-legends, touring pros who never made any of the rich-kid amateur teams, guys who might leave their spoons in their coffee while they drank.

The Masters didn't *bar* black people. Frankly, it wasn't thought necessary. In fact, it did let them carry the bags.

Now, one way you can get in the Masters is by winning the championship of Formosa or making a good showing at Kuala Lumpur. Plus, you can be *invited* by a vote of former champions.

Former champions have often voted out of sentiment. Cronies who had fallen on evil days—to say nothing of in sand traps and lateral water hazards—got in on this kind of pass.

As a two-time tour winner, a guy who had been a victim of 20 years of injustice, and a surrogate for his people who have been victims of 200 years of same, it occurred to me, a sense of shame might have directed that vote to Charlie Sifford this year. Charlie is not *any* black man, and this would not be tokenism, he is a tour winner under circumstances as adverse as for any athlete who ever lived. Like a Bulgarian immigrant getting in a spelling bee.

Art Wall Jr.—and let's hear it for him!—voted for Charlie Sifford. As far as I know, that gave Charlie a total of one. The other guys voted for Bob Murphy.

Now, I'm all for the Irish. But we've been in the country clubs for a long time now. Not as long as West Virginians, to be sure, but long enough.

What's more, Bob Murphy was already safely in the Masters! He was second on a point list that would admit all the way through six! It was like sending money to Rockefeller or rice to China.

The Masters invites select foreigners, as noted. The official position of the Masters is that they "allow ourselves a bit more latitude with foreign players because, in most cases, they do not have the opportunity to prove themselves against USA players."

How's that again, fellows?! Who was more "foreign" than Charlie Sifford till he was over 40? He could play if he was raised on a camel or a fjord or a castle in Spain. In a tobacco patch in Carolina, no.

But, pshaw! He had an unnatural advantage: He was raised in America.

Charlie had one last chance down here at Greensboro. At the age of 46, all he had to do was beat out this field of 141 young studs. Charlie threw a 74 at the course in the opening round. On this easy track it might as well be 94.

Charlie signed his scorecard, then turned and said to this reporter bitterly: "Now they can keep their tournament down there lily-white."

Wait a minute, Charlie! You forgot the caddies.

*1969*

★   ★   ★

# If You're Expecting One-Liners

OK, BANG the drum slowly, professor. Muffle the cymbals. Kill the laugh track. You might say that Old Blue Eye is back. But that's as funny as this is going to get.

I feel I owe my friends an explanation as to where I've been all these weeks. Believe me, I would rather have been in a press box.

I lost an old friend the other day. He was blue-eyed, impish, he cried a lot with me, laughed a lot with me, saw a great many things with me. I don't know why he left me. Boredom, perhaps.

We read a lot of books together, we did a lot of crossword puzzles together, we saw films together. He had a pretty exciting life. He saw Babe Ruth hit a home run when we were both 12 years old. He saw Willie Mays steal second base, he saw Maury Wills steal his 104th base. He saw Rocky Marciano get up. I thought he led a pretty good life.

One night a long time ago he saw this pretty lady who laughed a lot, played the piano and he couldn't look away from her. Later he looked on as I married this pretty lady. He saw her through 34 years. He loved to see her laugh, he loved to see her happy.

You see, the friend I lost was my eye. My good eye. The other eye, the right one, we've been carrying for years. We just let him tag along like Don Quixote's nag. It's been a long time since he could read the number on a halfback or tell whether a ball was fair or foul or even which fighter was down.

So, one blue eye is missing and the other misses a lot.

So my best friend left me, at least temporarily, in a twilight world where it's always 8 o'clock on a summer night.

He stole away like a thief in the night and he took a lot with him. But not everything. He left a lot of memories. He couldn't take those with him. He just took the future with him and the present. He couldn't take the past.

I don't know why he had to go. I thought we were pals. I thought the things we did together we enjoyed doing together. Sure, we cried together. There were things to cry about.

But it was a long, good relationship, a happy one. It went all the way back to the days when we arranged all the marbles in a circle in the dirt in the lots in Connecticut. We played one o'cat baseball. We saw curveballs together, trying to hit them or catch them. We looked through a catcher's mask together. We were partners in every sense of the word.

He recorded the happy moments, the miracle of children, the beauty of a Pacific sunset, snow-capped mountains, faces on Christmas morning. He allowed me to hit fly balls to young sons in uniforms two sizes too large, to see a pretty daughter march in halftime parades.

He allowed me to see most of the major sports events of our time. I suppose I should be grateful that he didn't drift away when I was 12 or 15 or 29 but stuck around over 50 years until we had a vault of memories. Still, I'm only human. I'd like to see again, if possible, Rocky Marciano with his nose bleeding, behind on points and the other guy coming.

I guess I would like to see a Reggie Jackson with the count 3 and 2 and the Series on the line, guessing fastball. I guess I'd like to see Rod Carew with men on first and second and no place to put him, and the pitcher wishing he were standing in the rain someplace, reluctant to let go of the ball.

I'd like to see Stan Musial crouched around a curveball one more time. I'd like to see Don Drysdale trying not to laugh as a young hitter came up there with both feet in the bucket.

I'd like to see Sandy Koufax just once more facing Willie Mays with a no-hitter on the line. I'd like to see Maury Wills with a big lead against a pitcher with a good move. I'd like to see Roberto Clemente with the ball and a guy trying to go from first to third. I'd like to see Pete Rose sliding into home head-first.

I'd like once more to see Henry Aaron standing there with that quiet bat, a study in deadliness. I'd like to see Bob Gibson scowling at a hitter as if he had some nerve just to pick up a bat. I'd like to see Elroy Hirsch going out for a long one from Bob Waterfield, Johnny Unitas in high-cuts picking apart a zone defense. I'd like to see Casey Stengel walking to the mound on his gnarled old legs to take the pitcher out, beckoning his gnarled old finger behind his back.

I'd like to see Sugar Ray Robinson or Muhammad Ali giving a recital, a ballet, not a fight. Also, to be sure, I'd like to see a sky full of stars, moonlight on the water, and yes, the tips of a royal flush peaking out as I fan out a poker hand, and yes, a straight two-foot putt.

Come to think of it, I'm lucky. I saw all of those things. I see them yet.

*1979*

★  ★  ★

# All-Time Greatest Name

THERE HAVE been lots of great names in baseball history. Napoleon Lajoie (pronounced "Lash-oh-way"), Grover Cleveland Alexander, the only guy in the game with either three first names or three last names, "Germany" Schaefer, "Dummy" Hoy, "Ping" Bodie, Sibby Sisti. And Cletus Elwood Poffenberger and William Adolph Wambsganss weren't bad.

But, for sheer unadulterated alliteration, the all-time baseball name belongs to Van Lingle Mungo. You can't even say it, you've got to sing it. It sounds like something a guy would be singing from the rigging of a banana boat coming into port, or like the rumblings of a steel band. It's part calypso, part hog-call. The consonants just tinkle along like a runaway calliope.

A tunesmith was so taken with the sound of it, he wrote a whole song around it, making Van Mungo the only big league player I know of other than Joe DiMaggio to get a song written about him.

There will be a lot of big stars at the annual Old-timers Game at Dodger Stadium this Sunday. DiMag will be there. Willie Mays, Sandy Koufax, Duke Snider and Henry Aaron will, too. But, the really big excitement will be the presence of the man whose name is a song, Van Lingle Mungo.

The reasons are quite personal. You see, whenever I come across the name Van Lingle Mungo, immediately I'm 40 years younger. In fact, it's a hot day in the '30s and I'm seated in the bleachers in a ball-park in Hartford, Connecticut. The mighty Hartford Senators are playing a July 4 doubleheader against the dreaded, despised, treacherous New Haven Profs for the Eastern League first-half championship.

Justice is triumphing because, on the mound for the home nine is the invincible Van Lingle Mungo, the best pitcher ever to throw in that league, the possessor of an unhittable fastball and a curve that swoops over the plate like a diving pelican. He strikes out 12 of the villainous New Havens that day, including their vaunted superstar from Yale, the footballer-turned-baseball player, Bruce Caldwell, three times. Hartford wins the pennant by 11½ games. There is joy in Mudville and the sun is shining bright in Bulkeley Stadium.

Why is it the heroes of our youth are always more mythic, larger than life, than those we acquire later in life? Aren't you sure that senators and presidents and ministers were better when you were a boy? Don't you secretly think Dempsey and Louis were really the *last* heavyweight champions? Weren't Gable and Cagney *stars*? And players in films today just actors? Weren't the winters colder, summers hotter, days longer, nights darker, then? Hasn't the world shrunk since you grew up?

So it was with Van Mungo and me. He and Jimmie Foxx, the slugger, were genuine, 14-karat legit bubble gum card carriers' heroes. No one has quite made it since.

Van Mungo didn't make the Hall of Fame. His lifetime record was a so-so 120-won, 115-lost. You say "so-so" until you understand Van Lingle took his fastball and smoking curve onto one of the most pathetic of major league rosters. The Brooklyn Dodgers of the '30s were known journalistically as "The Daffiness Boys," "The Flatbush Follies" and other riotus epithets. Mungo lost a no-hit game once with two outs in the ninth when the second baseman dropped a pop fly. "The *scorer* ruled it a hit because the sun got in his eyes," Mungo recalls.

Mungo twice won 18 games with this collection of comedians and twice won 16 games. The club was mired in the second division throughout that decade, but Mungo was a workhorse, usually pitching well over 300 innings. He usually led the league in games started—38 one season, 37 another—and finished 22 of them each year. He led the league in strikeouts one year (1936) when the club finished next to last.

The Dodgers of the era had a lot of players nicknamed "Rabbit," to give you an idea of their power and, even in their bandbox ballpark, the team leader in homers in 1936 had exactly four. Mel Ott, by himself, hit more home runs than Van Mungo's Dodgers.

No less an authority than Billy Herman, a Hall of Fame second baseman who batted against the likes of Dizzy Dean, Bob Feller, Lefty Gomez, Lefty Grove and Lon Warneke, says, "I think Van Lingle Mungo was possibly the fastest pitcher I ever saw."

I talked to the fastest pitcher Herman ever saw by phone down at his farm in Pageland, South Carolina, where he said he was sitting on his porch watching the bulldozers turn his old farm into condominiums. He remembered the old Hartford Senators well, he said, if not the kid in the bleachers.

"We had a better team down there than the one I went to in Brooklyn," he recalls. "I always thought they called them 'Dodgers' in Brooklyn because of the way they dodged fly balls. Only, sometimes, they didn't. Sometimes the balls hit them in the head."

Van Mungo says he never expected to have songs written about him like *Sweet Sue* or *Sweet Adeline*. "But I got out of baseball because of ulcers. I got five of them. I got 'em in service during the war, but the Army didn't buy that. They just said I ought to of chewed my food better."

Did he wish he had been traded to a contending club? "Well, I would have liked that. In my prime, that is. I went to the Giants late, after the war. You see, I always got to pitch against the big boys. I always got Dean, Hubbell, Vander Meer, Warneke and Schumacher. Those fellows. I pitched the game that knocked the Giants out of the pennant in 1934 after their manager, Bill Terry, had asked, 'Is Brooklyn still in the league?' Beat 'em, 5–1. They clocked my fastball at 109 miles an hour in those days. I tell you, it sang on the way to the plate."

Naturally, Van Lingle Mungo is the only pitcher in the history of the game whose name and fastball were both hummers.

*1980*

## SANDY GRADY

When Larry Merchant was preaching revolution as the *Philadelphia Daily News*'s sports editor, one of his first hires was a wordsmith out of North Carolina named Sandy Grady (1927–2015). The idea was to infuse the home of the Liberty Bell and the cheesesteak with Grady's southern lyricism. He was such a hit that two years after his arrival in 1957, the city's *Evening Bulletin* hired him away from the *News* and made him a columnist. It was an era when native son Wilt Chamberlain cast his seven-foot shadow across basketball, the Warriors and Eagles won championships, and the 1964 Phillies flopped infamously. Grady captured it all with high style and velvet-shiv humor. Then, in 1970, he walked away from sports and returned to the *News* to write a Washington column for the rest of his career. But even after his death, there were still Philadelphians who would tell you their favorite sports columnist was Sandy Grady.

★　★　★

# Cool World of Basketball's Wilt

*By the river . . . 'neath the sha-dy tree,*
*Just my baby . . . Ju-hust my baby and me,*
*We hug—kiss—cuddle close,*
*By the river, 'neath the shady tree.*

W ITH THOSE immortal lyrics, basketball's biggest day since the peach basket arrived. Wilt Chamberlain, having left the NBA a smoking, wrecked captive nation in 53 easy games, was naturally restless for new continents to enslave. What, indeed, remained but American Bandstand?

Promptly at 3:30, Ghengis Khan arrived in his honey-beige convertible at the TV studio. Wilt was obviously ready for this new opponent. His black pants were creased sharp as a butcher's blade. Mustache trimmed. Larynx ready for battle.

There were preliminary, warmup squeals from about 75 goose-pimpled nymphlets waiting in the Market St. cold. Wilt's purposeful stride carried him past the squeakers, into the office of Dick Clark's producer. Already in the main studio, rock 'n' roll litany had started, punctuated by a voice saying, "No gum, kids; drop your gum at the door."

Wilt sat on a low couch, relaxed as an old razor strop, talking proudly of his record sales. "I hear they've been sold out in Philadelphia for five days. They're pressing a fresh batch. I may cut a new one. My family's always laughed at me singing. I did this just to make 'em stop laughing."

In the arena, the battlefield was ready. It is a surprisingly small room, lights hanging like sausages in a meat house, cables and cameras everywhere, Dick Clark in pancake makeup ruling the dais, about 150 youthful music lovers squirming in the bleachers along one wall. "Now we're going to have one of the great athletes of all time," Clark instructed his cub pack, while film clips of Wilt flitted across a monitor screen.

At 4.16 the blue curtains parted and Wilt Chamberlain met American youth. Like Wilt vs. Bill Russell, this was no contest. American youth succumbed without a fight. There was a mighty squeal, as if a flock of field mice had invaded a girls' locker room. Clark, visibly impressed, looked up at Wilt like the first explorer who sighted Pikes Peak.

"Look at Wilt," said a balding producer. "The guy's got it. He loves this stuff."

Casual, towering, glittering in his miraculous coat—a five-button, tweed Chesterfield with black satin lapels, big enough to fit Spooky Cadet, Wilt's horse—Chamberlain had the juveniles bedazzled. Then his fingers snapped. His body swayed. This was the tap-off . . .

*By the river . . . 'neath the sha-dy tree,*
*Just my baby . . . Ju-hust my baby and me,*
*We sing—cling—everything,*
*By the river, 'neath the shady tree.*

The squealers hit their highest Cs when Wilt began a stylish shuffle to the rhythm, rocking gracefully as a hook shot. Wilt fast-broke into the last chorus, then signed autographs behind a fake soda fountain while the Bandstanders danced—a mob scene in which tots grapple for camera position while wearing cataleptic stares.

"Boy, that was a weird feeling," Clark told a producer during the candy commercial. "I tried to interview the guy standing up (Clark's 5'9") and he was out of sight."

"Now you know how Russell feels."

While the dolls in short skirts and lads in duck haircuts wrestled to the strains of "Chattanooga Shoeshine Boy," Wilt ambled out to make the plane to Syracuse. "I like the other side of the record, 'That's Easy to Say,' much better," said the artist. "I try to sound a little like Lloyd Price. He's the greatest."

"Where did you pick up the dance steps, Wilt?"

"Oh, I used to do that for a few bucks at Kutsher's. You know, samba, rhumba, fancy stuff. One night Guy Rodgers and I got the floor at the Copa and wowed 'em. Oh, I'm a tough dancer, man. No defense can stop me."

Rumbling with laughter, a rock 'n' roll album under his arm, shaking the hands of teen-age idolators, he fled down the corridor. It had been another day in the cool, unlimited world of Wilt Chamberlain.

*Ev-ery Sunday . . . by the bright sunshine,*
*Chicken in the basket . . . all the time;*
*Then in the evenin', when the sun goes down,*
*We hold tight, strollin' back to town.*

*1960*

★ ★ ★

# A Visit to Managers' Terrace

NOW, IN that elegant ballyard phrase, The Lump Is Coming Up, the famed Big Apple called fear. Someone is choking, and it seems fair to name the culprits.

Oh, not John Callison, who swears he doesn't give a hoot for magic numbers. Not Wes Covington, whose cold malevolence toward that right-field scoreboard may yet make it kindling wood. Not Rich Allen, who would laugh if caught in a paddleless canoe in a typhoon. Not Gene Mauch, who thinks pressure is a word for hydraulic engineers, not his brave, noble pros.

The fans are running scared. There were 20,067 anxiety cases in the Connie Mack snakepit last night, and that means 40,134 sweaty palms and shaky knees. A man touring the grandstand had not heard such groaning and cussing and screeching since the last Italian movie. You can't blame the burghers, who remember 1950, a year most of the Phils spent in Algebra I.

They piled out of the parking lots this crisp night, laughing like kids arriving at a wiener roast. There was a fat moon over Lehigh Av., the Phils had a six-and-a-half game lead and all was perfect in the Mauchian world. By 11 P.M., having watched John Tsitouris torment the Phils, 1–0, they hit the sidewalk with the tight mouths, like people who had seen a train hit a car.

It was all splendid until Cincinnati's Chico Ruiz stole home in the sixth. The ladies waved their Phillies pennants as pertly as U. of Miami cheerleaders swing pom poms, and you've never seen so many guys in Phillies souvenir caps whooping it up. A guy in Lower Section 18 blew a bugle, and it was fun to yell "Charge!" Then suddenly there were a lot of 50¢ hoagies and 25¢ pizza slices jammed in constricted throats.

They began snarling at each batter who lurched hopelessly toward John Tsitouris, who has the pitching motion of your Aunt Maud swatting a mosquito, which made it worse. They booed Art Mahaffey, who left the game biting a fingernail thoughtfully, having heard this music before. They booed each other when customers dropped foul balls. Only in Philadelphia.

But to savor the deep, mortal terror of the last innings, you had to visit the Managers' Terrace. This is the concrete half-moon running behind the box seat-reserved seats, where about 500 guys stand to watch through mesh wire. They manage every inning, and if that idiot Mauch would listen to them he would be 20 games ahead.

These are weather-beaten types, smoking cigars with the name bands left on, wearing colored jackets bearing the names of their bowling teams—"Bombers" or "Champions, 1958." Some of them have malformed left arms from holding the voice of By Saam close to their ears. On Managers' Terrace, though, there are no silly pennants or "Go, Phillies, Go" pins. It has been a hard, weary season for them, and there is no time for jazzy ostentation when you are managing a pennant club.

For the last three innings, they were in trouble on the Managers' Terrace. They wanted a run off Tsitouris profoundly. They tried everything. Three of them, who were observed managing desperately, will be called The Minister, The Advisor and The Judge.

The minister prayed to each Phillies deity for deliverance from suffering. He opened the sixth by pleading for mercy from Wes Covington: "C'mon, Wes baby, please get a hit off'n this bum." The Advisor was quick with solid counsel: "Step outta the box and make him nervous, Wes, then knock one off the wall." Covington heard him, and did it. Then John Herrnstein struck out, and The Judge delivered his verdict: "Herrnstein, you no-good bum, I'm gonna send you to Little Rock and bring up Shockley."

The Judge seemed fair about each case. Going to Little Rock was like being sentenced to Eastern Penitentiary, but The Judge was coldly dispassionate about Herrnstein's crime.

The Minister begged Mahaffey not to walk the bases loaded in the seventh. The Advisor yelled to Mauch to get Bobby Locke in there, which Mauch did, thank heavens. The Judge sent Mahaffey to the Three-I League, where he will only be allowed to pitch on Halloween and Lincoln's Birthday.

There was a scary moment in the ninth, because Bobby Shantz pitched well, and The Judge was tempted to fire Mauch for not starting Shantz. There was deep, mute fright down in the stands, though, where people—they often pronounced his name like a sneeze—were saying, "Boy, that Tsitouris is an inhuman machine." They knew his name on Managers' Terrace, okay. They called him Tourist, Curious or Zurich.

They managed hard in the last of the ninth. The Minister beseeched Covington, and got a head-first double. The Advisor told Tony Taylor to walk on a 3–2 count, which he did. Ruben Amaro struck out to end it, and The Judge said with a magisterial rue, "I'm gonna put that bum in the Little League until he learns to swing a bat."

The mob, suddenly pale and aghast, moved slowly out the wickets. "C'mon, Phils, and I can't stand much more of this—you gotta wrap it up," entreated The Minister. "Next time Mauch should know better," said The Advisor. "He's gotta bunt or steal the run like the Reds did."

On the portables, By Saam's voice was saying regretfully that Tsitouris had pitched a wonderful game.

"That Saam would go to a hanging," said The Judge, "and call it wonderful. The bums are gonna blow it if they don't look out."

The moon over Lehigh Av. slid ominously behind a cloud as the worried burghers hit the parking lots. The guys from Managers' Terrace chomped their cigars dourly and said they would now play it one game at a time.

*1964*

★　★　★

# The Mob Hit .000

I N AN hour there would be a fight. Not many thought so, though. Under the shabby Garden marquee, the heat and hot dog fumes were thick as gauze. The mob, shirts circled with sweat, ties hung slack, pale skin beaded, milled in the 8th Avenue gloom like moths suspended from a July streetlamp.

Two cabs smacked doors and the mob watched the debate through hooded, dull eyes. It was 95 degrees under the marquee, and $5 could get a pew in the (slightly) air-conditioned Garden. On display were Joe-ee Archuh and Eh-mil Griffit', but the mob had an unchampionship view. . . .

"Gotta be a nothin' fight, Griffit' is lazy. Archuh is a cutie. Nobody come to fight nobody."

And: "If it's close, Archuh steals it. He'll have all the Irish raisin' hell for him. They'll give it to the bum."

And: "All Archuh can do is run and hope. The bum ain't in shape to go 15. He'll run out of gas. Hey, you evah see Mickey Walker fight?"

No, but Walker was wrong too, if that's any comfort. After the curbside dialectics, 13,176 paid their way past the perspiring Pinkertons. If they were dodging the heat, the 13,176 only found more inside the ring, where Archer and Griffith nearly blew every fuse in Manhattan. It was the best fight in years, and the mob blew points one, two and three. The mob hit .000.

They were accurate on only one minor point. The Garden was wild for Joey, Joey, Joey. It's the only pep rally I've ever attended for a busted-beak, high-school dropout. "Let's go, Jo-ey!" the chant began when Archer revealed his Irish-green britches. Later, whooping for every Archer jab, every Archer escape from a rope-side fusillade, they reminded me of Mets' fans—you know, the New Breed kids, ecstatic over a double play, knowing they'll be doomed in the ninth inning.

Not that I could really hear Archer's Army. Sorry, chief. Two rows back sat most of Griffith's relatives. Sat is a bad verb. Emelda, Emile's momma whom he calls Chubby Checkers, was bouncing and shouting in a black floppy hat. Cousin Bernard was putting a loud voodoo on Archer. And eight sweaty cops encircled them when the Irish began yelling insults. But everybody was grinning. It was that kind of night.

And when it happened, Archer was all the publicity guys promised him, with those big yellow posters, "Last Chance for the Irish!" He was in the Corbett and Tunney and Conn image, looking frail with an aura of courage. Even at eight pounds lighter, Griffith seemed more menacing, powerful, muscles bunched, a bulldog with a greyhound. "Let's go, Joe-ee!" they sang in the darkened arena, and Archer did, astonishing them.

When he had walked out of the midtown hotel with his brother Jimmy—once his idol, once a fighter, now his manager, long hair yellow—Archer said, "Okay, all or nothin'." For a guy who knows percentages, who owns stocks and Charlai cattle and small-time real estate, he threw it all away for a gambling hour. After the second round, Archer put it all on the table. He went for Griffith's head, and Emile sensed the game, and what ensued was a dialogue through the 15th round, glittering, thoughtful, desperate. Splash! went the hooks, and small showers of sweat flew in the lights.

Archer's body was reddened by the pounding, then the color TV was enriched by a cut high over his right eye, Hollywoodish, harmless. Both of them were trying for home runs, but Griffith was connecting most often. Now Emile tried to slash and swipe at the cut in the ninth, and the Archer buffs' boos rang in the dark. "Stick and move," said Joey's brother classically. He did too, floating, jabbing, enjoying a couple of rounds that had the balcony's wild approval, but everyone knew Joey had to win the last three.

"Good round for Archer," said one press-row thinker, keeping score. "Good round for Griffith, you mean," said another. "Good round for everybody," said a third, because the Garden was caught now in the rhythm of their small war. And in the ring of cops, her big hat ajar,

Momma Emelda was yelling, "Take your time, son. Finish him off, son. That's my son, everybody." I had Emile ahead 8–7 on the edge of the last round, but the debates will last until the inevitable rematch.

"He butted me and it oughta cost him," said Archer, surrounded by the Irish Mafia, mouths like downturned parentheses. "Yeah, I'll fight him again. I won this one 9–5."

Judges and Griffith disagreed. "If I butt him, I'm sorry. It was a punch," said Emile, oddly subdued. "No I was never dizzy. Why you say he hurt me? He never did. When they yell for Joey, he take more chances. Better for me. Hey, he's a wonderful boxer. . . ."

Past the dives and pawnshops and juice stands of 8th Avenue, the mob poured now. Who won? In the electric guitar blare where the Caribbean backers did 7,000 versions of the Watusi, it was Griffith. By the long oak bars owned by names such as McGrogan and Donnelly and Slattery, it was Archer.

Nobody was left under the lightless marquee of the Garden now. The hot dog stand went dark, and the cabs hissed past, and the air turned cooler. It was also that kind of night.

*1966*

## PETER FINNEY

Peter Finney's sports column was as much a part of the New Orleans experience as the music of Professor Longhair and a po' boy at Dome-liese's. For sixty-eight years, on the *States, States-Item,* and *Times-Picayune,* Finney (1927–2016) captured the improbable highs and mind-bending lows of every legal game that could be found in his good-timing hometown. He grew up in the French Quarter, was an altar boy at St. Louis Cathedral, graduated from Jesuit High School and Loyola University, and got the story no one else could about Billy Cannon's historic Halloween night run for LSU in 1959. Finney always asked the right questions but never with malice aforethought. He was too nice a guy for malice even when Saints fans protested their team's gross incompetence by wearing paper bags over their heads. "All I do is write," he said. "I've never had to work a day in my life." No wonder he was always smiling.

★  ★  ★

# "Bounced Right into My Arms": Cannon Planned to Let It Roll

B ATON ROUGE—Let's just start by saying that's the way the ball bounces.

There was a moment of excruciating suspense when 67,500 souls fixed their eyes on the red handkerchief after Billy Cannon's classic 89-yard touchdown rumble Saturday night.

But then the referee's arms went up, and a thunderous cheer split the heavens. . . . Ole Miss was in motion . . . and the score would be OK: the Tigers 7 and the Rebels 3.

That was enough to shake strong hearts . . . but think of the outbreak of seizures had Cannon announced to the multitude his thoughts as Jake Gibbs' 47-yard fourth-quarter kick fell out of the skies.

"Until the last second, I wasn't going to play that punt," said Cannon. "I was going to let it roll. . . . Gibbs didn't kick this one as long as the others, and it was sort of dribbling toward me.

"Ole Miss was covering well, and I didn't feel like taking chances. . . . I had fumbled already and given 'em three points.

"But then, right at the end, the ball took a high bounce and fell right into my arms. . . . I took two steps forward and started running."

Movies of perhaps the finest clutch run in SEC history give the lie to Cannon's postgame modesty that "all the credit should go to the blockers."

True to some extent, Billy received two vital blocks—one from Lynn LeBlanc and one from Ed McCreedy.

But the film clearly shows Cannon being hit a half-dozen times along his treacherous route down the sideline past the Ole Miss bench.

The first tackler cracked at the 20-yard line, the second at the 23 and two more at the 25.

At the 30, end Jerry Daniels made contact and Cannon carried him 5 yards, where he was hit once again.

A heroic figure in defeat, Gibbs made a valiant try at a shoestring job at midfield . . . Cannon shook him off.

"I knew I had it around the Ole Miss 30," he said. "When I saw Johnny Robinson looking back for someone to block, I felt this was it . . . just don't stub your toe. . . ."

Cannon claimed he was oblivious to the tremendous roar accompanying his journey.

"But once I crossed the goal line, I kinda got tuned in all of a sudden and seemed to hear everyone at once. . . . I got hit hard in the game, but not much harder than by those guys who jumped me in the end zone. . . . I was lucky to get out alive."

"It was the finest run I've ever seen since I've been in football," said a breathless Paul Dietzel, LSU's coach. "No back in the country could have made that run except Billy Cannon."

That, of course, was the salient part of 1959's "game of the year."

The concluding chapter of this "made in Hollywood" spectacular was LSU's third goal-line stand of the evening.

In the first quarter, Cannon fumbled after a 15-yard thrust, and Ole Miss recovered on the LSU 31. The Rebs could get no farther than the 3 and, on fourth down, Bob Khayat booted a field goal from the 12.

A bobble shortly before halftime by fullback Earl Gros at the LSU 29 opened the door for a march to the 7, which was frustrated by the Chinese Bandits.

After Cannon's touchdown and Wendell Harris' extra point, Johnny Vaught called sophomore quarterback Doug Elmore from the bullpen, and starting on the Reb 32, he began making like an accomplished field general.

When Ole Miss pushed to the 23, Dietzel removed the Bandits and sent in the White team, which had a five-minute rest.

But the Rebs made them retreat to the 7, where they played a first-and-goal—a carbon copy of last year's situation in the second quarter.

Three plays carried Vaught's red-shirted marauders to the 2, but on fourth down, Elmore tried left end, where he was greeted first by Warren Rabb and then by Cannon.

The run died a yard short of immortality.

"I thought he'd try that rollout," said Rabb. "He ran the same play a few moments earlier and got a first down. . . . I moved over a little and was waiting."

Thirty-three seconds later, the game ended with LSU's goal-line still uncrossed after 38 quarters.

The Tigers' dressing room was a cross between a Turkish bath and the tunnel of love.

Dietzel's perspiring athletes were like a bunch of delirious school-boys, planting kisses with reckless abandon and embracing one another with bear hugs.

The most eloquent quote of the night came from Go team guard Mike Stupka, who came over and put his arm around the most exhausted Tiger of them all.

"Thank you, Billy," he whispered . . . and then went his way.

Don Purvis, clutching the game ball, said, "I wouldn't take a million dollars for this football. I mean it."

1959

★  ★  ★

# Just Call Me Gorgeous

"YOU'LL HAVE to excuse my appearance," said the fellow whose well-scarred dome was flanked by two cauliflower ears and topped with wavy, white locks. "Today is Sunday and all the beauty parlors are closed."

I had caught Gorgeous George with his hair down.

Rather than express outrage at such misfortune (Gorgeous also needed a manicure and his orchid shirt was a bit rumpled), he was all charm and candor.

In the course of an hour, you learned that the man who a decade ago built wrestling into a $36-million-a-year bonanza was part showman, businessman, historian and athlete.

Showmanship definitely takes preference.

The act he stages tomorrow night at the Municipal Auditorium blends cleanliness and color and, because it coincided with the advent of television, it launched the wrestling boom.

It begins when his valet, in cutaway, striped pants and derby, enters the ring carrying a silver tray on which rests a huge spray gun. A bath mat is draped around his arm.

After he sprays the ring, ropes and neighboring areas, George ("just call me Gorgeous") enters in a robe that stretches from his neck to the floor. His hair is in ringlets. As he walks, he inspects his manicure and sometimes tosses a golden bobby pin into an audience that is a mixture of cheers and catcalls.

The match begins, and always Gorgeous' curls become involved. The result is of no particular significance: sometimes he loses, most of the time he wins.

"Are all wrestling matches fixed?" I wanted to know.

"Well, you'd just as soon ask me if I beat my wife or lie on my income tax return," said Gorgeous.

"We're all entertainers, but don't you believe all the boys making top money can't wrestle. They've got scars to prove it. You look them over closely. I say they're athletes."

Financially, the top attractions are in the class with people like Williams, Musial, Mantle and Mays.

"I'll put it to you this way," says Gorgeous. "If I could have made the money I made and paid taxes like they used to back in the '30s, I'd be a multi-millionaire."

Wrestling revenue has bought Gorgeous a turkey ranch and three homes (all painted orchid) in California.

"I've been on all kinds of TV shows and I'm the only wrestler ever featured in a movie—*Alias the Champ*. The next project is a book on my life."

Gorgeous makes like a historian when he explains he is not the first long-haired wrestler to wander on the scene.

"We had four presidents—Washington, Lincoln, Buchanan and Teddy Roosevelt—who were wrestlers. Lincoln was a pro. He wrestled a guy named Jim Anderson here in New Orleans for $10. At least that's what Robert Reep says in his book, *Lincoln at New Salem*. Check me on it."

It was Washington's picture on the dollar bill that started Gorgeous on his curly locks trail.

It took the 43-year-old, 210-pound native of Seward, Neb., a long time, however, before he could make his buffoonery pay dividends.

He quit school at an early age and took odd jobs—packing strawberries, grinding oil well bits, repairing typewriters and chopping cotton.

He left home at 19, to wrestle for peanuts.

"Your hands were your breadwinners," he said. "Many a night I'd lay in a cheap hotel, hungry and broke, wishing I were home."

His rise began in 1941 in Eugene, Ore., when he decided to get a pair of royal blue trunks with sequins and a $250 robe purchased with his winnings. Both were startling departures from the customary sweat-stained garb of the day.

Some fans grabbed his neatly folded robe off his chair and tossed it all around the auditorium. By the time he got it back, it was in shreds. Gorgeous was so mad he challenged the whole house.

The fans raised a rumpus and suddenly George was in demand. It was at Eugene, too, that George heard a lady fan remark: "My, isn't he gorgeous?"

A bell rang—George Wagner had a first name.

The spray gun gimmick first appeared in Columbus, Ohio, because a doctor warned Gorgeous about a severe mat burn on his knee.

"It got so much attention when we were doing it merely to disinfect the ring as a safety measure that we decided to dress it up," George said. "Hence the valet."

Next step came one day in Honolulu when Gorgeous, bothered by his long hair getting in his eyes, decided to get a permanent. Three hundred people soon gathered outside the salon, and that night he was a sensation.

"Every 10 days," he says, "I need a touch-up job. I'm in every day for a wave, and that's $6 or $7 a crack, so I've got my overhead. Funny, huh?"

George the athlete, who idolizes Strangler Lewis, says he has mastered 90 holds—his favorite being the flying mare. In this one, he'll get a headlock, twist his legs and then jump in the air while spinning. This jerks his opponent off the ground—he falls—and Gorgeous falls on top.

It isn't always that simple. One night, Leo Nomellini, the former all-American tackle, threw a flying tackle at Gorgeous and rendered him unconscious.

"They carried me from the ring on a stretcher and, as I was moving through the crowd, all those irate husbands started kicking me—they're my biggest enemies."

Few are faster on the gimmick-uptake than Gorgeous. A while back he was a guest on the Jack Paar show and swore Paar into his fan club, making the comedian promise he would never mistake a "Georgie pin" for a common bobby pin.

The next night Paar walked off the show and headed for Hong Kong.

"Was it your perfume that drove him to the Orient?"

"No, never," he replied. "I use Chanel No. 10, you know. Why be half safe?"

*1960*

★   ★   ★

# It Could Have Been Worse . . .

N O, THERE have been worse disasters.
- In 1887, a flood in China left 900,000 dead.
- In 1556, an earthquake, also in China, killed 830,000.
- In 1737, an earthquake, this one in India, was responsible for 300,000 fatalities.

So keep this in mind when you contemplate the score—Tampa Bay 33, New Orleans 14. Keep in mind Johnstown, the Hindenburg, the Titanic. Little Big Horn.

Was not Tampa Bay the best 0–26 team in professional football?

Hadn't it already broken loose for three points in six home games this season?

Although the coach had complained his team could not score against a strong wind, who was to say it could not score, again and again and again, in the windless Superdome and controlled 70-degree weather?

Doesn't anyone believe in the law of averages?

And New Orleans hospitality?

The Buccaneers had suffered enough. They were beginning to give Jean Lafitte, Captain Hook and Long John Silver, not to mention Short John McKay, a bad name.

Ask yourself: Is there anything more saintly than losing to the worst team in the league, a 12-point underdog, by 19 points?

In their Monday Morning Quarterback Club, you may be sure Peter and Paul, Matthew, Mark, Luke and John are blessing their namesakes for playing the role of Good Samaritan.

"It's better to give than receive."

In this case, six interceptions, three of them accounting for all of the Bucs' points in the second half.

"Blessed are the meek."

In this case, a Saints' offense which kept giving Tampa the ball in the plus side of the field by not making a first down during the first 24 minutes.

"Allow others to do unto you what you have been trying to do unto others."

In this case, win.

"Blessed are the no-shows."

In this case, 4,140 missing from the crowd of 40,124.

Are you there, Hank Stram?

"No question this is the lowest I've ever been as a coach."

Stram said it with feeling and, in saying it, he spoke for the 11-year-old franchise.

Until yesterday, there were two other contenders in the race for what you might term abysmal milestones: a 62–7 loss to Atlanta in the opening game of '73, a 42–17 loss to Chicago to cap a 2–12 finish in '75.

Now the Bucs go to the head of the list.

"You can't believe how ready this team was to play before the game," Stram was saying. "They were raising so much hell in the dressing room, I thought some players were fighting.

"But we go out there and strangle by the thumb. As soon as they got those points, we could feel it. The longer we went without points, the more pumped up they became."

Even at halftime, down 0–13, Stram said the mood was good. But that changed in a hurry on the Saints' second play of the third period when Mike Washington picked off a Bobby Scott pass in the flat and scooted uncontested 45 yards.

"It was a quick out," explained John Gilliam. "The guy gambled and it paid off. If Bobby had checked, and then thrown, we would have had six instead of them."

But Scott had looked right and then turned and threw left—in one motion. He had no string on the ball, and the Bucs had all the points they needed.

In essence, the Saints lost this one weeks ago, when they began compiling a tome of breakdowns—offense, defense, special teams. They have found so many ways to lose, they expect to lose, which made it no surprise they began to press when the Bucs got out in front, 6–0.

You don't allow teams to run back punts all the way (Packers and Chargers), trick you on a fake field goal (Cards), hit the upright on placekicks (Packers and 49ers), return critical kickoffs into scoring position (Jets) without it taking its toll.

Hank Stram has not done what you would expect a coach to do: bring his team strongly down the stretch. It has been just the opposite.

While the Saints do not have the personnel of a contender, they have not executed with the kind of precision you expect from a franchise making even modest progress.

Where did Stram lose the handle this year? Has he been too soft? Too timid about making changes?

Those are questions Stram must ponder. Also, owner John Mecom Jr. will have to ask himself that in a post-season appraisal. Mecom left yesterday's game in the fourth quarter and headed for Florida—not Tampa.

"He will review the entire situation after the Atlanta game," explained one club official, looking ahead to the end of the season.

For now, the brightest news is the Saints' magic number is one.

1977

## JIM KLOBUCHAR

There was once a sports columnist in Minneapolis who moonlighted as unofficial general manager of the city's first NBA franchise, the pre–Los Angeles Lakers, which didn't say much for his paper's concern about conflict of interest. When Jim Klobuchar (b. 1928) became a columnist at the *Star*, he showed the town that a writer was better off by far if he wasn't in a team's pocket. Klobuchar was aggressive, opinionated, and, best of all, good. So good, in fact, that the sports page couldn't hold him and he became a general-interest columnist for what was now the *Star Tribune*. But on NFL Sundays, public demand brought him back to write about the Vikings, the team he had covered since its inception in 1961. Not many sportswriters develop that loyal a following. Even fewer raise a U.S. senator, but Klobuchar did—his daughter Amy.

★   ★   ★

# The Dragon vs. a Scrambling St. George

G REEN BAY, Wisconsin—Like Marley's Ghost in a camel-hair coat, he fulminated on the sidelines, fists beating the air, while non-immortals in the stadium quailed.

The image of Vince Lombardi in mid-fury in Green Bay was so terrifying it appeared for a moment the officials were going to cede him the island of Sicily as a gesture of conciliation.

Lombardi is the Green Bay Packer coach and as such has authority to tell the leaves when to fall and the officials when to drop their laundry in Green Bay.

Lombardi is tough enough to make Julius Caesar call for a fair catch.

But Sunday along came Francis Tarkenton of the Minnesota Vikings, and it was St. George versus the dragon all over again.

This is one of the recurring morality plays of the National Football League. Lombardi, as the ranking field marshal in the NFL, annually designs a defensive plan of exquisite beauty and resourceful scope, all intended to stop the Viking offense.

Tarkenton immediately scrambles it into a misshapen ruin, like a mischievous kid tumbling sand castles at the beach. This offends Lombardi's esthetic sensitivity and at times, like Sunday afternoon, wins the ball game for the Vikings.

But rarely do they meet head-to-head as they did Sunday in the pale yellow light of the NFL's version of the late show.

With the Vikings on offense in the first half, somebody dropped a penalty flag. Confusion overtook the officials.

"No. 77 is downfield," one of them howled.

Lombardi demanded a march-off against the Vikings. An official edged tentatively toward the Packer bench, but, not having received formal permission to address the coach, did not immediately speak.

Lombardi gestured toward the Viking goal line. The officials picked up the ball.

Tarkenton ran to them screaming.

"Who was downfield?" he demanded of an official.

"No. 77," somebody said.

"That guy," Tarkenton explained, "is wearing a green shirt. He belongs to the Packers. He can stay downfield all he wants. We're the guys on offense, and our No. 77 (Gary Larsen) is on the bench.

"Are you guys running the ball game or is Lombardi?"

Time elapsed agonizingly while everybody pondered the question. They finally bowed to the purity of Tarkenton's logic and let the play stand up.

It was one of those games, of course, which would have had everything if they had allowed the clock custodian a few more minutes at the controls. As it was, he nearly spilled into Ed Sullivan's time.

In the process he added a new dimension to the NFL's cast of characters, the scrambling timekeeper.

He got the usual inspiration from Tarkenton, who delivered the crucial play by running the Packer pursuit into the air-blowers and then waving to Jim Phillips before throwing. When Tarkenton waves once, it means the receiver should reverse field. When he waves twice, it means the receiver should run another 15 yards, cut between the tarpaulin and Gate 5, and come back toward the goal posts.

To Phillips, he waved four times, the maximum emergency wave.

"I already had run north, east, west and south," Phillips explained. "If he waved one more time I would have taken the river."

When it was over, Lombardi sat in his office, astonishingly controlled and forgiving. He was thoughtful and cordial to visitors, but you shuddered to think about the fate of the Packer defensive line on Tuesday.

He walked over to Norm Van Brocklin and addressed him pleasantly. Normally, when Van Brocklin and Lombardi meet, they hold their hands near their belts like Jack Palance and keep the wall behind them.

Van Brocklin has never made a production out of acknowledging his peers or superiors in the NFL, but Lombardi he respects, sometimes with a snarl and sometimes with a wisecrack. Sunday he did it with absolute humility.

"We beat," he told Lombardi, "the best."

"Your team played well," Lombardi said. "It's a credit to you, coach."

Van Brocklin would have given five grand for that on the market.

"Vince Lombardi," he told a pal, "has got class."

But downtown in Green Bay, they weren't so sure about the Packers.

In Green Bay, young couples don't whisper sweet endearments over candlelit dinners.

"Honey," a half-oiled brunette asked her date in the Tuxedo Bar, "what happened to the Packers?"

The guy said, "Sweetie, we just weren't getting that rush on Tarkenton. Now you got to give the Vikings credit. They're tough. I think they ought to become one of our traditional rivals."

"But we've only been playing the Vikings for six years," she said softly.

"Honey," the guy said, "the way Tarkenton does it to us, it's traditional."

I wandered into a downtown supper club and asked a waitress for directions. She was carrying a tray and tried to dodge. I dodged, too, but the wrong way and we bumped.

"How do you like that?" she said. "In Minneapolis, even the mashers scramble."

*1966*

★   ★   ★

# Joe Namath Slays the Knights

THERE IS an easy rhythm and ring to it, a sound of chivalry, as we link yet another new immortal today to the idols of our youth, Frank Merriwell, Sir Galahad, Tom Mix—and now Joe Namath.

I know there will be purists who argue that time has not yet confirmed Joe's right to enshrinement into this brotherhood of gallantry and good works. And that further, it is entirely possible that Joe would disrupt his investiture proceedings at the round table by claiming that he knows at least five knights who handle their lances better than Galahad and that Mix couldn't hold his liquor.

We may as well accept it. In 2½ hours of football Sunday, Joe dissolved the myths of centuries that had nurtured our simple faith in the ultimate triumph of virtue. At the very minimum, you grew up to expect virtue to get at least a tie, as symbolized by Ara Parseghian of Notre Dame two years ago and re-affirmed by Bud Grant a year ago.

But today, in the wash of Sunday's Super Bowl victory by the New York Jets over Baltimore and the National Football League, we have to take a hard look at all of our adolescent fantasies, swallow bravely and tell the kids of America:

"Well, at least he doesn't drink Scotch during the half, which ought to be a very good lesson to you on the benefits of sacrifice and self-discipline."

What we have here then is the prototype of a new vintage matinee hero, a Jack Armstrong on the rocks.

The fairy tales, my melancholy friends, are dead. The same thing would have happened if the sheriff outshot Robin Hood at the annual hole-in-one archery festival on the downs. Namath beating the Colts, tradition and Jimmy the Greek of Vegas, all in 2½ hours, is no less shattering to mankind's ongoing belief in justice-with-mercy than Perry Mason losing to Hamilton Berger.

How are you going to explain it to the kids? You might as well tell them that Bob Richards is a tobacco auctioneer on the side or that Vern Gagne wears falsie biceps.

The whole concept of the morality play in the movies, on television and on the playing field may have to be revised in the light of Joe's conquest on Sunday. The Dodge boys will switch to dark hats. Bud Wilkinson might have to go to snuff. You will have to take your 8-year-old aside for a manly dialogue and inform him quite frankly: "Percy, the ball game IS over before the final whistle, especially if they've got the 18th commercial still to put on and they're outa field goal range anyhow."

Now you may argue that Joe Namath is a roisterer, a loudmouth, a freako in styles, a vulgar conversationalist; that he accomplished the nearly-impossible in this special kind of endeavor by getting kicked off a Bear Bryant–coached team at Alabama; that he is a crass commercialist, an arrogant brawler and furthermore that he doesn't drink Beep.

All of these things Joe might modestly acknowledge. Unfortunately, he plays football rather well.

The trouble is, we are confused about how to cast Joe in the pro football version of the morality play. Until a few days ago Joe was the Menace. He offended the fair-minded men with his braggadocio and he offended the women by suggesting that a female sportswriter was a bitch, a point on which the women might at least be willing to keep an open mind. We may now have to cast him as the Fu Manchu Prophet, the Quarterback from Manchuria.

Regrettably, Namath delivered. Despite all of our admiration for his skills and his defiance of convention, however, we have to concede that he could not have done it alone. The Colts, by carefully husbanding their resources, managed to save all of their atrocious football for the championship game. They played on a consistent and inspired level of ineptness that suggested that they could not have been that bad by themselves from start to finish—somebody must have been injecting them with boredom pills during timeouts.

An epoch is over, people. We were gulled by the brawny Colt linebacker who was so tough he was supposed to eat the panes out of the bus windows. Instead, we yield the seat of honor to Namath, who ran out of panes a long time ago and is now ready to start running over the pedestrians.

Send him a carton of Wheaties, Big G.

*1969*

# DAVE ANDERSON

Dave Anderson (1929–2018) was one of those sportswriters a new-comer to the business could go to school on, a paragon of dignity in the rowdiest locker room and a true craftsman every time he sat down to put words on paper. He seemed destined to become part of history when, as a copy boy at *The New York Sun*, he opened the crate contain-ing the portable typewriter W. C. Heinz had used to cover World War II. Anderson made history himself a few years later when he became the last reporter to cover the Dodgers for the *Brooklyn Eagle*. In 1966, after a tour of duty at the *New York Journal-American*, he got called up to the big leagues, *The New York Times*. He flourished whether he was writing about baseball, golf, football, or hockey. His reward was twofold: a promotion to sports columnist in 1971 and a Pulitzer for commentary ten years after that.

★ ★ ★

# The Sound of 715

ATLANTA, APRIL 8—In the decades to come, the memory of the scene might blur. But the memory of the sound will remain with every-one who was here. Not the sound of the cheers, or the sound of Henry Aaron saying, "I'm thankful to God it's all over," but the sound of Henry Aaron's bat when it hit the baseball tonight. The sound that's baseball's version of a thunderclap, the sound of a home run, in his case the sound of the 715th home run. The sound momentarily was the only sound in the expectant silence of 53,775 customers at Atlanta Stadium and then, as the sound faded, the ball soared high and deep toward the left-center-field fence. And over it. On the infield basepaths, Henry Aaron was trotting now, trotting past Babe Ruth into history in his 21st season. On his first swing in tonight's game, the 40-year-old outfielder of the Atlanta Braves had hit another home run, just as he had hit his record-tying home run on his first swing at Cincinnati in last Thursday's season opener. At home plate, surrounded by an ovation that came down around him as if it were a waterfall of appreciation, he was met by his teammates who attempted to lift him onto their shoulders. But he slipped off into the arms of his father, Herbert Sr., and his mother, Estella, who had hurried out of the special box for the Aaron family near the Braves' dugout.

"I never knew," Aaron would say later, "that my mother could hug so tight."

Moments later he was accepting a diamond wrist watch from the commissioner of baseball, Bowie Kuhn, but not from Kuhn himself. Rather than expose himself to the boos of the Atlanta populace, Kuhn had dispatched an ambassador, Monte Irvin, to the scene of the pre-game festivities in the event the 715th home run occurred. When it did, Irvin presented the watch and when he was introduced as being from the commissioner's office, the boos roared. In his jubilation, Henry Aaron smiled.

"I was smiling from the boos," he would say later. That's all he would say because that's the way Henry Aaron is. Henry Aaron doesn't gloat. Quietly, he has resented Kuhn's attitude toward him, whether real or imagined. It began when Kuhn ignored his 700th home run last season and it simmered when Kuhn ordered Eddie Mathews to use him in the starting line-up in Cincinnati yesterday after the Braves' manager had planned to preserve him for the Atlanta audience. Kuhn was correct in that ultimatum, because the Braves were defying the integrity of baseball.

But the commissioner was wrong tonight in not being here. He had stood up gallantly, but suddenly he had sat down again. Henry Aaron should have ordered the commissioner to be here.

"I thought the line-up card was taken out of Eddie Matthews' hand," the man with 715 home runs said. "I believe I should've been given the privilege of deciding for myself."

It's unfortunate that controversy somewhat clouded Henry Aaron's moment. It's also untypical. Of all our superstars, Henry Aaron has been perhaps the most uncontroversial. But time will blow those clouds away. Soon only his home runs will be important, not where he hit them, not where the commissioner was. His eventual total of home runs will be his monument, although they represent only a portion of his stature as a hitter.

With a normally productive season, in what he insists will be his last, Henry Aaron probably will hold six major-league career records for home runs, runs batted in, total bases, extra base hits, games and times at bat. Ty Cobb will retain the records for hits, runs, batting average and stolen bases. Babe Ruth will hold the records for slugging average and walks. Through the years, Cobb and the Babe were the ultimate in hitting, but now they must move over.

"With a good year," Henry Aaron has said, "I'll hold six records, Cobb will hold four and Ruth two."

Perhaps that will convince the skeptics who minimize his accomplishments as a hitter. Some of the skeptics are traditionalists, some are racists. Statistically, their argument is that Henry Aaron needed 2,896 more times at bat than Babe Ruth in order to break the home-run record. Those skeptics ignore Henry Aaron's durability and consistency, attributes as important as Babe Ruth's charisma. And when his 715th home run soared over the fence tonight, Henry Aaron never lost his dignity, his essence as a person.

"You don't know what a weight it was off my shoulders," he said later, "a tremendous weight."

Now the weight will be transferred to the hitter who someday challenges Henry Aaron, if that hitter appears.

*1974*

# BUD COLLINS

To casual tennis fans who saw him on TV from Wimbledon, he was the man wearing the wildly colored psychedelic pants. To Abbie Hoffman, the athletically-inclined Sixties radical, he was the tennis coach at Brandeis University. To writers making their first visit to a tennis tournament large or small, he was the unofficial host who answered as many questions as they could ask. Most of all, though, Bud Collins (1929–2016) was, as *Sports Illustrated*'s Frank Deford called him, "the very soul of the game." At *The Boston Globe* from 1963 to 2011, Collins wrote about everything from boxing and travel to politics and the Vietnam War. But it was tennis that inspired his nicknames for players ("Fräulein Forehand") and let him bear witness to the brilliance of the Chris Everts and Roger Federers of the world. And yet love never inspired delusion. As Collins himself said, "Either the ball goes over the net or it doesn't."

★ ★ ★

# Evert Smashing, Wins Battle of Wimbledon

I N SWEPT the zephyr from the plains of New South Wales, charging to the net for one last volley. It was Evonne Goolagong's final shot at holding off a grim reaper in white dress, that hatchetwoman called Chrissie.

Goolagong plunked her volley to midcourt rather than sharply hitting it away, and all she could do was shrug at the concluding stroke:

a two-fisted Evertian lob that sailed over the Aussie and landed in the dust just short of the baseline.

Not until then, the match point two hours distant from the beginning of this crackling battle for female supremacy in a game called tennis, could you be sure who would win. Christine Marie Evert, once and now again champion of Wimbledon (6–3, 4–6, 8–6), and the Aussie, Goolagong, both had innumerable moments of brilliance. But Evonne's athletic ability couldn't carry her to a second title, even though she was ahead, 2–0, in the third set, and had break points for 3–1.

Ultimately the Big W went to the woman with the iron innards, the young labor leader who was made for this kind of test. It was one of the ironies of the hot and gusty afternoon in Center Court that the twenty-one-year-old Evert who wanted this title above all, will lead her flock—the Women's Tennis Association, of which she is president—in a snub of Wimbledon in 1977, "unless we get equal parity with the men in prize money." Evert insisting the cash "means nothing," but that the women merit just as much of that nothing as the guys, earned $18,000.

When Ilie Nastase and Björn Borg collided for the men's championship first prize was $22,500.

Another irony was that despite Evert's incredible strokemaking, her clever forays to the net, and crunching volleys—frequently taking the attack away from the customary attacker, Goolagong—she couldn't win the full-house crowd of 14,000. London has adored Sunshine Supergirl Goolagong since 1971 when, as a nineteen-year-old, she danced and glided to the championship, dethroning Margaret Court.

"I got mad because they were so one-sided," Evert said, "and I think that helped me." The audience lamented each loss of a point by Goolagong and applauded madly when she scored, even for Evert's mistakes.

Evert, however, isn't looking for warmth when she goes to work. She supplies her own with barrages from the baseline, and is always a cool hand. "When Evonne won the second set, I really lost heart. I didn't feel like a winner," she said, although her appearance and performance belied the feeling.

She seems to need only herself. "Last year my dad [teaching pro Jimmy Evert of Fort Lauderdale] was here, and I think I tried too hard to win it for him. He stayed home this time, and I gave him a nice surprise. I think that down in his heart he believed I could never beat Evonne on grass—but he wouldn't let that on to me. He cried when I called him right after the match."

Nevertheless, there was support and help for Evert, who won her first Wimbledon two years ago over Olga Morozova. As Princess America became the queen, the old queen in abdication, Billie Jean King, cheered her successor on from the friends' box. "Billie Jean and Rosie Casals kept motioning me to get into the net and it made the difference at the end," said a smiling Evert, who has conquered her fear of frying at the net.

She raced forward on strong forehands, and finished the points with bludgeoning forehand volleys to rise from 15–40 at 1–2 in the last set, and canceled the third break point in that critical four deuce game with a ringing forehand winner.

"Chris put me off by volleying so well—she's never done that against me before," said Goolagong, who probably had sailed through to the final too easily, losing no sets. She wasn't aggressive enough, letting herself get caught up in too many backcourt rallies, during which both mastered the dry, crumbling court and the bad bounces better than any of the men.

"It came down to a battle of the minds—who would hang in there longer," said that death-grip hanger, Evert. "I was a little smarter, a little tighter on the big points. I played them better."

Goolagong agreed. "I didn't do my best volleying when I had to."

From 0–2, Evert streaked to 3–2. Thereafter it was all marvelously hectic, the most exciting and best played final since Court tipped King six years ago, 14–12, 11–9. Goolagong took Chris's serve and it was 3–3. She kept going to 4–3 on her own, riding out two break points.

Evert crashed her groundies to 4–4, and leaped for a serve-breaking volley. There she was at 5–4, and it was time for Goolagong's toughest stand.

"For some reason I didn't have the adrenaline flowing in that game. I wasn't excited," Evert said. "Evonne was." The Aussie banged out a break in four points, and stepped ahead again, 6–5.

The rest was Evert. Goolagong had 40–30 in the thirteenth game, but Evert bashed an overhead, and Goolagong played two loose points. "I knew I'd think about this for a year if I didn't beat her," said Chris, who served it out from 7–6. Evonne fought to 30–all, shocked her following by socking a simple forehand return over the baseline, and was interred by that closing lob.

"It wasn't the same Evonne who beat me in the Virginia Slims final," said Evert after snapping Goolagong's 26-match streak, including two involving herself.

"There wasn't quite the look I see in her eyes when she's super-tough."

Evert's eyes were blazing combatively, especially down the stretch, as she increased her own winning streak to 17, recapturing her No. 1 status and made Goolagong one of a handful to lose three Wimbledon finals.

It has been four years since these two launched The Rivalry of the Seventies as kids in the same playpen. Goolagong won then, also a gripping three-setter, establishing the tone for their planetary feud, and she won their three subsequent meetings on grass.

Evert, however, leads, 17–11, and says, "It's easier without Billie Jean here in the singles. Just her presence made us all tense."

The men's doubles went to the Mexican-American alliance of Raul Ramirez and Brian Gottfried, 3–6, 6–3, 8–6, 2–6, 7–5, over Aussies Geoff Masters and Snake Case, but that was anticlimactic to Evert.

The hatchetwoman is in charge, and—look out, ladies—her blade can only get sharper.

*1976*

★ ★ ★

# Boxing Grieves Loss of
# 5th Street Gym

M IAMI BEACH—and this is the Ballad of the Sad Classroom:

*Readin', 'ritin', 'rithmetic'*
*Don't make the grades here,*
*Prof. Dundee marks "A" if you stick*
*Jabs in the other guy's ear.*

*Many a two-fisted scholar*
*Studied for punchin' PhD,*
*Whether Pep-clever or brawler*
*None matched poet laureate Ali.*

*But bang the drum slowly,*
*Toll the mournful count to ten,*
*Wreckin' ball comin' like Rocky:*
*Obliteratin'; School's out, Amen.*

It's no fun to contemplate the razing of citadels of learning, the destruction of laboratories, the disappearance of a classroom where the prodigy and valedictorian of the 5th Street Gym, Muhammad Ali, was nurtured, along with numerous other advanced-degree head breakers.

"Double-tough lifetakers," Sam Silverman used to laud such *cum laude* pugilists.

You stand at the corner of Washington and 5th, South End of Miami Beach, and only stillness that seems a death rattle drifts from the open second story windows. For forty years the rattle of punching bags emanated from those slits to mingle with sunbeams and traffic din. The place, a big, low-ceilinged room, about 130-by-60, could be called the Harvard of the Sweet Science without overly offending the highly tolerant proprietors, the Dundee Brothers: the dean, Chris, and Professor Angelo (although Harvard may not quite rate as the 5th Street Gym of the fine arts). Chris promoted fights, Angelo tutored the fighters.

Like Harvard, it did attract students from around the globe, a magnet and landmark such as Widener Library. Imagine the Widener being torn down and you can grasp the enormity of the 5th Street Gym's demise. Think of the maestros of manhandling who trained here for their recitals—champions named Sugar Ray (Robinson and Leonard), Willie Pastrano, Carmen Basilio, Luis Rodríguez, Sugar Ramos, Joey Maxim, José Nápoles, Ralph Dupas . . . too many to recount. And, of course, the titan himself: arrived as Cassius Clay, becoming the greatest of all American athletes—Muhammad Ali.

How can this be, this room gutted and quiet, waiting for the breaking ball to knock the two-story building flatter than Ali did George Foreman early one mysterious morning in Zaire nineteen years ago? "Rumble in the Jungle!" Ali called his reascension to the heavyweight throne.

"You gonna rumble young man!" his witch doctor, Bundini Brown, would screech over and over. And, man, didn't he rumble?

But Ali got old and tired too fast, and so has his study hall which, its owners say, will be more useful destroyed and transformed to an American architectural classic—a parking lot.

"It was falling apart, but I wanted to save it, have it renovated," says the pedagogue of pedagogues, trainer Angelo Dundee. "But the owners, nobody else did. I felt awful when it closed. I offered to bring my fighters back here . . . but . . . no go. Sad. Everybody in the world of boxing knew the 5th Street Gym. It was . . ." He stops, not wanting to be too sentimental about a reformed Chinese restaurant, a place where egg rolls preceded tough eggs as features.

It was what a gym should be—stained and grungy, a seedy parlor for palookas and princes of the science. A shabby ivory tower. You had to climb stairs to reach higher learning. It has ever been thus. The distinguished gyms were stale, aromatic walkups where fresh air was suspect. Stillman's in New York. The New Gardens on Friend Street in Boston. All gone now.

Dundee is a little apologetic about his new "gym-uh-nasium," as the fight set often pronounced such studios. "North of here, in Hollywood, it's in a health club. First floor."

"Too antiseptic, and lowdown," is the verdict of Dr. Ferdie Pacheco, Dundee's friend and Ali's onetime physician.

"No termites," confesses Dundee, who was in Ali's corner from the start. "I'd warn newcomers to 5th Street about the man-eating termites, and that we might go through the floor at any moment," he smiles.

Incomprehensible that the Miami Beach city fathers would allow this historic treasure to vanish. Especially since it's right around the corner from the revived and celebrated neighborhood called the art deco district, roamed by commercials-making camera crews from everywhere. The mayor must be as hardheaded as the stone crabs for which nearby Joe's is renowned.

So the Sad Classroom is going, going . . .

Beau Jack, the 72-year-old ex–lightweight champ, sits amid rubble and ghosts in a corner, keeping a "sad, sad" deathbed vigil until the wreckers arrive. "So many good men here. Now nothing. It's terrible."

It wasn't always sad. The classroom was noisy and electrified by Ali's presence, his confidence and sense of fun. He showed up in 1960, says Dundee. "He said, 'Angelo, get all your bums ready for me. I'll take 'em all on.' He was a great learner.

"He lived in the ghetto in Overtown over in Miami then. Every day he'd run here, over the causeway. Until they got to know him the cops would stop him, suspicious of a young black kid running the bridge. You know how that goes."

He was beautiful in 1964, entertaining visitors to the gym, bragging captivatingly about how he'd whup that big old ugly bear, Sonny Liston, and take the title.

Nobody believed except Ali, Dundee and John Gillooly, the droll Bostonian who columnized for the *Record* and was almost alone in correctly picking the upstart whom he called "Gaseous Cassius."

Liston, the *Record*, Gillooly have departed. Ali has slowed to an elderly pace. And school's out at his classroom.

*1994*

## JERRY IZENBERG

Of all the newspaper sports columnists working today, choking down cold press-box coffee as they contend with brutal deadlines, truculent athletes, and their downy-cheeked editors' demands that they tweet, the reigning warhorse is Jerry Izenberg (b. 1930). He has cut back to one column a week for the *The Star-Ledger* in Newark, but still makes it to the Super Bowl and the Kentucky Derby, possesses a fine sense of outrage, and has a story for everyone he meets. Stanley Woodward, the legendary sports editor who hired him more than six decades ago, would be proud. Izenberg has maintained the master's values, in particular social consciousness and an abiding love for characters and language. Had his turn at the *New York Herald Tribune* in the 1960s led to a career in Manhattan, his star might have shined brighter. But judging by the magnitude of his work, it has been quite enough to be Jerry Izenberg.

★   ★   ★

# The Promoter

H E SITS at his desk and stares through the unwashed window at the gray lump that is 44th Street. It is beginning to drizzle outside but most of the good that might have come from last night's show was already mortally wounded. It had begun to die in the early-morning dampness.

Now it is early afternoon and in three hours he will pick up the bulky envelope filled with tickets and he will lock the iron-gray wall cabinet and he will walk down the dirty fourteenth-floor corridor to the elevator. He will drive out to Sunnyside Gardens and he will have all night to think of the people who will not be there.

He has been thinking about them for two days now but he will forget them when the dawn breaks in on his next sleepless night. He will forget them and start worrying about the ones who will not be there the next time he goes.

Irving Cohen is a fight promoter. Once he was a manager and his eyes change ever so slightly when he ticks off the names . . . Rocky Graziano . . . Walter Cartier . . . Irish Bob Murphy. That was in another world. Now he is his own promoter and his own matchmaker and sometimes his own ticket-taker and his own usher.

The operation runs every Tuesday but this week he has a bonus show on Friday night because the circus is in the Garden and the big television camera has to live somewhere and they are giving him his shot. It is the only show of the season on which he will make money.

The rest of the time Sunnyside Gardens will die its weekly economic death. It has as much chance in the modern world as a buggy-whip factory but it trains young fighters and so Madison Square Garden picks up the deficit and helps Irving Cohen make his weekly nut.

Last night he had José Torres in the main event and he should have sold out the joint but yesterday it rained and Irving Cohen knew right then that he was hurting.

"We got three types of customers at Sunnyside," he said yesterday afternoon, turning away from the dirty window and his weather watch. "We charge $1.50, $2.50, and $3.50. The $1.50 guy, he comes because it is Tuesday and there is a fight and this is what he has to do. But when the weather is lousy, well, the $3.50 guy, he doesn't come. He is a businessman. He won't go across the street to see a fight if it rains. He can stay home and watch television. Tonight, he will stay home."

This is the way it is and Irving Cohen knows it. He also knows that he has had a lot of rainy Tuesday nights this season, which began last October and will run through the first week in May. He has an option to pick up five more dates but he will not exercise it. He says he is very tired.

On Monday night, the night before he had Torres going for him, he watched the late show and he watched the late late show and then he watched something else but he is not sure what it was.

"You worry. You worry that tomorrow you will go to the office and there will be a phone call and one of your fighters is going to cancel out. God forbid he should be a star bout fighter. Then you're dead. Monday I found a substitute in Paterson and another in New York but they were on the undercard. Where do you find a substitute for a main event the day of the fight?"

So all night long Irving Cohen tossed and turned and around 4:30 he dozed off and his wife, Jean, tiptoed out of bed and shut off the television. At 8 A.M. yesterday he was awake and he looked out the window and he felt the dampness and saw the wet streets and he still felt lousy.

"Where you going?" Jean Cohen asked him.

"I gotta go to the office."

"So," Jean Cohen said, "sit and have coffee. Sit and eat something. You don't eat now, you wouldn't eat later. Sit down."

Irving Cohen is sixty years old and has been over this course so many times before and he will be over it again so many more times. So he sat and had coffee.

"I get to the office and nobody canceled out, thank God. So then I go to the commission for the weigh-in. You gotta hope they all make the weight but mostly you gotta hope they all show up. We don't pay Garden prices. A four-rounder gets $50 with us. At the Garden he gets $150. A six-rounder gets $100 with us. At the Garden he gets five times that. So you want to know about the heartaches of a small promoter? So that's it. From 10:45 until 12:15 it's hell. The commission office is on West 47th, and you stand by that elevator hoping and praying until every last one of them shows. Then all you got to do is hope they show that night at Sunnyside."

It has been a long season for Irving Cohen. He needs $3,000 to break even and an average show draws $2,200. He will tell you that his small club is an artistic success and he will point to kids like Johnny Persol, who jumped from Sunnyside to a main event at the Garden. He will also tell you that business is lousy, which it is, and then he will look at the rain.

The television card this Friday is the saver. Last year, he had three of them. This year, he has one. There is a thin white stubble on his face because he did not shave yesterday morning and, as he says, he looks tired.

"You worry," he says, sitting in the middle of all those fight posters in his office. "You worry about the weather and the fighters and the customers and you worry about the decisions because the people will blame you for that too.

"Back when I was a manager," he says, "a small promoter could do all right because then you had the neighborhood rivalries. Now you don't even have the neighborhoods."

And then he turned around and looked out the window again.

"Today is gone, I hope it don't rain Friday."

*1964*

★   ★   ★

# Courage Is Riding Out a 1,600-Pound Tornado

THIS WAS a couple of nights ago, when the beers were short and the talk was long and the veterans were trying to single out the most courageous feat they had ever seen from the safety of a press box. This is, of course, an impossible task.

On the other hand, it brought to mind Mr. Freckles Brown, simply because nobody else at the bar had seen or heard of him, and it opened the wellspring of memory just enough to make a man think that no matter how you rate his sport, he is worth a mention any time the subject of sheer competitive courage surfaces.

Freckles was a rodeo bull-rider. His career, which incredibly did not reach its zenith until he was forty-six years old, was a throwback to the time when real cowboys spent the entire winter in the line camps, curled up in their soogans (which were unwashed but well-inhabited quilts), dreaming of canned peaches and free women and the beautiful return of spring, which would send them off the ranch and back to the arenas.

The calendar, and the modern truck (which eliminated the need for a line camp), dictated that Freckles missed that slice of life but, emotionally, he was clearly one of them. So when rodeo moved into a new world where the band played "Georgie Girl" instead of "Home on the Range," Freckles never paid much attention to the new breed of cowboy that came out of rodeo schools and supermarket checkout jobs.

The first time a man met him was back in 1967 at the national finals in Oklahoma City, where, just four years short of his fiftieth birthday, he had come to ride a bull.

Some things do not change.

The bull was a big, ugly, red-and-white-faced Braford—a strange cross between a Brahma and a Hereford. A rodeo bull is no family terrier, turning on the neighborhood kids because they have tied a can to his tail. Hit-and-run is not his ball game. He will throw you, and then keep on coming back at you until the rodeo clown jumps in front and sticks out his butt to draw the bull's attention.

So, on that night one man will never forget, here was old Freckles, and here was Tornado, who weighed 1,600 pounds. They had sent 300 cowboys out of the chute on Tornado's back during his career, and none of them had survived the six-second whistle.

Freckles was going out to ride him at an age when most of us have put taking out the garbage under the heading of strenuous exercise. He was going to ride him for two reasons: The first was to protect the mortgage on 500 acres over on the Muddy Boggy River in Soper, Oklahoma.

Nobody handed Freckles the down payment on that acreage. It was paid for with three decades of riding the Tornados of his world, one broken neck, and enough broken legs to stock the spare-parts department at the Mayo Clinic.

He was also going to ride him because nobody else in the world ever had—and in Freckles's mind this was, therefore, his Super Bowl, his World Series, and his heavyweight championship.

When the chute banged open, Freckles was looking down at that big, red hump of a neck, and he was telling himself over and over to remember that this was what the cowboys call a "spinner," and that sooner or later he would jerk that huge body to the right, rip backward, and try to nail the man on his back.

Freckles fought him. He rode him past the whistle, and when it blew, everyone in the joint was standing and shrieking as Freckles cut clear. Then he was walking away.

Freckles's walk was his signature. He was so bow-legged that if you stood him next to somebody who was knock-kneed they would have spelled "ox." He was walking away, and waving his hat, and 12,000 people had seen a miracle.

The next day a man told him that he almost expected his grandchildren would see Freckles at work one day. "Not likely," Freckles drawled, but you could see the thought intrigued him.

That night, he announced his retirement. A rodeo official named Dave Stout laughed in his face. "Freckles, you ain't gonna quit," he said, and then turned to another man and explained: "He can get up on a bull and do something very few folks in the world can do. Last week he told me that when he comes out of the chute, sittin' on the bull's back, he feels just like the emperor of Japan. No, I'd say catch him after he's turned fifty, and he'll be doin' exactly what you saw him do last night."

When a man next saw him again, four years later, Freckles, indeed, was fifty. Some retirement. Just six months earlier, in a place called Lenapooh, Oklahoma, a bull with the imaginative name of Number 46 caught him leaning the wrong way and smashed his ankle.

He and Ronnie Bowman drove fifty miles that night to where

Freckles had parked his car. Then Ronnie packed the ankle in ice. Freckles drove the remaining 200 miles.

When he limped through the door, Edith Brown, who was the resident Soper, Oklahoma, expert on Freckles, through marriage, shook her head and said, "Damn, Brown, you done it again."

Finally, he quit. There don't seem to be any more Freckleses around the sport these days. The Old West is dead, along with people like Pete Knight, who once lay dying on the hard dirt floor of a tiny arena in Hayward, California, after a bronc named Duster had kicked a piece of rib into his lung. The year was 1937; ironically, it was the first year Freckles Brown went off to ride bulls for money.

When the first man to reach him asked Pete if it hurt, he replied, "You're damned right it does. Now help me get the hell up, because this is downright embarrassing."

Once, in a quiet moment, a man asked Freckles if he'd been afraid back in Oklahoma City on the night he went out to master Tornado.

"Hell," Freckles said, "only two kinds of folks don't have the sense to be afraid—the first are crazy and the second are dead. It's the way you handle it that counts."

Case closed.

*1985*


★   ★   ★

# Just Color Doug's Day Beautiful

S AN DIEGO—You can draw any sociological implication you want out of what Doug Williams did here yesterday if you feel you must, but please do the rest of us a favor and find yourself a closet somewhere for that kind of nonsensical monologue.

If you think anything else besides the fate of the Redskins was riding on his throwing arm yesterday, that's your problem. He didn't come in here having to throw the ball any farther or better because of who he is.

"It's my belief," Joe Gibbs went out of his way to point out after Williams' magnificent performance—340 yards and four touchdown passes—"that America is long past that."

Doug Williams came to San Diego for one reason and one reason only. He came to try to win a football game. And he won it with the kind of day few quarterbacks have ever had anywhere, anytime, any place.

Make no mistake about it. Williams was a quarterback long before he got here and long before the week-long barrage of inane questions generated by a plantation mentality that insisted on linking his job and his skin color.

Despite an early ten-point deficit . . . despite a script that seemed to dictate in the very first quarter that John Elway was destined to rise above San Diego as though he were part Houdini, part Prince Valiant, and straight out of Central Casting . . . despite a sickening moment near the end of that period when Williams went down on the Jack Murphy Stadium grass, his legs spread-eagled like a pair of scissors, and had to leave the game for one series of downs . . . despite it all, once the Redskin offensive line began to assert itself, Williams steadily emerged as the quarterback he knew in his heart he was long before he ever came here.

On Wednesday, Richie Petitbon, a Redskins assistant coach, watched Williams work on the practice field at Cal–San Diego, shook his head and kept his thoughts to himself.

"It was almost too good to be true. I have never seen a quarterback look as good in a practice session as Doug did," Petitbon finally confided to Gibbs.

On Friday, Eddie Robinson, who had never had a quarterback in the Super Bowl before and who coached Williams for four seasons at Grambling, arrived as his former player's guest.

"Don't worry about him," Robinson said. "There's nothing this game is going to ask for that he already doesn't have."

Nor were they worried down in Zachary, Louisiana. At B.J.'s Seafood on Highway 19, they had a forty-five-inch TV screen in the back room, a $5.99 catfish-fillet special on the grill, and what must have seemed like half the population of Williams's hometown crowded into the joint, waiting to see the guy they knew was a quarterback as far back as the nights when they would cram into the sardine can of a stadium where Chaneyville High played its home games.

Nobody had to tell any of them Doug Williams was a quarterback. The annual Zachary Sausage Festival each May may be the town's hot event but it's an outside bet that there will be a Doug Williams Day on the horizon to give the festival a run for its money.

But, for all that, a lot of people knew there was a lot that a lot of other people didn't want to know. They took some convincing, and in the span of fifteen minutes of some of the finest football any quarterback has ever played, Doug Williams put the exclamation mark on his statement.

When he went down and limped off the field, there were those who felt he would not be back. The Redskins had a horrible field position, they couldn't get started (he was 3-for-8 at the time), and a lot of second-guessers expected his replacement Jay Schroeder, to be in to stay.

Such people know nothing of Williams, and Joe Gibbs is not among them. They are people who do not understand the real tests of toughness. Doug Williams does.

In the spring of 1984, Williams, his wife, Janice, and their new baby visited her folks. Janice was standing by the refrigerator when, without warning, she collapsed. She died a month later of a brain tumor.

Nobody will ever quite understand the pain Doug Williams survived. People who know him best will tell you there were times when he, himself, couldn't measure it. But survive he did. And nobody bothered to ask whether a black quarterback could make it through that.

Yesterday's injury was a hyperextension of his left knee. By the second half, he was wearing a brace and extra tape. But, on the first possession of the second period, there was no time for that. And, as if that weren't bad enough, he had spent three hours in a dentist's chair the night before, undergoing root-canal surgery. But he sucked it up and went back to war.

Unless you spent yesterday in a cave interviewing troglodytes, you are aware of what Doug Williams did in that brief fifteen-minute span: touchdown passes of eighty, twenty-seven, fifty, and eight yards— thirty-five points in five minutes, forty-seven seconds of possession.

Yesterday, Doug Williams was more than a quarterback—he was an artist, standing tall behind an offensive line that wrapped him in cotton candy, coated him with Teflon sweat, and surrounded him after every scoring pass with the kind of emotion shared only by warriors trying to climb the same mountain.

There were 73,302 people in Jack Murphy Stadium, and not one cared a damn about the sociology of the winning quarterback. They knew what they were seeing—and it wasn't pigmentation; it was brilliance.

"I didn't come here as a black quarterback," Williams said after he was through dominating Super Bowl XXII, reaffirming what a lot of people who do not deal in folk myths knew all along.

"I came here," he said, "as the quarterback of the Washington Redskins."

He left as the MVP of the Super Bowl.

*1988*

# LARRY MERCHANT

Before making his mark as a fearless boxing analyst for HBO and after spending a decade as the crusading sports editor of the *Philadelphia Daily News*, Larry Merchant (b. 1931) wrote three columns a week that provided the heartbeat for the pre–Rupert Murdoch *New York Post*'s stellar sports section from 1966 to 1975. Hip and knowing, iconoclastic and socially conscious, Merchant could leave readers rolling with laughter in the aisles of subway cars or scorch the earth with outrage ignited by intellect. He once said his bosses at the *Post* would have been happy if he only wrote about Muhammad Ali, Joe Namath, and whatever hairy-chested hero had seized the moment, but the predictable wasn't for him. If it was, he never would have written a column about getting ready for opening day of the baseball season with Marianne Moore, a renowned poet and the quintessential Larry Merchant subject.

★　★　★

# Ali Baby

T IS said that truth is the first victim of war. The furor over Muhammad Ali at least grievously wounds a few truths about him.

Those who view him as evil incarnate, as a threat to Western civilization and as a poor misguided child, those who interpret his every move or statement through a one-dimensional Muslim prism, miss the essential Ali Baby. They have blinded themselves to the fun that still gushes from him.

One of the interesting sidelights to his predraft physical this week was the remark of one of the young men with him that he seemed so entertaining and down-home because "he was away from the Muslims." Why must we believe that the bogeymen we create are as humorless as we are?

The Muslims in their undertaker tidiness are indeed a grim lot in public. But they could no more gag Ali Baby than they could convert Floyd Patterson. They are, in fact, his best audience. Membership in the sect does not automatically exclude laughter—except among the nonbelievers who never laughed at him to begin with.

This is in evidence any time Ali Baby can be observed for, say, ten minutes. He still makes people laugh. When the professional cynics see this, they shake their heads and murmur, "Tsk, tsk, he could've been a credit to his race."

When he was in town to fight Zora Folley, Ali was asked some non-sensical questions simply to measure his mood. Willie Mays, asked the same questions once, was suspicious and uncooperative. Ali Baby took off on wild paper-plane flights of fantasy.

What's your favorite number?

"Nine. Yes, nine. I used to like to write nines in school. I like the way nine looks, a circle and a curl. My favorite two numbers are sixty-six. I believe there's a prophetic meaning in numbers."

If you had to give up ice cream or steak, which would you choose?

"Steak. You can always eat hamburger, roast beef, lamb and veal. I like ice cream too much. Chocolate and vanilla. Integrated."

Which would you rather have, a big dog or a little dog?

"I had a little dog when I was young, a little white dog with spots. We called him Spot. He was a sick dog. He died. If I got a dog now I'd want a big dog, a great big dog. Woof, woof."

A second essential of Ali Baby that is generally missed is that while he may be relatively unlettered he sees things less as a child than with a child's open curiosity, an unadulterated adult. Thus, when he was matched with George Chuvalo, he identified him as a "White Hope," scandalizing the boxing community, which acknowledged it privately. Thus, when Howard Cosell patronized him with, "You're a bright boy, Muhammad," he shot back, "You're not as dumb as you look."

Dumb Ali Baby isn't. Naive maybe, especially about some aspects of the Muslims, but doesn't naiveté and/or faith go hand in hand with all religious conviction? What makes him "brainwashed" while others are merely pious or zealous?

He is not an intellectual. It is easy target practice to shoot his arguments full of holes. But that doesn't mean he can't make more sense than respected muck-a-mucks on some issues. "We are fighting for the freedom of the Vietnamese. Why can't I have freedom of religion?" Argue with that.

He challenges our values. He makes us uncomfortable. Which is why the American Civil Liberties Union had to come to his aid this week, charging he was being punished by boxing authorities who stripped him of his title because of his unpopular political and social beliefs.

Ali Baby isn't wise beyond wisdom and good beyond goodness. He has shown flashes of the ugly side of himself. But in sum he is a young man of the times who is making a mark on the times that the times are better for.

1967

★   ★   ★

# Poetry in Motion

M ARIANNE MOORE, the poet, eighty years young, got up from the chair to fetch her baseball glove. It was in her bedroom, where every kid keeps his, or her, glove.

"It's a fielder's glove," she said, trying it on her right hand, then her left. Her hands are small and delicate, like fine ivory, and she laughed at the sight of that saddle-sized hunk of leather reaching halfway up her arm. "It's a little big for me. . . . Wait, I'll get my baseball too. I have two of them."

She disappeared into her bedroom again, fetching both baseballs, presumably from under her pillow. She called them "horsehide."

Marianne Moore is not in the habit of taking spring training in her apartment in Greenwich Village—"I like to go to Saint Petersburg," she said—but it seemed like a sensible concession to time. She doesn't have to cover as much ground as she used to. "I was a left fielder," she said. "I wasn't very good."

From out of left field though she has been given an honor she deems more astounding than all the honorary degrees and poetry prizes bestowed on her. She is going to throw out the first ball at Yankee Stadium.

"My goodness," Marianne Moore said. "I thought that was reserved for presidents and governors."

It was, when it was safe for presidents and governors to show up in public. It was, before Mike Burke took over the Yankees for CBS. Mike Burke has been trying to put the team together again and redo their image while he's at it. Last year there was that paint job on the stadium, powdery white with blue eyeshade for the old dowager. This year there are shrimp pink foul poles and Marianne Moore. It's hard to root against shrimp pink foul poles and Marianne Moore.

Mike Burke gave her the glove and the balls, to get her soupbone in shape, to work out the kinks, to be ready to go nine, in fact, Yankee pitching being what it is.

"He gave me everything but the mound and home plate," she said. She has a catcher, her brother. "My brother said I should return the glove after the game, but I'm going to keep it. He told me to throw the ball in a nice arc so the photographers can get their pictures, but I think I'll throw it around the knees; that's where they tell pitchers to throw it. You know what Campanella told the photographers when they asked him to smile? 'I haven't heard anything funny.' "

Roy Campanella was Marianne Moore's favorite ballplayer. Her brother took her to Ebbets Field. "Karl Spooner was pitching. Campanella went out to talk to him. He had an awkward look, but he moved with celerity."

Marianne Moore sees baseball with her own beautiful blue eyes. She doesn't see batting averages and strategy. She sees a game played by people. A very long time ago she taught commercial law at the Carlisle School in Carlisle, Pennsylvania, and she had a student named Jim Thorpe. She watched him play football and do it all in track and field, but what she remembered was, "He was a gentleman. I called him James. It would have seemed condescending, I thought, to call him Jim."

There is a story, an anecdote, a piece of character exposure, that goes with all her favorites and unfavorites.

"A guard in the bank of Williamsburgh told me Campanella was thinking of his son, who had got in trouble, when he had his car accident.

"Elston Howard is my second favorite. I remember reading that he got $30 to play his first game and he couldn't believe anyone could get paid for doing what he loved to do. I named my pet alligator after him. Isn't that awful?

"I did a radio show with Mary Margaret McBride. She told me Willie Mays had been a guest too. He talked about his big new house in San Francisco. She asked him how he was furnishing it. He said, 'French Provincial.' "

She said that neither Mickey Mantle nor Babe Ruth appealed to her, although she admired them as athletes. Mantle seems "gruff" and "never hits a home run when I expect him to." Ruth was "boorish."

The game itself, as a thing apart, touches another sensibility in Marianne Moore.

"It's the dexterity and accuracy that I like most about it. The nimble movements of the first baseman, the way a ball lights in his glove. The way an outfielder catches one backhanded. But I don't like the double play; the execution is nice, but someone is always disappointed.

"Whenever I feel gloomy I watch a game. The people aren't sheep. The grass is so green. I'm annoyed only that I never get a foul ball; it always rolls down the screen."

Marianne Moore tapped her glove. Next Tuesday might be the day.

*1968*

★   ★   ★

# Hustler Outhustled

A LL RIGHT, men, quit brooding and get to the dishes. Make sure the beds have hospital corners. And on the way to the supermarket why don't you stop off at the doctor's office for a little vasectomy? We've been the unfair sex for millennia. Last night we surrendered unconditionally.

Bobby Riggs, carrying the banner of male chauvinism, went down in flames.

Billie Jean King, carrying the banner of women's liberation, shot him down.

In a once-in-a-lifetime promotion that would have made P. T. Barnum and Tex Rickard swoon, she-is-woman beat he-is-man in straight sets 6–4, 6–3, 6–3.

Before the largest audience ever to witness a tennis match, or a circus—30,472 in the Astrodome and many millions on television, in thirty-six countries—Billie Jean King reduced the oinking Bobby Riggs to a ham sandwich. She ate him up and picked her teeth with his racket.

"I said I was a fifty-five-year-old man with one foot in the grave," Riggs said. "It's one and a half now."

Billie Jean King was simply too good for Bobby Riggs. He had taken his magnificent "Battle of the Sexes" hustle as far as it could go—until it got to a woman who could play the game and not the stakes. A hustler is someone who isn't intimidated by the stakes. That is a definition of a great athlete as well. Billie Jean King is a great athlete. She was raised in a competitive environment to do exactly what she did last night—be at her best when the money, a $100,000 jackpot and lots of commercial "fringies," as she calls them, was on the table.

"There's something in my psyche, my personality," Billie Jean King said, "that gets me up for the main event."

"Under the pressure and tension," admitted Riggs, a legendary money player, "she did better than I did."

Riggs knew it was a game on the second point, a textbook rally of lobs, volleys, drop shots, backhands and forehands. Riggs hit enough good shots to win a set against the country club suckers who love to lose to him. But he lost the point to Billie Jean on some amazing recoveries. "Her quickness," he said, "was too much for me." And he wasn't wearing galoshes or holding a dog on a leash or doing any of those exotic handicaps he dreams up for his hustles.

His only handicap was her. The only thing he beat her at was huckstering.

When they arrived at center court, she borne like an Egyptian queen, he wheeled in a rickshaw, as though it was a summit meeting of Cleopatra and Confucius, she could only sigh a "God!" at the hokeyness, but he rose to the occasion by remembering, "Where's my Hai Karate after-shave?" She stripped off a blue sweatsuit and emerged resplendent in a pastel blue dress with rhinestones and sequins across the shoulders. He, shameless, wore a windbreaker with "Sugar Daddy" (a candy sponsor) emblazoned on the back. The two plugs were worth a reported $95,000 to him.

A couple of hours later Billie Jean King looked like she could run the Boston Marathon and Bobby Riggs looked like he had both feet in the grave. She toyed with him, like a daughter now tweaking her father's cheek, now jabbing him in the ribs, now mussing his hair. His entourage of trainers and medicine men rubbed ice on his legs and arms and forehead as though he were a beaten fighter. What he was, was a tired old man.

"I feel this is the culmination of my career," she said. "Ever since I was eleven years old and I couldn't get in a tennis picture because I didn't have tennis dress, and I thought tennis was a game only for the rich and the white. I wanted to change the game."

So the short and happy resurrection of Bobby Riggs comes to an end and the folk herohood of Billie Jean King begins. For his farewell he leaned over and nibbled on her ear.

*1973*

## WELLS TWOMBLY

To see Wells Twombly (1935–1977) at work, a glass of something eighty proof beside his typewriter and a rascally smile on his flushed face, was to know you were looking at a writer convinced no one could write better than he could. He hoboed around the newspaper world—*Valley Times Today* in Los Angeles, *Houston Chronicle, Detroit Free Press*—until he barged through the door at the *San Francisco Examiner* in 1969 and found a home for his ornate literary style. Locked in a mortal combat with the who-what-where mentality that ruled newspapers, Twombly didn't hesitate to use symbolism or the adjectives that a writer in *Esquire* said he applied to his prose "the way older women apply rouge." Unimpressed, Reggie Jackson, baseball's self-promoting slugger, once announced that Twombly would be lucky to interview him. No, Twombly replied, Reggie would be lucky to be interviewed *by* him. Twombly prevailed.

★  ★  ★

# Gallery of Goats

WHISTLING HAPPILY through a tangle of twisted teeth, the keeper shuffled down the corridor, searching for the proper key in the stale darkness. A huge ring of brass keys, hanging from his belt, clanked as he moved. His frail hands trembled with excitement. A sinister gleam brightened his mean little eyes. There hadn't been an installation ceremony in years and the keeper had come to the conclusion that the gallery might have to be closed forever.

Now he stood outside that hated den of infamy, fumbling in his pocket for the familiar brass key with the carving of the dark prince himself on the handle. Ah, there it was. How comfortable it felt in the keeper's sweaty palm. The lock protested as it turned. The thick metal door, almost atrophied with rust, creaked open painfully. The keeper snapped on the light and looked around at his collection. Here and there on long dusty benches other eyes blinked back at him. In the corners spiders and scorpions scurried, thoroughly unaccustomed to anything but darkness.

This was the gallery of goats, created by dapper Richards Vidmer, a brilliant New York sports writer of a generation ago, who felt that there ought to be some reasonable alternative to the Hall of Fame. Built solidly out of equal parts of imagination and printer's ink, the gallery had weathered the passing years magnificently. And now it was time to bring the membership rolls up to date again.

"All right, you dolts, move over and make room," the keeper shouted, hardly concealing his fiendish delight. His fingers played lightly over the handle of his whip as he talked. "Shove down there, Roy Reigels. You thought you were some kind of dummy to run the wrong way in the Rose Bowl. But that was nothing. There wasn't any television then, so nobody could see your stupidity. What's more, 600 million Chinese didn't even know there was such a sport as football."

Down the line the keeper went, stopping in front of another inmate. He curled back his lip and flashed some yellow fangs at the tormented soul.

"How about you, Hippo Vaughn? Hardly anybody remembers what a terrible sense of timing you had. When was your big day? Oh, yes, back in 1917. You were pitching for the Chicago Cubs and you threw a no-hitter. You lost in the tenth inning. In all the history of baseball, nobody has been ignorant enough to pitch a no-hit game the same day somebody else was no-hitting your team. Get back, stupid."

Farther down the bench, a wistful little figure sat. His eyes were focused toward some lost horizon. The keeper chuckled venomously.

"And here's Bill Shoemaker, the greatest jockey of modern times. Bet Shoe and you won't go wrong, will you? Heh! Heh! Do you think they'll ever let you forget the time you reined up Gallant Man at the sixteenth pole and blew the Kentucky Derby? Push down there, Shoe, you dope."

Now the keeper spotted another prominent member of the gallery. He stopped and threw back his head and howled like a beast of hell.

"Harvey Haddix! You used to be our prize exhibit, but not any more. No sir. You're small potatoes now. All you did was pitch a perfect game against Milwaukee for 12 innings. Then you lost in the thirteenth. Remember that? Well, how could you forget?"

Everywhere the keeper looked he saw the great goats of the past. There was Ralph Branca, who threw the home run ball to Bobby Thomson. There sat the Braves scout who recommended that the front office wait awhile before offering a contract to this kid Willie Mays. There was Fred Williamson, the Kansas City defensive back who bragged that he was going to hammer the Green Bay Packers to bits in the first Super Bowl. All of them slumped there like concrete figures in some infernal sauna bath.

Now the keeper turned and flung the door open wide. He crooked a twisted finger to the man standing outside. "This way, Mr. Wright. This is the place. Step lively now. This is your new home." And in walked Stanley Wright, smiling bravely through his tears. The keeper rattled his keys and demanded strict attention.

"Gentlemen," he said. "This is Stanley Wright, one of America's leading track coaches. This is a man who has always prided himself on his meticulous nature. A great detail-man, this Mr. Wright. At the 20th Olympic Games he made himself an immortal goat. It was up to him to get two 9.9 sprinters, Reynaud Robinson and Ed Hart, to the 100-meter qualifying heat. He blew it completely. He misread the starting times. Why? Well, it seems they were printed in military style, you know, 'Oh-sixteen-hundred hours.' The two kids got to the stadium late and were disqualified."

The other gallery members gasped. Quietly, the referee involved in the famous long count in Chicago that cheated Jack Dempsey out of the heavyweight title got up and moved down to make room.

"Naturally, Coach Wright was sorry. But how do you explain that to two kids who worked four years for nothing?" said the keeper. "Now let's see where we should put our newest goat.

"H-m-m-m-m. Let's be democratic. Where do the rest of you guys think he belongs?"

Silently, the other goats stood up. These were the greatest nincompoops in all of athletic history. Without bothering to take a vote they shifted one space to the left, leaving Stanley Wright a place right next to the door. The keeper arched his ancient neck and let out a roar so terrible it stopped the blood in mid-vein. Then he slammed the door shut, leaving Stanley Wright there with his tears for all eternity.

1972

★   ★   ★

# Super Hero

IN NATURE, there are certain movements so swift and so graceful that no mortal can adequately describe what has taken place. In the upper branches of a fir tree, a squirrel goes bounding from level to level, his eyes focused on the horizon, his heart pounding gently with the vibrations of the earth itself. Beyond a copse of birches, a doe stirs. Somewhere inside her she knows that a hunter is waiting, hip-deep in the snow. Swiftly, she turns and goes leaping through the drifts.

No man living is skillful enough to describe exactly how Roberto Clemente moved through the meadows of our land for 18 summers. His was a special style and grace. It was a smooth motion, fluid and compact. Most of the people who bought tickets to watch him play right field for the Pittsburgh Pirates never seemed to appreciate what he could do. They accepted it. But they never appreciated it. Pay $3.50 and see Roberto do the impossible. He was brilliant, to use a phrase that doesn't really do justice to his memory.

No athlete of Clemente's quality has been taken for granted quite so shamelessly. The customers applauded him like human beings who had seen too much television. Magic was dead. The super-sensational was too ordinary. Perfection was their birthright. They paid their money and they sat there as baseballs went sailing off toward a glove that never made a mistake. It was far too easy, far too sweet. Roberto just couldn't make the game of baseball look hard enough.

Hit the ball to right at Pittsburgh and forget it. Try to run to second on that slim figure in the outfield and you could count on the ball being there ahead of you. It was so lovely, so automatic that God Himself must have designed the play. Offensively, Clemente was one of the best of his generation. He rated right there with Mickey Mantle, Stan Musial, Willie Mays, Henry Aaron, etc. He was a walking immortal. He ran. He threw. He hit.

Trouble was that Roberto Clemente could never communicate his true self. It was his opinion that newspapermen had a stringent pecking order. They regarded baseball players in the following way: On top were the American whites, followed rapidly by the American blacks. Next were the Latin whites. Way down at the bottom were the Latin blacks. They were nobody's children.

"I feel that I would be considered to be a much better athlete if I were not a black Latin," he told a newspaperman one sorrowful evening in Pittsburgh two years ago when the Pirates were winning the World Series.

"I play as good as anybody. Maybe I play as good as anybody who plays the game. But I am not loved. I don't need to be loved. I just wish that it would happen. There are many people like me who would like that to happen. I wish it for them. Do you know what I mean?"

Trouble was that few people truly understood what he was talking about. Even his colleagues on the Pittsburgh Pirates admitted that they weren't just sure how to take him. They didn't know if he was a self-serving egotist or a humanitarian who honestly loved his neighbors. Always Roberto Clemente seemed to be tiptoeing along a chalk line.

"This was the most decent man I've ever known," said pitcher Steve Blass. "And nobody ever seemed to understand him. Maybe there was a language barrier, I don't know. He was absolutely selfless. He'd talk about his physical problems and writers would make jokes. What he was trying to say was that Latins and blacks play hurt just like everybody else. They didn't get that. They said he was a hypochondriac."

When the Pirates got into the World Series, Clemente got a dozen hits. He was splendid beyond belief. After each game he would talk seriously to writers. Certainly he wanted credit for himself. Why? Not for personal glory, but because he wanted a forum for his beliefs. He had this wild notion about a sports city in his native Puerto Rico where indigent children could live. They could grow to manhood with the high ideals of competitive athletes to guide them. Their whole lives would be changed by the opportunity to play games, to get a decent meal, to wear clean clothes.

"This is my dream," he said. "I do not know exactly what this sports city will be like, but it will be beautiful. It will be open to everybody. No matter what they are. After I open the first one in Puerto Rico I will open others. I will do this thing because that is what God meant me to do. Baseball is just something that will give me a chance to do this."

And Roberto Clemente believed he had this mission to perform for mankind. When the Governor of Puerto Rico asked him to head the island's relief fund for the Managua earthquake victims, he threw himself into the project with a passion.

Here was one of the finest baseball players who ever lived and he went from door to door in the richer sections of San Juan, asking for donations. He raised $150,000 in cash and thousands extra in material goods. Roberto filled up the Santurce ball park with clothing and food. Clemente said he would personally take them to Nicaragua. He meant it.

The time came to transport those items. The airplane rose slowly from the runway, headed out to sea, made a desperate turn, and fell into the water. Thus died a humanitarian. Thus died a real man. Thus died a very fine baseball player. Not necessarily in that order.

*1973*

★   ★   ★

# There Was Only One Casey

ON CASUAL inspection, the old man looked like a woodcarver's first attempt at a gargoyle. The face was crude and drooping, even when it was new. The eyes were watery and mournful, like a human basset hound. The ears were large and foolish. The hands were hopelessly gnarled. The legs looked like two Christmas stockings stuffed with oranges.

Luckily, greatness doesn't necessarily come in attractive wrappings. Up close, the old man was genuinely beautiful, not exactly in the category of Robert Redford, but beautiful just the same. It was the beauty of a rare antique, tenderly rendered and gracefully aged. It was the beauty of a three hundred-year-old handcrafted pipe, rubbed by a thousand hands and redolent of a thousand aromatic tobaccos. This was a precious original and, of the millions of words that will be written about Charles Dillon Stengel in the next few days, none of them will quite do him justice.

He was one of a handful of baseball characters whose reputations did not exceed their true personalities. The fact is that Yogi Berra was never anything but a quiet, humorless, somewhat grumpy New Jersey businessman, whose humor was largely created by Joe Garagiola anyway. Bo Belinsky was just another charming scoundrel who liked girls, which made him about as kooky as five-sixths of America's male population. Dizzy Dean was a big depression-era redneck who loved beer. As a young man he was bumptious. As a senior citizen, he was a bore.

But the Casey Stengel of real life was better than the Casey Stengel of the printed page. The problem was a mechanical one, which was never solved. He could not be properly transmitted. However, the best literary men of his time worked on it. Oh, how they worked. Still, it never came out quite right, especially the rambling, shattered syntax of his speech, which was a flagrant put-on. Only a very few people understood what Stengel was doing. He led them through a merry maze built entirely of semantic disgraces. He did it on purpose.

Early one morning when he was between jobs, he sat in the tower at Wrigley Field in Los Angeles trying to make Gene Autry a pauper by sucking up so much free booze that the singing cowboy would have to get his guitar and make a comeback. The more he tucked away, the more lucid he became. A twenty-five-year-old baseball writer who covered the Los Angeles Angels and delivered a column nobody read out in the San Fernando Valley was utterly amazed. "That jargon of yours is just a joke," he gasped.

"Son," said Casey in that gravel-driveway voice of his. "This is gonna be our little secret, isn't it?"

The man was a clever and articulate comic who spoke two languages. When he was unguarded he would talk in this straightforward, highly lucid English, which nobody paid any attention to. When there were reporters and other assorted individuals present he spoke in tongues. It was a tangled rat's nest of verbiage that bore only a scanty resemblance to the Mother Tongue so heartily endorsed by the queen of England. Even the mightiest of journalists cowed when he turned on the juice.

When he was managing the wretched New York Mets of the early 1960s he attempted to describe what the fans were like. It was a fine, feathered piece of literature. "These fans are very rabid like they were very collegiate or something because it takes four hours for us to leave our dressing room after a game, which is good because the concession people sell a lot of hot dogs, which is good for our business and I like that. I expect that very soon they will carry one of my players out on their shoulders like he just caught a touchdown for Yale. They are very patient and that's good. These fellows of ours are going to keep right on improving because they are better than most folks think and not as bad as they used to be, because it would be hard to be as bad as that."

There were people who thought Charles Dillon Stengel was a bad manager, just because he had wretched teams in Boston, Brooklyn, and New York. They said that Harpo Marx could have won ten pennants in 12 years with the Yankee clubs that Casey had. That was a mistake. Oh, occasionally he would fall asleep on the bench during night games when he was fronting for the Mets, but that was strictly an epilogue to his years with the Yankees. Even that most cynical of athletes-turned-author, Jim Bouton, said that Stengel knew exactly what he was doing when he had Mickey Mantle and Whitey Ford working for him.

There was this pitcher named Hal Stowe who thought that all he had to do to make the major-league roster was to act like he belonged. He did none of the things other rookies were asked to do. He drank and went to dinner with Mantle and Ford. He did not run in the outfield and he made no overt attempt to impress Stengel. There was one place open on the roster, but Stowe failed to qualify.

"It's true that Hal Stowe pitched pretty good this spring," said Stengel in straight language. "But I noticed that he never ran in the outfield, that he never did all the things he was supposed to do. He never really hustled and he never really worked at it. That's why he didn't make the squad cut, he could bull-bleep everybody but the manager."

Just two years later, Stowe used the same act and managed to put a move on Ralph Houk, the hand-clapping, cigar-chewing militarist who replaced Stengel. The pitcher went north and opened the season with the Yankees because Houk thought he looked and acted like a big leaguer and that was very, very important. Stengel was not so easily confused. When he worked for the Mets the club came up with a nineteen-year-old first baseman named Greg Goossen, whom everybody gurgled about.

"In ten years, Greg Goossen has a great chance of being twenty-nine years old," he said. It wasn't cruel. It was accurate. Sure enough, just ten years later, Goossen did turn twenty-nine, but not with any major-league baseball club.

One afternoon before a World Series game, Stengel took a young Mickey Mantle out to right field at the old ball park in Brooklyn and started to explain how to play caroms off the concave wall. Mantle wanted to know how his manager knew so much about it.

"I used to play right field for the Dodgers!" growled Stengel. "Do you think I was born old?"

So there will be a World Series this year and Casey Stengel will not be present. He was always good for a story. One afternoon it was raining in Baltimore and there he stood with a foot on the rail. "Pardon me, Casey," said a columnist, "it's lousy outside and I need help." He went on for an hour.

Standing nearby was a slim, quivering journalist from a small-town paper. When he was through rescuing the veteran, he turned to the rookie, gave him about 15 minutes and ended up with: "Listen, I got a secret, exclusive story I don't want to give to nobody else. I go to bed late and get up early. You gotta meet me at 6 A.M., but bring some Scotch and we'll break things together."

The man was beautiful. If he's dead, it is only a rumor. Don't bother to print it.

*1975*

## ROBERT LIPSYTE

Robert Lipsyte (b. 1938) didn't plan on staying at *The New York Times* when he became a copyboy there. He was a precocious nineteen-year-old Columbia University graduate who dreamed of living in California and writing novels and screenplays. He wound up on the baseball beat anyway. Then it was decided that *The Times*'s regular boxing writer couldn't be wasted covering the anticipated mismatch between Sonny Liston and a motor-mouthed kid named Cassius Clay, so Lipsyte found himself thrust into one of the defining sports stories of the twentieth century. He parlayed the opportunity into a job as a columnist and became one of the leaders of a new wave that upset applecarts and inspired critical thinking. He eventually left daily journalism to write fiction and nonfiction and work in public television. But when Muhammad Ali, the former Cassius Clay, died in 2016, *The Times* knew whom it wanted to write his page-one obituary: Lipsyte.

★ ★ ★

# Clay Wins Title in Seventh-Round Upset as Liston Is Halted by Shoulder Injury

MIAMI BEACH—Incredibly, the loud-mouthed bragging, insulting youngster had been telling the truth all along. Cassius Clay won the world heavyweight title tonight when a bleeding Sonny Liston, his left shoulder injured, was unable to answer the bell for the seventh round.

Immediately after he had been announced as the new heavyweight champion of the world, Clay yelled to the newsmen covering the fight: "Eat your words." Only three of 46 sports writers covering the fight had picked him to win.

A crowd of 8,297, on its feet through the early rounds at Convention Hall, sat stunned during the one-minute rest period between the sixth and seventh rounds. Only Clay seemed to know what had happened; he threw up his hands and danced a little jig in the center of the ring.

The victory was scored as a technical knockout in the seventh round, one round less than Clay had predicted. Liston seemingly had injured the shoulder in the first round while swinging and missing with jabs and hooks at the elusive 22-year-old.

The fight was Clay's from the start. The tall, swift youngster, his hands carelessly low, backed away from Liston's jabs, circled around Liston's dangerous left hook and opened a nasty gash under Liston's left eye.

He never let Liston tie him up for short, brutal body punches, and although he faltered several times, he refused to allow himself to be cornered. His long left jab kept bouncing off Liston's face. From the beginning, it was hard to believe.

The men had moved briskly into combat, Liston stalking, moving flat-footedly forward. He fell short with two jabs, brushed Clay back with a grazing right to the stomach and landed a solid right to the stomach. The crowd leaned forward for the imminent destruction of the young poet.

But the kid hadn't lied. All those interminable refrains of "float like a butterfly, sting like a bee," had been more than foolish songs. The kid was floating. He leaned back from Liston's jabs and hooks, backed into the ropes, then spun out and away. He moved clockwise around Liston, taunting that terrible left hook, his hands still low.

Then he stung, late in the first round, sticking his left in Liston's face and following with a quick barrage to Liston's head. They continued for long seconds after the bell, unable to hear the inadequate ring above the roar of the crowd.

It must have been somewhere in that round that Liston's shoulder was hurt.

[Jack Nilon, Liston's manager, said at the hospital that the former champion had hurt the shoulder during training, The Associated Press reported. He said Liston did not spar Feb. 3, 4, 5 and 14 because of the injury. Asked why he hadn't postponed the fight, Nilon said, "We thought we could get away with it."]

He strained forward with over-eager hooks that struck only air. For a moment, in the second round, Liston pummeled Clay against the ropes, but again, Cassius spun out and away.

Then the young man began to rumble as he had promised. His quick left jabs penetrated Liston's defenses, and he followed with right hands. He leaned forward as he fired rights and lefts at Liston's expressionless face. Liston began to bleed from a crescent-shaped cut high on the left cheekbone.

Like a bull hurt and maddened by the picadors' lances, Liston charged forward. The heavy muscles worked under his smooth, broad back as he virtually hurled his 218 pounds at the dodging, bobbing, dancing Clay.

His heavy arms swiped forward and he threw illegal backhand punches in his bear-like lunges. Once, Clay leaned the wrong way and Liston tagged him with a long left.

Cassius was staggered, but Liston was hurt and tired. He could not move in to press his advantage.

And now, a strange murmur began to ripple through the half-empty arena and people on blue metal chairs began to look at one another. Something like human electricity danced and flowed as the spectators suddenly realized that even if Cassius lost, he was no fraud. His style was unorthodox, but. . . .

There was little action in the fourth, as Cassius continued to circle. Once he opened his eyes wide as a Liston jab fell short, and it seemed as if he were mocking the heavy-footed hunter. As it turned out, Cassius could barely see.

He began complaining to Angelo Dundee, his trainer, at the end of the round. Something had gotten into his eyes, from Liston's glove, from the sponge, somewhere. But he went out for the fifth anyway, and all Dundee could do was shout, "Stay way from him, stay away."

Clay tried to stay away. Sensing something, Liston bulled forward, slamming Cassius with a left hook in the nose and lefts and rights to the body. Blinking furiously, Clay kept circling away. He never hit back.

Both fighters were sluggish in the fifth round, breathing heavily. Liston's face was still impassive, but the grooves along his forehead seemed deeper, and the snorting breaths through his nose harsher.

He seemed even more tired in the sixth as Clay's eyes cleared and the younger man bore in, then leaped away, jabbing and hooking and landing a solid right to Liston's jaw. Clay's jabs were slipping through at will now, bouncing off that rock-like face, opening the cut under the left eye.

Liston walked heavily back to his corner at the end of the sixth. He did not sit down immediately. Then as Liston did sit down, Clay came dancing out to the center of the ring, waving his arms, all alone. It seemed like a long time before Drew (Bundini) Brown, his assistant trainer, was hugging him and Dundee was dancing up and down, and Jack Nilon, Liston's adviser, was wrapping yards of tape around the former champion's left shoulder.

"I just can't go back," a Liston aide reported Sonny to have said.

And then the crowd was cheering and booing, which is something like laughing and crying because it was the wildest thing they had ever seen. It didn't make sense. For weeks, Clay had played the fool and been tagged at will by unworthy sparring partners. This morning, at the weigh-in, he had acted bizarre and disturbed.

And tonight, he had been cool and fast and without fear.

Until the knockout, the officials had had the fight a draw. Referee Barney Felix had scored the six rounds 57–57 on the 10-point-must system. Judge Bill Lovitt scored it 58–56 for Liston, and Judge Gus Jacobsen 58–56 for Clay.

But points didn't really matter after all. Poetry and youth and joy had triumphed over the 8–1 odds. And until it had happened (and perhaps until they can look it up) people laughed at the thought that a night like this could happen.

The crowd had cheered lustily at 9:59 P.M., when Cassius came jogging down the aisle toward the ring, his face impassive, wearing a hip-length terry-cloth white robe on which was emblazoned, The Lip. Nobody even snickered, for everyone knew Clay to be a braggart, not to be taken seriously.

He leaped through the ropes in a sudden motion, then waited in the ring for six minutes before Liston started down the aisle, shadow-boxing in a corner of the ring. He did not talk or shout. Liston, in a long, white robe, glared out from a white hood and climbed heavily through the ropes.

"Wipe my face off, hey, wipe my face off," said Clay to Dundee. The trainer was staring at the implacable Liston, and didn't hear Clay until he had repeated himself.

Both men stood in their corners serenely, as the inevitable parade of notables—Rocky Marciano, Sugar Ray Robinson, et al—shook their gloved hands. Sonny, in white trunks with a black stripe and his name across a thigh, seemed malevolent and invincible. Clay, in white trunks with red piping, seemed only big.

Earlier, rumors had swept Convention Hall that Cassius was not going to show, that the thin line of hysteria he had trod during the morning weigh-in had become full-scale fear.

But even as the rumor mounted (that he was in a plane, en route to Mexico), Cassius was standing quietly in a far corner of the arena. He was waiting for his brother, Rudolph Valentino Clay, to make his professional debut.

Few people noticed him. He was dressed in a tight-fitting black tropical suit and wore a black bow tie on his ruffled, white dress shirt.

Clay was surrounded by aides—Brown; Archie Robinson, his personal secretary; and Dundee. Dundee was carrying a blue suitcase and Bundini kept a hand on Clay's back, as if he might have to restrain him at any moment.

But Clay hardly moved. Despite his height (6 feet 3 inches) he often had to stand on tiptoe to watch the action in the far-off ring. Once, when Rudy floored his opponent, Chip Johnson of Naples, Fla., in the second round, Clay shouted some encouragement. Otherwise he was silent.

Even during the one-minute rest periods between rounds, Cassius stared at the ring. His face seemed tense and alert, but his body was unmoving. At the end of the four-round bout, when it was announced that Rudy had won, Cassius turned abruptly, without saying a word, and followed a phalanx of Miami policemen with flashy gunbutts out of the arena and into his dressing room.

Once there, at about 9:15 P.M., he was re-examined by Dr. Robbins.

At the weigh-in, Dr. Robbins had said that Clay's pulse rate was around 120, more than double his norm of 54. Forty-five minutes before the fight, Clay's pulse was 64, the same as Liston's. Sonny had arrived at the hall a few minutes after 8 P.M. and gone to his dressing room to rest.

*1964*

★   ★   ★

# The Medal

WALKING UP the post office steps in the brilliant, chilly afternoon, Dick Tiger said: "If they ask me how much it's worth, what should I say?"

His companion shrugged. "We should try to pawn it and find out."
"I'll say a million dollars." Tiger laughed. It was the first time he had
laughed. "I'll say fifty or a hundred, just so it gets there."

He stood on line at the registry window, a small black hat perched
on his head, his body muffled in a fur-lined coat. He has always seemed
overdressed in America, always a little colder than everyone else. Once
he said it all went back to the four years he lived in England, training in
drafty gyms as he boxed on the Liverpool-Blackpool circuit.

The clerk behind the registry wicket hefted the package and shook
his head. "No good, you got Scotch Tape on it. Go around the corner,
they'll give you some brown paper."

Another line. Tiger has always been such a patient man, waiting for
bouts, waiting for return bouts, waiting for a crack at a world championship. He had won two, the middleweight and the light-heavyweight,
and lost them both, and now, at the age of 40, he is picking up fights
where he can while waiting for one more title shot.

"If there had been no war," he said earlier that morning, "I would
be retired by now. But . . . well . . ." he smiled and spread his hands.
"I'm not getting rich or investing money. Now is just for daily bread
and praying the war is over. I cannot complain. I am not the only one
who lost property."

A clerk handed Tiger a long strip of gummed brown paper and a wet
sponge in a dish. Tiger took it to a writing desk and began to tear the
brown paper into small strips, his thick fingers careful and precise. He
had always taped and bandaged his own hands, rare for a champion
boxer. He had done many things himself. He was always considered a
very tight man with money and with intimacies. Unfailingly courte-
ous and cooperative, but dowdy and reserved. His money all went to
Nigeria, to his wife, seven children and his large family circle, and
into buildings and shops. Until the country exploded into war, he was
a rich man.

"Well," he said, finishing the package, "now I know there is something else I can do."

There was another wait at the registry window. Tiger studied the package. It was addressed to the British Ambassador, in Washington, and inside was the medal with the pink ribbon, now grimy, he had received in a ceremony in Lagos six years ago. The medal, Member of the Order of the British Empire, had begun to grow heavy in his mind. In a letter accompanying the medal, he had written:

"I am hereby returning the O.B.E. because every time I look at it I think of millions of men, women and children who died and are still dying in Biafra because of the arms and ammunition the British Government is sending to Nigeria and its continued moral support of this genocide against the people of Biafra."

He had signed it, Dick Tiger Ihetu. He had been christened Richard Ihetu, Ibo for "what I want." Dick Tiger became his ring name in early battles against such local gladiators as Easy Dynamite and Mighty Joe Young. But bombs had fallen and blood had been spilled and babies had starved in the towns of his youth, and when he spoke of his country it was no longer with the earnest chamber of commerce pitch he had used only a few years ago.

"If you look at Africa now," he had said earlier last Friday morning, "there is fighting and trouble in every country that once was under the British Government. They were forced to give the countries independence, but they gave it with the left hand and now are trying to take it back with the right hand."

He stopped suddenly. "I am not a politician. I don't want people to say, ah, there's a dumb fighter who does not speak good English talking."

He had wanted to return the medal for some time, he said. But it was not until he read two weeks ago that John Lennon, the Beatle, returned his O.B.E. for reasons that included Britain's involvement in the Nigerian civil war, that he decided to mail back his medal.

"Okay," snapped the registry clerk, flipping the small package. "What's in it?"

"A medal," said Tiger softly.

"What?"

"A medal."

"What's it worth?"

Tiger shrugged. "I don't know. Fifty, hundred dollars?"

"No value," said the clerk, to himself. He weighed it, registered it, asked Tiger if he wanted it to go air mail. Tiger said, yes.

"One sixty."

Tiger gave him two dollar bills, and counted his change. He readjusted his scarf as he walked out into the bright street, and smiled, and shook his companion's hand and could only say, "Well . . ." and shrug, and start down the steps.

*1969*

## BILL NACK

Bill Nack (1941–2018), the most poetic of sportswriters, was covering such unpoetic subjects as politics and sewers for *Newsday* when he climbed atop a desk at a 1971 Christmas party and recited the winners of every Kentucky Derby from memory. The Long Island daily's editor, a devout horseplayer, watched in awe, and not long afterward Nack found himself with a new assignment, writing about, as he put it, "the whole horse." A little more than two years later, he was chronicling Secretariat's Triple Crown and writing a book about it that was made into a movie. Nack became a general sports columnist, gleefully harpooning Yankee owner George Steinbrenner's bloated ego and the Nero-esque overtones of Super Bowl insanity. But *Sports Illustrated* beckoned in 1979 with time, space, and money that he couldn't turn down. When he left twenty-three years later, having had his byline upgraded to William Nack and having written about everything from the horses to boxing to chess, he was more than one of the magazine's legends. He was beloved.

★ ★ ★

# First a Hush, Then Awe

E LMONT—It ended with a single stentorian burst of applause, with screams so sudden they seemed startled out of people, and they began when Ron Turcotte pushed Secretariat to ever-widening leads of 28, 30 and finally 31 lengths in the Belmont Stakes.

It ended, too, when Turcotte jumped off in the winner's circle and groom Edward Sweat led Secretariat past the crowds from which long and sometimes braceleted arms reached out for the chestnut colt as he passed nearby. Hands slapped his muscular body. Hands shot up in fists. Hands were cupped over faces. Hands were holding hands and gesturing elation and awe.

It also ended when Sweat led Secretariat through the long tunnel from the winner's circle to the saddling enclosure, the big colt sweating heavily, his eyes darting left and right as the thousands of people lining the enclosure sent up cheer after cheer and shouted his name over and over. "Spectacular, just sensational," said trainer Elliott Burch as Sweat led Secretariat past him through the paddock and out the paddock gate to the tunnel between the racetrack and the stable area.

Secretariat had won the Triple Crown—he had won the last leg of the crown in record time, 2-1/5 seconds faster than any other Belmont winner had ever run the distance—so it was still ending, as if it would never end, as Sweat took him through the tunnel, still ending as crowds followed him on both sides, behind him, in front of him, as he walked with that fine sense of bearing he has toward the barn where he would have a saliva and a urinalysis, routine tests for drugging.

Trainers gathered in the testing barn and looked at the colt as Ed Sweat washed him off with water, scraped him with a water scraper, and the trainers laughed when George (Charlie) Davis—the colt's regular exercise boy who was holding him while Sweat scraped—kissed the colt on his nose.

"He's a great horse," said John Campo, who trained the second place finisher, Twice a Prince.

"He is," said H. Allen Jerkens, one of America's top trainers, who stood outside the test barn fence with his daughter, Julie, just to get a closer look at Secretariat.

This was nearing the end of a long day for Secretariat, the close of a day in which he ran faster than any horse has ever run 1½ miles—the classic distance—in the history of the American turf. There he was, near the end of his day, drenched with sweat and water, an object now of adulation and awe, and a tired and thirsty horse whose day began more than 12 hours earlier, in a barn 100 yards away, in silence.

It began in the dark of the morning while he slept.

It was 3:56 A.M., and in barn five at Belmont Park a Pinkerton guard, Joe Fanning, stood framed against the lighted open doorway of trainer Lucien Laurin's tackroom. A motorcycle backfired on Hempstead Turnpike, but the stalls of the horses in barn 5 quickly sunk back into quiet darkness, as suspended as deep breaths. Nightwatchman Clem Kenyon had already fed Secretariat his quart of early morning oats, hanging the tub in his stall, when John Harris materialized beneath a street lamp on his way to his job as a groom for Laurin. "This is going to be the big day," Harris said. "We run four horses . . . we got a horse in the first race, and then we got Spanish Riddle and Angle Light and" . . . there was a pause, a smile, and he added, ". . . And the big horse."

Down the shed row Secretariat was beginning the day in stall seven. Harris and the other stablehands were about to begin their days of the Belmont Stakes. Harris stretched, disappearing into a room nearby, and in the doorway light the Pinkerton vanished in the darkness toward Secretariat's stall, returning an instant later to stand guard. Soon birds began rioting in the trees, the sky bluing, and horses stirred inside their stalls and it was nearing 5 A.M.

The colt was lying down then, resting like a good horse, when the 2-year-old Capito—half-brother to Riva Ridge—poked his head from neighboring stall nine and looked about. Other heads quickly popped outdoors. Riva Ridge looked up both ends of the shed. Then stable foreman Henry Hoeffner arrived, pulling up in his car, and in a second he was strolling up the shed toward Secretariat's stall. As Hoeffner walked past the tackroom, Secretariat thrust his blazed face and massive chestnut neck from the door, giving Hoeffner the eye. Hoeffner stopped, looked the colt up and down, and walked away, It was 5:12 A.M., and a beginning.

So the rhythm of the workaday routine began. Soon Edward Sweat, the groom of Secretariat, drove up in his car and climbed out in search of a cup of coffee. "I'm ready," said Sweat, sipping it as he walked into the barn. "I'm ready as I can get." Sweat set the cup on the windowsill in front of Secretariat's stall.

"Well," he announced out loud to the shed, "let me get old Big Red ready here." The colt peered at Sweat, his ears pricked forward as he listened for the words, and he watched Sweat carefully as the groom picked up a fork and walked to the stall. There Sweat stopped, smiled as he raised his hands like an 1890 pugilist and said to the colt, "Come on, Red, get back in there so I can do some work." The colt moved backward slowly, and Sweat ducked into the stall to work. It was 5:40 A.M.

So Sweat quickly got the colt ready for Secretariat's morning stroll, his only exercise on the morning of the day of the biggest race in his life. Sweat brushed the colt down, rubbing his glossy sides and back and shoulders. "He looks good this morning," said Sweat, walking toward the stall. "We'll take him out right now. Hey, Big Red, here I am, here I come." It was 5:57 A.M. when he finished working on him and the colt's regular exercise boy, Charlie Davis, led him from his stall to the outside walking ring. And Secretariat put on his show.

Laurin himself arrived five minutes later, and the pace of the morning work seemed to pick up sharply, with Laurin going to the racetrack to see horses work, returning to the shed and office, stopping to look in on Secretariat when he passed the stall. And the colt gazed upon the hubbub as if it were just a mere abstraction. He backed into his stall, came to the door again, backed in again. The morning was swept up by rakes and swished into little corners by brooms, and he watched it all quietly. Sweat gave the colt a quart of oats at 10:30 A.M., three quarts less than he does on non-racing days. Secretariat stood in the back of the stall, as if brooding. "Now he don't want to be bothered," said Sweat.

Work wound down. Stablehands went to eat, the stable emptying and the life of the racetrack easing back. Only Sweat crouched outside the shed washing towels at 10:20 A.M., beginning the long wait for the end of the afternoon.

The colt was in his stall all through the late morning and early afternoon, alone but for Ed Sweat working in front of the stall and an occasional groom walking by and Tom Trotter Jr., the Pinkerton who replaced Fanning, standing on guard near the stall. The afternoon pressed on, with horses passing the Laurin barn to and from the races at the track.

It grew late. And suddenly Edward Sweat dipped into the stall and started to get the colt ready, and the colt knew it. Again, the colt's rations for the afternoon meal were cut, the tip-off that he would battle with other horses in a horse race. Sweat moved into the stall, brushing him and rubbing him, putting a shine on the coat, a luster. Then McClain, the assistant trainer, with a serious set to his face, strode through the crowd that gathered at the open end of the shed and said, "You all are going to have to step back, please, step back now. The horse won't be able to walk through with a crowd here." The crowd stepped back. It was 4:07 P.M.

George Davis jumped suddenly on the pony Billy Silver, walking him to the door of the shed to wait for Secretariat and the post parade. Angle Light, the colt who had beaten Secretariat in the Wood April 21, was led back sweating and sandy from the seventh race, finishing out of the money in that race before the Belmont.

At 5:10 P.M., the loudspeaker in the stable area shouted that horses should be brought to the paddock for the eighth race, the Belmont. Then, out walked Secretariat and Sweat, with cameras clicking in the crowd. "Take it, Ed, take it," someone yelled.

Ed Sweat nodded and smiled and walked Secretariat through the tunnel to the paddock for saddling. All around the paddock, the crowds applauded, cheered, with one fan yelling, "Go get 'em, Secretariat." It was nearing post time.

The jockeys came out, and Turcotte jumped on the big colt and the crowd cheered harder, more boisterously than before, and Turcotte smiled faintly, then seemed to stiffen his face. It was no time to take a bow.

It was time to ride in the horse race of his life; a time to whip and beat all horses, and to do it with the ease of breaking sticks. And it was a time to understand that some things are a long time ending, and for some they may never end at all. "He's the greatest," Davis said, kissing the colt on the nose.

1973

## DAVE KINDRED

If there is a logical successor to Red Smith in terms of sense and sensibility, it is Dave Kindred (b. 1941). For fifty years, he tended to the language and the people (and racehorses) he wrote about with a craftsman's precision. He captured what other writers didn't because he abided by a credo of his own making: "If you pay attention, you'll see something you've never seen before." Every newspaper that employed Kindred—*The Courier-Journal* in Louisville, *The Washington Post, The National, The Atlanta Journal-Constitution*—was better for the diligence that made his column mandatory reading whether he was at the Super Bowl or a bush-league ballpark. He ultimately wrote *Sound and Fury*, a penetrating book examining the relationship between Muhammad Ali and Howard Cosell. Though now retired, Kindred continues to write about a girls' high school basketball team in Morton, Illinois (pop. 16,000), posting his dispatches on Facebook and a local website. He gets paid in Milk Duds.

★   ★   ★

# Willie Pastrano

THE OLD fighter is talking.
"I look at ordinary people in their suits, them with no scars on their face, and I'm different from these people."

Willie Pastrano is the old fighter, once a world champion, the light heavyweight champion for two years in the early 1960s. Though lit by the thin winter sun of a late New Orleans afternoon, the old fighter's face belongs to darkness.

"I don't fit in with them people. I'm where everybody's got scar tissue on their eyes and got noses like saddles. I go to these old-timers' conventions, old fighters like me, and I see the scar tissue and all them flat noses. They're beautiful. Galento, may he rest in peace. Giardello, LaMotta, Carmen Basilio. What a sweetheart Basilio is. They talk like me, like they got rocks in their throats. Beautiful."

This is Willie Pastrano, who once sat at tea with the Queen of England. Willie Pastrano, who knew a man who sawed people into pieces for disposal. Willie Pastrano, who made $100,000 in his last fight and a year later robbed houses and yachts, "sneaking in like a . . . dog," to buy the heroin he needed with his daily breakfast of gin and vodka, razor-blade soup.

"I was," Willie Pastrano said, "the living dead."

He quit talking.

The old fighter made the sign of the cross.

In a deserted firehouse with a threadbare ring, Willie Pastrano works as the boxing coach of the New Orleans Recreation Department. At the Superdome, a $4.80 cab ride away, Sugar Ray Leonard gets $7 million this week and Roberto Duran $10 million. Willie Pastrano, for his week's work, will clear $69.50.

He's broke, yes. "But look," he said, "I've had money, I've been rich." He'd rather be what he is now. Happy. He's happy to be alive. He is 45 years old, and sharpies will tell it was 8–5 against Willie Pastrano ever getting so old. Heroin addicts don't win many times.

"Just saying 'heroin' makes me feel like I taste it in the back of my mouth," Pastrano said. "I go to the doctor's office and see a syringe, it makes me sick to my stomach. You never really kick it. You always got the yen. You always got to fight. I'm the champ at fighting the junk."

At 190 pounds Willie Pastrano is only 15 pounds over the light-heavyweight limit. There is a spring in his step. A weightlifter now, he is in good shape. The son of an Italian father and a Cajun mother,

Pastrano has a square-cut face of mottled browns and blacks. Thin lines of scars wiggle through his eyebrows, and long-healed wounds are marked by tiny craters on his cheekbones. Doctors twice have done surgery on his left eye, and now he wears sunglasses because the eye is always red.

And if the eye is red, people think they know. It's a detached retina, but people think the red in his eye means Willie is on the horse again. On the heroin.

He goes to churches now to tell the people without scars on their faces that he was a heroin addict.

He tells them the junk put him in three mental institutions and three hospitals. They wanted to tape wires to his forehead and shoot electricity through his brain. He said no. No electroshock for a world champion. He would beat the stuff on his own.

It's the toughest fight of his life, he says, and he is winning.

Pastrano lost his championship the third time he defended, losing to José Torres in March, 1965. Fighting was the only thing Pastrano ever did right. A fat little kid, shamed by his father, who beat him with a belt for not striking back at neighborhood bullies who taunted him as "jelly shaking on a plate," Pastrano went to a boxing gym to lose weight. In the process, he found talent.

Never a puncher, always a clever stylist, Pastrano fought 18 years before winning the championship from Harold Johnson. On the way up, he had tea with the Queen and Prince Philip while in London to fight; he moved with good fighters such as Kid Gavilan, Benny Paret, Jimmy Ellis and Ralph Dupas, and he had $30,000 in the bank after he lost the title to Torres.

"When I lost the title, I got down on myself," Pastrano said. "I was lonely. I had nobody. I had nothing. So I opened my doors to the wrong people. I let in anybody, just so there'd be people around. For three years after I lost my title, I didn't know who the hell I was."

Who the wrong people were: "Killers, dope dealers, people who sawed up bodies. I didn't know it at the time. I thought one guy owned a gas station and another guy was a salesman. Then one day I went to visit this one guy. I walked through his house and out to the back, to his utility shed, and I saw him through a crack in the door."

What he saw: "He had on rubber gloves and an apron. He had a hacksaw, and his hands were full of blood. I started to say, 'Hi,' and that's when I saw the foot cut off. I puked."

For three years, Pastrano used heroin daily. "It wasn't the heroin I wanted. It was the boxing thing. Boxers should be rehabilitated like Vietnam veterans. Boxers have been to war and are psychologically scarred. You got fighters acting like they're punch-drunk when they're not, just to get attention. Like Beau Jack shining shoes in front of a hotel in Miami. He ain't punch-drunk. He just misses the applause. With the applause, you come to life."

Without that affirmation of existence, Pastrano needed big money for the only high available to him. Heroin.

"I didn't have nothing left from my $30,000, so I was always look-ing to get money. You needed money because you needed heroin to feel normal. Your body gets to need it like food. I had gin and vodka for breakfast. And heroin. I did 'b and e's' for the money. Breaking and entering. I robbed places across the street from police stations. I robbed houses, I robbed yachts. I never used a weapon, not once. I was sneaking in like a . . . dog."

He went cold turkey in 1969, Pastrano said, and there followed 10 years of wandering. Las Vegas, Oklahoma City, Miami. A trail of tears. Dupas dragged his right leg and became a hermit. Ellis and Gavilan are blind in one eye. Paret is dead, killed in the ring. And Willie Pastrano, their friend, once a champion of the world, worked as a bouncer in strip joints, 2 o'clock in the afternoon 'til 2 the next morning, six days a week. Worked some as a chip runner in Vegas, did some greeting at a greasy spoon in Reno.

Back in his hometown of New Orleans, Pastrano has worked the last year with the city recreation department down at the Magazine Street gym. Yellowed newspaper clippings are stuck to the walls. History is on those dirty walls: Cassius Clay at 13, Tony Galento falling through the ropes against Jack Dempsey, Willie Pastrano in with Archie Moore.

Sitting at the back of the gym, Pastrano watches a handful of plainly pitiable fighters. They should be pumping gas somewhere. They are in Pastrano's gym desperately dreaming. Because a manager reneged on a deal, Pastrano has taken over managing his first fighter, Chubby Johnson, 22, who will be on the Leonard-Duran undercard.

"They say old boxers ought to get away from boxing," Pastrano said. "I don't want to be a manager. But a guy backed out on Chubby and now I got him. Okay, I'm a manager. So all right. Boxing is what I am."

Then Pastrano said, "You know what Duran did the other day during a workout?"

Duran did this: Duran looked into the crowd and raised his gloved fist in salute.

"I looked around to see who he was waving to," Pastrano said.

The old fighter's face left the darkness a moment. "It was for me."

*1980*

★　★　★

# Ben Crenshaw

H IS BOY would win the Masters and Charlie Crenshaw loved it. He's an old man now, 70, who has seen his boy hurt too many times. Ben Crenshaw was to be the next Nicklaus. He won the first pro tournament he played. But in a decade of frustration, he never won a major championship. No Opens, no PGAs, no Masters. His marriage fell apart and Ben blamed himself because he gave his heart more to the game than to his marriage. His swing fell apart and a hundred friends tried to help put it back together. Then, late on a lovely Sunday afternoon, Charlie Crenshaw knew his boy would win the Masters and the old man wept.

Spring days die softly here. Sunlight fades to the pink of a baby's cheeks. When the sun goes down behind a stand of strong pine trees, the dying light moves across the ground in random patterns that, if we are lucky, paint a picture we will remember always. Such a light, filtered through the pines, fell across Ben Crenshaw's face shortly after 5 o'clock Sunday afternoon. The light touched Ben's blond hair. For a moment, he was golden.

He had won the Masters. There were three holes to play, but he had won it. He had a three-stroke lead. He had made a 12-foot birdie putt at the 15th hole. There his father, Charlie, a Texas lawyer, beefy and rough-cut, allowed himself a small celebration. Walking behind the huge gallery, walking alone, he threw his fists wide, for just a second, and then clasped his hands behind his back again, walking on.

Only three holes to go then, and Charlie Crenshaw stood by a pine tree a dozen yards from the 16th green. It's a 170-yard hole with a pond guarding its left side. "Keep this one dry, baby," Charlie Crenshaw said. He said it aloud, but he said it to no one. He said it to himself and he said it to his boy 170 yards away. Ben Crenshaw would win his first Masters unless, by his own failings, he lost it.

He had lost other big ones he wanted. He came to his game loving it. He ran his hands over maps of the Old Course at St. Andrews, where the game was born. He knows about Old Tom Morris and Young Tom Morris, Francis Ouimet and Bobby Jones. He can show you the spot at Augusta where Gene Sarazen did it. But it seemed, in the cruelest turn, that this gentle little man loved too much. Maybe it would be easier to win if he came to work stone ignorant rather than knowing where the footprints led.

"When you lose the PGA in a playoff . . . when you hit it into the water on the 71st hole of the U.S. Open and miss a playoff by a shot . . . when you double-bogey the 71st hole of the British Open to lose that tournament, you start wondering."

Ben Crenshaw said those words an hour after winning the Masters this time. He spoke of 1975 in the U.S. Open at Medinah, 1979 in the PGA at Oakland Hills and '79 in the British Open at Royal Sandwich. Six times in the majors, twice in the Masters, Crenshaw has finished second.

"You start wondering if you can hold yourself together."

*Keep this one dry, baby.*

Charlie Crenshaw stood by the 16th hole. His boy put his tee shot on dry land. Then Ben Crenshaw walked to the green. With thousands of people applauding, with the sweet sound washing over him, with the dying sunlight golden on his face, Ben Crenshaw smiled. And his daddy, next to a pine tree behind a thousand people, said, "It's great when they cheer for your kid like that. Man."

With his heavy hands, Charlie Crenshaw wiped away tears.

This was it. "Lady Fate or Dame Fortune takes somebody by the hand and leads them through," Charlie Crenshaw said to a reporter who found him in the crowd. "She's been with Ben all week. He's hit shots through trees and out of trees. . . . He's had the greatest putting round I've ever seen. That one at 10, my Lord. . . . When David Graham made two putts in the '79 PGA just to stay in the playoff, to keep Ben from being a champion, it couldn't have been David Graham by himself. That lady just has to be with you."

Charlie Crenshaw laughed. "That lady has been all over Ben so many times this week."

At the 10th hole, Crenshaw had made a 60-foot putt that broke eight feet, rolling on an arc of improbable design to an intersection with the hole, a dot in the great distance. If Graham beat Crenshaw in '79 with two playoff putts, Crenshaw beat Tom Kite here with that 60-foot improbability. Kite botched the 10th hole five minutes later and dumped a killing shot into Rae's Creek 15 minutes after that.

When the 60-footer at the 10th fell, Ben Crenshaw said he thought, as his father had, "Maybe this is my day." This is what they wanted for 20 years. Charlie, never more than a hacker himself, bought his son a putter for his 15th birthday at home in Austin. Ben still uses it, though with a new shaft ("It got broken when I was 16. It ran up a tree or something").

This is the day Charlie Crenshaw thought of two years ago when his boy was in trouble. Ben had fallen to 83rd on the money list. The boy who would be king was a sad commoner. A hundred friends, earned by his humility and kindnesses, tried to help. He tried a hundred new swings. Then he tried what always had worked. He talked to his father.

Charlie Crenshaw remembers the talk. "I told him the Lord gave him his swing. Just like He gives a gift to a great artist or a pianist. I told him, 'Just go up and hit it, don't analyze it.'"

So in 1983 Ben Crenshaw won his first tournament in three years. And now, at age 32, he has won the Masters. Ben Crenshaw stood in the dusk at a victory ceremony. He thanked his friends. "If I could cut out a piece of my heart and give it to you, I would," he said. And he said, "I am so happy my father is here. I am very fortunate to have the father I do. He's a gentleman and I have tried to live the life he would want me to."

Ben Crenshaw's last piece of golf work Sunday was to sign his score-card in a tent beside the 18th green. As he came out of the tent, the champion saw his father and walked to him, arms open. They hugged for a long, long time, with the boy burying his face in his father's shoulder.

*1984*

★　★　★

# Walter Payton

S WEETNESS NO more. Walter Payton is gone. The ball last settled into his hands on a little pass when the Bears asked him to do one more miracle, after all these years one more miracle, a little one, a matter of eight yards for a first down in the last minute. And when Payton made seven yards—forced out of bounds by tacklers closing down on him—it was over, a man's lifework done.

A life's work, running with a football in your hands? Yes, if you're Walter Payton. If you came from the hardscrabble nowhere of Mississippi, if in 13 pro football years you became the greatest runner ever, if your dignity graced the game more than any game deserved, then, yes, a life's work not only well done but uniquely done, a work of immortality.

Whatever the score on this icicle of a January day, it doesn't matter. Nor does it matter that the Redskins and not the Bears have moved nearer the Super Bowl. We have seen the last day's football work of Walter Payton, a runner of heavenly gait, a man they called "Sweetness," whose gentle manner and lilting voice belied the iron of his will and body.

A yard short, the game lost, Walter Payton walked off a football field for the last time. Players from both sides touched him, no words needed, for everyone knew this was it, the 13 years done, Payton retiring at age 33, a young man but still an old runner, the quickness that delivered so many miracles now gone.

The game ended around him. Payton alone stayed on the Bears' bench. In massive old Soldier Field with its Roman columns, a single man sat on the bench. Payton let his hands fall together between his knees. He tugged at the fingertips of the gritty gloves a ballcarrier wears on wintry days by the Chicago lakeshore. He sat with his head bowed, and from behind him came the voices of fans: "We love you, Walter." . . . "Thank you, Walter." An old man raged against the dying of the light, "One more year, Walter. You can still do it."

Walter Payton, a millionaire, has talked about buying an NFL franchise. The Bears have invited him into the front office. There's a world out there for him. So when he saw the sidelines of time and age closing down on him, he decided it was time to go. He shares the NFL rushing record of nine straight 100-yard games; he has done it 77 times, but not once in his last 20 games.

He had 85 yards this day on 18 carries. For a step here, a step there, the years fell away, and we saw what Walter Payton had been when every step was taken with a winged foot. This day's work done, a life's work done, the workman sat on his team's bench at the side of an empty field in a great stadium. He would say, "I didn't want to hurry the moment."

From somewhere behind him came a woman's shout, "Chicago loves you, Walter." And he rose to leave, with 25,000 people chanting in farewell, "Wal-ter . . . Wal-ter."

As if by habit, Payton moved onto the field, walking near the hash-mark, one last time moving toward the end zone. He never looked up, never raised his eyes, until he entered a dark tunnel. Then he blinked against tears. He had left records everywhere. Now he had left himself behind. Sweetness no more.

He came to his locker in a corner of the Bears' room. He sat in his uniform. He still wore his helmet. He let his head fall back against a wall, and a teammate said, "You OK?"

Payton's tiny voice, his eyes closed, still in his uniform: "I'm just taking my time taking it off. This is the last time I take it off."

An old Chicago newspaperman, Bill Gleason, Payton's friend, sat by him. Of two dozen reporters there, none spoke. Then Payton said to Gleason, "You going to miss me?"

"Absolutely," Gleason said. "What I'm going to remember is how much fun you were."

Payton said, "That's the main reason I was playing, to have fun."

He later would stand in front of a press conference and say, "The last 13 years for me have been a lot of good times and a lot of bad times. There were times when I wanted to quit and times when there'd be no quit in me. . . . The bottom line is, God blessed me. I've truly been blessed."

Ready to leave the locker room a last time, Walter Payton put his gear into a bag slowly. He clicked shut the clasp of a watch heavy with diamonds. He touched his neck with a spray of perfume, and then, with a little laugh, sweetness indeed, he sprayed a few puffs of the stuff on the sportswriters at his side, the perfume battling Bill Gleason's cigar.

*1988*

## LEIGH MONTVILLE

In eighteen years as a *Boston Globe* sports columnist, Leigh Montville (b. 1943) doled out laughs and left readers shaking their heads in admiration. "Everyone else looks at things from the ground floor," a colleague said. "Leigh writes like he's got his own hot air balloon." You can feel the change in altitude when you read what he had to say about his first dizzying all-nighter watching ESPN and the mojo expended in pursuit of game-winning homers. Montville went on to write for *Sports Illustrated* for nine years and is now, after best-seller success with books on Babe Ruth, Ted Williams, and Muhammad Ali, one of the country's foremost sports biographers. Not bad for someone who fancies himself more the spiritual kin of Woody Allen than of Woodward and Bernstein.

★  ★  ★

# The Tube That Won't Let You Up

A GUY named Leroy Witherspoon came dribbling across my eyes at 3 in the afternoon. The clock was ticking down. The crowd was going wild. I was going wild.

Five . . . four . . . three. Leroy let it go. Two . . . one. The ball went through the hoop. A definite swish. A 30-footer.

"Did you see that?" I asked.

Silence.

"Did you see it!" I demanded.

I was alone. I was sick.

I was screaming about something that had happened almost two days earlier. I was screaming about the fact that Potsdam State had tied Augustana College to send the Division 3 NCAA basketball final into overtime. I don't know where Augustana is located. I am a little hazy about Potsdam. I knew none of the players involved. I did know that Potsdam won in overtime. I knew that tape-delayed fact already, having read it two days earlier on the scores page of a newspaper.

I still was screaming.

Never in my worst sports junkie moments, not even on a spectacular fall afternoon, the family out in the leaves, me in the living room with a football game involving the nondescript Kansas City Chiefs or the St. Louis Cardinals or the Detroit Lions, had I felt this bad. This was Florida. People in Boston would kill to be 20 feet outside my motel room door, sitting at the pool on a workday Wednesday afternoon with a piña colada and a smile in the 80-degree sunshine. I was watching Leroy and Potsdam on my glow-in-the-dark little television, located two feet from the flyswatter and the Gideon Bible.

Help me, Father, for I have sinned.

I was hooked on ESPN.

I never had seen it before, you know? I had heard rumors. *They have it in Malden. My brother has it in Springfield. Twenty-four hours of televised sports every day of the week.* I always had said I wanted it. I demanded it. Bring me the cable. Bring me 24 hours of sports every day. Bring it and bring it now. I was outraged that my area of the United States was so tardy in receiving this greatest technological breakthrough in the history of mankind.

I found now that I couldn't stand it.

Or, worse yet, that I couldn't handle it.

ESPN, which went onto the air in September of 1979, just pumps those sports at you. Sports you never knew existed. Sports you never cared existed. Ask me if I would walk across the street to watch Potsdam play Augustana and I would laugh. Ask me if I didn't have to walk anywhere, just turn the knob . . . I watched track from New Zealand,

auto racing from Bristol, Tenn., Division 2—or was it Division 3?—
swim championships from some steamy pool, a taped tennis match
from Rotterdam that I saw three separate times, Jimmy Connors
against Sandy Mayer.

It was just so easy. Get up in the morning and turn on the set. A
fight is on! Freddie Roach of Dedham, no less. Sit and watch. Go somewhere, do something, return to the room to shave, turn on the set
again. Gymnastics! Do something else. Prepare to go to bed . . . no,
turn on the set. Just to check. Sports Center! Every score of every game
ever played! Followed by soccer from England, Crystal Palace against
Tottenham Hotspurs. By God, that's old Mike Flanagan of the Tea Men
out there! Fall asleep as the action fades to more New Zealand track.

I began to feel as if I were on a diet of honey-dip glazed doughnuts.
Excuse me.

I began to feel physically ill. If too much is not good for you, as
mother always said, this definitely was too much. The set controls you.
There is no time, nor inclination, to watch the rest of television anymore. Not even the news. There is no inclination to read books, newspapers, anything. Turn the knob. Watch the games. No need to talk.

I called ESPN yesterday to see what I would be missing today
because my week in that motel room has ended. I will be missing:
midnight, Martin Luther King Games, decathlon I; 1 A.M., Auto Racing 1980, A Look Back, A Look Ahead; 2:30 A.M., SportsCenter; 3 A.M.,
Top Rank Boxing from Philadelphia; 5:30 A.M., NCAA Volleyball,
Golden Dome Classic semifinal; 7 A.M., SportsCenter; 8 A.M., Professional Rodeo from Mesquite, Texas; 10 A.M., SportsCenter; 11 A.M.,
NCAA Gymnastics, Div. 2. That's just half the day, with shows like
Arizona State baseball and Superstar Volleyball Cup and the Virginia
500 to follow in the afternoon and night.

"How many homes are you in now?" I asked the ESPN man.

"Eight-point-nine million," he replied. "We project we'll be in 30 to
35 million by the middle of the '80s."

"And the long-distance future? Do you expect you'll be in every
home before 1990 as the cable moves down every street in America?"

"We would think so."

My palms sweat at the thought.

I have seen the future and it is Leroy Witherspoon on a sunny Wednesday afternoon.

*1981*

★   ★   ★

# It Ain't Over till It's Over

ANAHEIM, CALIF.—The future stared them in the face. The visiting men in gray baseball suits looked here and there and everywhere and could see the grim fate that waited for them. One pitch away.

"Get your equipment," the policemen said in the far reaches of the bullpen. "We'll take you out the back way, through the corridor."

One pitch away. All of Southern California seemed to hang from the triple-decked stands of Anaheim Stadium, waiting to romp across the neatly mowed field in a civic celebration. The California Angels were going to win the American League championship yesterday afternoon and head along in story and song to the World Series.

The Boston Red Sox were not.

"I looked across the field and I could see everyone in the Angels' dugout getting ready to celebrate," Red Sox reserve Dave Stapleton said. "Gene Mauch. Everyone. They had those nice little smiles that you get before you start hugging everyone."

Dave Henderson of the Red Sox was the hitter and Donnie Moore of the Angels was the pitcher and the count was two balls and two strikes, two outs in the ninth, and the Red Sox were as close to dead as possible without the 5–4 score being official and sent across the country. One pitch away. How could you be closer?

"The television platform was all set up to interview the losers in the clubhouse," Red Sox designated hitter Don Baylor said. "They'd set it up as early as the second inning. They'd been getting it set all day. I'd come in here and the technicians would be making plans."

Noise rolled around the square ballpark as a constant. Kids could be seen in the outfield, their legs already hanging over the fence as they prepared to rush onto the field in joy. A line of orange-coated ushers protected each of the baselines. A line of cops protected the Red Sox dugout and bullpen.

"It's crazy," Red Sox catcher Rich Gedman said. "They don't allow anyone onto the field for anything for the entire game, and then, in the ninth inning, the biggest time, there are all these people everywhere. Get 'em out of there."

"We had trouble seeing in the bullpen, there were so many cops out there," reliever Steve Crawford said. "There must have been 150 cops and ushers, all standing around, watching the game with us."

Each of the players in this bullpen group was doing a curious thing. Each of them was holding his hat in front of him, upside down. A line of baseball players, holding hats.

"Almost like you do when you're begging," reliever Joe Sambito said.

The ritual was developed early in the year. For luck. Any time the count on the batter reached 2 and 2 and there were two outs, everyone in the bullpen removed his hat and held it this way for luck. The Ritual of The Hats.

"What do you do if the batter fouls off the pitch and the count still is 2 and 2?" Sambito was asked.

"You put them back on your head for a moment, then remove them again," the pitcher said. "You always have to reload The Hats after a foul ball. Don't you know anything about baseball?"

Rituals were everywhere. Gloves were stationed in certain places on the dugout bench. Fingers were crossed in certain ways. John McNamara was crouched on the front step, taking the good view. Haywood Sullivan was standing in the right-field seats where he had been standing for most of the long game. Everyone was hanging, looking in the midst of this. One pitch away.

"Was anybody saying anything in the dugout?" designated hitter Baylor was asked later.

"Some guys were," he said. "I remember Dwight Evans saying at the top of the inning, 'We've got more baseball to play.' That was the thought I think we all wanted to have. More baseball to play."

More baseball to play? Not really. This was going to be a sad end to another installment of the perpetual Boston baseball saga. This was going to be the three-game blowout on the West Coast, the undignified early exit in the playoffs, four games to one. The lasting memory would be the grim 4–3 loss in 11 innings late on Saturday night, the game that should have been won, the game that dropped away when Jim Rice lost that ball in the lights in the ninth.

The poets charmed by the team's melodramatic past surely were already at work. Updike had the paper in the typewriter. Two kids in center field had a bedsheet sign that read, "Another Boston Choke." The old thousand-pound weight was being returned to the back of every player who wore the uniform.

One more pitch.

"I was watching in the clubhouse," said reliever Bob Stanley, who had been in the game and stung by a succession of blood-stained base hits for three runs. "Right at that television over there. Roger Clemens, Oil Can Boyd and me. We never changed our seats. For luck.

"I was really mad at myself. I was just hoping something good would happen."

One more pitch. The team had been trailing, 5–2, at the start of the inning. Baylor had homered with Stapleton on base to cut the lead to a run. Gedman was on first after being hit by a pitch, his hand still throbbing. Henderson was at the plate. Two and two. He fouled a pitch, then fouled another. The caps went on. The caps went off. The fingers stayed crossed.

Donnie Moore threw the baseball. Dave Henderson swung. One more pitch.

"Did you hear that the champagne corks already had been popped in the Angels' locker room?" owner Haywood Sullivan said as he sat in a corner of the clubhouse excitement after Henderson's homer had given the Red Sox life after certain death in this game of playoff games and headed them to an eventual 7–6 win over the Angels to bring the series back to Boston tomorrow.

"That's what I heard. With two outs, some of the kids in the clubhouse were popping the champagne so each player would have a bottle ready when he came in."

Sometimes one more pitch is more than enough. Not very often, but sometimes.

*1986*

## JOHN SCHULIAN

John Schulian (b. 1945) made his debut as a sportswriter in *Sports Illustrated* with a freelance story about a boxing promoter in Baltimore who ran a gym above a strip joint. A little more than a year later, in 1975, *The Washington Post* hired Schulian to make a certain Nixonian football coach's life miserable. Eighteen months after that, Schulian became the lead sports columnist of the *Chicago Daily News*, and a columnist he remained in tours with the *Chicago Sun-Times* and *Philadelphia Daily News*. He left newspapers for Hollywood in 1986 and wrote for such TV dramas as *Miami Vice*, *Wiseguy*, and *Midnight Caller* before he scored as co-creator of the international hit *Xena: Warrior Princess*. Along the way, Schulian wrote extensively for *GQ* and *SI*. He is the author of the novel *A Better Goodbye* and three collections of his journalism, and has edited five sportswriting anthologies, including this one.

★　★　★

# Pistol Pete: Parting Shot Full of Sorrow

BOSTON GARDEN creaks with age and smells of mankind's excesses, yet Pete Maravich always thought of it as his salvation. To call it home was to be a Celtic and to be a Celtic was to be a winner, and there was no seeing beyond such idealism until Maravich was out on the old dump's hallowed parquet floor at last. Only then did he realize that once you are haunted, you are haunted for keeps.

Even when he was under the thirteen NBA championship banners that hang from the Garden's rafters, Maravich couldn't free himself from the specter of his father. Press Maravich, a vagabond college coach, had molded his son to superstar specifications and undone himself in the process. "His life ages a man before his time," the *wunderkind* called Pistol Pete once said. But it was harder by far on the woman who bore Press Maravich his famous son.

She couldn't stand the days and nights alone and the crank calls meant to harass the coach and prodigy who spent too few hours under the same roof with her. She paid the cost of other people's fame for as long as she could, and then she ran out of psychological currency. One suicide later, Pete Maravich was without a mother.

The whole sad story was etched on his face, a visage so devoid of joy that a stranger seeing it for the first time would never believe how much happiness Maravich created with his phantasmagoric shooting and psychedelic passing. He belonged to the same breed of irrepressible showmen as Earl Monroe and Julius Erving, yet his small, pinched mouth wasn't made for smiling. Greatness, quite simply, was not a commodity to be enjoyed when you looked at it through Maravich's deceptively innocent eyes. The circles beneath them and the worry lines above them told you that, and if you still didn't believe it, he would tell you in his own words.

"I'm in a cold business," he said midway through the journey that took him to four NBA cities but never to a jewelry store for the championship ring he coveted. "I don't like the conniving, the flesh-peddling, all the dirty things."

So it was no surprise to hear that Maravich called it a career at thirty-one the other day. He was in Boston, the would-be promised land he found his way to last season. The Celtics were still saying they needed his savvy and his sniper's eye in their backcourt, but he would have none of it. He was leaving and not coming back, and the reason should have been obvious: His innocence had finally succumbed to his disillusionment.

The battle had raged inside Maravich for each of his ten years as a professional, leaving him weary and suspicious of everyone, maybe even himself. He disliked dressing rooms for considering serious questions, and on those occasions when he found a quieter setting for an interview, he would tell the reporter, "It was better this way, wasn't it?" It was better, but for Maravich, it wasn't the best.

The best was when he had a basketball in his hands and nothing on his mind except drawing mobs of kids into steaming high school gyms with the wizardry no one else has equaled. "I can dribble six balls at one time, juggle three, and spin two on my finger," he used to say. His lessons in showmanship began when he was four years old, and from then on, basketball would be as much showbiz to him as it was sweat. But not everybody appreciated it.

"If you're lucky," Maravich once said, "50 percent of the people will love your act."

And the others?

"I guess they hate you."

The truth hit Pistol Pete at Louisiana State. He was pulling up his floppy gray socks, dancing to the music of John Fred and the Playboy Band, and short-circuiting scoreboards by averaging 44.2 points a game for his college career. The bad feelings had something to do with the behind-the-back passes he heaved into the third row and something to do with his being his father's robot.

And the bad feelings only got worse in the NBA. In Atlanta a sweet team turned sour because its underpaid black star begrudged Maravich his fat paycheck. "Nobody wanted anything to do with the rich little white boy," he said afterward. The longer he stayed in the league, bouncing from Atlanta to New Orleans to Utah, the stronger the suspicions became that the rich little white boy was a loser. "I have this reputation, this stigma," he would say, thinking all the while that the Celtics were the cure.

Maybe they would have been ten years ago, or even five. But by the time Maravich showed up in Boston last season, his brilliance was a memory. A surgically repaired right knee had cost him precious steps and a stretch in Utah's doghouse had coated his jump shot with rust. In a career fraught with frustration, perhaps that was the biggest frustration of all: He was in the company of winners and he couldn't contribute the way he wanted to.

It was a cruel indignity, yet one that an abundance of high-salaried athletes are willing to endure. Maravich was better than that. "I've shot too many baskets," he told the Celtics the other day, and then he left. His exit was quiet and tasteful, marred only by the familiar voice of his star-making father. Press Maravich used the occasion to say his son should still be what he was raised to be—a general manager, a big shot, someone special. God's mercy on Pistol Pete.

*1980*

★  ★  ★

# The Proud Warrior

L AS VEGAS—Blood cascaded down Marvelous Marvin Hagler's nose, leaving a stripe thick enough to divide a highway. And yet the sight and feel of the relentless crimson ooze moved Hagler in a way that bore no relation to anything modern, automated, or federally funded. Suddenly he was jerked out of 1985 and back into a time when warriors wore loincloths instead of boxing trunks and did their hunting without benefit of eight-ounce gloves. He was a primitive and that splash down the middle of his face wasn't blood. It was war paint.

The more it flowed, the more savage Hagler became. And the more savage he became, the more you wondered if this hellish explosion hadn't been building inside him for all of his thirty years. Or is he really thirty-two, the way Thomas Hearns kept insisting? For all Hearns knew, Hagler might have been born two thousand years ago if the violence that poured out of him last night was any measure. And there was no time for Hearns to renew the debate now.

He was trapped inside the third-round nightmare that would end his dream of becoming the world's middleweight champion. The roar of the crowd had moved him to try slugging it out with Hagler, and now it was an angry, unbearable hum in his ears. Every time he tried to take a step to safety, Hagler was there punching him—punching, punching, punching until the spidery challenger must have thought he was trapped in a thunderstorm of leather.

This wasn't the way anyone expected Hagler to fight. Hagler was supposed to be cautious in the early rounds, jabbing, moving in and out, a conservative who would make Ronald Reagan look like a social-ist by comparison. That was why the champion had looked so bad in groping to a decision over Roberto Duran thirteen months ago. That was why Hearns's stock had skyrocketed when he caught Duran on the rebound and splattered that vicious little wharf rat across the canvas like a bad painting. But it counted for nothing now as Hagler turned the gaudy outdoor ring behind Caesars Palace into the kind of hellhole the beautiful people aren't supposed to know about.

As Bo Derek, Joan Rivers, and a host of TV stars who aren't worthy of the name gaped and gawked, the champion woke up memories of dingy arenas where the air is solid cigar smoke, human flesh is the leading commodity, and the showers never work. It can be a miserable business, the fight racket, and maybe Hearns forgot that inescapable truth when he got a load of the money he and Hagler were making. The price tags on this one were $5.6 million for the champion and $5.4 million for the challenger, and you can get your head turned around by a payday like that. You can think you are better than you really are. You can think your sweat doesn't stink. And if you do, your thoughts aren't worth a penny.

"Tommy is very cocky," said Hagler, who knows that fortunes don't come easily, "and I had something for him."

Make that some *things.*

The first of them was a leaping right hand that sent Hearns reeling across the ring. Then there was another right that sailed over gloves that were barely at half-mast and bounced the challenger's brain around the inside of his noggin. Hagler punctuated the barrage with a left hand that missed—what an irony for a great southpaw puncher—and then he went back to his right for the last time. Hearns was done.

He lay on the canvas with nothing moving except his heaving chest as referee Richard Steele stood above him, tolling his destiny. At nine he was up, but it didn't matter. "His eyes were glazed and his legs were wobbly," Steele said. There was no point in pushing the issue beyond 2:01 of the third round. Thomas Hearns was finished and Marvelous Marvin Hagler was still champion.

"Yeah, I'm still the champion," he said. "But I had to fight like a challenger."

And he was magnificent.

So was Hearns—for a while. Maybe he was just setting himself up for what matchmaker Teddy Brenner called "a tomahawk followed by an ax." Maybe he was just giving Sugar Ray Leonard, the only other man to beat him, an opening to belittle him "for thinking he could knock everybody out." But the first round that he and Hagler wove last night was a tapestry of violence—beautiful, beguiling violence.

They went for each other's throats, and they refused to retreat. If Hagler was rattling Hearns's ribs, Hearns was hammering Hagler's head. If Hearns was making Hagler taste blood, Hagler was filling Hearns's mouth with a fist. Back and forth they went, never pausing for a break, never looking for a break. The result wasn't Pryor and Arguello. It wasn't Ali and Frazier. It wasn't Robinson and LaMotta. It was all of them rolled into one.

Just as he had said he would, the five-nine-and-a-half Hagler turned into a giant. He was giving away four years in age, three and a half inches in height, and three and a half inches in reach, and none of it mattered. He got cut on the forehead in the first—"A butt," grumbled one of his trainers, Pat Petronelli—and that didn't matter, either. He was getting bigger and bigger, and as the round thundered to an end, he whacked Hearns with a left that drove him into a neutral corner and widened his eyes with surprise and unwanted knowledge. Now the challenger knew who the boss was.

"Marvin took away Tommy's right hand, that was the key," Petronelli said. "He ran right through that right hand, and when he knew he could do that, he knew he could do anything. He took away Tommy's legs and he took away Tommy's heart."

The only thing that could have stopped Hagler was his own blood. It poured from the gash in his forehead, and there was more to come when Hearns opened the scar tissue under his right eye. The ring physician studied the damage between the first and second rounds, and the referee did likewise at the start of the third. But Hagler—the single-minded destroyer who had WAR written on the baseball cap he wore throughout training—never paused in his attack. "I was afraid they might stop the fight," he said, "but you know, when I see blood, I turn into a bull."

So Hagler raged and Hearns fell in the round he had predicted for the victory that eluded him. The challenger wound up helpless in the referee's arms and the champion moved within three of Carlos Monzon's record of fourteen successful title defenses. And that was as it should have been. "I hope Tommy will say I'm the better man now," Hagler said. Whether the loser did or didn't hardly mattered, though. The rest of the world knew the truth—the world that Hagler rules as king of the middleweights.

Never mind that this was the sixty-fifth fight of his career. He had never been royalty before. But when he walked into his post-fight press conference, he was embraced by the new major domo at Caesars Palace. And everything around him seemed musical, even the sound of promoter Bob Arum introducing the sagging Hearns while he, Marvelous Marvin Hagler, donned his championship finery in the sanctuary of his dressing room. Hagler was moving at his own pace now, deciding when he would step back outside into the loving glow of the television lights, enjoying it all so much that he scarcely noticed the stretcher he passed on his way out the door and into the night. No stretchers for him. Only a chariot would do.

*1985*

## DIANE K. SHAH

Steve Carlton, a brilliant but media-averse pitcher for the Philadelphia Phillies, spent much of the 1970s and '80s refusing to speak to the press, and he got away with it until Diane K. Shah (b. 1945) of the *Los Angeles Herald Examiner* let it be known he had things backwards. *She* wasn't speaking to *him*. Shah made her point with the grace and whimsy typical of her work as the first woman to have her name up in lights as a big-city sports columnist. Of course she had to be talked into leaving *Newsweek* when the *Herald Ex*'s editor recruited her in 1981. But once she said yes, she sailed through locker rooms and press boxes, tall and elegant, with a style that told one and all there was more in her life than the column. Six years later, she proved it by resigning and returning to the world of books and magazines.

★   ★   ★

# At 7-Foot-2, Is Abdul-Jabbar Above It All?

TO ANYONE not familiar with the Laker Family Saga, the episode in which Kareem Abdul-Jabbar confronts owner Jerry Buss in his office at the Forum must have seemed confusing. Apparently Kareem was unhappy about something, but before the final fade to black, the two parties stepped out of the doctor's office and beamed at each other.

"Fortunately, after talking with Dr. Buss," Kareem noted in the closing moments, "I realize the situation hasn't gotten that extreme."

And Dr. Buss said, "I am glad that Kareem had the presence of mind to make matters clear."

What matters? Since the local papers do not carry plot synopses of the show, I decided to go to The Man himself.

A meeting was arranged, and Tom Collins, Kareem's agent, offered some helpful advice. "Don't count on a whole hour," he said. "More likely you'll get half an hour. You might want to start out by talking about history with Kareem or rugs or the Egyptian mare he just bought. But remember, when he starts to fidget, that's it. Leave as quickly as possible.

"And," Collins added, "don't expect much eye contact."

Kareem entered the room and sat down at the conference table. Quicker than a fast-break, he swiveled his chair around until he was facing the window—and I was facing the back of his neck.

QUESTION: What was the part about Magic Johnson's contract causing concern?

VOICE: When you get five people who can play domineering basketball together, you have something special. It's not wise to tamper with that.

Q: How did Magic's contract tamper with that? I must have fallen asleep during that part.

V: In 1971, Milwaukee won the championship. Then they traded Greg Smith, a 6-foot-5 power forward. Milwaukee never won the championship again. It was a glaring example of mismanagement. This thing with Earvin brought back bad memories of mismanagement.

Q: "How so?" I made a mental note to catch the Greg Smith episode in the summer reruns.

V: The way Magic's contract became known. Nobody knew what the contract meant. Earvin could be the general manager if he wanted, or the coach.

Q: You didn't really believe that you would walk into camp next month and find Magic standing there with a whistle around his neck?

V: No. But nobody knew for sure.

Suddenly, Kareem whipped around. "We didn't know," he said again and spread his hands in a gesture of helplessness . . . I glanced at my watch . . . or was it a warning fidget?

Kareem: We know how close Earvin and Dr. Buss are. So I wondered how does this affect me? Is my status on this team reliant on what I do on the court or how friendly I am with the boss?

Kareem swiveled back round.

V: Nobody could really understand what Earvin's job was. The way it seemed when it came out was as if Dr. Buss just adopted Magic and he could do what he wanted. The team was just something for Magic to play with.

Q: But why did you go see Dr. Buss exactly?

V: I'm the captain. Guys were calling me up.

Q: How many?

Kareem began rubbing his hands on the arms of the chair. I'm not that good at reading strategies, but it looked like a possible power fidget.

V: Two.

Q: And what did you tell Dr. Buss?

V: I tried to let him know the way you do things is very important. It's a danger if he makes too many bad decisions.

Q: How do you think he liked you telling him that?

V: I don't know. I am, after all, no more than an employee. I was walking on thin ice.

Q: And you said if this thing with Magic's contract was not cleared up you wanted to be traded?

V: That's professional pride. I said if the climate isn't right where good basketball could be developed, I would go somewhere where it was right.

At last I was beginning to see bare outlines of a plot—sort of. Unfortunately, Kareem was fidgeting so so badly by now I feared he would fall out of his chair.

Q: So to sum up . . .

Kareem stood to deliver the denouement. "People should be allowed space to be human, and to excel."

Then he was gone. Thirty minutes to the second. Perhaps the show should expand to an hour.

*1981*

★   ★   ★

# Oh, No! Not Another Boring Interview with Steve Carlton

H AVING RECENTLY passed a statistical benchmark, that is, having just written my 300th column, I find I am besieged by athletes begging me to interview them. I know that only 15 other sports columnists in the history of journalism have reached this plateau, but I must say this constant round of interviews does grow wearisome. Every time a new team comes to town it's the same thing. You'd think all the athletes could just get together and agree to one mass interview.

To make matters worse, I once again find myself covering the play-offs. So now the requests for interviews have intensified all the more. Yesterday morning, no sooner had I reached my office when the phone rang.

"Yeah," I said.

"Er, Miss Shah? This is Steve Carlton with the Philadelphia Phillies. I was wondering . . ."

"I haven't even had my coffee yet," I grumbled. "Don't you guys ever sleep?"

"I'm sorry," said Carlton. "It's just that I was, er, wondering if you would have time today to interview me."

"What team did you say you were from?"

"The Phillies. I'm a pitcher."

"Oh, right, I remember. But haven't I interviewed you before? When the Phillies won the 1980 World Series or after you got your 300th win? I'm sure I did."

"Actually, you didn't," Carlton said. "I was rather hoping you would, but you always walk right past me. I've even sent you notes requesting interviews, but you never reply."

"You know how many games there are in a season?" I said.

"Yes," said Carlton meekly. "But I felt I had to give it a shot."

"So what is it you want me to interview you about?" I said, trying not to sound bored.

"Well you could ask me about my tough conditioning program," he said. "The Kung Fu and pushing my arm into a tub of rice. Or how many more years I'm going to pitch. Or what I think about the playoffs."

"Same old stuff," I said, stifling a yawn. "You'd think occasionally one of you guys would come up with something new to say."

"Perhaps you could ask me about being an oenophile," Carlton suggested.

"Don't try to impress me with big words," I snapped. "I hate looking things up in the dictionary."

"Oh," said Carlton deflatedly. "Well, er, I did lead the league in strikeouts. With 275."

"Are you a Cy Young candidate then?"

"No," he said sadly. "That would be John Denny. He pitches Wednesday night."

"Don't take this personally," I said, "but readers would probably be more interested in finding out what he has to say."

"I wouldn't need much time," Carlton pleaded. "Although I usually like as much time with the writer as possible."

"I've heard that before," I sighed. "You athletes think the longer the interview the better the story. Only I'm not getting paid to shoot the breeze with you guys. I get paid to write a column. I know it's important to your line of work to get interviewed, so I try to accommodate you when I can. But it's not in my contract here at the paper to just sit around doing interviews all day."

"I'll try to be as brief as possible," said Carlton. "Perhaps we could have lunch or a cup of coffee before the game."

"Absolutely not," I screamed. "You want me to talk to you, we'll talk at the ballpark. I hate when athletes try to interfere with my private life."

"Fine," said Carlton. "What time should I meet you?"

"Well, let's see. I'll get out to Dodger Stadium about two-and-a-half hours before game time. Then I have to go up to the press box and set up my word processing machine. I have to find a plug and take the machine out of its case and make sure it works. This is a special time for me. I don't like to be rushed."

"How about after you finish word processing practice?"

"No, 'cause then I like to stroll around the batting cage chatting with my colleagues from the other papers. It's really annoying when an athlete comes over and interrupts. Some of the best jokes I hear are said at the batting cage."

"After that?" said Carlton hopefully.

"No," I went on. "Next I have to stop in Tom Lasorda's office. I need to check out the food and which celebrities have come by. And then I have to run through the Dodger clubhouse and say hello to everyone 'cause they expect hometown writers to be friendly to them."

"Gee," said Carlton. "This is really important to me. It's the playoffs."

"Tell you what," I said. "I'll send an intermediary. I'll get Vin Scully to interview you. He'll give the tape to Steve Brener, the Dodger publicist, and he'll screen the best answers out."

"I really appreciate this," said Carlton.

"Sure," I said. "By the way, what did you say your name was?"

*1983*

## BOB RYAN

You can find the picture on the Internet: a young, mustachioed, and apparently unflappable Bob Ryan (b. 1946) rolling a sheet of paper into his portable typewriter as Celtics fans young and old cluster behind him on press row, waiting to watch as he writes the game story they will read in the next day's *Boston Globe.* That's how big Ryan was in the 1970s and '80s. Maybe not as big as the team he covered, but big enough to have chronicled it with such bombast, humor, and hoop wisdom that he made the city and his own paper care about the Celtics. In forty-four years on the *Globe,* the last twenty-three as a columnist, Ryan covered Super Bowls, World Series, Final Fours, and the Olympics, but it was always the Celtics who provided the most inspiration. "There aren't many people," he said, "who could write a game story the way I wrote 'em." Here are two such stories that prove he wasn't bragging.

★　★　★

# Celtics Steal It: Bulls Fall in 2 OTs, 135–131

ONLY ONE man in the history of the NBA play-offs knows what it feels like to score 63 points at the highest level of competition and be denied the sweet smell of team success. But the hoop world knows that every other player and every other team is on borrowed time. The Celtics, Lakers, Hawks, Rockets and every other 1986 title aspirant had better seize whatever opportunity they can—Now!—because we are clearly at the dawn of the Age of Jordan.

"I would never have called him the greatest player I'd ever seen if I didn't mean it," said Larry Bird after yesterday's exhilarating, stimulating, emotional, exhausting and altogether brilliant contest. "It's just God disguised as Michael Jordan."

Bird's equation of Jordan to the Deity is understandable in light of Jordan's record-breaking 63-point effort in the Garden (a display that surpassed Elgin Baylor's 1962 play-off standard of 61), but let the record show that Bird was able to speak in the pleasant afterglow of victory. Despite all Jordan's virtuosity, the Celtics constructed a 2–0 series lead by walking (staggering would be a more apt description) off with a 135–131 double-overtime triumph in what could accurately be described as an epic contest.

They play 'em and we rate 'em, and there is no question that this game will make the Top 5, and maybe even the Top 3, of Greatest Celtic Play-off Games Ever among the Garden cognoscenti. This was pure athletic theater, and not until Orlando Woolridge air-balled a desperation three-pointer with two seconds remaining in the second OT was there a legitimate chance for any Celtic owner, general manager, coach, player or fan to relax and light up that mental cigar. As long as Mr. Jordan is known to be present in this hemisphere, no rival lead is safe, no palm is dry, no throat swallows easily and no stomach is settled. A man who scores 63 points *out of the flow* is a man to fear, respect and idolize.

But justice, as we witnessed in Holmes-Spinks II, has nothing to do with winning and losing, for despite Jordan's 22 field goals and 63 points, he didn't make the biggest basket of the long, long afternoon. Jerry Sichting, a player whose game is to Jordan's as a 1955 Studebaker is to a 1986 Porsche, had that honor. For it was Sichting who took an inside-out pass from Kevin McHale and did what he has done faithfully all year—swished the foul line jumper. That basket broke the game's 13th tie and gave the Celtics a 133–131 lead with 57 seconds left in the second OT. And when Jordan missed a left baseline jumper on the next Chicago possession, Robert Parish rebounded.

The ball went to Bird (36 points, 12 rebounds, 8 assists), who orchestrated a two-man game on the right wing with Parish. "As soon as he set the pick and rolled, I gave it to him," said Bird, unconcerned that Parish had not scored a jumper all night and had established a bad case of the oopsies in his infrequent drives to the hoop. "When he goes, you've got to give him the ball. You don't worry about Robert Parish. I never do, because he's made lots of big plays for this team."

That's no lie, and this time he took the pass and swished a 12-foot moon shot on the right baseline to give Boston a four-point lead (135–131) with nine seconds remaining.

In any game such as this, there is invariably an individual of whom it can safely be said, "Without him, this would *definitely* have been an L." Yesterday afternoon, that man was the oft-maligned Danny Ainge.

You never would have pegged Ainge as a potential hero midway through the third quarter. He hadn't even scored a point by the time the aggressive young Bulls claimed their final 10-point lead (69–59). But before the period was over, he had erupted for 13, including 11 in the final 2:36, the last three of which came on a three-pointer that brought the struggling Celtics within one at 84–83.

Ainge would wind up with 24, and he would score two giant baskets, the first a left-handed lane drive that would tie the score at 125–125 with 12 seconds left in the first OT, and the second an open 18-footer that would give Boston a brief 131–127 lead in the second OT, a lead that was quickly wiped out via two quick hoops by the irrepressible Jordan.

Chicago abandoned the first-game strategy of continual Jordan isolations, and he proved how brilliant he was by performing even better in the context of a normal offense than he did when 90 percent of the action was directed his way. The Bulls took the lead at 4–2 and clung to it stubbornly until a clock-beating 28-foot three-pointer by Bird gave Boston the lead at 93–92 and created the first of nine consecutive lead changes through 102–100, Boston (an inside-out three-pointer by Bird from McHale).

Boston did everything but summon the ghost of Walter Brown in an attempt to knock out the Bulls, but the visitors would not succumb. A 108–104 fourth-quarter lead soon turned into a 111–110 Chicago advantage on the Jordan basket that gave him an even 50 points. A 116–113 lead with 45 seconds remaining in regulation (an Ainge-to-McHale alley-oop) evaporated when Charles Oakley hit a free throw with 34 seconds left, leading to the sequence (Bird miss, Parish momentary rebound and Chicago steal/strip/maul/who-knows-what-but-no-call) that set up the game's most controversial happening.

Leading, 116–114, with six seconds left, the Celtics had to dig in one last time to preserve the lead. With about one second left, Jordan up-faked Dennis Johnson and threw up a three-pointer that clanged off the rim as McHale arrived on the scene. Referee Ed Middleton called a foul on McHale after the shot. Did Jordan get hit? Did he spread-eagle smartly upon release and hit McHale? Do you ever make a call like this? Middleton did, and Jordan, naturally, sank both shots to create OT No. 1.

The Bulls surged ahead by four (123–119) on a Jordan three-point play with 1:39 left, but Sichting canned a corner jumper (missing the affixed free throw) and Ainge came through with that clutch drive. Jordan missed an unmolested left-side jumper and Bird rebounded with two seconds left. A Bird three-pointer was long and the weary troops entered the second OT.

Way, way back in this one, many amazing things had gone on. For example, Bill Walton (who fouled out with 6:10 left in regulation) grabbed 13 rebounds in 13 first-half minutes. Sidney Green and Oakley had made breathtaking tap-ins. Bird, after going 0 for 5 in the first quarter and then hyperextending his right pinkie (forcing him to play with it taped to its neighbor), came out to hit nine of his next 11 shots, including two three-pointers. McHale scored a fourth-quarter basket while actually sitting on Dave Corzine. And every primary Celtic had gotten himself into foul trouble (the first six guys, Walton being No. 6, compiled 31 fouls).

All the while, Jordan just kept scoring. And scoring. And scoring. This way. That way. Horizontally. Vertically. Diagonally. In ways never conceived of by Hank Luisetti, Joe Fulks, Paul Arizin or even World B. Free. And, reminded Parish, "It's not like he was doing it in a summer league."

A question now arises: What is Michael Jordan capable of doing in his *own* building? Two-and-zero looks about 100 times better than 1–1 right now.

*1986*

★  ★  ★

# Celtics' Crowning Glory: Bird Buries Rockets

THE HOUSTON ROCKETS were like an unwary couple pulled over on the highway for going 3 miles over the speed limit by a burly Georgia cop with the mirrored sunglasses.

It wasn't their day. The cop's name was Bird. The bailiff's name was Bird. The court stenographer's name was Bird. The judge's name was Bird. And the executioner's name was—guess what?—Bird.

Welcome to Bird Country, boys, and while you're at it, why don't you congratulate the Boston Celtics on the occasion of their 16th NBA championship? He didn't make *every* shot, or grab *every* rebound, or account for *every* assist, or make *every* steal, or sell *every* hot dog, but he plugged himself into every conceivable aspect of the game to the extent that all the other players had to do was feed off his energy level. "Let's face it," said Kevin McHale, "when you play with a guy like Larry Bird, it gives you a lot of confidence."

Yesterday's final was Boston 114, Houston 97. The Celtics never trailed. There were no ties. The closest spread in the final 2½ periods was 11. With 7:20 remaining, it was up to 30 at 97–67. The suffocating Boston defense held Houston to 35 percent shooting in the first three periods.

The tone of the game was established in the first minute and a half. Ralph Sampson (who was to no-shows what Buddy Rich is to drummers) missed the first Houston shot and referee Jake O'Donnell called a loose-ball foul on Robert Reid. Whoa . . . there were no questionable loose-ball fouls called on the Rockets in Houston during Game 5.

Dennis Johnson drove to the basket, and McHale (29 points, 10 rebounds) shoved it back in with the underside of his left hand. Whoa . . . the Celtics weren't getting second shots in Houston. Houston set up, and Bird stole a Rodney McCray pass to start a fast break. McHale finished off with a silly-looking runner that bounced around a few times and fell in. Whoa . . . the rims in Houston would have kicked that baby all the way to Galveston, or so it seemed. Gee, it's great to be back home again.

Johnson, guarding Reid for the first time in the series (he simply asked K.C. Jones for the assignment), made him feel as if he were wearing a rain-soaked overcoat. The man who had 13 assists by halftime of Game 5 had 2 points and 2 assists by this intermission.

Down deep, McHale was swallowing the villainous Sampson (1-for-8 first half), Robert Parish was denying Akeem Olajuwon, and Bird was somehow or other playing McCray, Sampson, Olajuwon, Reid, Lewis Lloyd and every other Rocket this side of Zaid Abdul-Aziz.

"It was just tough defense from start to finish," said DJ. "Tenacious. They couldn't stand it."

By the first Houston timeout (14–6, Boston, at 8:32), the Rockets had more turnovers (5) than field goals attempted (4). At 20–9, the Rockets called for a 20-second timeout, as the Celtics had picked up 12 points via fast breaks and 4 more via second shots. It was pretty clear that the man in charge had put a whole new record on the turntable than the wall of noise he had on there the other night. This was a song the Celtics could dance to.

"The game just started totally different than the ones in Houston," reflected Jerry Sichting, who was a part of a big second-quarter unit. "We came out and picked up on defense. We should never have let it happen down there, but we knew how to correct the problem."

After Bird fed McHale for a dunk to make it 22–10, the Rockets made the first of two significant runs. Olajuwon brought them back with three consecutive steals on passes intended for Bill Walton, who at that point probably wished he could have traded places with Jerry Garcia's guitar pick.

"Here I was, just in the game, and I lose the ball three straight times," said Walton. "All I was thinking was that Larry was going over to K.C. and saying, 'Get that guy out of here!'" Walton would stick around to submit 10 points and 8 rebounds.

But Houston never could pull ahead. The Rockets got within one at 22–21 (McCray layup after Olajuwon steal No. 3) and 24–23 (McCray right-back fast-break layup). When McCray missed an attached free throw, Olajuwon grabbed the rebound and missed a turnaround. It would be Houston's last chance to go ahead.

By period's end, the Boston lead was up to 29–23. Houston crept back within three at 31–28, only to see the game get completely away from them in the next 5:28 as the unit of Bird, McHale, Parish, Sichting and the invaluable Danny Ainge (19 points, 4 assists, 2 steals and 7-for-9 shooting) ran off a 16–4 spurt to make it 47–32.

By halftime, Bird was well on the way to his third triple-double of the playoffs and second of the Finals with 16 points, 8 rebounds, 8 assists, 3 steals and the wettest, dirtiest, grungiest-looking uniform since Pepper Martin's in the '31 Series. He had involved himself in every conceivable operation during an emotional half of basketball, once bringing back John Havlicek memories with a fast-break leaner from the foul line and another time even winning a first-period jump ball from Olajuwon.

It was 55–38 at the half, and the only reason it wasn't worse was Boston's atrocious foul shooting (11 for 21 in the first half). Seventeen is a nice margin, but the Celtics weren't merely interested in maintaining it. Embarrassed by the goings-on in Game 5, they wanted scalps.

And so did the fanatical crowd, which had gotten on Sampson from the beginning, and wanted a game to place in the all-time memory bank. The fun really began at 59–45 when Parish hit Ainge for an inside-out, left-corner, buzzer-beating three-point swisher. Sampson (one field goal in the first 32 minutes) missed a hook and Ainge converted on a three-on-one fast break. Bird stuck in a three-pointer from the left with the arc of a Wade Boggs line drive (69–49). DJ made a power left-handed right-to-left drive. Parish hit a moon shot. The Celtics led by 21 (82–61) after three.

Bird had one great crowd-pleasing move left in his repertoire. In his seven years, he has done a lot of outrageous things, but what he did at 84–61 ranks right near the top of anyone's list. He received a behind-the-back pass from Walton on the left baseline, fumbled the ball, realized the 24-second clock was near expiration, and instead of dribbling toward the hoop for a potential foul, he started making his way through an obstacle course to the three-point line in the next corner. Arriving at his destination, he turned and swished a three-pointer. The sound that followed only remotely could be described as noise.

Bird finished with 29 points, 11 rebounds and 12 assists, and he was awarded the Sport magazine MVP award. He had promised the world beforehand that "everything's gonna be just fine," and, as usual, he had delivered. Marveled Houston's Jim Petersen, "I saw him take on five guys by himself. He's the best. At times, he doesn't seem to need teammates."

"Larry Bird," said K.C. Jones, "is where he wants to be. He has reached the pinnacle of basketball."

And so have the Celtics, whose victory yesterday was the 47th in 48 tries on the parquet, and who finished the season with 38 consecutive victories at home. "They weren't beating us here today," said McHale.

"They hurt us the worst way they could in Game 5. They hurt our pride. It's not often that 12 guys together have on their game face, but that's what happened today."

And they'll all admit that one face was a little grimmer, a little meaner and a little more meaningful than all the others. "Nothing Larry Bird does surprises me," declared Bill Walton, "and everything he does impresses me."

Which is very similar to the way the NBA has viewed the Celtics as a whole for the past 29 years.

*1986*

# THOMAS BOSWELL

Thomas Boswell (b. 1947) hired on as a copyboy at *The Washington Post* thinking it was a temporary stop on his way to law school. That was in 1969, and he hasn't left yet. In the years since, he has succeeded Shirley Povich as the most beloved sportswriter in the nation's capital. Povich himself, in what turned out to be his last column, called Boswell baseball's "unmatched chronicler-philosopher." Though he brings the same high standards for clear thinking and memorable prose to golf, it was baseball that gave a national profile to the hometown kid who grew up rooting for Washington Senators slugger Roy Sievers. Boswell was a proponent of metrics before they had a name and he campaigned long, hard, and successfully for the return of big-league baseball to the city. He never wonders what kind of lawyer he would have been.

★   ★   ★

# Something to Shout About

PERFECTION.
The sky above Memorial Stadium was pale blue and utterly empty today. Not even a cloud could get in free. The air was an ideal, invigorating autumnal 70 degrees. Scientists might call such conditions "standard temperature and pressure." Baseball fans, however, would call this fervid pennant-race afternoon one of raging high fever and almost unbearable pressure.

Occasionally, what should happen does happen.

Today in Memorial Stadium, it did.

On the penultimate day of a gloriously improbable pennant race, the Baltimore Orioles, baseball's symbol of intelligence and economy, finally caught the mighty Milwaukee Brewers, symbol of numbing slugging power.

Now, after this day's 11–3 Oriole victory over Milwaukee, the two teams with the best records in baseball, the two clubs that have battled each other for six months, find themselves breathlessly deadlocked after 161 games at 94–67. These Orioles and Brewers will meet one more time here on Sunday at 3:05 P.M.

The starting pitchers will be two gentlemen with serious claims on bronze busts in Cooperstown: Baltimore's 263-game winner Jim Palmer, who's won 13 of his last 14 decisions, and Milwaukee's Don Sutton, winner of 257 games. All this in the final regular-season game of the final season of the Orioles' manager, Earl Weaver.

To the winner goes the American League East Division championship.

If that winner be Baltimore, then the Orioles will also find a splendid place in baseball history. No club since the professional game first breathed in 1869 has ever swept a season-ending, four-game series to win a championship by one game.

To stretch the point still further, Baltimore would have gained five games in the standings in the final five contests of the season; that, too, would be a first in baseball annals.

"We've gone from extinction to a tie for first place in less than 48 hours," said a stunned Hank Peters, Baltimore's general manager, recalling how bleak the team's chances looked before they scored four last-gasp runs in the ninth inning to beat the Tigers in Detroit, 6–5, Thursday night.

More than that. When the final Brewer out this afternoon was recorded at 5:25 P.M., it meant that Baltimore had beaten Milwaukee three times in just a few minutes less than 24 hours.

To Sunday's loser will go a winter of the bitterest grief.

If that loser be the Brewers, then this exceptional team—the club with the most staggering offensive statistics since the '52 Brooklyn

Dodger Boys of Summer—will run the risk of being remembered, and reminded forever, for having the worst late-season collapse on record.

It would be a spurious infamy—simply the sort of star-crossed, uptight, five-game losing streak which any team can have, but one which, in this case, would come at the least propitious time imaginable. What has happened to the Brewers here has been so sudden, more like a series of natural disasters than baseball games, that somehow they hardly seem culpable.

As the Brewers left Memorial Stadium this evening, they had the look of 25 Androcles looking for the face of a friendly lion in this dizzy, deafening den.

"SWEEP, SWEEP, SWEEP," bellowed this standing crowd of 47,235 as the Brewers trudged to their quarters. Then, as usual, the chants of "O-R-I-O-L-E-S."

To say that the Brewers now face a colossal bit of soul-searching would be an understatement of the first order.

In these 24 Hours of The Oriole, the Baltimoreans have won, 8–3, 7–1 and, now, 11–3. Every time the Brewers have shown the least sign of resistance or will, the Orioles have redoubled their pummeling of the Brewers' suspect pitchers in their next at bat.

The most staggering statistic from these three games is that the Orioles have had 46 hits—18 of them today—and 58 men on base in just 24 innings. Every time the Brewers look up, the bases are drunk with fowl. Sooner or later, somebody's got to score. Keep enough pressure on and accidents will happen.

Those who think such abnormalities cannot continue were not present in Fenway Park in September 1978 when, with similar stakes on the table, the New York Yankees humiliated Boston by a total score of 42–9 over four days. That was the Boston Massacre. This might be the Baltimore Bushwack.

Several unique psychological burdens hang over the Brewers' heads.

First, all evidence says that they simply play miserably against Baltimore. The Orioles have won nine of 12 meetings. Baltimore has hit

.325 for the year against the Brewers while Milwaukee has batted just
.238 against the Orioles. These Brewers, who dominate the lists of
major league leaders in almost every statistical category, have 51 fewer
base hits than Baltimore in their dozen meetings. The top five men in
the Brewer order were two for 18 today.

Given all this, the Brewers, who've been in first place for the last 60
days, must ask themselves the gravest of all athletic questions between
two fine teams: Given what has happened, do we really deserve to win?

At the moment, the Orioles—who have gone 33–10, including 17
come-from-behind wins, since they began a sprint Aug 20—now have
the sort of statistical aura that might bespeak superiority.

Next, the Brewers have been trying desperately to put on the skids
ever since they arrived here.

"This has gone far enough," said Gorman Thomas before the game
today.

"If there's such a thing as overconfidence," said Brewer General
Manager Harry Dalton, "then we've pushed them to the brink."

The Brewers seem caught by the first baseball Law of Motion:
over the long haul, the sport is a game of statistical norms, but, over
the intense short haul of a pennant race, it's largely adrenaline, luck,
momentum, unpredictability. In other words, this is the time of year
for streaks, collapses, heroism. Ask the world champion Los Angeles
Dodgers, who appeared to have the NL West wrapped up until they
lost eight straight.

At one level, this weekend has been, and will be, just a jubilant
gathering of the baseball fans and clans.

However, to the participants, it's a form of pastoral torture. Baltimore Manager Weaver, whose imminent retirement may be serving
as an inspiration to his team, is so tight that you could play "Dueling
Banjos" on the lines on his forehead.

Underneath all these major chords, this symphony of a final show-
down has one tantalizingly bizarre *leitmotif.*

None of this should ever have happened.

Back in June, Milwaukee catcher Ted Simmons thought that a John Lowenstein strikeout had ended an inning, so, he casually rolled the ball back toward the mound. Before Simmons realized there were only two outs, a pair of Baltimore runners had advanced a base. The next man singled home two runs, instead of just one. The game ended in a 2–2 tie instead of a 2–1 Milwaukee victory, when rains arrived after nine innings.

But for that tie, which was replayed here as part of Friday's doubleheader, the Brewers would already be AL East champions.

Baseball historians will instantly note the similarity of the famous Merkle Boner of 1908 when Fred Merkle cost the New York Giants a midseason victory over the Chicago Cubs when he neglected to touch first base after an apparent game-winning hit. Instead of a victory, the game went down as a tie and the Giants, forced to replay the contest at season's end, lost the pennant to the Cubs by a single game.

Perhaps such plays, such baseball miracles, come along once in a lifetime.

*1982*

★   ★   ★

# Nicklaus a Master Again

A UGUSTA, GA.—Some things cannot possibly happen, because they are both too improbable and too perfect. The U.S. hockey team cannot beat the Russians in the 1980 Olympics. Jack Nicklaus cannot shoot 65 to win the Masters at age forty-six. Nothing else comes immediately to mind.

Other periods have their Louis-Schmeling memories and the like, events that require only shorthand phrases for a total evocation. For those whose frame of reference begins since World War II, few events in sport will command a higher place—for drama, for sentiment and for value—than what Nicklaus accomplished this evening in the 50th Masters. A golden victory for a Golden Bear.

Now we have a new benchmark for ennobling emotion in games. What Nicklaus achieved, deep in the dogwood, goes beyond mere excellence. His superiority at golf was established long ago. This afternoon was special because Nicklaus called on reserves of poise, of strength, of judgment under enormous pressure, which go to the heart of human dignity. When the youngest and strongest of athletes would have given up, five shots behind the leaders with just ten holes to play, Nicklaus said to caddie Jack Jr., "If I'm going to do anything, I better start doing it."

Even rarer than his golf shot-making, Nicklaus brought, as he has always brought, a regal sense of joy in combat that is the core of great sportsmanship. Where others suffer in the creation of their athletic deeds, Nicklaus exudes both utter concentration and complete pleasure. Others say their prayers in Amen Corner, Nicklaus sings hallelujah. "I haven't had this much fun in six years. " Nicklaus, the mature adult who knows deferred gratification to the bone, will wait and work years for one long vital day of the purest adrenaline-filled life.

Golf is the game of failure. More than any of our other sports, golf incorporates both the capricious and the cruel. Ted Williams once said to Sam Snead: "Golf's not that hard. The ball doesn't move." "No," replied Snead, "but we have to play our foul balls." In the last six years, during which he has won only two tournaments out of nearly a hundred attempts, Nicklaus has had to play many foul balls. Only those who follow his career meticulously know how many crucial short putts he has missed, how many shots that he once depended upon have failed him, how many chances to win he has kicked away. And only those who know him can have seen the pain of self-inflicted mediocrity. Playing tournament golf without sufficient practice is like walking downstairs in pitch darkness. And finding time for golf is often nearly impossible for the man who Chi Chi Rodriguez said "is a legend in his spare time."

Devoting days to his family and five children has been a joy. "To have your own son with you to share an experience like that is so great for him, so great for me. I have great admiration for him. He's done a wonderful job of handling the burden of my name." Typically, Nicklaus's first phone call this morning was from his son Steve, who said, "Whataya think, Pop? 'Bout a 65 wins it?" "That's the number I had in mind," replied the old man. "Then let's go shoot it," said Steve.

Less pleasure to Nicklaus has been the building of a $300-million empire, based on golf course design, club manufacturing, clothing lines and dozens of subsidiary businesses. In the last six months, Nicklaus increased his burdens by becoming his own chief executive officer in the wake of some overseas losses. He put his hands on the machinery every day. But not always on his golf clubs.

To what depths of talent and temperament did Jack Nicklaus reach this warm breeze-swept afternoon on the course that his hero, Bobby Jones, designed? Two weeks ago, he pronounced his game a wreck. One week ago, he said, "I've finally started hitting the ball solidly again." One day ago, he said, "I haven't made a putt all week." Yet, when the moment presented itself, he grasped it, felt its texture, turned it to his advantage, fed off it while others were being devoured. "This is a young man's golf course," he said. "Greens fast as glass. Pins on the knobs. Every putt breaks two feet. It's long and hard to walk. The crowds make for lots of emotion, which drains you."

Nicklaus paused. He had no explanation. Something so improbable and so perfect that it could not possibly happen had actually come to pass. He was the center of it, yet could not fully understand. Brought face-to-face with the mystery of his own personality, he could only fall back on that boyish high-pitched giggle and wry smile.

"Obviously," he said, "I'm just tickled pink."

*1986*

★  ★  ★

# The Rocket's Descent

N OW, ROGER CLEMENS joins Barry Bonds in baseball's version of hell. It's a slow burn that lasts a lifetime, then, after death, lingers as long as the game is played and tongues can wag. In baseball, a man's triumphs and his sins are immortal. The pursuit of one often leads to the other. And those misdeeds are seldom as dark as their endless punishment.

Shoeless Joe Jackson, an illiterate outfielder who hit like a demon in the 1919 World Series, but neglected to blow the whistle on his crooked teammates, died with his good name as black as their Sox. Pete Rose, who bet on his team, but never against it, finally confessed. It could be good for his soul, and buys him dinner at my house any night, but may never get him into Cooperstown. Now, they have company: two giants of our time, just as humbled, though no less tarnished.

Yesterday, the only man with seven Cy Young Awards came crashing down the mountain of baseball's gods and ended in a heap beside the only man with seven most valuable player awards. What a sport. Half the players of the last 20 years may have cheated, but who gets nailed? The greatest slugger since Babe Ruth and the greatest power pitcher since Walter Johnson.

Clemens and Bonds now stand before us like twin symbols of the Steroid Age: cheats, liars, ego monsters who were not satisfied with mere greatness and wealth but, as they aged, had to pass everyone in the record book, break every mark and do it with outsize bodies, unrecognizable from their youth, that practically screamed, "Catch me if you can." The whole sport whispered as both walked by. Now, everyone can speak aloud. Not because their guilt has been admitted or proven beyond any doubt, mind you. That would be too clean and easy for us, for baseball.

But the Rocket and Barry stand convicted in the court of public opinion, in Bonds's case by his flaxseed-oil defense and now, in this thunderclap Clemens catastrophe, by the direct I-injected-him-many-times-in-the-buttocks testimony of his own personal trainer. Clemens denied all charges vehemently. In a statement, he claimed that he is being slandered by "the uncorroborated allegations of a troubled man threatened with federal criminal prosecution."

Yet those nine pages of Mitchell report "slander" have been placed in the public's hand by baseball itself in 311 pages, plus attachments, blessed by the commissioner. Pete Rose had 10 times the chance against the Dowd report than Clemens has against the august Mitchell. What a public-relations mismatch: a tobacco-chewing, hot-tempered Texas right-hander against a former federal judge and Senate majority leader who helped bring peace to Northern Ireland. This time, the Rocket's out of gas and the bullpen is empty.

For more than a year, the Mitchell commission on performance-enhancing drugs appeared to expect to catch with five-pound test line, a defiant players' union and no subpoena power? Yet, apparently by dumb luck, a baseball drug peddler got caught, then rolled over on an insignificant scoundrel who happened to be Clemens's trainer. In a blink, baseball's blindfolded Ahabs found a whale in their seine. What's this? It feels like, it might be, oh my God, it's Clemens, hooked and gaffed, whether we want him or not.

"Bud, this is George. We're going to need a bigger boat."

Mitchell's opus was intended as many things. It was, of course, a severe front-to-back slam at the union for its 20 years of intransigence on drug testing. The charge is absolutely correct. Still, how self-serving can Commissioner Bud Selig be? He appoints Mitchell, closely affiliated with management in general and specifically with the Red Sox, to spend 21 months finding out who's guilty when he already knows that Don Fehr will get handcuffed in the last chapter.

And, of course, owners, mid-level baseball employees and even Selig get taken to ritual task. Oh, everybody should have acted faster, been smarter, seen the signs. But, gosh, how were we to know? Just because our players showed up for spring training like they'd spent the winter inhaling helium. Just because scouts in their reports and general managers discussing trades evaluated how much weight to give the "juice" factor.

Finally, naturally, because Congress knows a vote-grabber in an election year, the report serves as baseball's proactive shield against further embarrassing visits to Capitol Hill. I'm *shocked*, shocked, to discover that both Mitchell and Selig—who, just two hours later, endorsed every recommendation in the report—are passionately in favor of tougher "best-practices" drug testing. What a stunner. Why, right off the bat, Bud said there would be no more 24-hour warnings to clubs that a random drug test would be held the next day. You mean there were warnings for "random" tests? And MLB could have changed it unilaterally, but it took the Mitchell report before they did it? What impressive self-motivation.

However, the report's predictable functions—a punch in the nose to the union, a slap in the face to MLB, a predictable recitation of the usual (already revealed) steroid suspects and a T-bone steak to placate congressional watchdogs—were all obliterated by the discovery nobody expected. In the end, the Mitchell report will forever be the Clemens indictment.

Clemens plummeted from icon to fallen idol in a matter of hours. Even if he is innocent, as his lawyer claims, the damage is done. The report devotes nine scathing pages to him, far more than any other player. This is baseball's own officially commissioned history of its most tainted period. And who is its protagonist? Clemens.

How can that ever be undone? If Mark McGwire got only 25 percent of the Hall of Fame vote a year ago because he refused to answer questions before Congress—and, coupled with José Canseco's accusations, looked ashamed and guilty—then how does Clemens get elected when his own trainer and longtime friend says he injected him more than a dozen times?

Baseball and its fans may require a few days to digest the pairing of Bonds and Clemens, one player so prickly and against the grain, the other the ultimate good ol' boy. But the match is fitting because it makes us face the core of baseball's drug problem. At one end of the cheating spectrum, performance-enhancing drugs provided a last hope for marginal players clinging to a big league job. Their dilemma may touch us. We understand. Perhaps we sympathize. At the other extreme, among the greatest players, we harden our hearts. They had it all and threw it away for more money, more glory and more years in the spotlight.

That harsh judgment is true, but only by half. The fiercer the competitor, the greater the pride, the bigger the talent—in other words, the more qualities a man possesses that we claim to admire in a champion—the greater his fury will be at the thought of being beaten, outstripped, surpassed by another man. And the greater the chance that he will defy the rules, risk his health and "do what it takes" to win.

How like a superman to be above the law. How close to invulnerability to disregard your own health. How easy to confuse self-sacrifice for your team for a deeper and governing selfishness. How easy to mistake the sins of ego for the virtues of sport.

Such men would almost be heroic, if they weren't so tragic.

2007

## TONY KORNHEISER

Little-known facts about Tony Kornheiser (b. 1948) of ESPN's *Pardon the Interruption*: He broke into newspapers writing about rock 'n' roll, took the neatest notes of perhaps any sportswriter ever (in different colors of ink), and hated flying so much you would have thought he was Icarus without sunblock. Starting in 1970, Kornheiser wrote about basketball and tennis at *Newsday*, moved to *The New York Times* to write features and columns, and ended up doing more of the same at *The Washington Post* before the prospect of fame and money lured him to TV in 2001. He could get a laugh with a column about a basketball player he called "a shooter most foul" and make you feel the grief of a baseball lifer who had lost his son. Here, in a 1978 profile for the *Times*, Kornheiser peers deep inside the psyche of Reggie Jackson.

★ ★ ★

# Jackson's Lonely World

"What was it that Pasternak said? 'Once in every generation there's a fool who tells the truth exactly as he sees it.' That's Reggie."

*Jim Palmer*

REGGIE JACKSON is holding a cup of coffee in his right hand and a doughnut in his left hand. The first two fingers of his left hand are on the steering wheel of his silver and blue Rolls-Royce. He is backing the $80,000 Rolls—"six different positions on the seat; it's like sitting in your living room"—between a bus and a metal fence, working with a six-inch margin for error. He is doing this casually, the way a man might pour a glass of ice tea from a pitcher. With confidence, with don't-you-just-know-it confidence.

Jackson is on his way to Fort Myers, Fla., for a game against the Kansas City Royals, a three-hour drive from the Yankee camp at Fort Lauderdale. He has permission not to ride the team bus, not so special a privilege inasmuch as Billy Martin has given Thurman Munson, Graig Nettles, Sparky Lyle and Dick Tidrow, among others, the day off. Jackson never gets a day off. He is the Yankee who packs the house. He makes all spring-training trips, plays in every spring-training game, so the manager doesn't quibble with how he gets there. Anyway, the manager is also not on the bus; he is driving to the game with his pitching coach, Art Fowler.

"Needs gas," Jackson says, pulling into a service station.

The attendant's eyes dilate. It isn't often he sees an $80,000 Corniche. He fills the tank and begins washing the windshield.

"Sir, none of that soapy water, please. It's bad for the finish; it streaks." Jackson knows what's good and what's bad for this car. He washes it clean and wipes it down every day and waxes it every month. Himself. This car says just about everything about Reggie Jackson. It's big. It's expensive. It performs. And it has to have tender, loving care.

"Yes, sir," says the attendant. "This is purified water. Don't use the soapy stuff." He wipes a windshield blade. "I believe I'm about as good in my profession as you are in yours, if I can judge by your car here."

Jackson smiles. "Yes," he says, looking out through a window now so clean as to suggest no window at all. "Yes, I'll bet you are."

In minutes, he is heading west on State Road 84—Alligator Alley—cutting through a 75-mile stretch of Big Cypress Swamp. His eyes are scanning the trees for eagles and hawks. Suddenly he fixes on a patch of gray, hulking birds.

"See them?" he asks. "Vultures."

He rolls down the window on the driver's side and stares.

These are not pretty birds. They sit and wait for misfortune to happen. Jackson thinks about vultures. In the last seven seasons he has played for six division winners and four world champions. In the last 10 seasons he has averaged .270 in batting, 28 home runs and 84 runs batted in; last season the numbers were .286, 32 and 110. Maybe not automatic Hall of Fame, but, at the very least, impressive. The record shows that the man wins. "You'd think once in a while they might say it," Jackson says. "After 10 years, some of it ought to come back to you."

Jackson is easily hurt—too easily, most people suggest. But he had never felt quite the hurt he felt last season, his first in New York. Most of his teammates—and his manager—had a dislike for him, and they showed it by leaving him virtually alone on one side of the clubhouse. They had won a pennant without him, and they treated his coming and all the attention he received from the news media like an invasion. The press quickly got on him for his terrible defensive play and his mediocre offensive play early in the season. The fans gave him a booing unheard of in New York since the days of Roger Maris. Until the final game of the World Series, Jackson was the villain.

"Is 'hell' the right word?" he is asked.

"Double it," he answers.

The Rolls moves on, eating up road.

"They look at the money I make, and they say, 'The nigger don't deserve it; he never hit .300,'" Jackson says, beginning a monologue that lasts three miles, his voice rising and falling like that of a tent-city evangelist. "They see me working hard on my defense, and they say, 'The nigger's a showboat.' They see me sign autographs for two or three hours, and they say, 'The nigger just wants his name in the papers.'

"Do they ever say, 'The nigger can play'? That he wins? That he performs under pressure? Do they look at what I withstood and say, 'That nigger has fiber'? Just once I'd like to hear that; I'd like to hear someone say, 'Thanks, thanks for playing your butt off.' No, it's always, 'What's wrong with Reggie? He's a phony, a fake, not real, a glory hound, a man-ip-u-la-tor.' Why doesn't anybody say, 'The man can do it; he goes out and does it'?"

Jackson's reputation throughout the league baffles him.

"The worst in baseball," says Claudell Washington, a teammate on the Oakland championship squad of 1974. "Guys who don't even know him don't like him. They don't like his style. Most players are quiet; Reggie is always talking. The press goes to him for comments about players before going to the players themselves. And some of the things Reggie says. In my first year at Oakland, Reggie told the papers that I played outfield like I was trying to catch grenades. I don't think he means to hurt people, but he talks so much that he can't help it."

The consensus is that Jackson has the biggest ego, the biggest mouth and the most impeachable credentials of any superstar in baseball. For all his money, you can find few players who say they would trade places with him. What's more damaging, they don't think he cares.

"There's Reggie Jackson lovers and Reggie Jackson haters," says Billy Hunter, the Texas manager, who coached him in Baltimore. "I don't think he cares which way they go as long as they shout, 'Reggie!'"

Jackson listens. This is not making him happy. Vultures. He's hearing words and seeing vultures. He is surprised at the extent of his reputation. He doesn't want to acknowledge it.

"I'd like to say it isn't true," he says, conceding how it may well be. "Because I know I'm a good fella. I'm a good, clean, honest guy trying to be a good human being. If someone would take the time, he'd see it. But I'm resented, and apparently my way is abrasive. They doubt my motives. They don't believe me anymore."

His teammates—those who'll talk about him—say he has only himself to blame. They also say they respect the way he plays the game.

Munson, Nettles, Lyle and Tidrow refused to talk about him, but, Chris Chambliss suggested that what had probably happened to Jackson was that, in his desire to be unique, he created a monster that alienated his peers. Mickey Rivers said that last season "everything Reggie did was all right with everyone but the players." And Bucky Dent's observation was that "Reggie put himself in a position where he was damned if he did and damned if he didn't." But Dent also said:

"I was really happy for him when he hit the three homers in the last game of the Series. It was a real nice ending for him, especially after what he went through. I was new here myself, and, as quiet as I am, I even felt like cracking up last season."

For the first time in 30 miles, Jackson is smiling.

"Thank you," he says, as if Dent were in the back seat. "I am very appreciative that someone else saw it like that."

Jackson will talk about last season, but he must walk into it very slowly. The words are chosen carefully. They must be correct.

"Honest to God in heaven, I didn't think it would be like that," he says. "You think I'd have gone to the Yankees if I knew? Think a person wants to be disliked? I thought guys would say: 'Here's a man who played in the Series. He can help us. Let's go along with his program, because he's been there.'

"I missed it by 180 degrees. But it would've been easy to lay down and die, and I didn't. Those homers, they told me there's a God in heaven. They told me more about my character than my talent. You can't believe the pressure. You can't believe what it's like putting on that 44 and hearing them say, 'Go.' "

The easiest question in baseball is, What do you think of Reggie? Outside the Yankees, almost everyone has an opinion. Almost everyone prefaces his answer with this disclaimer: "I've always gotten along with him. When you get to know him, he's not a bad guy."

"The chocolate hot dog?" says Dock Ellis, briefly Jackson's teammate last season with the Yankees. "It's fashionable to knock Reggie, but down deep most guys are jealous of him."

"When it gets down to the nitty-gritty," says Paul Lindblad, a teammate at Oakland, "he comes to the top. There isn't a better pressure player in baseball."

"He can carry a team on his back," says Billy Hunter, "for a week to 10 days all by himself. The thing is, he doesn't adapt to a team; the team has to adapt to him."

"R.J., R.J.," says Claudell Washington, shaking his head. "He only cares about distance. Reggie never talks about the homers that just clear the fence; he's got to hit the longest ball ever. Got to be airport with Reggie, got to be out there on the airport runway. All he wants is for people to tell him, 'Buck, you're the strongest man that ever was.' Tell him that, and there's nothing he won't do for you. When he's going good, he's the best there is."

Jackson alternates between calling these critiques compliments and knocking the men who speak evil of him. He begs to be understood for his complexities, yet he seems to need to put others into tidy boxes. The criticism that bothers him most is Washington's—that he cares only for distance, that he could be a more nearly complete player if his ego weren't so invested in going downtown. Washington is not alone in this feeling; Billy Hunter, Ken Holtzman, Jim Palmer and Catfish Hunter say the same thing.

"It's hard for me to grasp," Jackson says, turning the Rolls off Alligator Alley onto Route 29 North, to Fort Myers. "I think it's my job to hit the long ball; whether I want to hit it 500 feet instead of 350, I struggle with. I'll take 40 or 50 homers that just clear a fence. But I can't hit .350 with 17 homers and 75 R.B.I.'s and be the asset I can be at .285 with 35 homers and 110 R.B.I.'s That's me, what I want to do.

"But I'll tell you this: For me to play nine innings a game and play every day for a manager like Billy Martin, I have to be a more complete player; he demands that. I've been working my butt off this spring to show him that I know I'm not too big to work on my defense and bunting. He makes me a better player."

Billy Martin, the magic name. The manager who almost fought with Jackson on national television in a dugout in Boston.

"Compared to last year, this year is heaven," says Martin.

Amen, says Jackson. All he wants to do is play ball.

This year his relationship with Martin is better. His relationship with Munson is better, by so much that they talk now; they could even go to dinner together should either care to. His relationship with all the Yankees is better. They've had a full season to realize who he is and how he acts and to get used to him.

What most of them learned in one season, Holtzman and Hunter had known for years. Holtzman and Hunter like him.

"Last year the players didn't understand how Reggie could have the kind of first half he had and still keep talking," says Hunter. "It was the same at Oakland."

"At Oakland, and at Baltimore," says Holtzman, who has spent the last six seasons as Jackson's teammate.

"You've got to disregard two-thirds of what you read in print that Reggie said," Hunter finds. "If you don't, he can really play with your head. Only about one-third matters anyway. The rest is just Reggie talking. What I think is that he tries too hard to be liked, and somewhere along the line it comes out wrong."

Jackson hears the words and seems to go into a trance.

"Yeah," he says. "Yeah, Cat's right."

This year, he says, it won't happen.

"I don't want turmoil," he says. "I'm going to do all I can to avoid turmoil, even if it means not standing up for my rights." He pauses for emphasis, in a sort of Jesse Jackson style. "First and foremost, I'm looking to stay out of trouble. Don't want nothing to do with it."

"But it'll find you, won't it?" he is asked.

"Always does," he says, exhaling ever so slightly as the Rolls pulls into the stadium lot at Fort Myers.

The uniform is tight and tapered, and he is into it in 15 minutes, ready to go. But the ride and the conversation have done his insides dirty. Too much past dredged up. He needs something to keep his stomach down.

"There's the man," calls Dave Nelson, the Royal infielder, coming over to Jackson. "Congratulations, congratulations on a helluva World Series. You deserve it."

Behind Nelson comes John Mayberry, the Royal slugger.

"Reggie!" Mayberry shouts.

"Rope, what's up?" Jackson says.

"You, man. You, with your bad self."

It is curious, but he seems most comfortable with members of other teams. With the Yankees, he is at his most comfortable at the batting cage, before games, when the other team's players are close. You sense that he is searching for vocal respect that only opposing players are willing to give him. It seems likely that still, even after his Ruthian World Series, some of his teammates are either too jealous or too stubborn to admit that they were wrong about his ability as a player.

In the clubhouse Jackson is hesitant. Even now there is a tenseness between him and many other Yankees. Yet, it may well be that he infers more hostility than actually exists.

"In the locker room I don't feel like I'm one of the guys," he says. "It's hard for me to say this. I'd like to fit in, but I don't. I don't know if I'll ever really be allowed to fit in. I need to be appreciated, even praised. I like to hear: 'Nice going. Great going. You're a helluva ballplayer.' But I walk in feeling disliked. Maybe I'm overdoing it. Like I never get on anybody in the clubhouse unless it's a situation where it's obvious that it's O.K. for me to say something. I stay in the background. I never talk to too many people, except maybe Fran Healy or Ray, the clubhouse attendant, or the press.

"I never small-talk with anyone; I don't feel that anyone cares to talk to me. So I kind of shut up. I'm always the one who has to initiate the conversation. Sometimes I hear my voice in the locker room, and I want to take it back. I don't want anyone to look at me or feel uncomfortable around me."

These words are hard to hear and harder, perhaps, to say.

And then there is a game to play. He is at peace playing baseball. He starts in right field and plays five innings, going to bat three times. Two outs and one R.B.I. single. The people, who react to him as they react to no other Yankee—loud boos, even louder cheers—are satisfied. He has been held down, but not out.

With permission to leave early, Jackson showers, dresses and goes to his car for the drive home. There is a crowd, as usual. He signs autographs and discusses the car, its paint job and the reason he likes to park it in the shade instead of the sun. Before leaving he takes a towel and wipes it down, wiping even the inside carpeting, making sure it is perfectly clean.

Forty miles outside Fort Myers he is playing his tape deck, and the chorus of the song repeats, "We're all in this together." Jackson is singing along. "All my life," he says, "I wanted a car like this. I know it's a rich man's car; I'm proud I can afford it."

"He should be happy," says Chris Chambliss. "He has everything he could want."

"Are you happy?" Jackson is asked.

"For print?" he answers as the car moves almost silently past the swamps on Alligator Alley.

*1978*

## RICK TELANDER

The normal progression for those who could make the jump used to be newspapers first, then *Sports Illustrated*. It was all about a writer finding a voice that told readers nobody else could have written what they were reading. But Rick Telander (b. 1948) found his voice long ago, when he wrote *Heaven Is a Playground*, his classic study of basketball dreams rewarded and thwarted. Then it was on to *SI*, where he spent twenty-two years as a star who was also a workhorse capable of handling any kind of story. He could have stayed at the magazine until they turned out the lights. But when the *Chicago Sun-Times* came to him in 1995 offering a job as senior sports columnist, Telander couldn't resist. He was a Peoria, Illinois, native, had been an All–Big 10 defensive back at Northwestern, and even lived in the Chicago area. The fit was a natural. So, it turned out, was writing a column.

★ ★ ★

# Making Their Points

ON TUESDAY, a young man named Dajuan Wagner scored one hundred points in a game, the first time a U.S. boys high school player had reached the century mark since 1979.

There was a lot of tongue-clucking about that display because, you know, not all of Wagner's one hundred points were needed.

Indeed, Wagner's school, Camden (New Jersey) High, beat Gloucester Township Technical School 157–67. So only eleven of Wagner's points would have sufficed for a victory.

Then we find out that on the same night, many miles away, a young man named Cedrick Hensley scored 101 points for Heritage Christian Academy of Texas City, Texas, in a 178–28 evisceration of Banff Christian School of Tomball, Texas.

Maybe it was Turn the Other Cheek Night for Banff. Who knows? But none of Hensley's points was necessary to send the Banff players home like flogged pilgrims.

Naturally, questions about sportsmanship came up. But they were dispelled like so many cattle gnats by Heritage Christian coach Jerome Tang.

According to the Associated Press, Tang urged Hensley to go for triple digits because, "He's having a surgical procedure done on Friday, and he will be out for about a week and a half."

Good thing Hensley wouldn't be out for a month. Tang might have had him go for three hundred.

"After he had fifty at the half," Tang said, "the kids said, 'We think we can get him one hundred.' They wanted to do this for him, and they sacrificed so that their teammate could accomplish something special."

Love that coach-speak.

Sacrifice. Something special.

But why go into the jargon at all?

Scoring one hundred points isn't that big a deal.

Hell, I've done it. Yes, I have.

Let me set the stage. It's the McGuane Park six-foot-and-under league in either 1974 or 1975. I'm playing for Henry's Sports & Bait Shop, a team made up of local Bridgeporters and a few of my football buddies from Northwestern. Our jerseys are reversible yellow and green and feature the proud logo of a man fishing in silhouette.

The old gym is so small that the games are four-on-four and the bench players have to stand. Spectators look in through the doorways. To take the ball out of bounds, you have to put your foot on the wall.

I'm a trifle taller than six-one, but I'm the shortest Henry's player on the floor at times. I don't want to name names, but Mark Krumptinger has to be six-two, and Frank Lutostanski is a whisker under six-three. But it's Bridgeport. There are various ways to measure.

We're playing Seemo's Schnozzles, and—how can I put this gently?—the Schnozzles are not in basketball shape. I'm pretty sure they are, well, let's say they've been visiting a tavern. Plus, they're all shorter than six feet.

At the half, Henry's is ahead something like 85–10, and we're all in double figures. What do we do to keep from being bored?

We look at the scorebook.

"Let's get somebody one hundred," somebody says.

I offer to be that person—my sacrifice, coach Tang—and away we go.

I had about thirty at the half, but now Henry's got serious. I didn't play defense, hovered at midcourt, took every outlet pass, and fired away. Nobody on Henry's shot except me, and every offensive rebound came flying back to me so that I felt like Kobe Bryant (who wasn't born yet) in his most orgasmic dream.

Still, I wasn't scoring fast enough, so I moved to the free-throw line. Then under the basket. Every now and then, a player would yell to the scorer, "What's he at?" It would take a while for the guy to calculate.

"Sixty-two."

Then later, "Seventy-nine."

By the time he said it, I had even more.

My lack of defense didn't matter. The Schnozzles, lurching and nauseous, were a team of self-checkers. They seemed to lose interest even in guarding me.

I don't want to say my arm got tired but it got numb. When the horn sounded, the scorer added up the little Xs that ran all over the page.

A hundred and eight, he said. "Or 107."

Were there any snoopy press members around, wanting to know whether Henry's had poured it on in an ugly display of vanity, cheapness, and downright cruelty?

No.

Was there anybody there to ask me whether I felt big now, like a real man?

No.

Did the Schnozzles mind?

I don't think they knew.

In fact, if anyone was harmed, it was me.

"They ran the clock straight through at the end," said Joe Zigulich, one of my teammates. "You were robbed."

Did my life change because of hitting a hundred?

I think so, but I'm not sure how. Other than buying all the beers that night.

*2001*

★　★　★

# Atkins a Study in Pride and Pain

K NOXVILLE, TENN.—I drive slowly past the small red-brick house on the narrow, winding road in the hills outside town.

I pull into a driveway a quarter-mile farther on. A dog barks somewhere. It's a few days before Christmas.

The dog stops. Silence.

I turn the car around, drive past the house again.

I don't know.

The house has its curtains drawn. There are two old cars in the carport, one of them very old, I'm guessing 30, 40 years. Fins. Rusty.

There's a wooden wheelchair ramp that looks weathered and unused leading to the front door. A "No Smoking" sign in the front-door window. Two tiny American flags on the wall next to the carport.

No lights on. No decorations.

Doug Atkins, 76, the legendary Hall of Fame defensive end for the Bears, lives here.

"I don't want to see anybody," he had told me during one of our phone conversations. People had their minds made up about a lot of stuff, he said. Predetermined. The country was going to hell. No middle class. Only rich and poor.

I didn't need to ask which side he fell on.

"I'm doing OK," he had said. "I cracked my hip awhile back. Never got well since then. I can walk with a cane, but it's getting rough. I got sick, and I've been poisoned from some of the medicine they gave me—lead poisoning. They don't put out the truth about medicines. So many crooks in the country nowadays—politicians, oil companies, pharmaceutical companies, lobbyists. A lot of people are worse off than I am. But I don't need to see any reporters."

Everybody knows that football is a rough game, that the NFL is the roughness polished bright and turned into performance art, the brutality into religion, the cracking bones into the percussive soundtrack that suits our times.

But not many know the toll the game takes when the players themselves, the artists, have left the stage.

A shocking number of the men, starting sometimes well before middle age, begin to limp, then hobble, then stop moving much at all.

Dementia, mood disorders, osteoarthritis, surgery, more surgery, pain—the wheel of football repercussion spins and spins.

And often, the longer a man played—meaning the better player he was—the worse his debilitation.

Doug Atkins played 17 years in the NFL, the best 12 for the Bears.

In that time, the long-legged, hickory-tough 6-8, 260-pounder did things that hadn't been done before on the gridiron. A scholarship basketball player at Tennessee as well as an All-America football player, Atkins sometimes jumped over blockers like a hurdler vaulting rolling logs.

He went out for track at Tennessee and won the Southeastern Conference high jump, clearing 6-6. In the NFL, he went to eight Pro Bowls from 1958 to 1966.

"I didn't know what I was doing in the high jump," he said on the phone. "In high school one time, I scissored 6-1½."

All that talent came together on the football field like a rainbow palette.

George Halas, Atkins' coach with the Bears and the man who helped found the NFL, said of the giant from Humboldt, Tenn., "There never was a better defensive end."

But now there's the embarrassment the game has exacted.

Mike Ditka hosts a golf tournament each year wherein Ditka and sponsors earmark money for Hall of Famers in need.

Sometimes it's a payout for surgical procedures or medicine.

Sometimes it's a wheelchair ramp.

One time it was for a tombstone.

"It's pitiful," says Ditka, tearing into the NFL's stingy pension plan for old-timers, the NFL players union and all PR aspects of the league. "Rip 'em all, I don't care."

The league's frugal pension plan is complicated, but it's simplified nicely by the fact that the veterans die at a swift pace.

There's a new pension agreement being put into place, but as of last year, NFL players who had reached age 55 might typically get between $200 and $425 a month.

Enough for aspirin, for sure.

While the current Bears swagger down the road to success and the NFL wallows in money, the old men who helped build the brand suffer in silence, often lame, often nearly destitute, their pride too great to allow pity.

Atkins had mesmerized me when I had asked him, please, just for me, to detail his injuries.

The groin pull that tore muscle off the bone, leaving a "hole" in his abdomen. "My fault," he said.

The big toe injury. The broken collarbone. The leg that snapped at the bottom of a pile. ("I got to the sideline, and it didn't feel right.")

The biceps that tore in half, Atkins' arm hanging limply.

"It's just a show muscle," he said, explaining why he never got it fixed.

"I see these old football players," says Dr. Victoria Brander, the head of Northwestern University's Arthritis Institute, "and every joint is ruined—their toes, ankles, knees, hips, fingers, elbows, shoulders. The supporting structure in the joints is gone. Their spines are collapsed. I see one former star who is bent like a 'C.'

"But they are noble. They played their game because they believed in something. They were warriors. They never complain."

I have gone past Atkins' house four times now. I take a deep breath. I dial his number on my cell phone.

His wife answers and gives him the phone. I just happen to be in the area, I say. Would he mind if I stopped by, maybe for a minute or two, on the way to the airport?

"Damn it, why do you all keep bothering me?" Atkins yells into the receiver. "I told you I was sick!"

And then the line is dead.

"These guys don't need much," Ditka will say later in barely controlled fury. "Your best players? Ever? Why can't the league give them enough to live out their lives in dignity? Is that so f—king hard?"

I drive on, feeling terrible, feeling cruel. I never should've imposed on Doug Atkins. On his pride.

In the midst of our bounty, I feel lost.

*2007*

## RICHARD HOFFER

Elegance can be elusive even when a sportswriter has all day to fuss over similes and metaphors. On deadline, the elusive often fades to impossibility as writer after writer resorts to the rickety prose of desperation. And yet Richard Hoffer (b. 1949) made the deadline pieces he wrote for the *Los Angeles Times* read as though he had worked out of a sumptuous garret and not some cramped, overheated press room with civilians who had no business there peering over his shoulder. Hoffer spent a decade as the ultimate stylist in *The Times*'s talent-rich sports department before moving to *Sports Illustrated* in 1989 and becoming its star boxing writer and all-purpose essayist. Boxing had been his specialty at *The Times*, too, but it is his story about gymnast Mary Lou Retton's 1984 Olympic triumph that became legend. Another writer might have needed hours to deliver something half as witty, incisive, nuanced, and literary. Hoffer produced a classic in forty minutes.

★ ★ ★

# Chacon Lives with a Dream
# and Relives a Nightmare

PALERMO, CALIF.—Bobby Chacon, one-time street-gang fighter, must now travel some 10 miles to find a street, about 60 more to find a fight. This is a long way from Pacoima, any way you look at it. From the San Fernando Valley to the Big Valley, from urban guerrilla to boxer to gentleman farmer.

Chacon has lived here two years, in a handsome "double-wide" mobile home. Palermo, no metroplis, is really just a four-way stop an hour's drive north of Sacramento. The Once-in-a-While barber shop, Engasser's Market, a Peacock service station and the Palermo Hardware constitute the downtown area. Chacon's home, at the end of several miles of twisting dirt road, may be said to constitute the suburbs.

He lives bounded by 20 acres of grassy meadows, some of it just now afire with purple wildflowers, some of it cooled by a rock-strewn, pool-pocked stream. Stands of oak populate the softly hilled horizon. There is a rabbit hutch some 100 yards from the home, a pig pen a bit farther. An aggressive goose, a turkey and two yapping dogs—a squat boxer and a chihuahua—form a kind of rural street gang. Or would, were there a street.

This is Chacon's landscape, a tranquil one with laughing kids—who produce the only sounds—and contented animals. It's a leafy playground is what it is, on this day alternately cooled by gentle breezes, warmed by unobstructed sunshine.

Yet it is not now an altogether happy picture, the Walden-like backdrop notwithstanding. For Chacon's interior landscape has been ravaged, the once-tranquil scenery within now a chaos of loss and guilt, personal rubble. And the most terrible landmark of all, the horror of a young wife, waiting for a call that never came, shooting herself in the head with a .22 caliber bullet, the record, "You Could Have Been With Me," spinning to a silent conclusion on the turntable.

Chacon has just completed the day's training at the Butte County Police Athletic League gym in nearby Oroville. He's working toward a May 4 fight with Rosendo Ramirez, a headliner on one of Babe Griffin's cards in Sacramento. Chacon, the featherweight champion in 1974 but an unpredictable fighter since losing the title in his first defense, hopes to be working for a title shot as well. He's 31 now and if time hasn't already run out, it is certainly running short.

At the gym he spars six rounds with some local amateurs, offering them as much instruction as he is deriving preparation ("You've got to keep your hands up—look how easy it is to get through—boom"). He uses the speed bag, jumps rope, does pushups, then finishes with 100 situps. By then the little gym is empty, the sparring partners and their wives, girlfriends and kids having left.

On his way to his own kids, he mounts the last hill in his gray-primer-painted '48 Chevy, a roostertail of dust hanging in the air behind him. This is still home to him and his three young children. Home, too, to memories both happy and horrible. He settles onto a couch and his two youngest, 6-year-old James and 8-year-old Chico, drape themselves around him, almost like the wedding rings he now wears on a gold chain around his neck.

A reporter who has been spending the day with Chacon asks questions about Chacon's grief and the story of his wife's suicide spills out, along, in time, with tears. A photographer records them—a wipe of the eye, a click of the camera. Good journalism, maybe. As human behavior goes, it's a bit shaky.

It is not a new story, anyway. Chacon told it to reporters the day after his wife Valorie's self-inflicted death more than a month ago. He had sat in a Sacramento motel room and had said that his 13-year marriage, a loving one by all accounts, had degenerated into a kind of war over his boxing. She had gotten him off the streets and into boxing, long ago. But now she wanted him out of the ring.

It may have begun with the beating an out-of-shape Chacon took several years ago at the hands of David Sotelo. Valorie, who had never seen her husband hurt, was as devastated by the damage as he was. She began insisting that he retire. Chacon resisted, but was haunted by her doubts about his future. He became an unpredictable performer, postponing important fights for vague reasons. He folded one show saying he wanted to leave camp to see his kids at play.

In the ring, he was still unpredictable. His manager, Jackie Barnett, remembers that Chacon, between rounds, would scan the ringside for his wife. Once or twice during a round, Chacon would clinch, spin his opponent, just to locate Valorie in the crowd.

Chacon either could not or would not give up boxing. His promises, even in their retelling, sound vague. He would stop after this fight, or that fight. At the end of this year, at the beginning of that. Or once he won the title. Or something.

There were these broken promises then. And other things—her loneliness, her low self-esteem. Who knows what? Early in the year, while Chacon was in Sacramento preparing for a fight, she attempted suicide with sleeping pills. Her brother had to break the door down to reach her. In the hospital she awoke in a rage at having failed. She tore the tubes from her arm, returned home and tore that apart. Chacon wasn't told until after his fight.

Doctors told Chacon she would try again. Chacon says it's funny that you can be told a thing like that and yet not really hear it. He didn't find out until later but Valorie was telling friends—everyone but him—of her desperation. The phone bills mounted as Valorie reached out. She told one friend that Bobby would fight again, but over her dead body. She told another that her husband would be better off in boxing without her. She told Barnett that she had a million-dollar ending for the Bobby Chacon story he was then trying to produce. "I'm going to kill myself," she told him.

Valorie took a trip to Hawaii, apparently looking for a job. Finding nothing but rejection, she returned. She was found wandering in the San Francisco airport. Chacon went and got her from a hospital in San Mateo. That night, back home, he lay with her on the floor, hugging her. He thought everything was all right.

But several days later he had to leave for Sacramento for yet another fight camp, and she couldn't believe it, that he was leaving so soon after her return. There were phone conversations in which Chacon promised to quit. But there were not enough phone calls, apparently. Valorie's mother was in the mobile home that day and she remembers Valorie waiting tensely by the phone. Late that morning, just as Chacon would have been going to train, Valorie abandoned her vigil, placed the record, "You Could Have Been With Me," on the turntable and went into her room and killed herself.

When Chacon reached her, she was still lying on the floor. "There she was," he says, "that little cutie. All that terrible blood. The blood just ran off. She looked pretty. I loved her so long—I only had love for her. I always loved her but I lost her . . ."

The next night Chacon climbed into the ring in Sacramento to fight Salvador Ugalde.

There is no explaining that, not even now, a month later. "All I know," he says, "is that it would keep me right for another day." For another day it did keep him right. But, having smashed Ugalde for a third-round knockout, there was little immediate redemption to be found in boxing. He returned to their home and cried for two weeks.

"She got tangled up in the web and the spider got her," Chacon says quietly, still haunted by her presence, still trying to locate her. "She was trying to figure out a lot of things those last few days but I didn't realize how she was slipping. It's funny—13 years, we knew each other to the bone, all the truths. She was my best friend. There was real love there. But you just don't hear things."

Chacon is at times furious with the inadequacy of his grief. At times he is just furious. "I was trying to make a good life for us," he says, recognizing his wife's suicide as an accusation, a blow he could neither fend nor return. "What was I going to be? A fireman? I wanted to make something out of my boxing. . . ."

He trails off, as he must do often during these awful recollections. "Now it's all too late and it doesn't really matter," he finally says. "Except late at night."

Chacon says he was visited by Valorie's spirit two days after her death. His account: He walked into the bedroom and he was blinded. "Val, I can't see," he said. But Chacon said she guided him to the bed, not saying a thing, and placed her arm around him. "It was a good feeling," he said, "a warm feeling. It was as if she was saying, 'You've got a tough road ahead of you.'"

And it is a tough road. He comes home from his training for a fight and walks into his house to see another woman, a married friend, taking care of his children. It seems to him he should be able to hug that person. There is that hole in his life.

But he still has those children. The younger two sleep with him at night, crowding him into a far corner of his queen-size bed. Eleven-year-old Jahna sometimes joins them. They do everything together, although, on this day they are doing it without Jahna, who has yet to return from play practice at school. Jahna plays the part of the bear who sings "The Bear Blues." Chacon and his two younger children know the "Bear Blues" by heart and, for the reporter and photographer, they sing together, "I'm not a very happy bear . . ."

He has his boxing. He says he has rededicated himself anew to that difficult and demanding sport. He says he threw his youth away on the game, doing it without reason. He won the title in spite of himself, he says. He'll win it again. In spite of everybody else.

Mostly, though, he has his grief, which is a kind of comfort after all, maybe the last available to him. "You wanted to see me cry," he says to the reporter. "It's all right; it's good to cry. I hadn't talked about these things since the night it happened. I hadn't thought about them. It felt good to talk about them and I'm glad we did. I never want to forget her."

*1982*

★　★　★

# Retton Vaults Past Szabo to Win Gold Medal

S HE'S A calculating coquettte. You give her a chance, she'll take your heart. She's a shrewd, brown-eyed gold digger. Yeah, you give her a chance, she'll take your gold, too.

Mary Lou Retton, who has restored pixie to our vocabulary, stole both Friday night, winning, in order, U.S. hearts and Romanian gold. The little sneak. Who saw her coming, padding down the runway in those size-3 feet?

Ordinarily you'd want to hang her from your rear-view mirror. But Friday night, much of America, certainly most of the 9,023 in Pauley Pavilion, wanted to suspend this 4-foot-9 doll in the stratosphere of Olympic tradition, where the heroes belong.

This is what she did, relying on all the nerve and cunning normally available to 16-year-old girls with crushes on Matt Dillon. Battling back in her final two events, needing perfect scores and no less, she beat Romania's Ecaterina Szabo by 5/100ths of a point and Romania's Pauca Simona by 5/10ths to win the women's all-around title, literally vaulting into history.

Some quick perspective: This is only the first individual Olympic medal ever won by a U.S. women's gymnast. Ever.

In the days and months and years that follow, this victory will no doubt be translated into a renewed boom in women's gymnastics, with new clubs opening and every pre-teen worth her pigtail paying money to learn how to somersault. Funny that the last big boom was in 1976, when another little pixie, Nadia Comaneci, transformed her sport. Try to picture seven-year-old Mary Lou, lying in her living room back in Fairmount, W. Va., watching Nadia, suddenly inspired. "I thought, 'Oh, my gosh, she's so wonderful,' " she said. "Who would have thought?"

Yeah, who would have thought? Nadia, a guest of honor at Pauley Pavilion for these Olympics, offering her silent benediction to the Romanian girls? Romania's star gymnast, Ecaterina Szabo, who began the night with a 10 and a 9.95 to take a quick .15 lead?

Only Retton, as nerveless as plant life, could have thought it. And did. She knew that the order of events indicated Szabo taking the early lead. What's to worry. While Szabo was performing in her strongest events, Retton was performing in her weakest. Wait for the finish to announce this winner. "It was the luck of the draw," she admitted.

Szabo, a gymnast who is much like Retton in form and style, began the evening with a 10 on beam. Retton was struggling through an uneven bars set with a 9.85. Suddenly Retton's preliminary lead (from the team event) of .15 was gone, wiped out. Then while Szabo was scoring 9.95 on her floor exercises, dancing to a whacky medley that alternated "Rhapsody in Blue" with "Camptown Races," Retton was getting a 9.8 on her least favorite apparatus, the beam. Szabo, the 17-year-old heir to Nadia, a veteran international competitor who placed third in the most recent World Championships, was leading America's ingenue by 15/100ths.

U.S. Coach Don Peters was unmoved by this apparent momentum. "I knew that after the first two events, Mary Lou might be behind, just because they were Szabo's strongest and Mary Lou's weakest. It was just a matter of order."

Then Szabo got a surprising 9.9 on vault, her legs slightly splayed as she dismounted. Retton took the floor, where her tumbling power is most evident and best rewarded. She vamped through the old song "Johnny, My Friend," playing the crowd shamelessly, grinning out of each somersault. A double layout somersault on her first pass. Grin. A double tuck. Grin. Another. Then a smile that revealed what must have been hundreds of the whitest teeth you ever saw. On the side, Peters held up all the fingers he had. The judges didn't have it in them to argue. A 10. Szabo's lead was cut to 5/100ths.

On the last rotation, Szabo was up on uneven bars first, while Retton cooled her heels waiting to vault. "I watched her on bars," Retton admitted. "It was a nice set, a clean set, but she took a step on her dismount, and I knew it was a 9.9. I knew I had it."

Oh, and who does your arithmetic, Mary Lou? She only had it if she scored a 10, as in perfect. A 9.95 tied her for the gold. Anything less and she was trying to beat Simona going for silver.

"I knew the takeoff was good," she said, recreating her event, "and I knew the vault was good. And I knew I'd stick it." The way people talked afterward, everybody seemed to know as much.

"It was the biggest vault ever," proclaimed her private coach in

Houston, former Romanian national coach Bela Karolyi, the Texan with the Transylvanian drawl. "When she hit the floor, there was no question."

Said Peters: "You have to give it a 10. It's the best vault I've ever seen."

Mary Lou didn't doubt as much. She pogoed halfway back to the runway for her second vault, arms in the air, arrested only by Karolyi himself who had vaulted the railing. As far as Peters was concerned, that was the only moment of suspense. "I thought we'd get slapped with a deduction," he said, noting that Karolyi, not officially on the U.S. staff, was performing what might look like a terrorist act to the judges. "But I guess that only happens in movies."

It was a 10, all right. Her second, meaningless one, was a 10 as well. Mary Lou, her eyelashes reaching into the first row, saluted the crowd, and a lot of people, as Peters always notes, "wanted to reach out and hug her."

Szabo stood quietly behind the horizontal bar, staring. Wistfully? Sadly? Who could know what those silver-dusted eyes were seeing.

Later Retton rolled the gold medal between her fingers, looking up into the stands, spotting parents, friends and fans. And her coaches talked about this prodigy, the new wave in gymnastics, "this chunky leetle thing," as Karolyi describes, "not quite a butterfly."

What they talked about, even more than her effervescence, was her nerve. Karolyi, the man who developed Nadia and who started, for that matter, Szabo before defecting to this country, talked in his usual hyperventilating chatter.

"She shows this fantastic ability, an aggressiveness," he said. "Who could do it? Who could come back and do it? Nadia was a great champion, but I am telling you Mary Lou is bigger. I guarantee no gymnast in the world could have done what Mary Lou has. To have that strong a personality is fantastic, unbelievable."

Peters, somewhat more subdued, agreed that there are few athletes as mentally strong as Mary Lou. "She thrives on pressure. She never gets tight," he said. "The pressure is what did it, when she needed those 10s. That kid thrives on it. A great champion."

Retton, finally put atop a chair so she could stand eye-to-eye with reporters, shrugged. "Yeah, I work best under pressure." What more was there to say? One thing that is unavailable to this 16-year-old is perspective. When you're that small, it can be hard to understand how you suddenly get so big.

*1984*

## DAVID ISRAEL

Brash, talented, and intent on challenging the status quo, David Israel (b. 1951) was twenty-three when he blew into Washington, D.C. *The Evening Star* had anointed him the country's youngest newspaper sports columnist, and he was as ready as he could be despite having little more than a year's experience covering college sports for the *Chicago Daily News*. Israel made his reputation by going after bigots, bad coaches, and every other variety of bonehead. When he took his column to the *Chicago Tribune* in 1978, the thrill of it all began to subside. Three years later, Israel headed to Los Angeles to write a city column for the *Herald Express* and pursue a future that would include writing and producing TV dramas, working as chief of staff at the 1984 Summer Olympics, and serving as chairman of the California Horse Racing Board. A splendid career but sportswriting's loss.

★ ★ ★

# Joe Pepitone: What Is He Doing for the Rest of His Life?

THE RACKET guys would come to the Copa almost every night in the early 1960s. They would come from the Bronx and Queens, from Brooklyn and Jersey. Always, they would be wearing sharkskin suits with thin lapels, white on white shirts, shoes with a high shine. These were not the Dons, the Mustache Petes from the old country. Not at all. These were their sons, the upwardly mobile hoods. The old guys, they knew business, but they did not know how to live. Their sons did. Big cars, dames, the Copa every night.

They would come to the Copa to be with the stars. They would go backstage and mingle. This certainly was the new breed. They liked to be seen. Among the stars they surrounded themselves with were ballplayers. Their favorite was a young kid with the New York Yankees, a first baseman from Brooklyn named Joe Pepitone.

Joe Pep loved them. He dressed like them and he talked like them. He knew how to live. He would stay out with them all night. When the Copa closed he would go with them to Rudy's, an after hours joint. He did not know anything of their business, and he did not want to know. But he loved their action.

"The people I grew up with were racket people," he explains. "You never heard anyone talk about Mantle or DiMaggio. The heroes were the guys on the corner. My cousin, Jimmy the Bug, was somebody very big. He was in numbers.

"I never wanted to be in rackets. I wasn't the bravest guy in the neighborhood. I was afraid of that set. I didn't want to live in fear of somebody blowing my head off. But they were still my people, and I liked to sit with them and go out with them. I loved them."

And they loved Pepitone back. They were careful it never got out that Pepitone was spending time with them. They kept it very quiet. Once the FBI called Pepitone in and asked him what he was doing with a certain guy. They asked him if he knew the man's business. He told them he knew the guy treated him nice and invited him over for dinner. He was never called in by the commissioner of baseball.

"You gotta make us Italians proud, Joey," they would say. "There aren't many Italians in the big leagues wit your kinda ability. We're countin' on ya."

At the time Pepitone was 21 and a rookie and playing behind Moose Skowron at first base for the Yankees. Joe's friends did not like this. They volunteered to give Skowron an accident.

"Joey," they said, "we'll just get in touch wit him after a game, and the next day ya got the job. No problem. He won't play real good with cracks in his legs."

It was not a joke. They were going to give Skowron an accident, but Pepitone persuaded them not to. That was going too far, even for young Joe Pep. It was one of the few times he realized a limit had been reached and it was time to stop.

They say that if Joe Pepitone knew how to stop more often he might have been a great baseball player. They say he might have been one of those guys you automatically talk about in the same sentence with the Hall of Fame. When he first came up they talked about him succeeding Mickey Mantle. Joe Pep could run, hit and field; he was a natural star. But he never made it.

He lasted 10½ seasons, playing mostly for the Yankees and the Chicago Cubs and a little for Houston and Atlanta. He hit about .260 and more than 200 home runs. Ordinary numbers. But Joe Pepitone was never just another ballplayer.

Now it was a rainy Sunday night in Washington, and Pepitone was wondering what he was doing here. Road trips used to be everything to Pepitone. He let them bust up his first two marriages. But now he wanted to be back with his wife and kid in Chicago. The suite in the Shoreham Hotel was right, a little bit gaudy and a little bit regal, done in deep pink and gold, but Pepitone just didn't feel comfortable.

"This is where we used to stay when I was with the Yankees," he said. "But I haven't been here in six years. That's a long time ago. I can't remember where we used to go. All I can remember is that this is the place Bouton said the Yankees used to go on the roof and look in the windows."

It was a real long time ago. Pepitone has not been a ballplayer for two years. He was here to promote a book he has just written about himself called "Joe, You Coulda Made Us Proud." The book is one of those things that they call candid. It's not about baseball, as much as it is about a kid becoming a man and trying to find himself and failing too many times. In some parts it does for Italians in Park Slope in Brooklyn what Philip Roth's "Portnoy's Complaint" did for Jews in Newark.

Pepitone was a kid who grew up confined and scared and did not know how to deal with freedom and money once he had a little of each as a teenage bonus baby with a bright baseball future. And for 10 years in the major leagues, he never ceased being that bonus baby. For 10 years he stayed out late. For 10 years he spent more money than he earned. For 10 years he thought ability could carry him anywhere. For 10 years he was a preening ego—one who would stand for endless minutes in front of a mirror, first to comb his hair, later to adjust his toupee. For 10 years it was one practical joke after another, one unfamiliar woman after another. For 10 years it was a party, nothing more, certainly nothing less.

For 10 years, Joe Pep drove managers nuts. So much unfulfilled potential, he had. So unstable, so undependable, he was.

Now he is 34, and looking for things to do with the rest of his life. He talks of opening another singles bar on Rush Street in Chicago. He had one before that was a success for about a year before it went bad. If he gets it this time, Joe Pep knows what to do. He is going to sell it as soon as it makes some money. He wants to have something left this time. From baseball he has nothing left except for a recognizable face and name and some memories. But when he looks back on what he has done with his life, Pepitone has few regrets.

"I stayed out every night," he remembers, "every night until four, five or six. Some days I would just go right to the ball park without sleeping. Now I think how I'd have been if I'd had the attitude of Tom Tresh or Bobby Richardson. What kind of player. I look back and I wonder if I would have been better. Maybe, I might have been worse.

"Since I've been out, I've had time to sit and think. It was tough going from $69,000 or $70,000 a year down to zip, I had to change my whole style of life. From the time I was 17 until I was 32, there was a party every night. But now it's been two years and I've been handling it."

Somehow, you have to wonder if Pepitone did not handle more of it right than he even gives himself credit for. He was a kid who played baseball as a game, which is all that it really is. He was a kid who played it all for fun, for laughs. Too few of them do that.

*1975*

★　★　★

# Butterfly . . . Tiger . . . Lion . . . Al McGuire Retires a Champ

ATLANTA—In 18 minutes, the game is going to begin, the game to decide the national collegiate basketball championship, the last game of Al McGuire's coaching career at Marquette University. The teams are out on the court warming up, but McGuire is still beneath the stands in the small dressing room his team is using.

Al McGuire is nervous now, very nervous. Norman Fischer, his business partner and close friend, and the team trainer and chaplain are with him in the room, but McGuire is paying them little attention. He is pacing now, six steps from one of the room's cinderblock walls to the other one, back and forth, ceaselessly pacing, and occasionally chewing on his finger nails.

Finally, McGuire stops and looks up and speaks.

"What's the name of that book about Devil's Island, the one that came out a few years ago?" he says.

"*Papillon,*" he is told.

"Yeah, it means butterfly in French, right?" he says. "In that book the guy told about pacing in his cell, about how he knew exactly how many steps it was from wall-to-wall, how he didn't even have to look to know when to turn around. The only difference with coaching is that the size of the locker rooms changes."

"You're like a tiger in a cage in a zoo," someone says. "They pace back and forth and they always know when to turn around."

"I'd rather be a lion right now," McGuire says. "What's that Sinatra line about the lion being majestic? You know, from that song with 'soar like an eagle.' Hey, I guess, he would be here, Sinatra, if Vegas had won and was playing us, huh?"

Vegas hadn't won, and now Marquette was going to be playing North Carolina. The Tar Heels had gone out for warm-ups at the same time as Marquette, but a manager says that now they've gone back into their locker room for some final words of encouragement from Dean Smith. McGuire does not bother with that second speech. He has already said everything he wants to. "This is it," he said. "I want to thank you all for everything you've done this year. Now go out and play." McGuire tells the manager to come back and tell him when North Carolina returns to the floor.

Two minutes before the game is to begin, the manager says that Carolina is back out on the court. McGuire pulls on the black vest and coat of his lucky suit, the one he has been wearing throughout the tournament without laundering, the one he will donate to an educational television station in Milwaukee to be auctioned. "OK, let's go," McGuire says to no one in particular.

Stern-faced, and nervously picking the nails of his index fingers, he marches out onto the court, where he is greeted by a standing ovation from Marquette fans. As the teams are introduced, McGuire is pensive and detached, applauding the introductions mindlessly, standing away from the huddle of his team.

Once the game stats, McGuire breaks out of his nervous trance and becomes involved. Disgusted early, he kicks the scorer's table and hurts the big toe of his left foot. Later he says he thinks the toe is busted, but that's good because it will keep him away from the golf course for a while and save him some money.

With about 12 minutes remaining in the first half and Marquette leading by a point, McGuire tells his team to set up in a zone defense.

The day before he decided the zone would be the best way to keep Phil Ford from doing too much damage against the Warriors. As the game progresses, he finds out his hunch was correct. North Carolina has trouble getting good shots against the zone, and in the second half, after it has outscored Marquette 18–4 in six minutes to tie the game at 45, Carolina discovers that the zone renders its four-corners useless.

"Every game is different," McGuire says later. "It's like pick-up sticks. You have to adjust as you go along to see how the sticks fall. That's why I don't get too involved in a game before it's played. You just have to figure out which sticks to pick up. Carolina went into a drought against our zone. Our zone normally doesn't work that well, but tonight it did and I stuck with it."

In the first half, Marquette is having no difficulty determining which sticks to pick up. Butch Lee is scoring, Bo Ellis is dominating the inside game and Marquette takes a 39–27 halftime lead.

The half goes so easily that McGuire doesn't even get called for a technical foul. Near the end of the half, he is angered by a call, paces, screams, and almost falls backward out of his chair. As he does his psycho number, his wife, Pat, sitting 10 rows up behind the Marquette bench, wearing her lucky black velvet jacket, stands up and screams, "Sit down, Al, sit down."

"She did that?" McGuire says later. "I didn't think I heard her. But maybe I did. Maybe that's what made me sit down."

The second half begins with a Carolina spurt. The pace of the game is quickened, and that is not good for Marquette. Twice, McGuire tries to slow the pace with time-outs. He is unsuccessful, until Carolina, attempting to draw Marquette out of a zone, slows itself down when it goes into the four-corners and holds the ball for three minutes before missing a shot.

The rest of the game belongs to Marquette, to Ellis and Lee, to Jimmy Boylan and Jerome Whitehead, and not even an odd technical foul called against Bernard Toone can prevent the Warriors from winning 67–59.

When the buzzer sounds, there is pandemonium. But McGuire is not part of it. He checks to make sure that the officials leave the floor with no second-thoughts, and then sinks into his chair.

"I feel washed out," he says later. "Normally alley fighters like me don't end up in silk lace. Normally they come close and wash out, but this time the numbers came up right.

"I was sitting there thinking why me? I was thinking of all the wet jocks and the socks. Of driving down Belmont Avenue in the car with the kids in it, going to a game. Of being freshman coach at Dartmouth. Of all the CYO's and the Y's. Of the fights in the different gyms. Of the locker rooms. Of the wildness of it all. I just have the team that won. I personally think Dean deserved it, not me.

"The two things I always wanted when I was young were to pack Madison Square Garden and to sit in the front of the bus. I got to sit in the bus when I became the freshman coach at Dartmouth 22 years ago. And 11 years ago I packed the Garden in the finals of the NIT against Southern Illinois when Walt Frazier and Dick Garrett were playing. I walked into the rotunda then and the guy was announcing standing room only."

As the celebrating continues on the court, as Ellis and Toone cut down the nets, McGuire disappears into the dressing room alone and with tears in his silver eyes. He has just done what he would call a Rocky number, a million-to-one shot. He has taken a team that lost seven games and won his first national championship in his last game as a coach. "I came in here to cry," McGuire says. "I'm not ashamed to cry. I just don't like to do it in front of people."

After a few minutes pass, McGuire returns to the court for the awards ceremony. When Ellis is called to receive his award, he stops to hug his coach and takes off the net that is draped around his neck and drapes it around McGuire's. Embarrassed, McGuire then takes the net and puts it around Whitehead's neck.

Before his name is called, McGuire signals to his family to come down onto the court so they can receive the award with him. When the public address announcer says, "Al McGuire," McGuire looks down at his jacket to make sure everything is right, and notices that the black coat is covered with specks of white cloth.

"God," Al McGuire says, "a lot of people must have lint on them."

1977

## MIKE DOWNEY

Mike Downey (b. 1951) got his first byline at a paper in Chicago's south suburbs when he was fourteen. Two years later, with college beyond his reach financially, he was a full-time reporter. Hired by the *Chicago Daily News* in 1975, Downey wrote such hilarious headlines that it seemed he would forever be stranded making other sportswriters look good. But the *Daily News* folded in '78 and he landed at the Second City's *Sun-Times*, where he covered basketball just long enough for the brain trust at the *Detroit Free Press* to realize he should be their lead sports columnist. He went on to write a column for the *Los Angeles Times* and *Chicago Tribune*, finding the humor even in Cal Ripken Jr's iron man streak but always ready to be serious when the moment called for it. The crime novelist Elmore Leonard name-checked Downey in *Be Cool*. First Lady Nancy Reagan sent jelly beans.

★   ★   ★

# When One Teardrop Is a Torrent of Hope

THE WARD is so quiet when Wayne Lukas gets there. Beeps from a few monitors. Pulses from a few phones. The nurses all know him, and by now he knows all of them.

Karen, on day duty. Kelly, on nights. Rendy, who called four times on Christmas Day to inquire how he was doing. They and the others, pulling 12-hour shifts. Sticking around afterward, simply to see if there was anything else they could do. Handing manuals on brain trauma to Wayne, so he could study up on the fate that had befallen his son. So he could understand what the monitors meant. So he could read the vital signs.

The nurses. They took Brady Wayne Lukas, age 3½, by the hand and led him into an anteroom of the Huntington Memorial Hospital to help *him* understand. Brady had been wondering why his daddy hadn't been home.

Jeff Lukas had always set aside one hour per night to read bedside stories to his boy. Ten days before Christmas, Brady's daddy did not come home. He was knocked down by a horse. He was knocked unconscious. He had lapsed into a coma and his condition was grave. Wayne Lukas had witnessed what had happened to his son through disbelieving eyes. Now his grandson wanted some answers.

"Where's my dad?" he asked.

So, they took Brady to the hospital.

He entered the room and saw his father on the bed, sleeping the deepest sleep.

"Wake him up," Brady said.

Wayne Lukas bent to touch his hand and said: "I would love to wake him up."

No one could. Jeff would only awaken on his own. Long days and longer nights would pass before there was even a glimmer of life. The stillness continued. The cerebral pressure fluctuated. He lost 39 pounds, unable to take nutrition, even intravenously. And then, a flicker of movement. A blink. A hint of comprehension.

Jeff's wife, Linda, squeezed his hand. His father, Wayne, whispered into his ear. He read the daily sports page to his son. He told of the phone calls, the faxes, the letters. One from Gerald Ford. One from George Steinbrenner. Bob Knight, checking in daily. Then that uplifting moment came when Jeff moved his hand. Not much, but he moved it.

The nurses. They took Brady Lukas to a room occupied by a mannequin. Tubes protruded from it, every which way. Wires were tethered to it, machines connected to it. They explained how oxygen is supplied to the human brain. They showed the boy a syringe, and how one works. They let him examine the model, explore it, ask questions. He asked what "head injury" meant. Brady is a sharp boy. He listens. He learns.

He returned to his father's room.

"Are you taking good care of my dad?" Brady asked.

Yes, they said.

"He has a head injury," Brady said.

Yes, they said.

"OK," Brady said.

And he began making tapes. At home, Brady spoke into a hand-held recorder, making conversation with his father. Now he would tell *him* bedtime stories. Day by day, he would fill up the tapes. He or his mother or grandfather would go to the hospital. One of them would press the recorder to Jeff Lukas' ear. They would never be sure how much he would hear. All they could do was check for a response. For life.

Christmas Eve came. The holidays had been all but forgotten. Wayne Lukas had tried to go about his business, training horses at Santa Anita, but the distraction made it difficult. Out the threshold of Barn 66, he had a clear view of the washing stall where Tabasco Cat, a magnificent horse, a potential Kentucky Derby horse, had broken free from his rein and gone galloping along the hardpan.

When Wayne Lukas heard the commotion outside his office around 8:30 on the morning of Dec. 15, he went outside in time to see his 36-year-old son stand in front of Tabasco Cat, trying to intercept the stampeding horse. Struck, he flipped into the air. Jeff's skull struck the gravel.

Wayne rushed to his side. "Call for an ambulance!" he shouted, and an exercise girl did. Riders and grooms came running. Wayne felt his son's forehead gently and spoke his name. There was no response.

The wait for the paramedics seemed endless, remembers Wayne, 58, one of the top trainers in the business. And then suddenly he had a vision, or at least what he thought was a vision. A woman in a crisp white dress. A nurse. What was she doing there so quickly, near the stables of a race track?

She turned out to be Denise Constantinide, not a nurse but a technician from the Dolly Green Nuclear Imaging Center, an equine facility on the Santa Anita grounds. She knelt and felt for a pulse. It was weak, but it was there.

It was some solace until the paramedics came. They prepared to take Jeff to a nearby clinic. No, one of the medics said, take him to Huntington, they have a trauma center there. Take him by helicopter. Wayne Lukas has this man's name. He hopes to thank him properly some day. He hopes this man helped save his son's life.

But first he must wait. The vigil continues. Wayne was so hopeful Thursday when he found out that Jeff had lifted his hand to his face. His condition had changed from critical to serious. But any emergency was possible. The brain pressure had risen dramatically when he was moved to another room for a CAT scan.

"Another day we finally had the cerebral pressure in check and then the pneumonia hit us," Wayne says, making his daily call to his son's side Friday. "Jeff's temperature shot up to 104. But today things look better. The scans look excellent. The nurses taught me how to read the scans. The scans look excellent today."

He is unnerved. He tries to work.

"It's probably therapeutic for me to talk about it," Wayne says later, in his office. The private phone number to Jeff's room is pinned to a bulletin board above him. He has horses running, horses he and Jeff have trained. He will go back to the hospital soon and read today's news to him. In the news this day, he sees that Virginia Kelley, the mother of President Clinton, has died of cancer.

"I was in Arkansas with her, at the races," Wayne says. "When I was about to leave, she said: 'Would you write on my program for me? Write something to Bill so that he'll know you and I spoke.' I've got Bill Clinton in a couple of my win pictures from races in Arkansas.

"So, I took her program and wrote: *Dear Bill: In thoroughbred racing, 85% of the production comes from the dam. So everything you have,* remember, you owe 85% of it to your mother. I'll bet he got a kick out of that."

The phone rings.

"Denny Crum! Hi, coach, how you doin'?" Wayne says. He chats with the Louisville basketball coach a while. Wayne once coached basketball. Bob Knight is as close a friend as he has. But so many have called. He gabs animatedly with Crum about horses and about his alma mater, Wisconsin, winning the Rose Bowl and then in hushed tones about Jeff, and thanks him for calling, hangs up and says: "Half the basketball coaches in the country must have called by now. These guys keep me sane."

It is not easy to behave normally. Everyone so wanted to make Christmas as normal as possible for Brady, for the brave boy who sat there making tapes. Brady turned off the recorder and wrote his letter to Santa Claus. He placed it next to a plate of cookies.

*Dear Santa,*
*The cookies are for you.*
*Please leave one present for my Dad.*
*Brady Lukas*

Christmas morning, Brady found his own present, an electric go-kart. He went for a ride. There is a fountain at the end of the street near his house. Brady drove the little car that far. Then he made another tape for his father.

The tape was taken to the hospital. It was pressed next to Jeff Lukas' ear.

His son's voice said: "Dad. I rode my go-kart down to the fountain today. Dad, I wore my helmet. No head injuries!"

A teardrop ran down Jeff Lukas' cheek.

He had heard.

*1994*

★  ★  ★

# He May Be Playing in *Year* 2131

Sept. 30, 2000
Dear Diary:
    Please, help me. I am so tired, I can hardly write. Today I played my 2,963rd baseball game in a row. I am 40 years old and my feet are killing me. My corns hurt, my calves hurt, my shins are sore and my thighs are as hard as an umpire's heart. I need rest. I need a day off. I need Ben-Gay.
    Today was the last day of the 2000 season. The Orioles stink. We are in last place, behind Boston, New York, Detroit, Toronto, Tokyo and Mexico City. I went two for four, but I could hardly run the bases. No way I can keep this up. Diary, tell me what to do. This must end.

*Cal*

★

April 27, 2001
Dear Diary:
    Game No. 3,000 is tonight. President Powell will be there. So will Vice President Rodham Clinton. I hear a lot of the old-timers will show up: DiMaggio, Mays, Aaron, Offerman. Here we go, another ceremony.
    Too bad they're tearing down Camden Yards next year to build a new park. Sure, it's falling apart. But I love the old parks best, don't you? I can't believe those graffiti punks spray-painted above the "Hit It Here" sign with the word *Don't*. Very funny. Anyway, I hope I can still hit the ball.

*Cal*

★

Oct. 1, 2002

Dear Diary:

Haven't written you in a while. Sorry. I can barely lift my arm. Hideo Nomo Jr. hit me with a pitch. These kids today; no respect.

Well, Diary, I have played 162 games per season, every season since way back in 1995. Yesterday was my 3,287th consecutive game. OK, so all I did was pinch-run for Anderson in the 16th inning when we ran out of players. So what? I'm in the box score. Man, I could use, like, 48 hours in a whirlpool.

*Cal*

★

March 21, 2004

Dear Diary:

Whoa, 3,500 games in a row. Doesn't seem possible. I'm hitting .333 and doctors want to study me, to see if I'm human or robot.

The Angels started Ken Griffey III last night. Told the kid, "I played with your grandfather." He laughed. He said, "If I slide into second base, better jump your old self over me, Gramps." Then he asked me about the olden days, back when we used wood bats. Fresh kid.

*Cal*

★

April 1, 2006

Dear Diary:

Spring training was a bear. My arteries are so hard, you could use them as cues to shoot pool. The artificial hip seems to be helping, but my plastic rotator cuff feels funny and these orthopedic cleats are really uncomfortable.

Skip suggested I try a 29-ounce bat. I'm not getting around on fastballs. Maybe I should go back to that priest in Tibet for more of those secret roots and herbs that keep me young. Today's my 3,774th consecutive game. I was up late last night. Leno did some funny jokes about the O.J. trial.

*Cal*

★

June 18, 2010
Dear Diary:
   Mercy. Somebody. Anybody. Help. Can't move. Can't run. Can't catch. Can't throw. Can't take any more. Isn't 4,500 games in a row plenty? Can't I go home now? They shoot shortstops, don't they? Read my lips: I . . . need . . . rest.
   Remember my kid, starting kindergarten the day I broke Lou Gehrig's record? Well, my kid's teaching at that school next term. Where did the time go? Me and the wife, the team gave us round-trip tickets on the shuttle to Neptune. I'm retiring this winter. Honest.

*Cal*

★

Nov. 1, 2020
Dear Diary:
   World Series ended today. Havana kicked Baltimore's butt, same as last year. But I did OK. Couple of homers, no errors. Feel fine. Could do this forever.
   The Smithsonian called. Wanted to know if I still had my glove from 1995. Wanted to know if I would donate it to the museum. Said I'd love to, but I can't. Still using it.

*Cal*
*1995*

## JANE LEAVY

Jane Leavy (b. 1951) couldn't settle on a career until her mother forced the issue. "I want to be a sportswriter," Leavy blurted, surprising them both. After writing her master's thesis on Red Smith, she found her way to *The Washington Post* in 1979 and had a distinguished nine-year run in which she survived anti-Semitic football coaches and athletes with advanced cases of arrested development. Leavy has since scored big in the book world with her comic novel *Squeeze Play* and her best-selling biography *Sandy Koufax: A Lefty's Legacy*. Another of her bestsellers, *The Last Boy*, may have had its genesis in her unsentimental but compassionate 1983 *Post* profile of Mickey Mantle in retirement. At the very least, interviewing him led to a career-changing discovery: Her gender could be more of a help than a hindrance. "I think there were some things," she said, "that none of these guys would tell men."

★ ★ ★

# The Man Baseball Forgot
# Plays the Hand He's Dealt

ATLANTIC CITY—Mickey Mantle has these recurring dreams. He's gliding down the runway with a vaulter's pole in his hands. And it's strange because he's never pole-vaulted in his life. Stranger still, his knees don't hurt and he's running as fast as he can.

He soars over the bar, giddy. He is so high, he can barely see the people on the ground. "When I get to the top, it's like I'm 50 stories high. I look down and there ain't nothing," he said.

Suddenly, he's free falling. Faster, faster. Terrified. But he always wakes up before he returns to earth. Cold and sweating.

Mickey Mantle awakens in Atlantic City, a place somewhere between decay and decadence. Downstairs in the Hi-Ho Casino, grim-looking women numbed by repetition line up behind slot machines, investing heavily in another kind of dream. They don't bother taking off their coats. It only takes three minutes to lose $10 in quarters. Sirens blare, bells ring, for someone else.

Inside, it is always night, a place for people who can't sleep and can't quit trying to win. Mantle's twin brothers are pit bosses in Las Vegas. His mother likes the slot machines so much they had to buy her a glove to protect her hand. But her son has been banned from baseball because of his affiliation with The Claridge Hotel and Casino.

Sometimes, he goes down there to sign autographs and say hello. But he won't be photographed dealing craps. And, late at night, you're more likely to find him in the hotel bar. "I don't sleep anymore," he said. "I wake up at 5:30 or 6. All those dreams."

Every night. In one, he's late for a game and he can hear the public address announcer saying, "Now batting, No. 7, Mickey Mantle." He can see Whitey and Billy and Casey but he can't get into the stadium because the gates are all locked. He doesn't need anyone to interpret that for him.

What do you do when the dream ends and you wake up 14 years later with a family to feed and time to kill?

You make a living being Mickey Mantle.

The Claridge Hotel opened in Dec. 1929, which was one sort of gamble. The casino opened 52 years later. In February, Mickey Mantle was hired as director of sports promotions, to play golf with the high rollers and sign autographs for the low rollers. His job is to be nice, which is nice work if you can get it.

It is one of life's great ironies that Mantle, who never quite felt at ease with the masses who adored him and sometimes couldn't find time for them, now gets paid—$100,000 for one year—to do both.

"I'm a lot nicer than I was," he said. "I care more about what people think than I used to. When I was playing ball, I didn't give a damn. Now I try to make people like me, maybe more than I should."

It is 1 A.M. Four Alabama boys see Mantle at a table in the country western bar. The biggest and blondest of them, who looks a bit like the Mick, holds out a pen for an autograph. "I'm a 30-year-old man," he says. "Would you mind? It's the price of fame."

Mantle, signing, says, "I get paid to do this."

Sometimes, people come up to him on planes and tell him how he brushed them off. "I don't feel bad," he said. "I'll give him an autograph now. I didn't shove him out of the way because I hated him. I wanted to get to the ballpark. Or maybe I thought I gave him one before.

"I was shy, scared, aloof. That's what they called it. I think the last 8 or 10 years with the Yankees I wasn't scared or shy. I was more of a public relations man for myself.

"I'll tell you what, though. Even though it's my job to be nice to people. It's not hard for me to do."

Mantle almost advertises his excesses. At 51, he is living proof that you can take the boy out of the locker room but you can't take the locker room out of the boy. The jokes are coarse, often unprintable.

But he can be vulgar one moment and eloquent the next. The contrast is startling, disconcerting. Mickey Mantle is still the greatest switch hitter baseball has ever known.

Who's better, Mickey Mantle or Willie Mays?

Mantle shakes his head. He was expecting something really tough: "If you didn't know either one of us and you opened the record book, what would it say? Damn Willie."

Mays is a goodwill ambassador for Bally's Park Place Casino Hotel, next door to the Claridge. Like Mantle, he can no longer be offically associated with major-league baseball because of the relationship with the casino. Their lives have long been intertwined but they haven't run into each other here. They haven't been in town at the same time.

Mays was blithe. He made baseball look so easy. Mantle was hurt. What should have been easy always looked so hard.

It began in 1951. He was heir apparent to Joe DiMaggio and Babe Ruth. But he was striking out too much. "Casey had to send me down to the minors," he said. "I went back to Kansas City. I got a hit my first time up and the next 22 I didn't even hit the ball. I was really down. I called my Dad. I said, 'Dad, I can't play.' He said, 'You wait right there.'

"I think he's coming up to give me a pep talk. He walks in the hotel room and starts throwing my stuff in a bag. I said, 'What's the matter?' He said, 'I thought I raised a man. You ain't nothing but a damned coward. You come back and work with me in the (zinc) mines.' He was crying. I was crying. I said, 'Let me try again.'"

Mutt Mantle, the best semipro ballplayer Commerce, Okla., ever knew, raised his son, and named his son (after Mickey Cochrane) to be a major leaguer. He spent $22 on a Marty Marion glove one Christmas when he was making $35 a week.

After his father left, Mantle hit .361 and rejoined the Yankees. They played the second game of the World Series that year at Yankee Stadium. "Willie Mays hit a popup," Mantle said. "Joe DiMaggio was playing center field and I was playing right. Casey had said Joe's heel was hurting him—it was his last year–and try and catch everything I could. I was running as hard as I could. At that time, I could outrun anybody. Just as I was getting ready to put my glove up, I heard him say, 'I got it.'

"Well, you don't want to run into Joe DiMaggio. So I slammed on the brakes. In the outfield, they have these sprinkler heads and they have rubber things over the top of 'em so they can drain out. My back spike caught right on the edge of the rubber thing and it wouldn't go with me. I was running so fast, my knee just went right out through the front of my leg."

Mutt Mantle, who was dying of Hodgkin's disease, saw his son get hurt that day. "The next morning it was so swollen, I couldn't even walk so he took me to the hospital," Mantle said. "He got out of the cab first. I couldn't put any weight on my legs, so I put my arm around his shoulder. This guy was as big as me, maybe bigger. When I jumped out, I put all my weight on him and he crumpled over on the sidewalk. His whole back was eaten up. I didn't know it but he hadn't slept in a bed because of his back for like six months. No one had told me.

"So we went to the hospital and we watched the rest of the series together. That's when they told me I'd better take him home and have him looked at because he's a lot sicker than I think. When I got home, I took him up to Mayo's Clinic in Rochester, Minn., and they cut him open and looked at him and said, 'Hey, Mick, take him home, let him do what he wants, he's not going to last much longer.'"

Mutt died the next spring at age 39. Mantle's grandfather and two uncles died of the same disease before they reached 40. "I'm the first Mantle boy that ever made it past 40," he said.

People said Mantle played every game like it was his last. "Maybe I thought about it, but it didn't bug me," he said. "I didn't sit around and say, 'I'm going to die.' "

Mantle's third son, Billy, the one named for Billy Martin, has Hodgkin's disease. He is 24. There are medical bills to pay. This is harder than his father. He turns away, flexing his thick, slugger's hands, trying to control the feelings. A tear appears on his cheek. "I don't want to talk about that, okay?" he said. "We're hoping he gets okay. I think he will. We're fighting it."

A caravan of golf carts lined up by the first tee of the Linwood Country Club waits for Mickey Mantle. "I don't walk," he said. "I can't walk."

It is a wonderful day for golf, but the round is as much for the invited press as it is for the invited high-rollers, whose value to the casino entitles them to 18 holes with the Mick.

The golfers fill the first four carts; camera crews from two networks fill three more and newspaper reporters bring up the rear. Mantle hits his first ball wide right. It ricochets off a tree and into the beach grass. Mantle sets off in pursuit. He's driving in circles looking for his ball; the television guys are driving in circles, looking to shoot him looking for his ball. "If you use this, it's going to be the dullest TV show ever put on the air," he says.

His second shot lands in a trap but he hits the green with his third.

As he kicks the sand back into place, he says, "This'd be a good job for Billy. He could get a lot of practice out here."

He's doing exactly what is expected of him and doing it well. "Hey, did you hear Steinbrenner gave Yogi a new million dollar contract?" he asks. "A dollar a year for a million years."

That reminds him of a Yogi-ism. One night, he says, Yogi and his wife were watching Steve McQueen in a late night movie "and Yogi said, 'He musta made that before he died.'"

Someone asks what Whitey Ford is doing these days. "'Bout like me," he says. "Waitin' to die." He laughs. "Just teasing. I see him two or three times a year. We're going to have a (baseball) card show at the hotel. We'll have Whitey and Billy and Roger (Maris). Roger's a good guy. Those were my three favorites."

In the summer of 1961, he and Maris chased each other and Babe Ruth's home run record across the country. Maris hit 61 and lost great gobs of hair. Mantle hit 54 and became a hero. "He beat Babe Ruth and he beat me, so everyone hated him," Mantle said. "Everywhere I'd go, I'd get a standing ovation. All I had to do is walk out of the dugout."

People send him the scrapbooks they have outgrown. He has 50 or 60 of them. Sometimes, early in the morning, when he can't sleep, he goes into the playroom where he keeps all his trophies, including the three MVP awards, and reads them. "It's like I'm reading about somebody else," he said.

Many of those people are in their 40s and running corporations. They have dispensable income and might just be dispensing it at casinos. Bill Dougall, president of the Claridge and a member of his foursome, approached Mantle about the job last November. "We're not trying to make money off him," he said. "The main thing is national exposure."

What better way to mitigate reservations about gambling than by bringing in the all-American boy? "What's amazing is my name is as good as it is," Mantle said. "When you think of Mickey Mantle, you think of Jack Armstrong. My dad named me Mickey Mantle, 'cept it sounds like a made up name."

Mantle has been here about six days a month since February. He'll be back in June for the Mickey Mantle Invitational Golf Tournament. "Mickey only comes when he's active and participating in an event," Dougall said. "We would never ask him just to be a part of the furniture."

Mantle says, "I would never do anything degrading to me or the hotel."

He finishes the round with a 79, low score, and a sore knee.

For such work, he was forced to sever relations with baseball. "He was not banned," a spokesman for Commissioner Bowie Kuhn said. "He can come back any time."

"I think he (Kuhn) had to do it," Mantle said. "He did it to Willie. I think he made his mistake when he did it to Willie. In the back of my mind, it bugs me a little. It sounds worse than it is."

He has been invited to the Yankees' Old Timers Day but he's not sure he wants to go. "I feel really kind of bad that no one took up for me except Billy," he said. "It's like, well, 'He's gone.'"

George Steinbrenner, owner of the Yankees, said, "I think it's a crying shame that two great center fielders, two of the greatest in the history of the game, are both unable to have an active part in baseball because of casinos. Gambling is part of the way of life in this country. The states have made it legal in casino form. By the same token, the commissioner has the right do what what he thinks is in the best interest of baseball.

"I feel for Mickey. I think it's more important to him than he thinks. I tried to send word through Billy that I didn't think it was a good idea. But a man has to feed a family, too."

It wasn't a difficult decision. "I knew I'd get banned," Mantle said. "What was I getting banned from? I've been out 14 years. All I'm doing is going to spring training as a batting instructor, which I wasn't. I was hanging around, same as now, signing autographs. I'm getting over $100,000 for being around. I like what I do.

"Why? I guess because there's not that much responsibility to it."

Most days, when he's home, he gets up, checks the Yankees' box score, stops by the office and heads for the golf course. He still does public relations work for the Reserve Life Insurance company, as he has for the last 10 years.

He never had any desire to coach. In 1978, he took his son, Mickey Mantle Jr., to spring training. "I didn't know how to work the batting machine," he said. "I put a ball in it. I had it turned up too high. The sonovabitch was going 120 miles an hour. It hit him on the knee. Damn near broke his leg.

"If he would have had my dad for a dad, he would have made a major league baseball player."

Mickey Mantle Jr. hit .198 in 70 games for the Alexandria Dukes that year. "My Dad always wanted one of us to play," he said a couple of years ago. "I thought I'd try it for his sake."

When Mickey Mantle Sr. was a boy, his father took him to Cardinal games in St. Louis, 300 miles away. "We'd go to the Fairgrounds Hotel by Sportsmen's Park where Musial and Slaughter ate breakfast," he said. "We'd just sit there and look at 'em. He never let me go over and get an autograph. Just to sit and look at 'em was unbelievable."

When he got to the Yankees, years later, George Weiss, the general manager, took him aside and said, if anyone asks, "just act like Joe DiMaggio is your hero and the Yankees are your favorite team, okay?"

Sure, Mantle said.

He played 18 years, hit 18 home runs in 12 World Series, a record he still holds. He says he should have quit in 1965. But he always wanted to play longer than he could, longer than he did. Every time he is introduced at a banquet and the speaker says, "he had a lifetime .298 average," he thinks, "you sonofabitch, quit saying it."

You remember the painful tableaus—Mantle collapsed in the base line, Mantle catching his spike in the cyclone fence in Baltimore, Mantle playing in the 1961 World Series with blood seeping through his uniform. "I didn't hurt as bad as everybody thought I did," he said. "I still ran down to first base faster than anyone."

But the knee feels like jelly now, with a calcium marble floating where cartilage ought to be. He may have to have knee replacement surgery. "Baseball was easy for Willie," Mantle said. "He loved it. You could see it in him. I did, too, when I felt good . . . I feel when I was good, I was better."

In his playing days, he never had a hangover. This morning, he has a headache. A guy comes over to ask for an autograph. Mantle puts on his half-spectacles. "I never will forget: I saw you strike out five times one day in 1950 in Boston against Mel Parnell," the guy says.

Mantle smiles and signs. After the guy leaves, he says, "There's an example of being nice. I wasn't even there in 1950."

He orders a beer. "Have you ever heard that song, 'Willie, Mickey and the Duke?' That guy made some money."

He begins to hum. "'Talking baseball. Willie, Mickey and the Duke.'"

His voice trails off. He doesn't know the words. "I know all the words to 'I Love Mickey,' " he says. "Teresa Brewer wrote it."

They recorded it together. " 'I love Mickey. Mickey who? The fellow with the celebrated swing.' You know what's on the other side? 'Keep Your Cotton Pickin' Paddies Offa My Heart.'"

It was 1956, the year he won the Triple Crown. He was on his way up. Life was a dream.

*1983*

## RALPH WILEY

Though the *Oakland Tribune* was only a launching pad for him, Ralph Wiley (1952–2004) rewarded it with the deft prose and clear thinking that opened doors for the African American sportswriters who followed him. He rose from copyboy to baseball writer to columnist at warp speed, coining the term "Billy Ball" to describe Billy Martin's managerial style and dissecting epic prizefights with a surgeon's eye and a corner man's wisdom. After leaving the *Tribune* in 1982, Wiley covered himself with more glory working for *Sports Illustrated* and ESPN.com, but it was as a cultural critic examining race in America that he seemed to have found his destiny. He wrote three books on the subject—*Why Black People Tend to Shout*, *What Black People Should Do Now*, and *Dark Witness*—as well as a screenplay that put a new spin on *Huckleberry Finn* but remains unproduced. "All a man's got," Wiley once wrote, "is the integrity of his work."

★　★　★

# Why Did Duran Do It?

R OBERTO DURAN is smarter than any of them gave him credit for. He got his way, and he will get his money. Some say fix. Whenever your man loses, fix is the easy way out. But I have no doubt that Duran intended to knock Ray Leonard's head off his shoulders when the fight began. After all, he is Roberto Duran.

But what Duran found in the ring sobered him. Leonard was fighting hard and impeccably. He was popping in that jab, and Duran could counter it only one time out of seven. To make matters worse, Leonard

316

was getting the best of it inside. Roberto found Ray, but was found himself even more often. And Leonard was not breathing hard.

Duran did not want to be embarrassed, as he was in the seventh round, by a man he still does not respect as a fistfighter, so he threw up his hands and robbed Leonard of his satisfaction. That was just like Duran.

Some say, "Well, Ali went thirteen rounds with a broken jaw," and then puff up as if they did this themselves. I say Duran is smarter. He could see the handwriting on *The Wall Street Journal*. He didn't want to go out sitting in his corner with two black eyes. Yeah, he quit, and anybody who wants to call him a coward is welcome to go down to Panama and tell him themselves. Duran will be there.

Then again, perhaps Duran gave up the ghost because he caught a glimpse of the tall, slenderish man with dispassionate eyes dressed in a cranberry suit. That would be Thomas Hearns and Duran would have been a mark for him. Thomas Hearns is the legacy, another kiss that Duran blows to Leonard.

"I'm here to dominate this division," said the king of Detroit. "I want the winner. Duran, the little short man, he's a midget, there's no way he could have beat me anyway. Sugar Ray? I really don't believe he's got the heart."

Hearns could steal the heart of the greatest welterweights. He is a physical strangeling, a 147-pounder who stands on ostrich legs with a heavyweight's reach and thunder in both hands. But you all know that by now. What you don't know is how Hearns would fight Ray Leonard. Listen.

"Our basic strategy against Ray would be to change up, to keep him off balance, box him," said Emanuel Steward, the trainer.

"I can't see no man 5-10 out-jabbing Tommy," said Steward, answering an Angelo Dundee charge that Leonard's jab would get there first. "They talk about Tommy's chin. I've watched him for twelve years, against Poles and Russians and Cubans. He's never been knocked down. One of his strongest assets is his chin.

"I have more headaches worrying about Wilfred Benitez than the others. He's hungry. He lost the title, and now he sees those big purses. It's a fight that Thomas needs."

Thomas says, "I'm not even thinking about Benitez. He would be no problem for me. He's the farthest thing from my mind." (They fight in January.)

Athletes have gotten better in every other sport, but I'm not so sure about boxing. Oh, I think the welterweights are as good now as they've ever been, from a strictly physical standpoint, but attitudes are different.

The promoters have no one to blame but themselves. In the old days, a title fight would be worth $25 or $30,000. Any champ worth his salt would run through that kind of money in no time, and be hungry for more. Now, with millions as a payday, the fighter has no reason to fight.

Thomas Hearns is a throwback to those days, mentally. Already he is building a mental animosity toward Ray Leonard. He wants Leonard bad.

Leonard is like Ali. Leonard has great physical skills. He still has the fastest hands in the division, and even Steward admits that he has a rock for a chin. But like Ali, Leonard wants to win and be paid. He doesn't necessarily want to fight. He does not enjoy being hit. He would rather pull his head back out of the way and avoid that, and I for one cannot find anything wrong with this evolution among great fighters. It will be less men slobbering on themselves in later life.

Hearns comes to fight, to destroy. He is still very hungry, for blood and money. As I say, Leonard has great skills, enough skills to make a fight of it. If both were angry and panged with hunger, they could stage one of the greatest fights of any era. But, attitudes being what they are, Hearns would kill Ray Leonard and only be sorry about it after the fact.

If Leonard is smart, he'll walk away, too.

*1980*

★ ★ ★

# The Undertaker Was Buried

THE SURVIVALISTS would hate Sugar Ray Leonard. The survivalists are those folk who have given up on civilization. They have run from the face of doom. They are fearful, nervous, afraid. They are not Ray Leonard's kind of people, obviously.

Thomas Hearns was the face of doom. In a one-to-one confrontation he was—is—as frightening as any bomb. But Leonard defused the bomb Wednesday night. He fought the fight of the master boxer who does what he must do. He fought Hearns with one eye. Hearns's left hand had closed the other. But, at the darkest hour, Leonard turned doom in on itself. He showed Thomas Hearns a mirror. Hearns was maneuvered into fighting Leonard's fight, and no mortal man can do that and stand for long.

That is now a point of historical fact. Two Sugars, please.

There was only a small window for Leonard to come through in this fight. That was evident in the first two rounds, when Leonard chose to circle and evade while Hearns, confident, held the middle ring. There was no way Leonard could win rounds from the perimeter, and he had lost those two.

The Room is a term borrowed from Muhammad Ali, who likened being hit into a state of semi-consciousness to being in a dark room, surrounded by, among other things, bats blowing saxophones. In the sixth round, Leonard sent Hearns to the Carlsbad Cavern Jazz Festival, in stereo.

Here is where Hearns proved his worth. Here is where he was knocked into the ropes, buckling and unaware. But he fought through the smoke. He came back to hurt Leonard. But the point had been made, and Thomas Hearns was a changed fighter after that. He did not like that Room. No air there.

So, from then on, Hearns fought from his toes, and Leonard stalked the center of the ring. Yes, Hearns proved from there until the fourteenth that indeed he could box, feint, and combinate. But he was on his toes. He was jabbing. He was exhorting the crowd. He was trying to be sweet, and he lost his power.

Meanwhile, Leonard's left hook was whittling Hearns's body, while Hearns was content to jab Leonard's swelling left eye. But Leonard's body attack pulled Hearns's arms down. And Hearns's blows, so telling early when he was putting body behind them, became mere flicks. He did not want to return to that Room. He stopped punching. He started jabbing, backing up.

The only question was, would Ray catch up before time ran out? He stayed in Hearns's face, so the tall man could not extend. The mutual respect now belonged mostly to Leonard. Hearns was doing the running.

Hearns won the tenth, eleventh, and twelfth, off the jab and his toes. It was the worst thing that could have happened to him. He came out in the thirteenth, and his whole being was directed toward Leonard's eye. He forgot his own.

It was a simple one-two that did it. Left-right, and Hearns was his. Leonard pounded Hearns through the ropes. The champion's face was a horrible mask of swollen eye and raging determination. He buried Hearns through the ropes near Hearns's corner. Hearns got up shaking his head, saying no, but Leonard's accumulated fury drove him back down again.

In the fourteenth, it was just a matter of finding the spot. Leonard hit Hearns flush with the right, again near Hearns's corner. Hearns was in the Room to stay. He did not go down, but he was out.

It was everything they said it would be.

When Hearns left the ring, he was unsteady, still feeling his way back into our world, the one we take for granted. In the ring, not even the shut eye could dull the luster of Ray Leonard's smile.

"That was a dull fight, a lousy fight," a sportswriter said to me as we entered the interview area. I had no patience. I found myself saying, "Well, what did you want? Death?"

No, not death, just a rematch. Ray did not want to ponder on such matters Wednesday night, and who can blame him? He had just nuked the nuker. He had just cancelled Doomsday. He had just turned in the fight of his life, in terms of tactics, strength, ability, intelligence, and heart. He had just buried the Undertaker, and there was no need to resurrect him, not just yet. At least let the eye stop hurting.

"I take my hat off to Mr. Hearns," said Leonard. "I don't have much to say [regarding a rematch]. I have just proven myself as the greatest welterweight in the world. But I say, in my book, we both are still champions."

A Hearns bettor crumpled his marker and, near tears, said, "And he was giving him a boxing lesson, too. Thomas was actually showing Ray how to box."

That was the problem. Nobody shows Ray Leonard how to box, and you can take that to the Room, and the bank.

*1981*

## MIKE LUPICA

Mike Lupica (b. 1952) came out of Boston College to cover the New York Knicks as though he had been born in Madison Square Garden. He was twenty-three and a star in the making at the *New York Post.* Two years later, in 1977, Lupica jumped to the city's other tabloid, the *Daily News,* to write a column that demanded to be read. There were echoes of Jimmy Breslin and Jimmy Cannon in his work, but there were also the fine touches of a writer who could capture a mood, paint a picture with words, and take a stand when the moment called for one. The *News's* crusty Dick Young showed his resentment by moving to the *Post* while Lupica moonlighted with an *Esquire* column, ESPN gigs, and books of every description. It's a common refrain that his newspaper work suffered as a result, but at his best Lupica was truly special.

★　★　★

# The Day the Music Died in Boston

THEY STOOD for a long time in Fenway Park when it was over, quietly at attention while the organist played marching music. The afternoon was gone, hope was gone, the season was gone, and the beautiful little park was again a tomb for its fans, as it has been in a lot of Octobers. On the field, a hated baseball team called the New York Yankees celebrated victory. The people kept staring at them dreamily. And no one moved. Maybe they thought that if they stayed the season would not be over.

There has always been a saying in Boston that while baseball isn't a matter of life and death, the Red Sox are. The Red Sox were dead. In the 163rd game of this special season, the Yankees had scored one more run. Rich Gossage had just thrown a fastball to Carl Yastrzemski in the bottom of the pennant race. Yastrzemski, a proud old hero who'd already knocked in two runs, popped that fastball up. There was not going to be one last series in Yankee Stadium, or Fenway Park, not one more swing of the bat for Yastrzemski or Jim Rice or anyone. The scoreboard said 5–4 Yankees. The Yankees were a run better. And no one wanted to leave Fenway.

The fans were paralyzed by all the ifs that must rule the last day of a pennant race like this one. If Lou Piniella had not made his great running catch off Fred Lynn with two on in the sixth. If the ball Piniella lost in the sun in the ninth, the one hit by Jerry Remy, didn't bounce right into Piniella's glove. If Bucky Dent had not turned into Bobby Thomson with his three-run homer. All those ifs. The organist kept playing the marching music.

"We're not the world champions for nothing," Lou Piniella would say in the winning clubhouse, when asked about all the little plays that enabled the Yankees to get a nose in front, like some kind of baseball Affirmed. "They played like world champions," Yastrzemski would say in the clubhouse at the other end of the runway.

The Yankees *had* played like world champions. Gossage held the Red Sox off in the end. A home run by Reginald Martinez Jackson provided the difference. The Yankees were going to Kansas City to begin a whole new passion play with their old friends, the Royals. They had done something quite difficult first. They had silenced Fenway Park.

The Red Sox' 14-game July lead was sad, ancient history. The gallant comeback that brought them to this tiebreaker playoff game, a comeback from a 3½-game deficit with only two weeks left, was wasted. All the pre-game partying on Boylston Street and in Kenmore Square and on Yawkey Way had turned into a magnificent wake. The best pennant race that anyone is going to see for a very long time had been won by the Yankees, by Ron Guidry and Dent and Piniella and Gossage and Jackson.

"Three seasons ended today," Jackson said in the clubhouse. "There was the first half. That belonged to the Red Sox. The second half belonged to us. And today? Today was a season all in itself."

Jackson smiled. His 400-foot, Reggie Jackson-model October home run in the eighth had ultimately meant victory for his team. Reggie is so used to all of this. He was a lock to be a central figure in yesterday's drama. He is one of the great money players of his time. He knew what a fine victory his team earned, a victory that began in July, when Bob Lemon became manager of the Yankees.

"I'm glad we don't have to play them anymore," Jackson said.

No one could endure any more of this Yankee–Red Sox material. The three seasons that Jackson talked about ended with a game that was several games, a full three-act production.

There was the first game, the one that took place over the first six innings, the one that had ex-Yankee Mike Torrez handling his old team, staked to a two-run lead by a Yastrzemski home run off Guidry, and a Rice RBI single. Then there was another game in the Yankee seventh, Act II, which saw Dent stun Fenway with a three-run homer that dropped into the bottom of the screen at the top of Fenway's famed Green Monster. Dent used a bat borrowed from Mickey Rivers, one sent out by Rivers in the middle of his at-bat. Dent had become another of baseball's unlikely heroes. The Yankees would leave the seventh ahead 4–2. Torrez was gone.

"I never did see the ball hit the screen," Dent said. These unlikely heroes are notoriously short-sighted.

Then there was the final game, the last act. Jackson's home run off Bob Stanley in the eighth. Two Red Sox runs in the eighth. The Red Sox getting two men on in the ninth as their fans began to dream grand dreams. But Rice hit a shot to Piniella, which Piniella saw, and caught. Yastrzemski popped up. It had been a beautiful excruciating game to end a wonderful season-long battle.

The game began with Guidry against Torrez. It had a home run from Yastrzemski, a big man in so many big games in his 18 seasons. It had Jackson, of course. And it ended with Gossage facing Rice and Yastrzemski with the winning runs on the bases. The game had everything. The season had everything.

The Good Lord must love his baseball.

By the time it was over, and the people had begun their painful October procession out of Fenway Park—a terrible New England ritual—Yastrzemski, who is 39 years old now, was standing in front of his locker talking about "terrible knots in my stomach." Torrez talked about how "in my heart, I know I did my best." Carlton Fisk slowly peeled off his clothes and talked about all the ifs.

"If that ball doesn't bounce up and hit Piniella right in the damn chest . . . , " Fisk said. He was talking about the ball Remy hit in the ninth. He had no answers. His voice trailed off. He turned to his locker and spit some tobacco into a paper cup.

"One run," Carlton Fisk said. "One run after 162 games, and they won and we lost, and what more can you say?"

"You don't bet on where they start," said Jackson. "You bet on where they finish."

They finished at Fenway Park on a diamond of an October afternoon. The Yankees went to Kansas City when it was over, the Red Sox and their fans went home. A lovely war ended at Fenway yesterday, a war decided by a run. The run made the ballpark quiet. It will stay quiet for a long time.

*1978*

★  ★  ★

# Connors Slams Death's Door Shut

THERE WERE three match points now for Jimmy Connors at Centre Court, at the finish of this match that was like his career. He had been as good as he could be against Mikael Pernfors, despite losing the first two sets, 6–1, 6–1. He had given as much as he could give. Someday, Björn Borg will wonder if he could have done more with his skill. John McEnroe wonders already. Connors will never wonder.

Jimmy Connors has gone the distance. Connors has squeezed this one extraordinary tennis game bone-dry. One more time yesterday, in one more big match, he forgot what year it was.

Billie Jean King said later, "Jimmy will never wake up in the middle of the night when he's 45 years old and ask, 'What if?' "

But there was still the last point to be won at Centre Court, at the end of an afternoon Centre Court will not forget. Connors is that big line from "The Untouchables": Never stop fighting until the fight is done. Connors knows. His right thigh was cramping. He is 34 years old, too old in a young man's game. He is an American man when they don't win anything in tennis. He took a last deep breath at Centre Court and served at Mikael Pernfors, and grunted as he came over the ball, and got ready to make sure the fight was done.

In the interview room, Connors was asked if the right thigh, which began to cramp in the fifth game of the fifth set, ever made him think he would not be able to finish. Connors threw a look at the questioner that was like a punch.

"I was always gonna finish," Jimmy Connors said. "Even if I had to crawl."

The serve went over the net and it came back and then here was Jimmy Connors leaning into one last backhand crosscourt, one of those backhands that magically got longer and meaner when it was

6–1, 6–1, 4–1 for Mikael Pernfors. Pernfors could have chased the backhand out of Centre Court and out to Church Road and never caught it.

It was over, after three hours and 39 minutes, at 7:56 on a London evening, as the last of the sun disappeared behind the Old Vic of a tennis theater. In one of the greatest comebacks in Wimbledon history, in tennis history, Connors had won, 1–6, 1–6, 7–5, 6–4, 6–2. Against all odds, against a player good enough to make the final of the French Open last year, Connors won his 91st singles match at Wimbledon and played himself into the quarterfinals.

"He is such a great hustler," Pernfors said. "If he gets the opportunity to come back, he's gonna take it."

"It has to be," said past champion Lew Hoad, "as good an effort as anybody has ever given here."

Connors is a champion. He is not a nice champion. But there is no rule to say you have to be. Connors has defaulted matches in his career. He has quit because of injuries. He has been vulgar, every bit the guttersnipe McEnroe has been at his worst. He has been a graceless loser and a snappish winner. There is a lot of Billy Martin in Jimmy Connors.

But across a career that really began in 1972, there has been so little quit in Connors. Borg was more talented. Borg had more serve, more speed, more topspin. McEnroe had all the shots the Lord can give; McEnroe was the whole orchestra. Connors was a groundstroker with heart, the way Chris Evert has been a groundstroker with heart. McEnroe beat up Borg; Borg didn't want to play any more. McEnroe became unstable, took a sabbatical, has a career in eclipse at the age of 28.

And Jimmy Connors keeps going. He is a tennis player. He keeps playing. Borg came along, then McEnroe. Connors was dismissed. Connors came back and won Wimbledon and the Open in 1982, eight years after he'd won his final Wimbledon, his first Open. Now he is 34, close to 35. He was the last American in the draw at the French Open.

He is the last American in the draw at Wimbledon. He plays Slobodan
Zivojinovic in the quarterfinals today.

"I can still play," Jimmy Connors said in the interview room.

He did not sit in a chair in the interview room. He did not want the
leg to begin cramping again. He leaned forward into the microphone.

"What I did today is all fine and good," he said. "But all it means is
now I'm in the hunt."

He was asked another question about the comeback and said, "The
best thing I did today was grind and fight."

We had heard it all before, in press rooms all over the world. It is
easy to joke about Connors talking about grinding and fighting, spill-
ing blood, all that. It is a routine. There is phony in Connors. It is too
easy to remember him grabbing his crotch, swearing at umpires, walking off the court against Ivan Lendl in the Lipton tournament last year.
It is easy to remember him skipping a ceremony for past champions at
the centenary Wimbledon in 1977.

He could have done it better off the court. There could have been
more grace, less mean spirits. But maybe those mean spirits helped
make him great, a champion, an American tennis immortal. The wonder boys go away. Connors keeps carrying the flag. Others would have
curled up into a little ball at Centre Court yesterday. Connors' tennis
obituary was being written in the press box: "Jimmy Connors, age 34,
perhaps made his last appearance at Centre Court yesterday . . ."

And Connors began to squeeze another day out of his tennis game,
another day out of this Wimbledon. He gave himself at least a chance
to win one more Wimbledon at a time when he has been counted
out again.

At Wimbledon, they will always talk about Jimmy Connors and
Pernfors and Connors making his stand after Pernfors had won 16 of
the first 19 games. The first set took 29 minutes. The second set took
29 minutes. It didn't take Pernfors long to get to 4–1 in the third. Then
Connors made his stand. Go figure the man's heart.

"I didn't have enough time to get embarrassed the first two sets,"
Connors said. "I was getting my butt beat."

But he came back and won yesterday. Once more, he filled Centre Court with his moxie, his grunting, his mouth, his groundstroking game, his heart most of all. The other guy had the lead. The other guy was 23. Didn't matter.

When it was 6–1, 6–1, a British reporter turned to me and said, "At least you're here for Connors' sunset." Ten minutes after the match, the sun set behind Centre Court. It went down. Not Connors. The twilight of his career is just like his career. Billie Jean is right. When it is over for Connors, there will be no questions, no might-have-beens.

*1987*

★ ★ ★

# Recalling Brother's Bravest Hour

I T IS a football Sunday. The Giants' game, their first home game since September 11, is on the television. So this is a day for the brother to remember football things. All days are hard, he says. You just hope tomorrow will hurt a little less, he says. At least, the football things make Chris Suhr smile. He is a kid on the Sundays he remembers. His brother Danny is so very much alive.

"I can hear his voice right now," Chris Suhr said yesterday. "I heard him wondering why the linebacker wasn't over in the flat where he was supposed to be. Why one of those SOBs wasn't covering the tight end closer. That sort of thing. Crying because one of the Giants would miss an assignment and the other team would score."

Chris Suhr is twenty-one months a fireman, no longer considered a rookie, in the department's regular rotation now. His brother Danny was with Engine Company 216, out of Williamsburg, Brooklyn. Danny Suhr was one of the first firemen killed on the morning of September 11, on his way with the rest of his company into tower two when someone who had fallen from tower two, or jumped, landed on top of him.

Then Father Mychal Judge, the Fire Department chaplain, was killed after giving Danny Suhr the last rites of the Catholic Church.

We have talked all the time since that day about how firemen and police officers and all the emergency workers are the real heroes of the city. Danny Suhr was always his kid brother's hero, long before he tried to lead everybody into tower two, back when he was No. 90 of James Madison High and No. 90 of the semipro Brooklyn Mariners, and captain of the Fire Department football team until he finally decided he was too old a couple of years ago, a couple of years before he became one of the firemen of the city who died much too young.

"He had that football mentality," Chris Suhr said. "Here I come. Rush the building the way you would the quarterback. He was always ready to go. You couldn't block him and you couldn't stop him. A little over six feet, maybe 250, maybe more. A square box of a guy."

Chris remembers the big game between the Fire Department team and the one from the NYPD back in 1993, remembers the Fire Department being down three touchdowns but then his brother, No. 90, forcing a fumble and making a big interception and bringing them all the way back for a 22–21 win.

"I think it might have been the last time the Fire Department beat them," Chris Suhr said.

These were good football memories for him, good ones, on a football Sunday much too quiet in the apartment. Chris Suhr said, "He loved the Giants, but he loved football more." This fall Danny Suhr, once All-City for Madison, had agreed to be a volunteer assistant coach at South Shore High for his old Madison teammate, Tom Salvato. The two Suhr brothers even played together in a touch-football league over on Randall's Island.

The Fire Department games were in the spring, Baker Field at Columbia sometimes, sometimes at St. John's. The Brooklyn Mariners played in the fall, on Saturdays usually. Danny Suhr played inside linebacker, some tight end. Sometimes he would be so sore the next day that he would get on the couch at the family's home on

East Nineteenth in Brooklyn, between Avenue R and Avenue S, St. Edmund's Parish, and stay there all afternoon watching pro football, the Giants and Jets both. Yelling about the coverage. Sometimes calling plays before they even happened.

"He was always the most advanced football guy in the room," his brother said yesterday. "He was great, my brother."

They all came in a hurry on Engine 216, on streets Danny Suhr knew around the World Trade Center because he used to go pick up his wife Nancy when she worked downtown. Nancy: the girl he'd fallen in love with when he was in the eighth grade and she was in the seventh, with whom he opened N&D Pizza, for Nancy and Danny, on Avenue U and Twenty-ninth. When he had gotten the call in Williamsburg he had left her a message, telling her he was on his way to the World Trade Center, and that he loved her; that he would see her later.

The engine pulled up near tower two and then No. 90 of Madison High and all his other teams, the square box of a guy, the linebacker who always wanted to be first to the quarterback or the ball, was running to get ahead of the other guys, wanting to be first in, probably thinking this was the fire of all their lives, until a part of the sky fell on him and killed him.

"He was everything on a football field except real fast," Pudgie Walsh, Danny Suhr's old coach with the Brooklyn Mariners and with the FDNY team, said yesterday. "He had to pick that day to be fast."

Danny Suhr was fast from the back step of Engine 216 on the eleventh of September. There were people inside who needed him.

"If my brother had somehow known that one of them in the company might have to die, over there trying to save people's lives, he would have said, 'I gotta go,'" Chris Suhr said. "He would have done what he did, called Nancy, and then he would have gone, never really believing this thing could stop him, either."

Chris Suhr has been working out of Rockaway, expects to be back soon with Engine Company 280 in Brooklyn. He was on vacation the morning of September 11 when he heard what had happened downtown. He got down there as soon as he could and when he did, he started to hear rumors about what had happened, not finding out for sure that his brother was gone until late in the afternoon.

"He wanted to save lives," Chris Suhr said. "And he did. The guys in his company are alive today because they were trying to give him CPR in the ambulance."

Chris Suhr said that before September 11, he and his brother made sure to attend line-of-duty funerals for firemen together. He said that as sad as those occasions were, they were also occasions of pride for both of them, and a chance to spend a few hours together, at a time in both their lives when that had become more difficult, even if they both still thought they had all the time in the world. They would both be in their dress uniforms, two big young guys from Brooklyn, the Suhr brothers, Chris a miniature version of Danny, side by side, honoring the family business, and maybe each other.

"Now I had to put on that uniform for him," Chris Suhr said. "And I have to keep putting it on for funerals, knowing he's not coming.

"You would have liked him," the brother said. "Everybody did." He went back to watching the football game, the only other voices in the room belonging to the announcers.

2001

# MARK KRAM, JR.

Mark Kram, Jr. (b. 1956) grew up as the son of a writer who was famed for his classic account of the Thrilla in Manila and pilloried for the ethical lapses that cost him his job at *Sports Illustrated*. The name they shared guaranteed a difficult road for the younger Kram, but he ignored the naysayers and successfully campaigned to resurrect his father's career. At the same time, after apprenticing in Baltimore and Detroit, he joined the *Philadelphia Daily News*'s legendary sports department in 1987 and spent the next twenty-six years writing the long, evocative features that became his calling card. One of them led to his first book, *Like Any Normal Day*, an award-winning look at brotherly love in the face of football-related tragedy. The piece reprinted here—a portrait of a boxer haunted by the man he killed in the ring—covers different emotional territory, but it resounds with what the Kram family will always be best known for: excellence.

★ ★ ★

# "I Want to Kill Him"

HACKENSACK, N.J.—Cold fear gripped George Khalid Jones as he boarded the Acela Express in Newark that summery day last July. Over and over he pondered: What would people say when he showed up in Washington at the funeral? Would they spot him in the crowded church and whisper among themselves, "*There he is. The guy who did it!*" He could feel their eyes upon him, the anger, the accusation, welling up from behind shiny pools of tears. And what would the widow say when she saw him? Would she become hysterical and scream, "*You killed him. You killed my husband!*" She would be there with her three children, suddenly fatherless because of him. How could he ever face them? How could he ever face any of them?

"George, come along with me to the funeral," Lou Duva, his promoter, had told him. "View the body, see the family, and go to the reception. Go down there and let people see you."

Two weeks had passed since Jones had stopped Beethavean "Honey Bee" Scottland in the 10th and final round of their light-heavyweight bout aboard the retired aircraft carrier USS Intrepid on the Hudson River in New York. Carried unconscious from the ring on a stretcher, Scottland underwent two surgeries at Bellevue Hospital Center: the first to gauge the pressure building up in his brain, the second to drain blood in an effort to relieve that pressure. He lingered in a coma for 6 days, during which Jones found himself overwhelmed with an ever-deepening anxiety. Nightmares filled what few hours of sleep he could get, spooky harbingers of the phone call that would finally come on July 2: Scottland was dead at age 26 of a subdural hematoma, a rupture of the veins between the brain and the skull. Uncertain if he could bring himself to attend the funeral 7 days later, if only because of the profound shame that had enveloped him, he agreed when Duva told him simply, "George, this is the right thing to do."

So they settled into their seats for their 3-hour journey, during which Jones somberly peered out his window at the passing factories and rivers. The then 79-year-old Duva looked over at Jones and said of Scottland, "It was his time, you know? Whether it happened in a boat or car or in the ring, God has a set time for everyone." He told Jones there had been an insurance policy on Scottland, that his widow and children would get "a nice piece of money."

The *New York Daily News* reported after the death that the promoter took out two insurance policies—a $20,000 medical policy and a $50,000 life policy. And Duva added this, "Remember: It could have happened to you." He told him boxing was a rough game, that he should get what he can out of it in the way of financial security and get out while he still had his faculties. Buy a house, get a college fund started. As they drew into Union Station, Duva said, "You have to leave this behind you today. You have to get closure."

A car picked them up at the curb and drove them to Metropolitan Baptist Church in Northwest Washington. Jones cautiously blended into the big crowd that had formed there, which included some boxers with whom he was friendly. They told him, "It happens. Keep your head up." Some relatives of Scotland were surprised to see him, but an uncle came up to Jones, held out a hand and said, "We're so happy to see you." The uncle told him that he should go on with his boxing career because "Bee would have wanted you to do that." The widow was equally gracious, her face sad yet forgiving. As he filed by the open coffin, which was surrounded by stands of flowers, he wondered how she and her children would be able to cope in the years to come. And suddenly it occurred to him: How could there ever be closure? *A piece of me is going along with him to the grave.*

Whenever a fighter kills another in the ring, he is always the forgotten victim, walled in by heavy shadows of guilt, fear and remorse. You cannot know how it feels until it has happened to you, which is why George Khalid Jones found himself so distressed when he picked up the sports section a few weeks ago and saw a quote from Mike Tyson. Outrageously, Tyson had said of Lennox Lewis, his opponent Saturday in Memphis, Tenn.: "My main objective is . . . to kill him. He should want to kill me, too, because I want to kill him." It sent a wave of terror through Jones, who said that while Tyson was probably only trying to psych himself up, he wondered if he truly knew what he was saying. Jones remembered what he had said a few days before the Scotland bout: that he had worked so hard in the gym that "I pray I don't kill anybody." They were only words then—typical prefight hype—but they have since come back to him as an unintended prophecy.

"Be careful what you say: It could come true," said Jones, seated at a corner table at an empty North Jersey diner. "And when it does come true, then you suddenly find yourself caught in a horrible nightmare. Sometimes you just say things, but you never think it'll happen."

The year that has passed since Beethavean Scottland expired has been a search for life after death for Jones, 34. When he came back from the funeral in Washington, he became overwhelmed by the tragedy that had befallen his opponent, who everyone said was "a good guy who loved his wife and children." Thoughts of his own mate and five children, of how precious they were to him, would leave him in a state of anguish, his tears streaming down the side of his handsome face. A voice inside his head told him: Quit boxing. Yet even as he packed up his gear and stowed it away in the attic, a part of him knew that the sport had provided him with the only piece of thread he ever had to weave a worthwhile existence. No one is exactly sure if he will ever be the same fighter—and that includes himself. But he is certain that "some good has come out of the death of Beethavean Scottland," if only that he now understands something that had eluded him for years: the value of life.

That has been a revelation to Jones, who grew up in circumstances where life had no value. With soulful eyes that exude a mannered gentility, Jones said his late father had 26 children with a variety of women and abandoned him while his mother was 6 months pregnant with him. He fell into drugs at an early age. Jailed at age 17 for shooting "a guy who tried to rob me and a friend on a corner" in 1985, Jones spent 4 years behind bars. Said his mother, Ruth Ann Jones-Mass, who remembered how a drug-crazed Jones once had to be led away in a straitjacket to the hospital to keep him from jumping off the roof: "Sometimes our children just go astray."

He sold drugs to support a gambling addiction and was arrested again in 1997. He came before a judge who told him, "Mr. Jones, you are a menace to society." So he went to prison again for a 4-year term, only this time he was leaving behind a woman, Naomi Del Valle, and their small children. Jones and Del Valle had been together since December 1991 and not a week passed that she did not go to the prison with her children. "Seeing him there was the hardest thing I ever had to do," said

Del Valle, employed in customer services by The Bank of New York. "I cried every visit, but I did every second of his time with him. I just knew there was a better person somewhere deep inside of him."

Some boxing talent was in there, too, if only he could clean himself up. He had begun boxing in jail in 1985 because he discovered that boxers received certain privileges, such as Sunday ice cream and unlimited cheeseburgers. He began to spar in some local gyms in early 1994, then turned pro that September against Marty Lindquist in Minnesota. He was supposed to go there as an "opponent"—which is to say he was supposed to lose—but he won a four-round decision. He then strung together 10 straight victories—including eight by knockout—when his career was interrupted by that 4-year jail stint, of which he served 34 months. When he came out again in May 2000, he clicked off four straight victories, three by knockout. His opponent for that ESPN2 "Tuesday Night Fights" date June 26 on the USS Intrepid was supposed to be David Telesco, but Telesco begged off with a broken nose sustained in training, and Scottland stepped in as his replacement.

"What would have happened if I had fought Telesco instead of Bee?" said Jones. "I ask myself 'What if . . .' every day."

The bell tolled: Ten strikes in honor of a popular boxing figure who had recently died. In the ring before his comeback fight against highly rated Eric Harding at the Mohegan Sun Casino in Connecticut, Jones suddenly found himself overwhelmed by the tragedy he had just endured. Walking into the ring that evening he had been fine—or thought he had been fine—but he had not expected there to be a call by the ring announcer for a moment of silence. As he stood there listening in his corner, he wondered to himself, "Man, is somebody playing a trick on me or what?" His eyes began to well up with tears.

"Every time I heard that bell 'ding,' the only thing I could think of was what had happened," Jones said. "And I began reliving the whole thing again."

Until he stepped into the ring on the USS Intrepid, Jones had been unacquainted with Scottland, a southpaw who fought out of a gym in suburban Washington called Round One Boxing. Scottland (20–6–2) worked as an exterminator to supplement his earnings from boxing, which were minimal in light of his inability to connect with a big promoter. He had married his childhood friend, Denise Lewis, and they had an 8-year-old daughter and two sons, ages 2 and 6. Ironically, the opponent he had been lined up to face for the Maryland State 168-pound belt last June 20, Dana Rucker, withdrew because of a hamstring injury, so Scottland was available when Duva began looking for a replacement for Telesco. Scottland had to jump up a weight class; he weighed in at 170, 4 pounds lighter than Jones. But Scottland jumped at the opportunity because it would pay him more than he had ever earned for a bout: $7,000 plus $1,000 in expenses. Said Jones, also a southpaw, "We both wanted the same thing: A shot at something better."

But it soon became clear that Scottland was in well over his head. By the end of the fourth round, CompuBox statistics showed Jones had landed 64 more punches than Scottland. During a 42-second span in the fifth round, Jones pummeled Scottland with 43 shots; Scottland landed only three. Cries of "Stop it! Stop it!" rang out from the crowd, and even ESPN2 commentator Max Kellerman observed, "This is how guys get seriously hurt." Ring physician Dr. Barry Jordan told referee Arthur Mercante Jr. before the eighth round not to allow Scottland to "take many more blows," but Scottland, who Mercante later said still was defending himself, rallied to narrowly win the eighth and ninth rounds. When the fighters came out at the beginning of the final round, Jones said Mercante told them as they touched gloves: "Show me who wants it more."

"And the only thing I could think was: 'I gotta get this guy out of here,' " Jones said. Scottland was felled by a combination with 45 seconds remaining and was immediately attended to by Jordan and two other doctors. Jones climbed up on the ring ropes to salute the crowd in victory.

But that joy turned to horror as it became obvious Scottland was seriously injured. While the doctors found him initially to be conscious, they said his condition quickly deteriorated. Concerned, Jones looked on as paramedics strapped Scottland to a stretcher, which they would have trouble squeezing into the elevator of the World War II–era Intrepid. As Jones walked back to his dressing room, he reminded himself, "This is just part of the game." Johnny Bos, his booking agent, assured him Scottland would be fine, but when Bos telephoned him later at home, the report he had was not an encouraging one. Nor were any of the subsequent reports from Bos, who called Jones six to eight times a day with updates. Said Jones, "All I could do was pray: *Please let him live.* It was the longest 6 days you could possibly imagine, then Johnny called to say, 'He died.'"

A depression fell over Jones that summer. He attended the funeral in Washington, but only when a close friend who had helped him conquer his gambling addiction told him, "What are you going to do? Are you going to punk out again, the way you always used to do? Or are you going to stand up and be a man?"

Going there had a soothing effect on him, yet if he discovered that others had forgiven him, he still was not at a point where he could forgive himself. When he attempted to go back to the gym a few weeks later, he broke down in tears and told Del Valle he was through. He began getting up late every day, at which point he would brush his teeth, then go back to sleep again. Del Valle told him, "This is not who you are. You have to get over this." And yet whenever Jones looked at her and his children, it reminded him of how Denise would never again be able to hold her husband, and how the children would never be able to say, "Daddy, we love you." Said Jones, "You know, it takes two parents to raise a child. No one knows that better than me." Weeks of inactivity had passed when Bos spoke up.

"George, you drive a cab for a living, and you hit someone, and they die, you have to get back in that cab and drive it again," Bos said. "This is the same thing. You have to get back in that cab."

You can never predict how certain fighters will come back after they have killed an opponent; fine talents such as Ray "Boom Boom" Mancini and Gabriel Ruelas were never the same again. In the case of Jones—who began training again in the fall—Bos said he never would have booked him against Harding last December if he had been aware of just how emotionally fragile he was. But Bos said he figured it could set him up for a big-money title shot against light-heavyweight champion Roy Jones Jr. A victory would give George an undefeated record with "the rep of killing an opponent," which Bos said could only enhance his desirability. But in the week before the Harding bout— for which George wore trunks emblazoned with the words "Bee" and "R.I.P."—he did a television interview in which he began crying. Asked in the interview how he has fared since the tragedy, he said: "This is the first time I have ever felt compassion." Bos was aghast.

Compassion is not an attractive feature in a fighter.

"Naaahhh," said Bos. "You do not want a compassionate fighter."

The Harding bout did not go well in any way. Duva, who ordinarily works the corner, was rushed to a hospital when his heart defibrillator malfunctioned. And then Jones fell to pieces during that unexpected moment of silence. While Jones would say later "the better man won that night," Bos said Jones was holding back with his punches, that he had Harding in early trouble but would not step in aggressively enough. Harding wobbled Jones toward the end of the sixth round, then finished the job in the seventh with a seven-punch combination. As Jones slid helplessly to the canvas, Del Valle looked on from her ringside seat and saw his eyes roll back into his head. "Oh God!" she yelled in terror. "Now this is happening to me!" Eleven-year-old daughter Aisha began crying hysterically. When Jones recovered back in his dressing room, Bos approached him and said, "This cannot be. Either you fight the way you're capable of or you're packing it in. I'm not letting you go out there and get hurt."

Bos said, "He called me and begged me for another chance."

He got it against Karl Willis in April. Jones (17–1, 13 KOs) fought well enough to win by a third-round technical knockout, but as Bos said, "Willis is no Eric Harding." Bos just said he told Jones to get some work in and that was what he did. Jones had command of the bout from the opening bell, got his punches off cleanly and said that he only once drifted back in time to the Scottland fight. It was when a fan stood up at his seat and shouted at him for everyone to hear: "Come on, George. Kill this guy."

Change has come over George Khalid Jones. Small things he does every day convince him of that. Once, he would have become enraged if another driver had cut him off. Today, he said he just shakes his head and sighs. In fact, he said you can slap him in the face and "the only thing I will do now is smile." It was not long ago, on a Saturday night, he happened to be watching the fights on television when it appeared to him that the referee should stop it. Suddenly, he began shouting frantically at the television screen: "Stop it! Stop it!" Only later did it occur to him he never would have done something like that before Scottland.

Preparing for a bout that could come as early as next month, he goes to the Police Athletic League in Hackensack every weekday at 4:30 P.M. He goes there after he gets off work at a printing plant, where he is the inventory manager. There, he works out until 6:30 or so and is surrounded by friends, every one of whom says what a fine fellow he is.

"I told him to get rid of those damn trunks he wore during the Harding fight," said an elderly trainer at the PAG. "All that does is bring up bad memories." Whenever Jones hears someone say that, he smiles politely and explains that Scottland is a part of him now, that he has dedicated his career to him. He hopes to help his widow in whatever way he can in the years ahead and even hopes to begin a college fund to help the children. Said Jones, "What I realized is that life is short, and you have to ask yourself: How do you want to be remembered?"

What Bos and others say is that Scottland died needlessly, that the bout should have been stopped in the early rounds. They say Scottland was a victim. His widow sued New York City, which owns the Intrepid, in March, for allowing her husband to be "unreasonably and violently pummeled." What has gone unsaid is that the burden of grief is a shared one, and that it extends far beyond the gravesite, where Jones stood that July day a year ago and peered into eternity. He did not "punk out," the way he once would have done, but faced up to a difficult thing and has become stronger—if not as a fighter, then as a man. Somehow he knows that Scottland has forgiven him. A certain inner peace has come with that realization. He can finally forgive himself.

2002

## BILL PLASCHKE

There was no doubt who the lead dog was among the reporters cover-ing the Los Angeles Dodgers when Bill Plaschke (b. 1958) was on the beat for the hometown *Times*. He had a passion for digging up stories and an engaging writing touch on deadline. When his bosses pointed him at the NFL, he didn't lose a step. Plaschke's reward, in 1997, after a decade on the paper, was a sports column of his own, a playground where he had the freedom to choose his subjects, create his own world, and, too often unfortunately, peel a grape with an ax. But he was lucky enough to be working in an era when columnists could write three or four times longer than normal when a subject cried out for special treatment. No better example of this phenomenon exists than the fol-lowing piece, Plaschke's exquisite, heartfelt portrait of a Dodger fan far braver than any of her heroes.

★　★　★

# Her Blue Haven

*Bill Plaschke predicted doom for the Dodgers in 2001. . . . Plaschke criticized. . . . Plaschke forgot. . . . Plaschke compared unfairly. . . . The Dodgers need encouragement, not negativity. . . .*

THAT WAS part of a 1,200-word screed e-mailed to me last December, a holiday package filled with colorful rips. It was not much differ-ent from other nasty letters I receive, with two exceptions.

This note contained more details than the usual "You're an idiot." It included on-base percentages and catchers' defensive statistics. It was written by someone who knew the Dodgers as well as I thought I did.

And this note was signed. The writer's name was Sarah Morris. She typed it at the bottom.

Most people hide behind tough words out of embarrassment or fear, but Sarah Morris was different. She had not only challenged me to a fight, but had done so with no strings or shadows.

I thought it was cute. I wrote her back. I told her I was impressed and ready for battle.

Little did I know that this would be the start of a most unusual relationship, which eight months later is being recounted from a most unusual place. I am writing this from the floor, Sarah Morris having knocked me flat with a punch I never saw coming.

*May I ask you a question? For two years I have been running my own Web site about the Dodgers. I write game reports and editorials. How did you become a baseball editorialist? That is my deam.*

This was Sarah's second e-mail, and it figured. Every time I smile at someone, they ask me for a job.

Her own Web site? That also figured. Everybody has a Web site. The Dodgers guess there are more than two dozen Web sites devoted to kissing the almighty blue.

So my expert wasn't really an expert, but rather a computer nerd looking for work. I didn't need any more pen pals with agendas.

But about that last line. I chewed my lower lip about it. The part about "my deam."

Maybe Sarah Morris was just a lousy typist. But maybe she was truly searching for something, yet was only one letter from finding it. Aren't all of us sometimes like that?

It was worth one more response. I wrote back, asking her to explain.

*I am 30 years old. . . . Because I have a physical handicap, it took me five years to complete my AA degree at Pasadena City College. . . . During the season I average 55 hours a week writing five to seven game reports, one or two editorials, researching and listening and/or watching the games.*

Physical handicap. I paused again. I was in no mood to discuss a physical handicap, whatever it was.

I have had these discussions before, discussions often becoming long, teary stories about overcoming obstacles.

Courageous people make me jealous. They make me cry. But at some point, they have also made me numb.

Then I read the part about her working 55 hours a week. Goodness. This woman didn't only follow the Dodgers, she covered them like a newspaper reporter.

But for whom? Sarah called her Web site "Dodger Place." I searched for it, and found nothing. I checked all the Dodger search links, and found nothing.

Then I reread her e-mail and discovered an address buried at the bottom: *members.tripod.com/spunkydodgers.*

I clicked there. It wasn't fancy, rather like a chalkboard, with block letters and big type.

There was a section of "News from a Fan." Another section of "Views by a Fan." But she covered the team with the seriousness of a writer.

The stories, while basic, were complete. Sarah's knowledge was evident.

But still, I wondered, how could anybody find it? Is anybody reading?

*Nobody ever signs my guestbook.*

Does anybody correspond?

*I get one letter a month.*

I read the Web site closer and realized that she does indeed receive about one letter a month—always from the same person.

So here was a physically handicapped woman, covering the Dodgers as extensively as any reporter in the country, yet writing for an obscure Web site with an impossible address, with a readership of about two.

That "deam" was missing a lot more than an r, I thought.

The days passed, winter moved toward spring, and I had more questions.

Sarah Morris always had answers.

*I started my own Web site in hopes of finding a job, but I have had no luck yet. I have gone to the Commission of Rehabilitation seeking help, but they say I'm too handicapped to be employed. I disagree.*

*So what if my maximum typing speed is eight words per minute because I use a head pointer to type? My brain works fine. I have dedication to my work. That is what makes people successful.*

*I don't know how to look for a job.*

A head pointer? I remember seeing one of those on a late-night commercial for a hospital for paralyzed people.

It looked frightening. But her stories didn't look frightening. They looked, well, normal.

Now I find out she wrote them with her head?

I asked her how long it took her to compose one of her usual 1,200-word filings.

*3–4 hours.*

While pondering that the average person can bang out a 1,200-word e-mail in about 30 minutes, I did something I've never before done with an Internet stranger.

I asked Sarah Morris to call me.

I wanted to talk about the Dodgers. I wanted to talk about her stories.

But, well, yeah, I mostly wanted to talk about why someone would cover a team off television, typing with her head for an invisible readership.

*I have a speech disability making it impossible to use the phone.*

That proved it. My first impression obviously had been correct. This was an elaborate hoax.

She didn't want to talk to me because, of course, she didn't exist.

I thought to myself, "This is why I never answer all my mail. This is why I will never go near a chat room."

The Internet has become more about mythology than technology, people inventing outrageous lives to compensate for ordinary realities.

So, I was an unwitting actor in a strange little play. This woman writer was probably a 45-year-old male plumber.

I decided to end the correspondence.

Then I received another e-mail.

The first sentence read, "There are some facts you might want to know . . ."

In words with an inflection that leaped off the screen, Sarah Morris spoke.

*My disability is cerebral palsy. . . . It affects motor control. . . . I have excessive movement, meaning when my brain tells my hands to hit a key, I would move my legs, hit the table, and six other keys in the process.*

This was only the beginning.

*When my mom explained my handicap, she told me I could accomplish anything that I wanted to if I worked three times as hard as other people.*

She wrote that she became a Dodger fan while growing up in Pasadena. In her sophomore year at Blair High, a junior varsity baseball coach, Mike Sellers, asked her to be the team statistician. Her special ed teacher discouraged it, but she did it anyway, sitting next to the bleachers with an electric typewriter and a head pointer.

*We had a game on a rainy day. The rain fell in the typewriter, making it unusable, so Mom wrote the stats when I told her. I earned two letters that I am proud of still.*

She wrote that her involvement in baseball had kept her in school—despite poor grades and hours of neck-straining homework.

*Baseball gave me something to work for. . . . I could do something that other kids couldn't. . . . Baseball saved me from becoming another statistic. That is when I decided I wanted to do something for the sport that has done so much for me.*

And about that speech disability?

*When I went to nursery school, teachers treated me dumb. This made me mad, but I got over it. I hate the meaning of "dumb" in the phrase "deaf and dumb." My speech disability is the most frustrating.*

OK, so I believed her. Sort of. It still sounded odd.

Who could do something like this? I figured she must be privileged. Who, in her supposed condition, could cover a baseball team without the best equipment and help?

I figured she had an elaborate setup somewhere. I was curious about it. I figured she couldn't live too far from Pasadena. I would drive over one day and we would chat.

*I live in Anderson, Texas. It's about 75 miles from Houston.*

Texas? She didn't explain. I didn't ask. But that seemed like a long flight to see a little rich girl bang on an expensive keyboard.

By now, it was spring training, and she was ranting about Gary Sheffield, and I was hanging out in Vero Beach, and I would have forgotten the whole thing.

Except Sarah Morris began sending me her stories. Every day, another story. Game stories, feature stories, some with missing words, others with typographical errors, but all with obvious effort.

Then, fate. The Lakers were involved in a playoff series in San Antonio, I had one free day, and she lived about three hours away.

I wrote her, asking if I could drive over to see her. She agreed, but much too quickly for my suspicious tastes, writing me with detailed directions involving farm roads and streets with no name.

I read the directions and again thought, this was weird. This could be dangerous. I wanted to back out.

Turns out, I wasn't the only one.

*I'm so nervous about tomorrow. I'm nothing special but a woman with disabilities. I don't know what makes a good journalism story. I don't know if I am it.*

I pulled out of my San Antonio hotel on a warm May morning and drove east across the stark Texas landscape. I followed Sarah's directions off the interstate and onto a desolate two-lane highway.

The road stretched through miles of scraggly fields, interrupted only by occasional feed stores, small white churches and blinking red lights.

I rolled into the small intersection that is Anderson, then took a right turn, down a narrow crumbling road, high weeds thwacking against the car's window.

After several miles, I turned down another crumbling road, pulling up in front of a rusted gate, which I had been instructed to open.

Now, on a winding dirt road dotted with potholes the size of small animals, I bounced for nearly a mile past grazing cows. Through the dust, I spotted what looked like an old toolshed.

But it wasn't a shed. It was a house, a decaying shanty covered by a tin roof and surrounded by weeds and junk.

I slowed and stared. Could this be right?

Then I saw, amid a clump of weeds near the front door, a rusted wheelchair.

*P.S. We have dogs.*

Do they ever. A couple of creatures with matted hair emerged from some bushes and surrounded the car, scratching and howling.

Finally, an older woman in an old T-shirt and skirt emerged from the front door and shooed the dogs away.

"I'm Sarah's mother," said Lois Morris, grabbing my smooth hand with a worn one. "She's waiting for you inside."

I walked out of the sunlight, opened a torn screen door, and moved into the shadows, where an 87-pound figure was curled up in a creaky wheelchair.

Her limbs twisted. Her head rolled. We could not hug. We could not even shake hands. She could only stare at me and smile.

But that smile! It cut through the gloom of the cracked wooden floor, the torn couch, the broken, cobwebbed windows.

A clutter of books and boxes filled the small rooms. There was a rabbit living in a cage next to an old refrigerator. From somewhere outside the house, you could hear the squeaking of rats.

Eventually I could bear to look at nothing else, so I stared at that smile, and it was so clear, so certain, it even cut through most of my doubts.

But still, even then, I wondered.

*This* is Sarah Morris?

She began shaking in her chair, emitting sounds. I thought she was coughing. She was, instead, speaking.

Her mother interpreted. Every sound was a different word or phrase.

"Huh (I) . . . huh-huh (want to show) . . . huh (you) . . . huh (something)."

Her mother rolled her through a path that cut through the piles of junk, up to an old desk on cinder blocks.

On the desk was a computer. Next to it was a TV. Nearby was a Dodger bobble-head doll of uncertain identity.

Her mother fastened a head pointer around her daughter's temples, its chin-strap stained dark brown from spilled Dr Pepper. Sarah then began carefully leaning over the computer and pecking.

On the monitor appeared the Dodger Place Web site. Sarah used her pointer to call up a story. Peck by peck, she began adding to that story. It was her trademark typeface, her trademark Dodger fan prose, something involving Paul Lo Duca, about whom she later wrote:

". . . Offensively, Lo Duca has been remarkable. Entering Friday's game, Lo Duca has batted .382 with five home runs and seventeen RBI. Last Tuesday Jim Tracy moved Lo Duca into the leadoff position. Since then, the Dodgers have won six and lost two. Lo Duca has an on-base percentage of .412. On Memorial Day Lo Duca had six hits, becoming the first Dodger to do so since Willie Davis on May 24, 1973. . . ."

She looked up and giggled. I looked down in wonder—and shame.

This was indeed Sarah Morris. The great Sarah Morris.

She began making more sounds, bouncing in her chair. Lois asked me to sit on a dusty chair. There were some things that needed explaining.

Times photographer Anacleto Rapping, who had been there earlier in the day, and I had been Sarah's first visitors since she moved here with her mother and younger sister from Pasadena nearly six years ago.

This shack was an inheritance from Sarah's grandmother. When Sarah's parents divorced, her mother, with no other prospects, settled here.

The adjustment from life in Southern California to the middle of a scrubby field more than 30 miles from the nearest supermarket was painful. Sarah was uprooted from a town of relative tolerance and accessibility to a place of many stares.

The place was so remote, when her mother had once dropped Sarah, helping her out of bed, and called 911, the emergency crew couldn't find the place.

"But the hardest thing for Sarah was leaving her Dodgers," Lois said.

So, she didn't. She used her disability money, and loans, to buy the computer, the television and the satellite dish that allows her to watch or listen to every game.

She doesn't have any nearby friends, and it's exhausting to spend the five hours required for shopping trips to the nearest Wal-Mart, so the Dodgers fill the void.

They challenge her on bad days, embrace her on good days, stay awake with her while she covers an extra-inning game at 2 A.M.

She covers so much baseball, she maintains the eerie schedule of a player, rarely awaking before 10 A.M., often eating dinner at midnight.

Through the cluttered house, the path for not only her wheelchair, but for the entire direction of her life, leads from her bedroom to the kitchen to the Dodgers.

The air-conditioning sometimes breaks, turning the house into a steam bath. Lois totaled their aging van last year when she hit a black cow on a starless night, then missed so much work that they barely had enough money for food.

Yet, Sarah spends nine hours, carefully constructing an analysis of Gary Sheffield, or two hours writing about a one-run victory in Colorado.

I asked what her Dodger Web page represented to her.

*Freedom.*

I asked how she feels when working.

*Happy. Useful.*

I had contacted Sarah Morris months earlier, looking for a fight. I realized now, watching her strain into the thick air of this dark room to type words that perhaps no other soul will read, that I had found that fight.

Only, it wasn't with Sarah. It was with myself. It is the same fight the sports world experiences daily in these times of cynicism and conspiracy theories.

The fight to believe. The fight to trust that athletics can still create heroes without rap sheets, virtue without chemicals, nobility with grace.

It is about the battle to return to the days when sports did not detract from life, but added to it, with its awesome power to enlighten and include.

In a place far from such doubt, with a mind filled with wonder, Sarah Morris brought me back.

I had not wanted to walk into those shadows. But two hours later, I did not want to leave.

Yet I did, because there was an airplane waiting, and an NBA playoff series to cover, big things, nonsense things.

Sarah asked her mother to wheel her outside. She was rolled to the edge of the weeds. I grasped one of her trembling hands. She grasped back with her smile.

I climbed into the car and rattled down the dirt road. Through the rear-view mirror, through the rising dust, I could see the back of Sarah Morris' bobbing head as she was wheeled back to that cinder-blocked desk.

For she, too, had a game to cover.

*If you see Karros, please tell him to watch his knees in 1999. He used to bend them more than now.*

Sarah sent me that e-mail recently. It was about the same time she'd sent me an e-mail saying she had finally saved enough money to begin attending a college about 45 minutes down the road in pursuit of her "deam."

I didn't get a chance to pass along her note to the slumping Karros, but it didn't matter.

A day later, he had a game-winning hit. The next game, a home run. The game after that, another homer.

If you watched him closely, you could see that he indeed was bending his knees again.

Eight months ago I wouldn't have believed it, but I could swear each leg formed the shape of an r.

*2001*

## MICHAEL WILBON

There's a mother lode of sidetracked sportswriting talent onscreen every time ESPN's *Pardon the Interruption* airs, and Tony Kornheiser is only half of it. The other half is his cohost and best friend, Michael Wilbon (b. 1958). In thirty years at *The Washington Post*, twenty of them as a columnist, Wilbon covered every sport worth writing about, stood tall in the face of brutal deadlines, and established himself as a premier storyteller. His main contribution, however, may have been his deft navigation of the cultural churn that has increasingly found its way into sports. Whether out of anger or disappointment, Wilbon had one of his finest moments as a columnist when he tore into the bitches-and-ho's disregard for women that landed Mike Tyson in prison. He painted the former heavyweight champion as what he was—a blight and an embarrassment—not because it was the politic thing to do but because it was the right thing.

★ ★ ★

# Entitled to Everything He Got

L A LÉCHÈRE, FRANCE—The results from Alpine skiing and pairs figure skating and the luge competition fall on deaf ears this day. The pictures and the words that matter come across the sea through CNN International and they all concern Mike Tyson. The lasting image is of that stairwell outside the courtroom in Indianapolis, where the gawkers line up like rubberneckers on the freeway, straining their necks to catch a glimpse of Tyson, the walking accident.

I'm sick of Mike Tyson and his sleaze, even 4,200 miles away. I'm sickened by the zealots who stand in the stairwell outside that court and shout encouragement at a man simply because he is a famous athlete, even though the victim could have been their sister, cousin or next-door neighbor. I'm sickened by a defense whose primary argument was, You knew he was a sex-crazed lunatic, how could you have gone anywhere near him? I'm sickened by his "boyz," his bodyguards who helped procure female companionship for Tyson. I'm sickened by the open-season-on-women atmosphere that would allow Tyson to fondle and grab and offend and frighten for years, to live unthreatened outside any boundaries of human decency.

I'm sickened by the people who ask, "Well if Willie Smith got off, how come Tyson has to go to jail?" as if their cases are the same, as if the legal system decides cases in bunches.

I'm sickened by those who want to absolve Tyson of any responsibility for his behavior because he was once impoverished and orphaned. There are endless men with fathers who barely finished grade school and could hardly afford shoes in the winter, but they didn't use that as an excuse to rape somebody.

I'm sickened by the people who want to make Tyson the victim of a racist conspiracy even though virtually any black woman who walks within arm's reach of him does so at risk.

I'm sickened by the gutless ministers in our communities who embrace him and alibi for him like awestruck groupies because he's a famous athlete, instead of demanding from their pulpits in the loudest voice imaginable that he clean up his grubby act. I'm even annoyed by the 18-year-old victim who, if she's as smart as everyone claims, would have to be living in a cave to not know her "date's" sorry history of deviance, though absolutely nothing she could have said or done would justify rape.

Most of all, I'm sickened by entitlement—this belief that because you're rich/famous/politically empowered/physically stronger than everybody else that any and everybody exists primarily for your pleasure.

Previous behavior may have been excluded from the just-ended trial, but not from this discussion. Tyson had settled out of court at least twice for matters involving sexual misbehavior. By conservative count, he allegedly grabbed or fondled nine women and tried to expose himself to the limousine driver in Indianapolis even before raping the 18-year-old woman. Remember back before the fight with Razor Ruddock, when Tyson said at a news conference (to Ruddock), "I'm going to make you my girlfriend"?

It sickens me that the current culture, especially as it regards the rich and famous, says that each party acted as he/she should have. Well she is supposed to make herself available to a rich, famous man, isn't she? And he, being rich and virile and invulnerable, is supposed to bed as many women as he can, isn't he? It's amazing how emboldened people have become with entitlement. Turn on your radio, hear Bell Biv Devoe rap the lyrics, "Me and the crew used to do her," and "Never trust a big butt and a smile."

This is the atmosphere Tyson runs in. "The Girl Ain't Nothin' But a Skeezer." "The Bitch Is Only After My Money." Tyson's behavior isn't just condoned in this disturbingly fast-growing subculture he inhabits, it's all but sanctioned. And if you don't see any connection, look no further than the courtroom in Indianapolis where singer Johnny Gill testified on Tyson's behalf.

The only thing sicker than this feeling of entitlement is the absence of strong voices lashing back with every available resource long before the result is rape. Where are the activists? Isn't there someone preaching that it's not okay to damn what you already know, damn the rap sheet, damn the out-of-court settlements that have already taken him off the hook, that it's not okay to make the exception because he's rich and famous?

In the current issue of *Vanity Fair* magazine, one of Tyson's buddies is quoted as saying that he and Tyson shared 24 women one night in Philadelphia. Another "aide" named John Horn lamented that the 18-year-old slipped through the cracks, you might say. "What we can do is screen the women better. If I was there or more of our crew was there, that woman would have had to answer some type of questions" he was quoted as saying.

We, not on the jury, had already used up all reasonable doubt with Mike Tyson. He put himself in the wrong place (again) and this certainly was the wrong time.

The recent public history of how men mistreat women began with Clarence Thomas. Though he committed no crime, he deserved and received every benefit of the doubt. Then, it was on to William Kennedy Smith, who got the benefit of the doubt, even though his accuser's weak case made the playing field so uneven. In Tyson's case, however, this rape is an extension of disrespectful, deviant behavior that's been allowed to continue for years. Finally, thankfully, somebody spoke up.

If the legal system wasn't perfectly served, universal justice seems to have been. To hell with his boxing career, and all the money he'd have thrown down the drain anyway, just like the tens of millions already wasted; there's a serious, ugly crisis at work here and Tyson's behavior is Exhibit A.

He made his prison bunk, now let him lie in it.

*1992*

★   ★   ★

# Winning Isn't Color-Coded

CHARLOTTE, N.C.—I'm rooting for Duke. Always do. This makes me a member of a small, tiny, wee little group: black people who root for Duke.

If you don't believe me, go ahead and conduct your own little poll. Ask 10 black people who they're rooting for in the Final Four and nine of them will give you the same answer: "Anybody but Duke." For the most part, people talk around the real issue and honest feelings stay in the closet.

Occasionally, I'll ask somebody black—could be a relative, a close friend, an ex-player—why he roots against Duke.

"Because they play too rough."

So did Georgetown, but you rooted for the Hoyas.

"Because they get every call from the officials."

So did Michael Jordan, but you rooted for him.

Finally, after you play this little game for five minutes or so, those real feelings slip out: "Because Duke is too . . . too . . . white."

When Johnny Dawkins and Tommy Amaker were the stars of the team, Duke was too white. When Danny Ferry and Christian Laettner were stars in succession, Duke was intolerably white.

And now, with Grant Hill leading the Blue Devils to yet another Final Four, Duke is still too white. All three of those generalizations are too prejudiced, too biased, too intolerable to be passed off as just silly. Last I checked, three of those five players are black.

Some people root for some teams for the strangest reasons: because the uniforms look nice, because the team colors are cool, because they like the style of play or so-and-so's nephew went there for two semesters. I don't care who people root for, but it's more instructive to find whom they root against. There are people in this country who are going to root against Georgetown simply and only because John Thompson and the vast majority of his players are black. There are fewer and fewer such sentiments about the Hoyas every year, but they're still out there and I've got the mail to prove it.

It's the same thing for Duke, just another race of people carrying different baggage. Duke has become the Boston Celtics of the college ranks, the basketball villain to too many black people. That thinking would be wrong even if Duke had an all-white team. But it's wrong and stupid because Duke's teams are never all white, never predominantly white. The irony—as I point out to blacks whenever they trash the Celtics without knowing they were the first NBA team to draft a black player, play an all-black team and hire a black coach—is that both the Celtics and Duke have provided black men with opportunities denied blacks by other organizations and colleges. And some of those other colleges we as black people root for.

Almost without exception, black kids who play basketball at Duke go to class, get their degrees on time and become contributing citizens. We won't root for them, but we'll root for, say, N.C. State, whose graduation rates for black players have been abysmal at times. What exactly qualifies an N.C. State to be "black" enough but Duke not to be? What's the criteria for being "too white"? One white starter? Two?

Is Grant Hill somehow not as black as, say, Scotty Thurman of Arkansas? How "white" can Duke be if its best player, Grant Hill, is the son of one of the most prominent African-American scholars/athletes/businessmen/entrepreneurs in the country? If Jeff Capel is "too white" that might come as a surprise to his father, the head basketball coach at historically black North Carolina A&T. You mean Gene Banks, Billy King, David Henderson, Kevin Strickland and Doug McNeely (Mike Krzyzewski's first recruit) don't count? And it can't possibly relate to playing for a black coach because a lot of those "too white" Boston Celtics teams played for Bill Russell and Tom Sanders and K.C. Jones. Tell kids these days that John Thompson played for the Celtics and that he once studied under Red Auerbach and they want to fight you.

On the back of certain models of Nike shoes are two statements: "Live Together" appears on one shoe. "Play Together" appears on the other. Nobody embodies these mottos more than Coach K's Duke teams. Nobody's teams shatter more stereotypes. He can have a tempestuous, leaping player such as Christian Laettner who is white, and a steady, thinking-man's playmaker in Tommy Amaker who is black, now a Duke assistant and one of the bright young coaching minds in the country.

The black players I've talked to about this issue over a period of years are perplexed. The most insightful thoughts I've heard on the topic have come from Laettner, who told me two years ago: "This is all about perception. I don't know if people resent us as much as they resent the way the team is portrayed by a lot of people in the media, this goody-two-shoes team that thinks it's better than other people. I never bought into it. I think the anger's just misdirected."

Hopefully, Laettner was right. If so, boo the TV announcer, boo the newspaper columnist who tells you Duke is good and UNLV is evil and that the Blue Devils are angelic and operate on higher moral ground. That kind of stereotyping builds resentment.

For the segment of the black community that feels so frustrated over generations of exclusion and therefore so proprietary about one of the few arenas black folks tend to rule, maybe it's time to transfer that passion from basketball to math and science. Many look at Duke and don't see the color-balance they want. I look at Duke and see basketball, season after season, at its best at the college level. And if Duke continues to play into the spring often enough, maybe the people who waste their time rooting for Duke to lose will grow so frustrated they'll get the point.

*1994*

## SALLY JENKINS

The apple didn't fall far from the tree where Sally Jenkins (b. 1960) and her legendary father Dan are concerned, but it did bounce in a different direction. Dan was an irreverent, wisecracking football and golf writer for *Sports Illustrated* who parlayed the craziness he witnessed into a solid-gold second career as what some Texas layabouts might call "a book arthur." Sally has written books, too, a dozen of them, but first, in 1984, she veered from the trail her father blazed and tackled the serious side of sports as a *Washington Post* feature writer and investigative reporter. In 1990 she jumped to *SI* only to return to *The Post* seven years later as a sports columnist who has proved she can be as compassionate as she can be intrepid. If something doesn't look right to Sally Jenkins, the devil can take the hindmost.

★   ★   ★

# Driving Home an Eternal Philosophy of Life

I N DALE EARNHARDT'S death, the larger meanings collide with lesser ones. Racing is a sport about progress, and perfectibility, but it's also about clans and running down dirt roads, looking for a fast way out of the dull inertia of small towns. It's a sport in which a kid with a ninth-grade education peers into the depths of an engine, and grasps the Newtonian concepts that can free him from pumping gas, but also possibly kill him.

Earnhardt died exemplifying a particular kind of manhood, one that not everybody will agree is sensible and worthwhile. In the modern world, an expert is more often than not defined as a bird-boned academic who is afraid of certain food groups. Earnhardt was an expert in exploring the edge of uncontrollability. In his line of work, the degree of error and the amount of forgiveness with which he worked were tiny, and when you live with those circumstances on a daily basis, it creates a certain kind of man, one who is perhaps only understood by other drivers, fighter pilots, steeplechasers, downhillers and high-beam steelworkers. It is perplexing to the rest of us, especially perplexing when drivers choose to pass the trade on to sons, but it's a good thing they do because it's not really a trade so much as an ethic.

Anyone who has been to the Daytona 500 knows that a car like Earnhardt's No. 3 doesn't start so much as it explodes. It could have been built by NASA; the only difference is that it was designed to stay on the ground. For Earnhardt, to drive that vehicle required a visceral belief in himself, and this is the definition of guts. It required an unreasoning faith in his capabilities, and, more important, it required Earnhardt to take complete responsibility for himself. That's unheard of nowadays. To call it a masculine virtue is not really done, but there it is. Dale Earnhardt had a great deal of character, old-fashioned and southern perhaps, but character nonetheless.

Drivers so often pass the ethic on to their progeny because to them racing is the same as living, and while it may seem an inexplicable ethic to you, it's not inexplicable to them: Earnhardt did to his son, and Bobby Allison did to his son, and Mario Andretti did to his son, and Al Unser did to his son, and Richard Petty did to his son, and Kyle Petty did to his son. Two of the scions and one of the fathers are now dead. Davey Allison was killed in 1993, and Kyle Petty lost his 19-year-old son, Adam, in a crash last spring at New Hampshire International Speedway. But to tell a son not to drive would be like telling him not to aspire. "What are we going to do in life? Are we going to sit around for something to happen, or are we going to make it happen?" said Tim Petty, a cousin.

It's beyond a philosophy, or a faith, it's simply as essential to them as breathing. They are consumed to ashes with the idea that if you give nothing, you get nothing. Better to waltz around the track even once than die still, which is why the Petty family has responded by becoming even more devoted than ever to the racetrack, and why Dale Earnhardt Jr. will keep driving. "Just because something bad happens, doesn't mean you quit," Kyle has said. Richard Petty has said, "It could happen crossing the street."

Casey Mears, 22, is a third-generation driver who competes on the Northern Lights Series. His grandfather, Bill Mears, started racing in Kansas in the 1940s, and his father, Roger, drove Indy cars, as did his renowned uncle, Rick. "I just knew more about racing than I knew about anything in the world," Casey says. He began racing his plastic Big Wheels when he was 2, doing circles in the backyard. He got into racing bicycles when he was 4, after that, and at 5 and 6, he began racing three-wheelers and quads. "From time I could walk I raced something, with pedals or training wheels," he says. "You assume certain risk and you realize there are possibilities of bad outcomes. The bottom line is, I absolutely love to get in a race car. Some things other people like to do are safer, but the fact that I absolutely love what I'm doing justifies, in my mind, the good and the bad."

With the death of Earnhardt there will be a great deal of discussion about safety and preventive measures, such as HANS, a device that stabilizes the driver's neck and head. But Earnhardt declined to wear one, according to his neurosurgeon, because he felt "trapped." He wanted the freedom to look around—and he understood that you can't legislate safety at 180 mph on the last turn of the last lap of the Daytona 500. The best way to be safe is to be excellent at it.

Did he court danger? Yes. But plenty of things are dangerous. The shallow ends of swimming pools. The weather. Other people. You know what a driver really fears? "Amateurs," Richard Petty once said. They fear the improbable far more than they do running a car on an oval track, for which they have trained and educated themselves their entire lives. "Most drivers are not very complicated, and they don't have a lot of complicated philosophical theories," says Lowe's Motor Speedway President H.A. "Humpy" Wheeler. "A lot of them believe in predestination, that when it's my time, I'll go."

At the Calvary Church in Charlotte yesterday, a service was held to celebrate Earnhardt's life, not mourn his death. While outsiders may puzzle over the meaning of his death, those closest to him will not. They won't ask if it was senseless, or why he did it, or why he wanted to pass racing on to his son. They might ask if it was the unpredictable that took Earnhardt, or the predetermined, or some collision between the two. But they won't search for the meaning. "As life is action and passion," Oliver Wendell Holmes said, "so a man must engage in the action and passion of his times, at peril of being judged not to have lived." We should all have such a meaningful death.

*2001*

★   ★   ★

# Only Medal for Bode Is Fool's Gold

S ESTRIERE, ITALY—For weeks now Nike has advised us to "Join Bode." Join him where? At the bar? That's one place you might find Bode Miller after the Turin Games, unless he's in his motor home, finding new ways to duck all that pressure he put on himself.

Miller is the biggest disappointment in the Winter Olympics, not because of the way he skied the mountain, but the way he acted at the bottom of it. The fact that he didn't win a medal at these Games, going 0 for 5 in the Alpine events, is beside the point. It's not the winning, it's the trying. The point is that he acted like he didn't try, and didn't care. Failing is forgivable. Getting fatter on beer while you're here is not.

If there has been a weaker performance by an American athlete on the international stage than that of Miller, I'm hard-pressed to think of one. To hear Miller tell it, he spent more time in Sestriere's nightclubs than he did in actual competition, which amounted to less than eight minutes. Miller's final Olympic event, the slalom, lasted all of 16 seconds. He bulled out of the start house, did a couple of quick scrimshaw turns, and promptly straddled a gate.

Fair enough—Miller has struggled in the slalom this season, finishing just two of eight races, and it was a tough course. Nine of the top 29 skiers in the competition did not finish. It was Miller's behavior afterward that sealed his reputation as the goat of the Games. He thrust his hands in the air, stuck out his tongue, and waggled in mock celebration. Then he skied off the course, avoiding the cameras and throngs of people at the bottom of the hill. When Associated Press reporter Jim Litke found him later, he declared, "Man, I rocked."

Then he delivered a disquisition on his Olympic experience. "It's been an awesome two weeks," Miller said. "I got to party and socialize at an Olympic level."

Let's review his awesome two weeks. Miller arrived in Turin sullen and defensive, and blew his chance in the downhill when he lost time on the bottom of the course, probably as a result of his lack of fitness. He blew another medal in the combined when he led after the downhill portion, but straddled a gate in the slalom. Next, he blew up a gate in the Super-G, and then insulted his rivals afterward by saying he wasn't one of those guys "who skies 70, 80 percent and gets on the podium."

Miller has worked awfully hard to reach this point; the relationship he has built with the public is the one he himself has constructed over many months. He was impossibly overhyped coming into the Winter Games between Nike's ad campaign, his autobiography, and those nipple-baring magazine covers, all of which he cooperated with and cashed in on. Miller took the world's biggest ego bath—until he realized it was going to be difficult to satisfy Olympic expectations, especially in a field chock full of Austrians.

Now he wants to distance himself from all the hype and commerce. "The expectations were other people's," he told the AP. "I'm comfortable with what I've accomplished, including at the Olympics."

The about-face has left Miller so confused that he can't get his stories straight. In one breath, he talks about giving it his all, and in the next, he talks about how hard he drank during the Games. "I just did it my way. I'm not a martyr, and I'm not a do-gooder. I just want to go out and rock. And man, I rocked here."

Or: "My quality of life is the priority. I wanted to have fun here, to enjoy the Olympic experience, not be holed up in a closet and not ever leave your room."

Miller's act has clearly worn on his coaches, and Bill Marolt, chief executive of the U.S. Ski and Snowboard Association, suggested that officials would have "a heart-to-heart" talk with Miller at the end of this season regarding his behavior. Nor would Marolt speculate if Miller would be back on the team. "I don't believe we should have conversations like this in the media," Marolt said. "But clearly it will be something we will address at the year's end, and I don't know where that will go right now."

What they should tell Miller is this: Everyone can sympathize with his struggle to meet unrealistic expectations. And everyone respects what Miller has done on skis, from his two silvers at the Salt Lake Games to the overall World Cup title last season. But nobody respects the Bode Miller who showed up here—maybe not even Miller himself—and unless he can compete respectably, he shouldn't return to the team. There are few things less worthy of respect than the athlete who pretends not to care about the outcome. It's a bail-out position, a protection and an excuse. If you pretend not to care, then no one can say you really lost. Miller never committed to these Olympics, never put his ante on the table. He sauntered around the Games as if he was just here to watch.

Which is mostly what he did.

*2006*

★ ★ ★

# George Huguely, Ben Roethlisberger, Lawrence Taylor: Male Athletes Encouraged to Do the Wrong Thing

G EORGE HUGUELY is said to have been a vicious drunk who menaced Yeardley Love, yet there has been no indication that any of his teammates said anything to police. Ben Roethlisberger seems to be a serial insulter of women, whose behavior is shielded by the off-duty cops he employs. And if the charges are true, Lawrence Taylor ignored the bruises on a 16-year-old girl's face as he had sex with her, never thinking to ask who beat her.

It's a bad stretch for women in the sports pages. After reading the news accounts and police reports, it's reasonable to ask: Should women fear athletes? Is there something in our sports culture that condones these assaults? It's a difficult, even upsetting question, because it risks demonizing scores of decent, guiltless men. But we've got to ask it, because something is going on here—there's a disturbing association, and surely we're just as obliged to address it as we are concussions.

"We can no longer dismiss these actions as representative of a few bad apples," says Jay Coakley, author of *Sport in Society: Issues and Controversies*, and a professor of sociology at the University of Colorado. "The evidence suggests that they are connected to particular group cultures that are in need of critical assessment."

What do we mean when we ask whether there was something in the lacrosse "cultura" that led to the murder of Yeardley Love? The Latin root of the word "culture" means "to grow." It means the attitudes, practices, and values that are implanted and nourished in a group or society.

There's a lot we still don't know about Huguely and his "brothers," but the attitudes and practices of at least some members of the

Virginia lacrosse team seem obvious: physical swagger, heavy drinking and fraternal silence.

In 2008, a drunken Huguely was so brutally combative with a female cop that she felt she had to Taser him. Last year, he assaulted a sleeping teammate who he believed had kissed Love, several former players say, and this year, he had other violent confrontations with Love herself, witnesses say.

We can argue about gaps in the system, but one constituency very likely knew about Huguely's behavior: his teammates and friends, the ones who watched him smash up windows and bottles and heard him rant about Love.

Why didn't they tackle him? Why didn't they turn him in?

Undoubtedly, many of the young men on the Virginia lacrosse team are fine human beings. I don't mean to question their decency. I don't mean to blame them.

But I do mean to ask those who knew of Huguely's behavior an important question. Why did they not treat Yeardley Love as their teammate, too?

Where were her brothers?

That doesn't just break the heart. It shatters it into a thousand pieces.

The allegations against Huguely, Roethlisberger and Taylor share something in common. In all of these cases, the alleged female victims were treated as undeserving of inclusion in the protected circle. They were "others" rather than insiders.

*Sports Illustrated*'s profile of Roethlisberger and the men who look after him is utterly damning. According to the magazine story, on the night that he allegedly accosted an over-served undergrad in a Milledgeville, Ga., restroom, Roethlisberger held up a tray of tequila shots and hollered, "All my bitches, take some shots!" He exposed himself at the bar. He forced his hand up someone's skirt. Yet police sergeant Jerry Blash described the alleged victim as "this drunken bitch," and Roethlisberger's bodyguards apparently blocked off the area. Protecting Roethlisberger, being "in" with him, took precedence over ethics.

"Who needs the bodyguard here?" Coakley asks incredulously. "What is the role of bodyguard? It's not to maintain male hegemony and privilege. It's to maintain order."

The charge of third-degree rape against Taylor prompts another question. Police allege that a 16-year-old runaway was beaten by a sex trafficker and brought to Taylor's hotel room, where, according to the police report, instead of protecting her, he allegedly protected himself with a condom. If Taylor is guilty, how could he have acted in such a depersonalizing way—unless he viewed her as more object than person?

According to Coakley, the data is clear: Certain types of all-male groups generally have higher rates of assault against women than the average, and their profile is unmistakable. They tend to include sports teams, fraternities, and military units, and they stress the physical subordination of others—and exclusiveness.

Common sense tells me that "sport" in general is not the culprit in all of this so much as excessive celebration and rewarding of it: binge drinking, women-as-trophies, the hubris resulting from exaggerated entitlement and years of being let off the hook. We are hatching physically gifted young men in incubators of besotted excess and a vocabulary of "bitches and hos."

What has happened to kindness, to the cordial pleasures of friendship between men and women in the sports world? Above all, what has happened to sexuality? When did the most sublime human exchange become more about power and status than romance? When did it become so pornographic and transactional, so implacably cold?

The truth is, women can't do anything about this problem. Men are the only ones who can change it—by taking responsibility for their locker room culture, and the behavior and language of their teammates. Nothing will change until the biggest stars in the clubhouse are mortally offended, until their grief and remorse over an assault trumps their solidarity.

*2010*

## JOE POSNANSKI

Not since the days of Red Smith and Jim Murray has a newspaper sports columnist been embraced with as much genuine affection as Joe Posnanski (b. 1967) was during his fourteen years as the anchor of *The Kansas City Star*'s splendid sports section. He left for *Sports Illustrated* in 2009, then bounced from the Sports on Earth website to NBC Sports to a tour of duty as MLB.com's national columnist. His latest stop is at The Athletic, the bumptious, ever-expanding all-sports website. While blogging voluminously at every stop, Posnanski has maintained a reverence for history, an open mind for the wonders of metrics, and a fascination with captivating personalities. To read his farewell to Negro Leagues legend Buck O'Neil is to be reminded that even in the twilight of newspapering as we have known it, there is still room on the sports page for art.

★ ★ ★

# RIP Buck O'Neil

IN A Lincoln Town Car on the way home from a funeral, Buck O'Neil said: "I don't want people to be sad when I die. I've lived a full life. Be sad for the kids who die."

So this will not be a sad column, I hope.

Buck O'Neil died Friday after a prolonged stay in a Kansas City hospital. He was 94 years old, almost 95. He lived a life for the ages. Buck used to say he had done it all—he hit the home run, he hit for the cycle, he traveled the world, he testified before Congress, he sang at the Baseball Hall of Fame, he made a hole-in-one in golf, he married the woman he loved, he shook hands with American presidents.

"And," he always reminded people, "I hugged Hillary."

Buck was the grandson of a slave. He grew up in Sarasota, Fla.—so far south, he used to say, that if he stepped backward he would have been a foreigner. He shined shoes. He worked in the celery fields. He could not attend Sarasota High because he was black.

"Damn," he said on one particularly hot Florida day in those celery fields, "there's got to be something better than this."

"That may have been the first time I ever swore," he would tell school kids across America. "But it was hot that day, children."

The lesson of Buck's story is that there is always something better—but he had to go out and get it. And he did. He played baseball. He was tall and had good reflexes. So he played first base, first for some semi-professional teams and then for the Kansas City Monarchs of the Negro Leagues. That, he said, was the time of his life.

It was a time when black players were not welcome to play in the major leagues, a bitter time for many. But Buck O'Neil did not know anything about bitterness. That was his gift. When others remembered Negro Leagues checks that bounced or playing fields with rocks on them, Buck O'Neil remembered listening to hot jazz on Saturday nights—"Charlie Parker, Count Basie, Duke Ellington," he used to say, as if there was magic in the names.

And more, he remembered playing baseball on warm Sunday afternoons with some of the best players who ever lived. He remembered playing with his friend Satchel Paige, the best pitcher he ever saw. Paige used to call him Nancy, and there's a long story that goes along with that, a story Buck O'Neil would tell 10,000 times in his long life. Suffice it to say, Satchel had a woman named Nancy, and he also had a fiancée named Lahoma, and once Lahoma heard Satchel knocking on another hotel door shouting, "Nancy! Nancy!"

Lahoma opened her door. And at that very same instant Buck opened his.

"Did you want something, Satchel?" Buck asked.

"Yes, Nancy," Satchel said. "What time is the game tomorrow?"

"And," Buck would say, "I've been Nancy ever since."

In those Negro Leagues days, Buck played baseball with Cool Papa Bell, who Buck said was so fast he once hit a line drive through a pitcher's legs and got hit with the ball as he slid into second base. He played baseball with Turkey Stearnes, a hitter who used to carry his bats around in violin cases and talk to them after games. "Why didn't you hit better?" he would ask them.

He played baseball with Josh Gibson, one of the great home run hitters who ever lived. Buck used to say that three times in his life he heard a different sound on a baseball field, a crack of the bat that sounded like dynamite. The first time, he was a young boy, and the hitter was Babe Ruth. The last time, he was an old man and a scout and the hitter was former Kansas City Royals star Bo Jackson.

The time in between was Josh Gibson.

Those baseball playing days burned brightly in Buck O'Neil's memory for the rest of his life. Buck was a pretty good player himself, a slick fielder and a fine hitter who once led the Negro Leagues in hitting. Toward the end of his playing days, he managed the Monarchs too. There, he ran across a shy young player from Texas who would sit in the back of the bus on those road trips and not say a word. Buck started to talk to him.

"Son," he told Ernie Banks, "you've got to love this game to play it."

Ernie Banks would become perhaps the most joyful player in the major leagues. They called him "Mr. Cub" in Chicago. He hit 500 home runs. He was inducted into the Baseball Hall of Fame. He was famous for saying, "It's a beautiful day. Let's play two."

"I learned that from Buck O'Neil," Banks said.

By the time Buck O'Neil managed in the Negro Leagues, things had changed. Jackie Robinson had broken through the color barrier, and many of the best African-American players were going to play in the minor leagues rather than the Negro Leagues. In 1955, the Chicago Cubs hired Buck to become a scout.

He became the first prominent black scout in the major leagues. His territory was the American South, and he spent most of his days around the historically black colleges. On those campuses, Buck O'Neil was bigger than life. "Everybody knew Buck O'Neil," said Lou Brock, a Hall of Famer Buck signed. "You could see everybody on the bench pointing and whispering, There's Mr. O'Neil. There he is. "

In 1962, he became the first African-American coach in the major leagues when the Cubs hired him. He was mostly responsible for working with the Cubs black players—Brock and Banks among them—and he never got the chance to work on the field as either a first or third-base coach. This bothered him a bit—as much as anything ever bothered Buck. He went back to scouting after a year and signed numerous star players, though what he remembered most was the time he and a fellow scout, Piper Davis, were looking for a game in Louisiana. They found a field and some lights and saw two guys standing in front.

"Is this where the game is?" Buck asked.

"Oh yeah," the guys said. "This is the game all right."

They walked toward the field and noticed there were no baseball players on the field. Instead, they saw a crowd overflowing with people in white sheets. There was a man standing on a truck wearing the outfit of the Grand Wizard.

"Piper," Buck said. "This ain't no ballgame. Let's get out of here."

They raced back to the car, hit the gas, and drove wildly past the two guys, who were laughing hysterically. About 10 miles down the road, Buck and Piper started laughing too. And Buck never stopped.

"Hatred," he always said. "It doesn't make any sense."

Buck loved telling Negro Leagues stories. For many years, he said, people didn't want to listen. People seemed offended somehow when he told them that Negro Leaguer Oscar Charleston was as good as Ty Cobb or his friend Hilton Smith might have been as good as Bob Feller. He kept telling the stories because he thought it was important.

"Sometimes," he said, "I think God may have kept me on this earth for a long time so I could bear witness to the Negro Leagues."

In 1994, he broke through. He was discovered—at age 83—by director Ken Burns, who gave him a starring role in his documentary "Baseball." In it, Buck told the same stories he had been telling for more than 40 years, but now people listened. People laughed. People cried. And Buck became a celebrity. He appeared on television talk shows, and wrote an autobiography (*I Was Right on Time*) and traveled the country to tell his story.

Two years later, he had the second-greatest day of his life. The new and expanded Negro Leagues Baseball Museum opened up on the famous corner of 18th and Vine—the same corner where on those long ago Saturday nights, Buck would listen to that great jazz and talk about the baseball games to come. He had spent many of his later years trying to make the museum a reality. The opening touched his heart.

"We spend so much of our lives honoring the people who crossed the bridge," Buck said. "Today we honor the people who built the bridge."

One day later, Buck lost his wife of 51 years, Ora. He would lose many friends in the last 10 years of his life. But he did not allow that to stop him from loving life. He traveled America, and kept bearing witness for those Negro Leaguers who had been forgotten or ignored. I know. I traveled with him. Buck appeared at every charity function he could fit into his schedule. He signed every autograph. He hugged every woman and tossed baseballs to every kid he saw wearing a baseball glove. This year, at 94 years old, he played in the Northern League All-Star Game. He would not stop. He could not.

"Moving," he said, "is the opposite of dying."

He started to feel tired in August, shortly after returning home from the Baseball Hall of Fame. Buck had not been elected to the Hall of Fame—he fell one or two votes short in a special election—and this set off something of a national firestorm. But Buck said he would not let it get him down. Nothing got him down. And he went to Cooperstown and led everyone in song. A few days later, he checked into the hospital for a short stay. He got out and said that he would have to slow down. A couple of weeks later, he checked back in.

The last time I saw him, he sat in a hospital bed, and he looked thin, his beautiful voice was a rasp. His memory was still sharp, and he grabbed my hand, and he whispered: "You are my friend." He deteriorated from there. Two weeks later he was gone.

But even though it's late at night and I can hardly see the keyboard because of the tears, I know Buck would not have wanted any of us to cry. So, instead, I will relive once more his greatest day. I heard him tell it a hundred times. It was Easter Sunday, 1943, Memphis, Tenn. The Monarchs were playing the Memphis Red Sox. First time up, Buck hit a double. Second time, he hit a single. Third time, he hit it over the right-field fence. Fourth time up, he hit the ball to left field, it bounced off the wall, and Buck rounded the bases. He could have had an inside-the-park home run, but he stopped at third.

"You know why?" he always asked.

"You wanted the cycle," I always said.

That night, he was in his room when a friend called him down to meet some schoolteachers who were in the hotel. Buck went down, saw a pretty young woman, and walked right up to her and said, "My name is Buck O'Neil. What's yours?" It was Ora. They would be married for 51 years.

"That was my best day," he said. "I hit for the cycle and I met my Ora."

"It was a good day," I said.

"It's been a good life," he said.

*2006*

★ ★ ★

# Sources and Acknowledgments

Great care has been taken to locate and acknowledge all owners of copyrighted material included in this book. If any such owner has inadvertently been omitted, acknowledgment will gladly be made in future printings.

W. O. McGeehan, Gertrude Ederle vs. the Channel; News of a Champion: *Wake Up the Echoes: From the Sports Pages of the New York Herald Tribune*, ed. Robert Barbour Cooke (Garden City, NY: Hanover House, 1956).

Damon Runyon, Stengel's Homer Wins It for Giants, 5–4: *New York American*, October 11, 1923. Copyright © 1923 by Damon Runyon. All Horse Players Die Broke: Damon Runyon, *Short Takes: Readers' Choice of the Best Columns of America's Favorite Newspaperman* (New York: Whitlesey House, 1946). Copyright © 1944 by King Features Syndicate, Inc. World rights reserved. Used by permission.

Grantland Rice, Senators Win Title, 4–3: *New York Herald Tribune*, October 11, 1924.

Ring Lardner, Mordecai Brown: The Reporter's Friend: *Chicago Tribune*, December 6, 1916. Kid's Strategy Goes Amuck as Jake Doesn't Die: Bell Syndicate, October 2, 1919. The Perils of Being a Football Writer: Bell Syndicate, November 6, 1921.

Heywood Broun, This Side of Paradise?: *Wake Up the Echoes: From the Sports Pages of the New York Herald Tribune*, ed. Robert Barbour Cooke (Garden City, NY: Hanover House, 1956). The Orthodox Champion: *Pieces of Hate and Other Enthusiasms* (New York: George H. Doran, 1922).

Frank Graham, A Show They Will Never Forget: *New York Sun*, June 25, 1938. Ex-Champion: *New York Journal-American*, December 5, 1945. Copyright © 1938, 1945 by Frank Graham. Used by permission of Frank Graham, Jr.

Westbrook Pegler, The Called Shot Heard Round the World: *Chicago Tribune*, October 2, 1932. Copyright © 1932 by *Chicago Tribune*. All rights reserved. Used by permission and protected by the Copyright Laws of the United States. The printing, copyright, redistribution, or retransmission of this content without express written permission is prohibited. The

Olympic Army: *New York World-Telegram*, February 17, 1936. Copyright © 1936. Used by permission.

Joe Palmer, Stymie—Common Folks; Samuel Doyle Riddle: Joe H. Palmer, *This Was Racing*, ed. Red Smith (New York: A. S. Barnes, 1953). Copyright © 1949, 1951 by Joe Palmer. Used by permission of the Estate of Joe Palmer.

Shirley Povich, Iron Horse "Breaks" as Athletic Greats Meet in His Honor; Larsen Pitches 1st Perfect Game in Series History: Shirley Povich, *All Those Mornings . . . At the Post* (Washington, D.C.: PublicAffairs, 2005). Copyright © 1939, 1956 by *The Washington Post*. All rights reserved. Used by permission and protected by the Copyright Laws of the United States. The printing, copyright, redistribution, or retransmission of this content without express written permission is prohibited.

Red Smith, A Horse You Had to Like; Next to Godliness: Red Smith, *Out of the Red* (Knopf, 1950). Miracle of Coogan's Bluff (1951): Red Smith, *Views of Sport* (New York: Knopf, 1954). Copyright © 1947, 1951 by Red Smith. Used by permission of The Literary Estate of Walter W. "Red" Smith.

Jimmy Cannon, DiMaggio: Jimmy Cannon, *Nobody Asked Me* (New York: Dial Press, 1951). You're Billy Graham: Jimmy Cannon, *Who Struck John?* (New York: Dial Press, 1956). Copyright © 1948, 1955. Used by permission of the *New York Post*. Doc Kearns: *Nobody Asked Me, But . . . The World of Jimmy Cannon*, ed. by Jack Cannon and Tom Cannon (New York: Holt, Rinehart & Winston, 1978). Copyright © 1963 by Jimmy Cannon.

Wendell Smith, It Was a Great Day in Jersey: *Pittsburgh Courier*, April 19, 1946. Copyright © 1946 by Wendell Smith.

W. C. Heinz, Down Memory Lane with the Babe: *New York Sun*, June 14, 1948. Death of a Racehorse: *New York Sun*, July 28, 1949. Copyright © 1948, 1949 by W. C. Heinz. Used by permission of Gayl B. Heinz.

Dick Young, Beloved Enemy: *New York Daily News*, September 30, 1946. Obit on the Dodgers: *New York Daily News*, October 9, 1957. Hutch: *New York Daily News*, November 12, 1964.

Emmett Watson, Goal-Line Stand in France Brings Freddy Back: *Seattle Times*, October 29, 1946. Copyright © 1946 by *The Seattle Times*. Used by permission. End of the Line for Leo: *Seattle Post-Intelligencer*, February 12, 1953. Copyright © 1953 by *Seattle Post-Intelligencer*. Used by permission.

Blackie Sherrod, Old Buster in Ivyland: Dallas *Times-Herald*, November 21, 1960. Changing Tastes; Zero Is Hero: *The Blackie Sherrod Collection* (Dallas, TX: Taylor Publishing Company, 1988). Copyright © 1960, 1978,

1980 by Blackie Sherrod. Used by permission of DeGolyer Library, Southern Methodist University, Blackie Sherrod Papers.

Jim Murray, As White as the Ku Klux Klan; If You're Expecting One-Liners; All-Time Greatest Name: *The Jim Murray Collection* (Dallas, TX: Taylor Publishing Company, 1988). Copyright © 1969, 1979, 1980 by *Los Angeles Times*. Used by permission.

Sandy Grady, Cool World of Basketball's Wilt: *Philadelphia Bulletin*, February 4, 1960. A Visit to Managers' Terrace: *Philadelphia Bulletin*, September 22, 1964. The Mob Hit .000: *Philadelphia Bulletin*, July 14, 1966. Copyright © 1960, 1964, 1966 by Sandy Grady. Used by permission of the Special Collections Research Center, Temple University Libraries, Philadelphia, PA.

Peter Finney, "Bounced Right into My Arms": Cannon Planned to Let It Roll; Just Call Me Gorgeous; It Could Have Been Worse . . .: *The Best of Peter Finney, Legendary New Orleans Sportswriter* (Baton Rouge: Louisiana State University Press, 2016). Copyright © 1959, 1960, 1977. Used by permission of Louisiana State University Press.

Jim Klobuchar, The Dragon vs. a Scrambling St. George: *The Zest (and Best) of Klobuchar: A Lively Safari into the Rollicking World of Jim Klobuchar* (Minneapolis, MN: M. Zelenovich, 1967). Joe Namath Slays the Knights: *The Playbacks of Jim Klobuchar* (Minneapolis, MN: Dillon Press, 1969). Copyright © 1966, 1969 by *Star Tribune*. Used by permission.

Dave Anderson, The Sound of 715: *The New York Times*, April 9, 1974. Copyright © 1974 by *The New York Times*. All rights reserved. Used by permission and protected by the Copyright Laws of the United States. The printing, copyright, redistribution, or retransmission of this content without express written permission is prohibited.

Bud Collins, Evert Smashing, Wins Battle of Wimbledon: *The Boston Globe*, July 3, 1976. Copyright © 1976 by Bud Collins. Used by permission of the Estate of Bud Collins. Boxing Grieves Loss of 5th Street Gym: *The Boston Globe*, April 23, 1996. Copyright © 1996 by Boston Globe Media Partners. All rights reserved. Used by permission and protected by the Copyright Laws of the United States. The printing, copyright, redistribution, or retransmission of this content without express written permission is prohibited.

Jerry Izenberg, The Promoter; Courage Is Riding Out a 1,600-Pound Tornado; Just Color Doug's Day Beautiful: *The Jerry Izenberg Collection* (Dallas, TX: Taylor Publishing Company, 1988). Copyright © 1964, 1985, 1988 by *The Star-Ledger*. Used by permission. All rights reserved.

Mike Downey, When One Teardrop Is a Torrent of Hope: *Los Angeles Times*, June 9, 1994; He May Be Playing in *Year* 2131: *Los Angeles Times*, September 8, 1995. Copyright © 1994, 1995 by *Los Angeles Times*. Used by permission.

Jane Leavy, The Man Baseball Forgot Plays the Hand He's Dealt: *The Washington Post*, May 8, 1983. Copyright © 1983 by Jane Leavy. Used by permission of the author.

Ralph Wiley, Why Did Duran Do It?; The Undertaker Was Buried: *Classic Wiley: A Lifetime of Punchers, Players, Punks, & Prophets* (New York: Hyperion, 2005). Copyright © 1980, 1981. Used by permission of the Estate of Ralph Wiley.

Mike Lupica, The Day the Music Died in Boston: *New York Daily News*, October 3, 1978. Connors Slams Death's Door Shut: *New York Daily News*, July 1, 1987. Recalling Brother's Bravest Hour: *New York Daily News*, October 1, 2001. Copyright © 1978, 1987, 2001 by Mike Lupica. Used by permission of the author.

Mark Kram, Jr.: "I Want to Kill Him": *Philadelphia Daily News*, June 5, 2002. Copyright © 2002 by the *Philadelphia Daily News*. Used by permission.

Bill Plaschke: Her Blue Haven: *Los Angeles Times*, August 19, 2001. Copyright © 2001 by *Los Angeles Times*. Used by permission.

Michael Wilbon, Entitled to Everything He Got: *The Washington Post*, February 12, 1992. Winning Isn't Color-Coded: *The Washington Post*, April 2, 1994. Copyright © 1992, 1994 by *The Washington Post*. All rights reserved. Used by permission and protected by the Copyright Laws of the United States. The printing, copyright, redistribution, or retransmission of this content without express written permission is prohibited.

Sally Jenkins, Driving Home an Eternal Philosophy of Life: *The Washington Post*, February 23, 2001. Only Medal for Bode Is Fool's Gold: *The Washington Post*, February 26, 2006. George Huguely, Ben Roethlisberger, Lawrence Taylor: Male Athletes Encouraged to Do the Wrong Thing: *The Washington Post*, May 8, 2010. Copyright © 2001, 2006, 2010 by *The Washington Post*. All rights reserved. Used by permission and protected by the Copyright Laws of the United States. The printing, copyright, redistribution, or retransmission of this content without express written permission is prohibited.

Joe Posnanski: RIP Buck O'Neil, *Kansas City Star*, March 16, 2014. Copyright © 2014 by McClatchy. All rights reserved. Used by permission and protected by the Copyright Laws of the United States. The printing, copyright, redistribution, or retransmission of this content without express written permission is prohibited.

★ ★ ★

# Index

The text of this book is set in 10 point Whitman, a relatively new typeface created by book designer Kent Lew, who was inspired by the typography of W. A. Dwiggins (1880–1956) and Eric Gill (1882–1940), and honored with a Type Directors Club Type Design Awards in 2002. The font used for the headnotes is Rotis Semi Sans, developed in 1988 by Otl Aicher. The paper is an acid-free Forest Stewardship Council–certified stock that exceeds the requirements for permanence of the American National Standards Institute. The binding material is Arrestox, a cotton-based cloth with an aqueous acrylic coating manufactured by Holliston, Church Hill, Tennessee. Text design by David Bullen Design. Design revisions and composition by Publishers' Design and Production Services, Sagamore Beach, Massachusetts. Printing and binding by McNaughton & Gunn, Saline, Michigan, with jackets furnished by Phoenix Color, Hagerstown, Maryland.